CANADIAN

CONTENT

CANADIAN

CONTENT

SARAH NORTON
NELL WALDMAN

SECOND · EDITION

HARCOURT
BRACE
CANADA

Harcourt Brace & Company, Canada
Toronto Montreal Fort Worth New York
Orlando Philadelphia San Diego
London Sydney Tokyo

Canadian Cataloguing in Publication Data
Main entry under title:
Canadian content

2nd ed.
Includes index.
ISBN 0-03-922859-2

1. College readers. 2. English language -
Rhetoric. I. Norton, Sarah, date. II. Waldman,
Nell Kozak, date.

PE1417.C351992   808'.0427   C91-094494-6

Editorial Director: Heather McWhinney
Developmental Editor: Tessa McWatt
Director of Publishing Services: Steve Lau
Editorial Manager: Liz Radojkovic
Editorial Co-ordinator: Sandra L. Meadow
Production Manager: Sue-Ann Becker
Production Assistant: Sandra Miller
Copy Editor: James Leahy
Cover Design: Landgraff Design Associates Ltd.
Cover Art (paper sculpture): Calvin Nicholls
Interior Design: Pronk & Associates
Typesetting and Assembly: Compeer Typographic Services Limited
Printing and Binding: Webcom Limited

∞   This book was printed in Canada on acid-free paper.

2 3 4 5   96 95 94

Preface

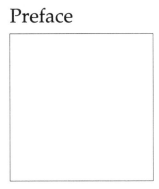

To the Instructor

Canadian Content, Second Edition, is a reader designed for Canadian college and university students taking a first-level composition course. Twenty-six of the fifty-six essays are new to this edition. In response to suggestions by readers of the first edition, the number of essays by women has been increased to twenty-two. Arranged according to rhetorical patterns, the essays are, for the most part, by or about Canadians. At this time in our country's history, it is appropriate—even urgent—to concentrate on the questions of who we are, where we have come from, and how we are similar to or different from our neighbours, so that we may choose intelligently where we want our common destiny to lead. A number of selections new to this edition focus on the uniqueness of being "Canadian." We hope they will provide students with new perspectives on and insight into our diverse community.

Prompted by readers and reviewers of the first edition, we have included readings and instructional text for all four traditional rhetorical modes: narration, description, exposition, and persuasion. Narrative and descriptive prose provide a useful starting point for many of our students because they are familiar with these forms from high school. Beyond this, both students and teachers will find powerful and affecting prose in the selections that constitute Unit One, Narration and Description. However, since most of the writing students will be required to do in school and on the job is expository, we have continued to emphasize the six basic expository strategies in this revision.

We acknowledge at the outset that the rhetorical patterns we treat in isolation are usually found in combination in most expository writing. In our experience, however, students find it helpful to analyze and practise these patterns of development one by one. When all have been mastered, students can then combine the strategies in various ways, depending on their subject and purpose.

To assist the students in their struggle to master clear, correct, and vigorous prose, we have arranged the units of this text in ascending order of difficulty. Units One to Seven deal first with narration and description—the patterns of development with which students are most familiar—then progress to more complex patterns: exemplification, process analysis, division and classification, comparison and contrast, cause and effect, and, finally, definition, which often requires the application of several of the preceding strategies. Unit Eight is devoted to argumentation, which also requires the command of a number of expository strategies. Finally, in Unit Nine, we include a number of fairly sophisticated essays in which the authors employ a variety of expository and persuasive techniques. Throughout the text, we emphasize that there is no single, "best" way of approaching a topic; there is always a variety of choices when organizing and developing an idea—depending on one's audience, subject, and purpose. In other words, we present the various rhetorical patterns not as formulas for the purpose of restricting or confining the student's thinking, but as methods of invention, as options to explore when thinking about the most effective approach to a subject.

For those instructors who prefer to organize their course around themes rather than rhetorical modes, we have supplied an alternate table of contents, entitled By Theme.

The essays within each unit are arranged from simplest to most complex; thus an instructor can assign readings suited to the level of the class, or can lead the students through a progressively challenging series of assignments in a single rhetorical mode. In choosing the essays for this text, we kept in mind three criteria: first, the selections had to be well written and neither very formal nor highly colloquial in tone. We looked for examples of good, middle-of-the-road, all-purpose standard English prose—the kind we want our students to learn to write. Second, the selection had to exemplify one of the modes: the structure and development had to illustrate clearly the pattern being presented. Third, we looked for pieces with a high interest level, selections that would stimulate thought, provoke class discussion, and promote our students' understanding of themselves, of others, and of the world around us.

Each unit begins with an introduction written in an informal, accessible style. Where possible, examples and allusions have been drawn from the students' culture—not only to make the point clear, but also to make the writing process less intimidating. We have tried throughout the book to demystify the writing process. The introductions encourage the student to ask specific questions about his or her subject and then to formulate a thesis statement that will summarize the whole essay in a single sentence. Whether or not the student ultimately includes this statement in the final paper— a strategy we encourage—the exercise of formulating the thesis statement serves to clarify both the student's thinking and the paper's organization. Many students resist composing a traditional essay outline; the thesis statement—which is an outline in miniature—ensures that the student has done the preliminary thinking and organizing that a clearly structured paper requires. Occasionally, students object to this "blueprint" approach to composition, protesting that "real writers don't write this way!" To be sure, novelists, poets, and many other professional writers do not approach writing this way. Nevertheless, as the essays in this text clearly illustrate, "real writers" do pay particular attention to the organization and development of their work.

Most of our students, of course, do not aspire to become professional writers. Their goal is to become competent writers within a profession. The key to competent writing is organization. Unfortunately, many students arrive at college without much training or practice in the structure of clear prose—hence our emphasis on structure throughout this text. Overwhelmingly, the majority of students are interested in and grateful for a practical, no-nonsense approach to writing such as the one presented here.

Immediately following the introduction in each unit, there is a short model essay that illustrates the form being presented. These model essays, all on the subject of education, also serve to illustrate the various introductory and concluding strategies that are summarized in the List of Useful Terms at the back of the book.

The readings themselves are followed by short biographical notes and by definitions of the most difficult words and allusions in the text. Please note that our "meanings" are not intended to be exhaustive dictionary definitions; we have defined the terms specifically as they appear in the context of the selection. The terms we have chosen to define are those that many students are likely to have difficulty with, terms that do not have contextual clues as to their meaning, and terms that are necessary to the reader's understanding of the essay. We expect students to use their dictionaries to clarify the meaning of other words they may not know.

Two sets of questions follow each essay. The questions under Structure and Strategy are designed to lead the students to an understanding of *form*: how the piece is put together and why the writing strategies employed are effective. The questions under Content and Purpose are designed to encourage the students' analysis of the *content* of the piece, to deepen their understanding of meaning. Terms that are included in the List of Useful Terms at the back of the book appear in capital letters in the questions; for example, if a question refers to the purpose of an ALLUSION, the typeface serves as a cue to consult the List of Useful Terms for an explanation of the word "allusion."

We have included a few Suggestions for Writing after each essay. These suggestions lead either to a paper with a form similar to that of the essay under discussion or to one that responds in some way to the content of the piece. We have deliberately kept the number of writing suggestions small, so that students and instructors will feel free to pursue their own responses to the form and content of the selections. There are also Additional Suggestions for Writing at the conclusion of each unit.

Acknowledgements

This book, like its predecessor, has been very much a team effort. We are indebted to numbers of users whose comments and suggestions have helped us shape the second edition; in particular, we thank Francie Aspinall, Ruth Colombo, Cynthia Flood, Brian Green, Tom Hartley, and Kate Porter for taking the time and trouble to send us selections that would not only illustrate a particular rhetorical mode but also interest students and provoke classroom discussion. We are indebted to our reviewers—Ian Lea, John Lucas, Anna Smol, Sabrina Reed, Reid Gilbert, Mary-Beth Knechtel, J. Howard Gibbon, Linda Stairet, and Joanne Buckley—who urged us to expand the Canadian focus and to include more selections by women. To our editor, Heather McWhinney, special thanks for her encouragement and patience. And finally, we extend our thanks to the thousands of students and teachers in high schools, colleges, and universities across Canada whose use and enjoyment of the first edition have made this second edition possible.

Publisher's Note to Instructors and Students

This textbook is a key component of your course. If you are the instructor of this course, you undoubtedly considered a number of texts carefully before choosing this as the one that would work best for your students and you. The authors and publishers spent considerable time and money to ensure its high quality, and we appreciate your recognition of this effort and accomplishment. Please note the copyright statement.

If you are a student, we are confident that this text will help you to meet the objectives of your course. It will also become a valuable addition to your personal library.

Since we want to hear what you think about this book, please be sure to send us the stamped reply card at the end of the text. This will help us to continue to publish high-quality books for your courses.

Contents

By Unit

Unit Three: Process Analysis: Explaining "How"   109

Unit Four: Division and Classification: Explaining Parts and Kinds   146

Unit Five: Comparison and Contrast: Explaining Similarities and Differences   176

Contents

By Theme

On Canada

On the Contemporary Scene

On the Cultural Mosaic

On History

On Leisure and Sports

On Morals and Ethics

On Politics

On Relationships

On Science and Technology

On Urban Life/On Rural Life

On Work

On Writing

1. How to Read with Understanding

Every college student knows how to read—sort of. The trouble is that most of us don't read very efficiently. We don't know how to adapt our reading style to our purpose. Most people aren't even aware that there are different kinds of reading suited to different purposes.

Basically, there are two different kinds of reading: *surface* reading, which is casual reading for pleasure or for easy-to-find facts. This is the kind of reading we engage in when we enjoy a novel, magazine, or newspaper. The second kind of reading is *deep* reading. This is the type required in college courses or on the job: reading to acquire knowledge, facts, and ideas, which we do to understand a topic because we need the information. This kind of reading has practical rather than recreational purposes. Both kinds of reading can bring us personal satisfaction, but one is undeniably more difficult than the other.

Deep reading, or analytical reading, is the kind that most of us don't do as well as we would like. As with any other skill, there is a technique involved that can, with practice, be mastered. In general, there are three basic guidelines to follow: figure out as much about the piece as you can *before* reading it; identify what you don't understand *while* reading it; and review the whole thing *after* reading it.

Specifically, there are seven steps to reading with understanding:

1. Remove Distractions.

Every year, teachers hear hundreds of students protest that they are able to read perfectly well while listening to music, watching television, talking on the phone, or filing their nails. These students are right. They can read, but they can't read for understanding. To read analytically, you have to focus your attention completely on the text. Reading for understanding is an *active* process, requiring your full concentration and participation. For example, you should learn to read with a pencil in your hand, if you don't already do so. Only half of the task of making the meaning clear belongs to the writer; the other half belongs to you. Understanding is something you have to work at.

Find a quiet spot, with a good reading light, where you can be alone with your book, your pencil, and your dictionary. We'll get to the dictionary later.

2. Preview Before You Read.

Human beings cannot learn facts, ideas, or even words in isolation. We need a context, a sense of the whole into which the new piece of information fits. The more familiar you are with the dimensions and content of the piece before you begin to read, the better able you will be to read with understanding—whether you're reading three sentences or three volumes.

Figure out as much as you can before beginning to read. How long is the piece? You'll want to estimate how much time you'll need to complete it. What's the title? The title usually points to something significant about the writer's topic or tone. Like the label on a candy bar, the title of an article tells you something about what's inside. Who wrote it? Knowing something about the author helps you predict what the essay might be about. Is the author dead or alive? What is his or her nationality: Canadian, American, or Tasmanian? Is he a humorist or a social critic? Or is she a journalist or an academic? Is the author a specialist in a particular field?

What about the body of the work? Does it include any diagrams or illustrations? Are there any subheadings that indicate the division of the material into main ideas? Finally, for the readings in this text, don't forget the context we've provided for you: the unit in which each essay is found gives you a clue to the kind of organization and development you can expect.

3. Read the Essay All the Way Through.

This is a very important step, and it isn't always easy. Most inexperienced readers have a fairly short attention span—about eight to ten minutes, or about the length of program time between commercials—and they need to train themselves to increase it. You need to read the piece all the way through in order to get a sense of the whole; otherwise, you cannot fully understand either the essay or its parts.

As you read the essays in this text, note the words marked with a °: it signals that the meaning of the word or phrase is given in the Words and Meanings section following the essay. If you're unfamiliar with the term, check the definition we offer and continue reading. Underline any other words whose meaning you cannot figure out from the context. You'll look them up later.

This first time through, withhold judgment. Don't allow your prejudices—in the root sense of the word, "prejudgments"—to affect your response at this stage. If you decide in advance that the topic is boring ("Who cares about baked beans?") or the style is too demanding ("I couldn't possibly understand anything titled 'The Huxleyan Warning'!"), you cheat yourself out of a potentially rewarding experience. Give the writer a chance; part of his or her responsibility is to make the writing interesting and accessible to the reader. Another point to keep in mind is that reading is like any other exercise: it gets easier, or at least less painful, with practice. You'll get better at it and soon be able to tackle increasingly difficult challenges.

You haven't forgotten your pencil, have you? Here's where it comes into the act. Try to identify the main parts of the essay as you read: the INTRODUCTION, the parts into which the body is divided, and the CONCLUSION. If they are obvious, underline the THESIS—often expressed in a thesis statement in the introduction—and each main point, usually expressed in the TOPIC SENTENCE of a PARAGRAPH. When you come across a sentence or passage you don't understand, put a question mark in the margin. Key terms that appear in CAPITALS in the introduction and in the questions are explained in the List of Useful Terms at the end of the book.

Good writers "set up" their material for you: they identify their subject early, and indicate the scope of their essay. They use various TRANSITIONS to signal to the reader that they have concluded one idea and are moving on to another. Note, however, that this first read-through is not the time to stop and analyze the structure and writing strategies in detail. You need to read the piece a second (or even a third) time to accomplish such analysis successfully.

If you've been practising what we've been suggesting so far, you will *not* have stopped to look up INTRODUCTION, CONCLUSION, THESIS, TOPIC SENTENCE, PARAGRAPH, or TRANSITION in the List of Useful Terms. The time to look up the meaning of these and any other unfamiliar terms is when you have finished reading through this whole section.

4. Look Up the Meaning of Any Words You Didn't Understand.

Here's where your dictionary comes in. Look up the words you underlined as you read through the essay—but don't just seize on the first definition given and assume this is the meaning the author intended. Read *all* the meanings given. Note that some words can be used both as nouns and as verbs; only one set of meanings will be appropriate in the context you are reading. When you're satisfied you've located the appropriate definition, jot it down in the margin beside the mystery word.

Now go back and reread any passages you noted with a question mark the first time through. Once you have figured out any vocabulary problems that initially bothered you, and now that you have an overview of the whole piece, you should find that the meaning of those confusing passages is much clearer.

5. Read the Questions Following the Essay.

After you've answered all your questions about the piece, go through the questions on Structure and Strategy and Content and Purpose that we have provided. You won't be able to answer them all at this point. The purpose of reading the questions now is to prepare yourself for a second, closer reading of the essay. These questions will guide you eventually to a thorough understanding of the essay. At this point, however, all you need to know are the sorts of questions you'll be considering after your second reading.

6. Read the Essay a Second Time—Slowly, Carefully.

Got your pencil ready? Identify the INTRODUCTION, the part of the essay that establishes the subject, the limits of the subject, and the writer's TONE. If you haven't already done so your first time through, underline the THESIS and main points. Make notes in the margins. Use the margins to jot down in point form an outline of the piece, to add supplementary—or contradictory—evidence, or to call attention to particularly significant or eloquently expressed ideas. Circle key TRANSITIONS. The physical act of writing as you read helps keep your attention focused on the article and can serve to deepen your understanding of both its content and its structure.

Think about the AUDIENCE the writer is addressing. Are you included in the group for whom the writer intended the essay? If not, you should remember that your reactions to and interpretations of the piece may differ from those of the intended readers. For example, if you are male, your response to Steinem's essay, "Erotica and Pornography: A Clear and Present Difference," will probably be somewhat different from that of the committed feminists who are Steinem's primary target.

During your second reading, identify the writer's main PURPOSE. Is it to inform, to persuade, or to entertain? Notice, too, how the writer develops the main points. Be sure you distinguish between the main ideas and the supporting details—the EXAMPLES, ILLUSTRATIONS, DEFINITIONS, ANALOGIES—that the writer has used to make the ideas clear to the reader. As you read, be conscious of the writer's TONE: is it humorous or serious, impassioned or objective, formal or informal? Good writers choose their tone very carefully, since it directly affects the reader's response, probably more than any other technical aspect of writing.

Finally, consider the CONCLUSION of the essay. Does it simply restate the thesis or expand on it in some way? Are you left with a sense of the essay's completeness, a feeling that all questions raised in the piece have been satisfactorily answered? Or do you feel that you've been left dangling, that some of the loose ends have yet to be tied up?

At this point, you have a decision to make. Are you satisfied that you understand the essay? Are the writer's purpose, thesis, main ideas, and method of development all clear to you? If so, go on to step 7. If not—as often happens when you are learning to read analytically, or when you encounter a particularly challenging piece—go back and read it through a third time.

7. Answer the Questions Following the Essay.

Consider the questions carefully, one by one, and prepare your answers. Refer to the essay often to keep yourself on the right track. Most of the questions don't have simple, or single, answers! Jot down your answers in point form or in short phrases in the margins of the text.

The purpose of the questions is to engage you as deeply as possible in the structure and meaning of each essay. As you analyze *what* the writer has said (the content and purpose) and *how* he or she has said it (the structure and strategies), you will come as close as you can to full understanding. At this point, you are ready to test your understanding in classroom discussion or through writing a paper of your own.

2. How to Write to Be Understood

Learning to read with understanding will help you write so that what you say is clearly understood. As you become conscious of the process readers use to make sense of a piece of writing, you will become increasingly skilful at predicting and satisfying the needs of *your* readers. For years, you've probably been told, "Keep your audience in mind as you write." By itself, this is not a particularly helpful piece of advice. You need to know not only *who your audience is*, including how much they know and how they feel about your subject, but also *how readers read*. These two pieces of knowledge are the keys to writing understandable prose. (We are assuming here that you have a firm grasp of your subject matter. You cannot write clearly and convincingly about something you don't really understand.)

As long as you know what you are writing about and whom you are writing for, there are five steps you can take to ensure your readers will understand what it is you have to say. The approach we're presenting here applies to all kinds of expository and persuasive writing; that is, to any piece of writing in which your purpose is to *explain* something—a process, a relationship, a complex idea—or to *persuade* your readers to think or act in a particular way.

Writing a paper is like going on a journey: it makes sense—and it's certainly more efficient—to fix on your destination and plan your route *before* you begin. Your subject is your destination. The main points determine the route you select to get to your destination. In other words, your main points determine the kind of paper you are going to write.

In this text, we explain eight of the most basic kinds of essay organization: eight different approaches to explaining a subject, eight different routes to a destination. Something we want to emphasize is that there is no *one way* to explain a subject. A **subject**, like a destination on a map, can be approached from many different directions.

Take the subject of education, for example. It is very broad, very general. Now, if you flip through the introductions to the first eight units of this book, you will see that each introduction ends with a model essay illustrating the organizational pattern explained in that unit. All of these model essays are on the subject of education, but they are all different. We've limited the subject eight different ways, chosen eight different sets of **main points**, eight different organizational patterns—eight different paths to the goal. Read these model essays carefully, and you'll discover how the pattern discussed in each unit can lend shape, coherence, and unity to the subject you're writing about.

As you will have discovered by now, people who are reading for information, for understanding, don't like surprises: no bumps or potholes, no sudden shifts in direction, no dead ends. They appreciate a well-marked, smooth path through the writer's prose. So your task is to identify the path for them, set them on it, and guide them through to the end. If you can keep them interested, even entertained, on their journey, so much the better. As you read through the essays in this book, you will encounter a variety of stylistic devices you can use to add interest and impact to your own writing.

Here are the five steps to clear, well-organized writing:
1. clarify your subject
2. identify the main points of your subject
3. write a thesis statement
4. develop the paragraphs
5. revise the paper.

If you follow these five steps carefully, in order, we guarantee that you will write papers that an attentive reader will be able to understand—and perhaps even enjoy!

Steps 1, 2, and 3 are the *preparation* stage of the writing process. Be warned: these three steps will take you as long as—if not longer than—steps 4 and 5, which involve the actual *writing*. There is a general rule that governs all expository and persuasive writing: the longer you spend on preparation, the less time the writing will take, and the better your paper will be.

Step 1: Clarify Your Subject.

The subject of your paper or report may be one assigned by a teacher or by your supervisor. Worse, you may have to come up with one on your own. Choosing a satisfactory subject can be the most difficult part of writing an easy-to-understand piece of prose. Inexperienced writers often choose a subject that is far bigger than either their knowledge or the space allotted to them can justify.

A suitable subject is one that is both *specific* and *supportable*. A thorough, detailed discussion of a single, specific topic is much more satisfying to read than a general, superficial treatment of a very broad topic. This is why Rick Groen chose to contrast Peter Gzowski and Johnny Carson rather than Canada and the United States in his essay, "Two Talk-Show Kings and a Tale of Two Countries" (see Unit Five). You can narrow a broad subject by applying one or more limiting factors to it. Think of your subject in terms of a specific *kind*, or *time*, or *place*, or *number*, or *person* associated with it. To contrast Canadian and American lifestyles, for example, Groen limited his subject in terms of person (two contrasting personalities who represent significant characteristics of their respective nations).

A subject is supportable if you can develop it with examples, facts, quotations, descriptions, anecdotes, comparisons, definitions, and other supporting details. These supporting details are called EVIDENCE; we will discuss its use more fully under Step 4, below. Evidence, combined with good organization, makes your discussion of a subject both clear and convincing.

Step 2: Identify the Main Points of Your Subject.

Once you have clarified your subject, think about the approach you're going to use to explain it. There are many possible ways of thinking and writing about any subject. In a short paper, you can deal effectively with only a few aspects of a subject, even a very specific one. But how do you decide what is the best approach to take? How do you decide which aspects of your subject to discuss and what main points to make and explain?

One way to sort through these choices is to do some preliminary research. Another technique some writers use is to jot down everything they can think of about their subject until they "freewrite" or "brainstorm" their way to an organizational pattern. Perhaps the surest way to approach a subject—especially if you're stuck for ideas—is to ask yourself some specific questions about it. Apply the following list of questions, one at a time, to your subject and see which question "fits" it best—which question calls up in your mind answers that approximate what it is you want to say. **(The symbol "S" stands for your subject.)**

If this is the question that fits	Then this is the kind of paper you will be writing
1. What does S look like? 2. How did S happen?	DESCRIPTION/NARRATION
3. What are some significant examples of S?	EXAMPLE

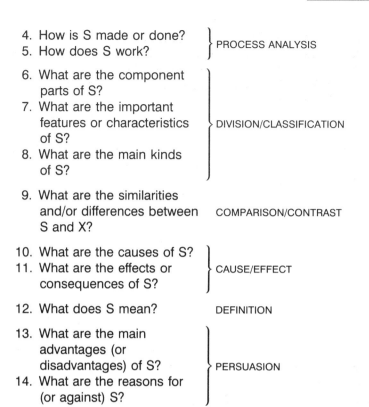

4. How is S made or done?
5. How does S work?
} PROCESS ANALYSIS

6. What are the component parts of S?
7. What are the important features or characteristics of S?
8. What are the main kinds of S?
} DIVISION/CLASSIFICATION

9. What are the similarities and/or differences between S and X?
COMPARISON/CONTRAST

10. What are the causes of S?
11. What are the effects or consequences of S?
} CAUSE/EFFECT

12. What does S mean?
DEFINITION

13. What are the main advantages (or disadvantages) of S?
14. What are the reasons for (or against) S?
} PERSUASION

These questions suggest eight different ways of looking at or thinking about a subject. When you discover the question that elicits the answers that are closest to what you know and want to write about, then you will have discovered what kind of paper you need to write. The answers to the best question are the aspects of the subject you will discuss; they become the main points of your paper. The eight different types of papers listed in the right-hand column above correspond to the rhetorical patterns presented in this text. To find out how to arrange and develop your main points to produce an effective paper, turn to the introduction of the appropriate unit.

Step 3: Write a Thesis Statement.

A thesis statement in your INTRODUCTION is the clearest way to organize a short paper of 350 to 800 words. It plans your paper for you, and it tells your reader what he or she is going to read about. Remember: "no surprises" is the watchword when you write, unless you're writing mystery stories. To continue the analogy between reading an essay and taking a trip, the thesis statement is a kind of map: it identifies both your destination and the route. Like a map, it keeps your reader (and you) on the right track.

To be specific, a thesis statement clearly tells your reader the subject of your paper, the main points you will discuss, and the order in which you will discuss them. Not all essays contain thesis statements. In some of the essays in this book, for example, you will notice that the THESIS is implied rather than explicitly stated. However, we recommend that you include a thesis statement in every paper you write. There is probably no writing strategy you can use that is more helpful to your readers' understanding of what you've written.

To write a thesis statement, you join your *subject* to the *main points* (arranged in an appropriate ORDER) by means of a linking word such as *are, because, since, include,* or a colon. Here is a simple formula, or blueprint, for a thesis statement (S stands for your *subject;* a, b, c, d stand for your *main points*):

> S consists of a, b, c, d . . . .

The introduction to each unit of this text contains a formula to follow when constructing a thesis statement for the particular type of paper presented in that unit.

Here are some examples of thesis statements taken from essays included in our collection:

"There are three dimensions of a complete life: length, breadth, and height." (*The Dimensions of a Complete Life*)

"Three passions, simple but overwhelmingly strong, have governed my life: the longing for love, the search for knowledge, and unbearable pity for the suffering of mankind." (*What I Have Lived For*)

"General education is an essential part of the curriculum because it enhances one's ability to build a career and to live a full life." (*Why Are We Reading This Stuff, Anyway?*)

"Most educators agree that the principal causes of failure in school are lack of basic skills, lack of study skills, and lack of motivation." (*Why Do They Fail?*)

Note that the main points in a thesis statement should be expressed in PARALLEL STRUCTURE. See the List of Useful Terms for an explanation of parallel structure.

Step 4: Develop the Paragraphs.

Each of your main points will be developed in a paragraph, sometimes in two or three paragraphs. Each paragraph should contain a TOPIC SENTENCE that clearly states the main idea or topic of that paragraph. Often, the topic sentence comes at the beginning of the paragraph so that the reader knows what to expect from the very beginning. The next five, six, or more sentences develop the topic. The key to making the paragraph unified (see UNITY) is to make sure that every one of the supporting sentences relates directly to the topic. An adequately developed paragraph includes enough supporting information to make the topic clear to the reader.

How do you decide what is the best way to develop a particular paragraph? How much support should you include? What kind of support should it be? To make these decisions, try putting yourself in your reader's place. What does he or she need to know in order to understand your point clearly? If you ask yourself the seven questions listed below, you'll be able to decide how to develop your topic sentence.

1. Is a *definition* needed? If you're using a term that may be unfamiliar to your readers, you should define it—phrasing it in your own words, please, rather than citing a quotation from a dictionary. The Introduction to Unit Seven will show you how to define terms.

2. Would two or three *examples* help clarify the point? Providing examples is probably the most common method of developing a topic. Readers may be confused or even suspicious when they read unsupported generalizations or statements of opinion. Providing specific, relevant examples will help them to understand your point. The Introduction to Unit Two will show you how to use examples effectively.

3. Is a *series of steps or stages* involved? Are you explaining a process to your reader? Sometimes the most logical way to make your point clear is to explain how something is done—that is, to relate, in order, the steps involved. The Introduction to Unit Three will give you detailed directions for this kind of development.

4. Would a *comparison* or *contrast* help make your explanation clearer? Your reader will find it easier to understand something new if you explain it in terms of something he or she is already familiar with. A *comparison* points out similarities between objects, people, or ideas; a *contrast* shows how the objects, people, or ideas are different. The Introduction to Unit Five provides a detailed description of this technique.

5. Would *specific details* be useful? Providing your reader with concrete, specific, descriptive details can be a very effective way of developing your topic. Such details create an image in the mind of the reader: of general appearance, size, shape, texture, or direction, for example. Descriptive details are also useful in creating or intensifying the mood you are trying to convey. In

some paragraphs, numerical facts or statistics are useful in supporting your point—just be sure your facts are correct and your statistics up-to-date! See the Introduction to Unit One for instructions on writing effective description.

6. Would *telling a story* be an effective way of getting your idea across? Everyone loves to read a story if it's well told and relevant to what's being discussed. Use of a personal anecdote to illustrate a point can be a very effective way of helping your readers not only understand your point but also remember it. A good story contains the basic narrative elements of event, place, and sequence; it also helps contribute to the tone and purpose of your essay. The Introduction to Unit One will give you guidelines to follow when using narration to develop a point.

7. Would a *quotation* or *paraphrase* be appropriate? Would your reader be convinced by reading the words of someone else who shares your opinion? Occasionally, you will find that another individual—an expert in a particular field, a well-known author, or a respected public figure—has said what you want to say so well that your own paper can only benefit from including it. Quotations, so long as they are kept short and not used too frequently, can also add EMPHASIS to an idea. Sometimes, you don't want to quote directly from another writer, but to rephrase the writer's idea in your own words. It's up to you to decide what the essential points are and then word them in a way suited to the needs of your paper. This technique is called paraphrasing. (The List of Useful Terms provides a fuller explanation of PARAPHRASE.)

Whenever you use a quotation or a paraphrase, of course, you *must* acknowledge your source out of respect for the writer. Otherwise, you are committing plagiarism—pretending that someone else's words or ideas are your own.

If you glance at the unit titles in the Contents, you will see that some of these methods of paragraph development are also structural principles on which whole essays can be based. Because of their multi-purpose character, it is essential that you become familiar and comfortable with all seven strategies.

The methods you choose to develop a point should be determined by your readers' needs and expectations. If you have a clear picture of your audience, you'll be able to choose the appropriate kinds and amount of development they require if they are to follow you with ease. You can, of course, use more than one method to develop a paragraph; sometimes a comparison can be effectively coupled with a quotation, for example. There is no fixed rule that governs the kind or number of development strategies required in any particular paragraph. The decision is yours. Your responsibility as a writer is to keep in mind what your readers know and what they need to know in order to understand the points you're making.

Once you have developed your main points, you will add two important paragraphs: the INTRODUCTION and CONCLUSION. All too often, these parts of a paper are dull, clumsy, or repetitive. But they shouldn't be and they needn't be. If carefully constructed, these paragraphs can effectively catch your reader's attention and clinch your argument. The List of Useful Terms contains specific strategies you can choose from in crafting a beginning and ending for your paper.

As you write your paragraphs, keep in mind that you want to make it as easy as possible for your reader to follow you through your paper. TRANSITIONS and TONE can make the difference between a confusing, annoying paper and an informative, pleasing one. *Transitions* are words or phrases that show the relationship between one point and the next, causing a paragraph (or a paper) to hang together and read smoothly. Transitions are like the turn signals on a car: they tell the person following you where you're going. The List of Useful Terms will give you suggestions for appropriate transitional phrases, depending on what kind of relationship between the ideas you want to signal.

Tone is the word used to describe a writer's attitude towards the subject and the reader. A writer may feel angry about a subject, or amused, or nostalgic, and this attitude is reflected in the words, examples, quotations, and other supporting details he or she chooses to explain the main points. Good writing is usually modulated in tone; the writer addresses the reader with respect, in a calm, reasonable way. Writing that is highly emotional in tone is not often very convincing to the readers: what gets communicated is the strength of the writer's feelings rather than the writer's depth of knowledge or validity of opinion about the subject.

Two suggestions may help you find and maintain the right tone. First, never insult your reader unintentionally with phrases such as "any idiot can see that . . . ," or "no sane person could believe . . . ," or even "it is obvious that. . . ." Remember that what seems obvious to you is not necessarily obvious to someone who has a limited knowledge of your subject or who disagrees with your opinion. Second, don't condescend—talk down—to your reader, and don't use heavy-handed sarcasm. On the other hand, you need not apologize for your opinion. You've thought about your subject and taken considerable time to develop it. Present your information in a positive rather than a hesitant way: avoid phrases such as "I tend to believe that . . . " or "I may be wrong, but. . . . " Have confidence in yourself and in your ideas.

Step 5: Revise the Paper.

At last, you've reached the final step in the writing process. Even though you are by now probably thoroughly sick of the whole project and very eager to be rid of it, *do not* omit this important final step. Revising, which means "looking back," is essential before your paper is ready to be sent out into the world. Ideally, you should revise several days after writing the paper. After a "cooling-off" period, you'll be able to see your work more objectively. If you reread it immediately after you've finished writing, you're likely to "read" what you *think* you've written—what's in your head rather than what's really on the page.

Thorough revision requires at least two reviews of your paper. The first time you go over it, read it aloud, slowly, from beginning to end, keeping your audience in mind as you read. Is your thesis clear? Are all the points adequately explained? Has anything been left out? Are the paragraphs unified and coherent? Are there any awkward sentences that should be rephrased?

The second time you read your paper through, read it with the Editing Checklist (on the inside of the back cover) in front of you for easy reference. Pay special attention to the points that tend to give you trouble; for example, sentence fragments, verb errors, apostrophes, or dangling modifiers. Most writers know their weaknesses. Unfortunately, it's human nature to focus on our strengths and try to gloss over our weaknesses. This is the reason why editing your work can be a painful process. Nevertheless, it is an absolutely essential task. You owe it both to yourself and to your reader to find and correct any errors in your writing.

If you are a poor speller, you will need to read your paper a third time. This time, read it through from the end to the beginning to check your spelling. Reading from back to front, you're forced to look at each word individually, not in context, and thus you are more likely to spot your spelling mistakes. If you are truly a hopeless speller, ask someone to identify the errors for you. Better yet, learn to use a spell-checking program on a word processor.

A final word of advice: whether you are in school or on the job, always make a copy of your paper before you hand it in. You wouldn't want to have to go through this whole process again if your paper got misplaced!

If you follow these five steps carefully, you and your reader will arrive at your destination without any accident, mishap, or wrong turns. The journey should be relatively painless for you, and informative—perhaps even enjoyable—for your reader.

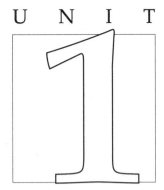

Narration and Description: Explaining in Terms of Time and Space

What? The Definition

What does it look like? How did it happen? When you write a paper, or a part of one, that answers these questions for your readers, you are writing description and narration. Both are rhetorical modes, and each can be used as an end in itself: description to reconstruct for the reader how something or someone appears; narration to tell a story or re-create an event. More usually, however, they are found together, used in support of an expository or persuasive objective. And that is how we encourage you to use description and narration in your writing—as adjuncts, or helpers, to your explanation, analysis, or argument.

In its simplest terms, a narrative relates a sequence of events: it tells a story. Skilfully done, narration does not merely *tell* the readers what happened; it *re-creates* the experience for them so that they may see and hear and feel exactly what it was like. Story telling is one of humanity's oldest and most powerful arts. Just the phrase, "Once upon a time . . . " is enough to capture almost everyone's attention. Novels and short stories are examples of narrative art, but they are based on fictional "events"—events that were created in the imagination of the writer. In this unit, we shall confine our attention to factual narration—events that actually happened in real life. We shall focus on the art of recounting a sequence of events in order to help explain or illustrate a point. In re-creating a series of events for the reader, good narration makes clear the causal connections between the stages of the action. The writer guides the reader through the story step by step. Process analysis and causal analysis (Units Three and Six) are also forms of narration in that they explain a chronological sequence of steps that result in a completed process.

If narration is based on the organizing principle of time—"What happened next?"—description is based on the principle of space: "Where is it?" "What does it look (sound, smell, taste, or feel) like?" Good descriptive writing creates a verbal picture for the reader; it reconstructs an image of someone or something. Note that words do not restrict the writer to visual description alone. Truly vivid descriptive writing appeals to more than just the readers' sense of sight. Michele Landsberg's article on the New York transit system, for example, evokes the sounds, the smells, and the feel of the subway, as well as its physical appearance.

Descriptive writing may be **objective** or **subjective**. Objective description is purely factual; the feelings of the writer do not enter into the written account. Lab reports and business proposals are examples of this kind of description. On the other hand, some descriptive writing is subjective or impressionistic; it creates a dominant impression based on the writer's values and feelings. For example, where a medical history would describe an Alzheimer's patient in objective terms, Michael Ignatieff's description of his afflicted mother is warm, personal, and deeply affecting.

Why? The Purpose

Narration and description are most often used to help explain a subject or develop a topic. Telling a story or creating a vivid sensory picture may be the most effective technique the writer can use to communicate clearly and memorably with the reader. For example, "Sophie" and "Growing Up Native" represent two very different pictures, two very different stories about life among First Nations peoples. But both Carr and Geddes rely on narration and description to convey to us their subject and their point of view. An essay on a very different subject, Tom Hawthorn's "Return of the Battle of the Monster Trucks" (in Further Readings) employs narration and description almost exclusively to create for us the experience of attending an off-road jamboree, an experience not many of us would have the opportunity—or perhaps the inclination—to enjoy in real life. His account makes the experience vivid, memorable, and fun.

Occasionally, a writer may choose to use narration or description by itself as the organizing principle of an essay. More usually, however, the two are used together to support an expository purpose, as is the case in the selections we've chosen for this unit. The writers' primary intent in these essays is to explain a subject or argue an opinion by means of stories and verbal pictures. "Growing Up Native," for instance, recounts the experiences of an Indian child growing up in the Yukon; Geddes's purpose is to convey both the supportive warmth of her extended family and the ravages of racism on families and individuals.

Narration and description, then, can be used in two ways. First, they can be employed together with other rhetorical techniques, in an article, essay, or report, in support of an overall expository purpose. A descriptive paragraph or narrative segment may develop a point in a uniquely effective way. Second, an entire essay may be developed as a narrative or descriptive piece. In either case, the writer needs to know and apply a few structural principles on which effective narration and description depend.

How? The Technique

To write a good narrative, whether it's a single paragraph or an entire paper, keep the following principles in mind:

1. Select appropriate details. What you leave out is as important as what you put in. How do you decide what is or is not "appropriate"? Every story has a purpose; you are telling the story to illustrate that purpose. Only details that are clearly and directly related to your purpose should be included. In any story, there are dozens or hundreds of events and particulars that could form part of the sequence. For instance, a narrative focusing on the perils of drug abuse could recount an addict's tale of increasing dependence and eventual resort to crime. While the roots of the addiction perhaps lie in childhood deprivation or abuse, it is neither possible nor appropriate to narrate the entire story of the addict's life. Your first task is to be selective. With your purpose clearly in mind, choose only those details that contribute directly to your point. Put yourself in your reader's place as you consider what to include and what to leave out. Is a particular event or physical detail indispensable to your reader's understanding? Does it relate clearly to your main point and contribute directly to the overall effect you are aiming for? If in doubt, leave it out. In telling a story, economy is just as important as the use of precise, vigorous language. We've all been bored to stupefac-

tion by storytellers who go on, and on, and on, delaying the point so long that by the time they do get to it—*if* they get to it— the listener's attention has long since wandered off in another direction.

2. Arrange the events of the story in the most effective time order. Once you've selected the significant details, consider how to arrange them to ensure maximum impact on the reader. How can you ensure the reader's interest right from the start? What should come first? What last? Is straight chronological order—a recounting of events in the order in which they occurred—called for? Or would the impact be greater if you began with an event that occurred in the middle of the chronological sequence, then introduced a flashback to fill in significant events that occurred prior to the point at which you began? This is the technique Michael Ignatieff chooses in "Deficits," for example. There is no single "best" arrangement of events in your story; once you've decided on the significant events you intend to include, experi- ment with a couple of different arrangements to determine which will produce the effect you're aiming for. Once you've settled on a time order, *stick to it*. Narratives usually rely on a certain amount of suspense to draw the readers through the story. Unless the time sequence is clear and logical, however, you're more likely to create confusion than suspense.

3. Use the same POINT OF VIEW (or angle of narration) throughout your paper. If an "I" is telling the story, don't shift in midstream to a "he" or a "she" or a "you." A consistent point of view is essential to the story's unity. Changing the point of view will only confuse your readers, who need to experience the story through a single narrative perspective.

4. Use TRANSITIONS to make your narrative coherent and to help your readers keep straight the relationships among events. Avoid stringing your sentences and paragraphs together with "and then . . . and then . . . and then," which will bore, if not annoy, your readers. Provide time markers that indicate where you are in the progression or development of the event: "after," "suddenly," "next," "as soon as," and "finally" are useful sig- nals that help your readers keep on track.

Writing effective description also involves adhering to organizational principles that direct and shape your writing. Here are three to keep in mind:

1. Before you begin to write, decide on the purpose of your descrip- tion. Is it your intention to create a factual, objective picture for

your reader? Or do you wish to create a dominant impression that reflects your personal values and feelings? Clarifying your purpose is necessary before you can select appropriate key points and an effective structure.

2.   Keeping your purpose in mind, select the physical details and words that will most effectively communicate the picture or impression you wish to convey. Good description evokes sensory impressions. You should include those features most likely to have a strong effect and memorable impact on your readers. Effective description often makes use of figurative language (see FIGURES OF SPEECH) to make the reader not only understand but also feel what the writer is describing.

3.   Once you have selected the details you wish to include, your next task is to arrange them in the most appropriate order, an order that is either inherent in the subject or dictated by the context. To describe a person, for instance, you could move from head to toe (not very interesting), or from external features to internal character. Or you could provide an overview—a general impression—before concentrating on the features most significant to your purpose. Note how Emily Carr organizes her description of Sophie (paragraph 5), for example. She proceeds from top to bottom and from general to particular—for a purpose.

If you were describing a photograph, you might introduce the details, in order, from left to right, or top to bottom, or from near to far—or vice versa. One pattern of organization is not necessarily better than another, although you are likely to have the greatest impact on your reader if you build from least important detail to the most important detail. (Just be sure your least important detail is described in language interesting enough to keep your reader awake!)

Writing narration and description may seem at first glance to be a relatively simple task. And it's true that you have probably had lots of experience with these forms in high school. Writing good narration and description—prose that has the intended effect on your readers, however—requires careful planning and close attention to detail. Mastering these rhetorical forms is well worth your time and effort, though, since most writing includes both narrative and descriptive passages. Because they answer the most fundamental questions readers ask—what is it like? what happened next?—narration and description are two of the most useful tools a writer can use to build understanding.

The essay below illustrates how narration and description can be used in combination to help communicate the writer's point.

New Year's in September

New Year's Day is the day after Labour Day. Every teacher knows this; so does every student. It is a fact of life for all of us who have not yet graduated from school. On that day in early September, teachers and students are partners in their excitement—often cunningly disguised under a layer of cynical ennui—at the annual New Beginning. As full of potential as a brand new spiral-bound notebook or an unsharpened pencil or an uncluttered desk, we assemble, determined to do better this year.

In the midst of this annual ritual, I find a moment to reflect on earlier first days, chosen from a staggering number now, since I have spent all but a handful of Labour Days in anticipation of school the next morning. Often my reflections fix on that day in 1971 when I faced my first class of college students. By that time, I'd had lots of first days: eight in primary school, five in high school, four in university, and two as a high school teacher. Many of them have been memorable, some pleasant, a few traumatic. But this first day in 1971 was the beginning of a new career: I was going to teach English to Theatre Arts students, and I was going to be great.

Aware that first impressions are all-important on these occasions, I pulled out all the stops and dressed resplendently in my green, double-breasted, pinstripe suit. This garment was my guarantee of a sensational start: the pants flared to a full twelve inches at the cuff (measurements in bell-bottomed pants do not have metric equivalents); the lapels were knife-edged and came out to *here*, where the heavily padded

Introduction (makes a general statement about a particular day)

Narrative begins here with a flashback to a specific instance of the general statement in Paragraph 1

Description (note the use of precise details that enable the reader to "see" the writer)

shoulders took over. The vest was paisley satin; the belt almost three inches wide and trimmed with a silver buckle that weighed two pounds; and the tie . . . is best left to your imagination. I finished off my ensemble with zippered boots that added a full inch to my 6'4" height. With my shiny new leather briefcase, recently trimmed shag haircut, and drooping Mexican bandit moustache, I presented the perfect picture of "with it" '70s professorial good taste.

Transition between descriptive passage and narrative

Those Theatre Arts students would be eating from my hand before I even began my carefully prepared introductory remarks.

Narrative resumes here

The Theatre School was a drive across town, and I left very early so I would have time to explore my new environment. The Theatre School was a dingy and decrepit old church, long since deemed uninhabitable by a decent God-fearing congregation. Directed by a sign pointing me to the ancient parish hall, I pulled open the grimy door and was greeted by the

Descriptive details appeal to several senses:

heady scent of old building mixed with

smell

fibreglass resin, paint, glue, sawdust, and a potpourri of unidentifiable odours.

hearing

Somewhere in the back of the building, a circular saw screamed frantically. I

sight

made my way along a bilious green hallway lined with brown lockers that looked as though they might have seen service in World War II. The glaring fluorescent lights, inches above my head, revealed the accumulated grime and abuse of many years. I crept past the woodshop where a set-building class was in progress. Banshees would have quailed before the agonized shrieks of that circular saw. What were they cutting in there? At the end of the hall, I found

touch

my classroom and tentatively pushed open the scarred wooden door. Large drafting tables and high stools filled most of the space; a blackboard and battered wooden desk at the front were the only evidence of potential academic function. Swallowing my disappointment and determined to make the best of it, I sat down at the desk to look through my notes and await my students.

Transition back to the narrative {

Narrative resumes here — Mercifully, the circular saw wailed its last and expired. For a moment there was silence; then I heard the babble of excited voices. I stood and set my face in what I hoped was a stern but sympathetic expression, prepared to impress my class. They arrived in a clump, as motley and colourful a group as ever trod the planks of a pirate ship. Dressed in a mind-boggling variety of torn and tattered blue jeans, checkered bell-bottoms, bright miniskirts, flowing granny dresses, garishly-coloured shirts, bandannas, hats, scarves and bangles, they swarmed into the room. Shouting and hooting in high spirits, chattering with neighbours or singing loudly and unselfconsciously, they selected their tables and perched on the high stools like bright, raucous birds. Before long, someone noticed me, and word quickly spread through the flock. Soon the room was silent. We spent several long, anxious moments staring at each other in wonder. They apparently had never seen anything quite like my suit; I certainly had never experienced anything like this gypsy mob. The silence grew, none of us sure how to begin. It was like a first meeting between alien races. Finally a late arrival broke the ice. A long-haired girl sauntered through the door and down the aisle to the front of the class. She was dressed in faded overalls and a yellow T-shirt displaying what looked like a

Descriptive details paint a picture of the class

Transition to narrative

Narrative continues and tension builds

Climactic incident breaks the ice — and the tension — with use of dialogue, the "punch line"

two-word obscenity (misspelled) across her chest. We eyed each other. She climbed onto a stool, grinned, and said, "Hi, I'm Peggy. You speak English?"

Conclusion (brings together descriptive details of place, time, and characters)

I didn't wear my green double-breasted pinstripe to the Theatre School again. In return, I was accepted and allowed to teach . . . so long as I didn't take myself too seriously. All in all, it was a happy arrangement—so happy, indeed, that I still think back on that long-abandoned old building with affection. Certainly, the structure was a fire trap and an eyesore, but somehow, despite—or maybe *because of*—their horrible environment, the students were among the most creative, the most dedicated, and the most fun I have experienced in my teaching career. They are scattered now all over the country, some of them probably still working in theatre. Wherever they are and whatever they are doing, they often get a quick and affectionate "Break a leg!" from a grateful teacher on our New Year's anniversary: the first Tuesday in September.

Last sentence echoes the introduction, contributing to unity

The Subways of New York

MICHELE LANDSBERG

Well before Bernie Goetz became a dubious national hero by trying to kill four black youths on the IRT° at Christmas in 1984, the New York subway had become a hellish metaphor.

While the subways of Moscow, Montreal, London, and Paris are

"The Subways of New York" from *This is New York, Honey!* by Michele Landsberg. Used by permission of the Canadian Publishers, McClelland and Stewart, Toronto.

celebrated as distinctive symbols of urban living, the New York subway strikes fear into the hearts of everyone who doesn't live here, and even most of those who do. (A survey in the Bronx revealed that 23 per cent of adults and 33 per cent of youths carry weapons when they go underground, knives being the side-arm of choice.)

3   As a fairly regular rider of the Terror of the Deep, also known as the Beast by some transit cops, I have to say it's not nearly so bad as it's cracked up to be. True, it has a staggering crime rate, by Canadian standards—eleven homicides, twenty-eight rapes, and thirteen thousand felonies in 1985—but all things are relative. There were, after all, two thousand murders above ground that year.

4   Like everything else in New York, the sheer scale of the thing is overwhelming: its size, speed, filth, even its corruption—one tunnel, still not open, has been under construction for twenty years. Three and a half million fares a day are deposited in turnstiles at 463 stations (and 118,000 more fare beaters jump over turnstiles or enter through exit gates); six thousand individually powered cars rattle along 687 miles of track at a top speed of forty miles an hour. Despite the fact that many of the cars are thirty years old and much of the equipment almost farcically outdated, close to 87 per cent of the trains arrive and depart on time.

5   The subway's terrible reputation is partly a subjective response to frightening surroundings. Nobody knows that better than I; on a visit to New York before I lived here, I took the subway for the first time to get back from the Brooklyn Museum. Flinching down a urine-soaked stairway to the murky depths, I asked directions from a stranger just as the train roared in.

6   "Don't get on the last ca-a-ar!" he screamed after me as I sprinted for the train. (The parlour car, as it's known, is the mobile headquarters for drug dealers.) I rode all the way to Manhattan in the heroic mood of one who has overcome great peril.

7   But the crime rate underground is in fact dropping, partly because of the four thousand transit police, at least one on every train after 8:00 P.M. "Of course," conceded° transit spokesman Bob Slovak, "an armed robbery in a train is a lot scarier, because there's nowhere to flee."

8   That thought does occur to me now and then as I joggle along in the stench, crowds, and graffiti grottiness°. It's hard not to feel menaced in a car that resembles a moving coal bin, where the few working lights flicker wanly, and every possible surface (including emergency exit instructions) is a black smear of illiterate spray-painted scrawl.

9   (By 1989, every car on the east side lines, which are making a determined pitch for Wall Street commuters, is a model of sprightly

newness. The cars with the hideously uncomfortable orange plastic seats, which don't fit anyone's derriere, are said to be Canadian made.)

The stations now have brightly lit "off-hours waiting areas" in 10 sight of the ticket booth, where late travellers grimly bunch together. Around them stretch Piranesi° vistas of vaulted gloom. Water drips from rusted overhead pipes to collect in rancid puddles on the stairways and between the tracks, scummed over with disintegrating candy wrappers and coffee cups. You imagine, though you rarely see, the rats.

The mad and the desperate are more visible. Beggars hiss at you 11 on the stairways; sleepers bundled by the walls have the pallor° of death, as though they haven't surfaced to the light in years . . . as indeed they may not have. Transit police call the homeless derelicts° who live in abandoned tunnels "skells," a hideously evocative word. On the Grand Central Shuttle the other day, passengers practised stony avoidance as a trance-eyed man, whose denim jacket announced "Con-Chon-Thon for Lord Jesus, Master Dragon," treated us to a wheezing religious rap.

It wasn't always like this. In 1912, workers excavating for the 12 new BMT were astonished to dig up the forgotten remains of the Beach Pneumatic Subway, the 1870 creation of Alfred Ely Beach. Any of us might have been amazed: that very first New York subway had a luxurious plush-seated car that ran a total of 312 feet under Broadway, propelled from behind by a huge fan. The carpeted— carpeted!—station was complete with paintings, a fountain, a grand piano, and Grecian statues holding up elegant globe lamps.

The current subway opened in 1904, and its first full day of 13 operation earned the headline "Rush Hour Blockade." Rush hour is still traumatic. The police have thirty-seven German shepherds ("They're not dogs, they're wolves," leered Mayor Ed Koch) who, despite their limitations—they can't pursue thieves up escalators— have an impressive arrest record, being trained to "bite and hold, rather than devour a person's flesh" according to a reassuring officer. But rush hour is still the peak crime time.

I admit that it sounds, and frequently smells, awful. In summer, 14 the heat, especially in stalled cars, is unbearable. The aging tracks are probably the world's noisiest. Still, improvements (rather like the work of Sisyphus°) are ongoing. I have actually ridden on a gleaming new graffiti-free silver express to Brooklyn, in which a mellifluous° conductor coaxingly announced, over a clear PA system, "Your local is waiting across the platform; step lively now to make your connection." The connection turned out to be a sinister, filthy shuttle in which restless teenagers passed ceaselessly from car to car, looking for easy marks.

15   Is this an indictment of the New York subway? No. Criss-crossing the city underground, I am always awed by the speed and convenience with which it transports its human freight, and I never fail to imagine the snarling, gridlocked traffic somewhere over my head. Part of New York's greatness is due to its huge, concentrated working population, and the city simply could not exist without the subway. Perhaps no city can be great without a subway.

16   Screeching, grinding, rattling, and roaring through the years, the subway still speaks hauntingly of the motto carved in stone at the City Hall station, a testament to that co-operative urban spirit: *Non nobis nati solum*—born not for ourselves alone.

$$\boxed{}$$

MICHELE LANDSBERG

Michele Landsberg (b. 1939) is a Canadian author, columnist, and feminist. Her books include *Women and Children First*, *Michele Landsberg's Guide to Children's Literature*, and *This Is New York, Honey!*, which recounts episodes from her three-year stint in New York City where her husband, Stephen Lewis, served as Canada's ambassador to the United Nations.

Paragraph

Words and Meanings

Paragraph	Term	Meaning
1	IRT:	Interborough Rapid Transit (the name of a New York subway line)
7	conceded:	admitted, acknowledged
8	grottiness:	grubby, dirty atmosphere
10	Piranesi:	eighteenth-century Italian artist who created wonderful engravings of ancient Greek and Roman archaeological finds
11	pallor:	unhealthy, pale colour
	derelicts:	people who have no home or money
14	Sisyphus:	mythological figure who was doomed forever to roll a huge rock to the top of a hill, only to have it roll back down again
	mellifluous:	pleasant-voiced

Structure and Strategy

1.   What senses does Landsberg appeal to in her description of the New York subway? Identify a couple of examples for each.

2. Which descriptive details do you find to be most effective in illustrating the "terrible reputation" of New York's subways?
3. Paragraphs 2, 3, and 4 are developed by means of statistics. What purpose do the numbers serve? What do they contribute to the points Landsberg is making about the transit system?
4. What is the purpose of paragraph 12? How does it contribute to the overall effect of the essay?

Content and Purpose

1. What is the THESIS of this essay? Is it stated or implied?
2. What is the purpose of Landsberg's ALLUSION to the myth of Sisyphus? What similarity is there between Sisyphus' doom and the maintenance of the subway system?
3. Paragraphs 15 and 16 seem to contradict the view of the transit system that Landsberg has created in the preceding paragraphs. What is Landsberg's opinion of the New York subway system?
4. What do you think Landsberg means when she writes, "Perhaps no city can be great without a subway." Do you agree with her?

Suggestions for Writing

1. Compare Landsberg's description of the New York transit system with your own experience of a transit system in a city other than New York.
2. Write an essay that describes in convincing detail a particular city location, or district, or system that evokes fear in the people who live there.

Sophie

EMILY CARR

Sophie's house was bare but clean. It had   1
three rooms. Later when it got cold Sophie's Frank would cut out all the partition walls. Sophie said, "Thlee 'loom, thlee stobe. One 'loom, one stobe." The floor of the house was clean scrubbed. It was chair, table, and bed for the family. There was one chair; the coal-oil lamp sat on that. Sophie pushed the babies into corners, spread my old clothes on the floor to appraise° them, and was satisfied. So,

"Sophie" from *Klee Wyck* by Emily Carr. Copyright 1941. Reprinted with the permission of Irwin Publishing, Inc.

having tested each other's trade-straightedness°, we began a long, long friendship—forty years. I have seen Sophie glad, sad, sick, and drunk. I have asked her why she did this or that thing—Indian ways that I did not understand—her answer was invariably, "Nice ladies always do." That was Sophie's ideal—being nice.

2   Every year Sophie had a new baby. Almost every year she buried one. Her little graves were dotted all over the cemetery. I never knew more than three of her twenty-one children to be alive at one time. By the time she was in her early fifties every child was dead and Sophie had cried her eyes dry. Then she took to drink.

3   "I got a new baby! I got a new baby!"

4   Sophie, seated on the floor of her house, saw me coming through the open door and waved the papoose cradle. Two little girls rolled round on the floor; the new baby was near her in a basket-cradle. Sophie took off the cloth tented over the basket and exhibited the baby, a lean, poor thing.

5   Sophie herself was small and spare. Her black hair sprang thick and strong on each side of the clean, straight parting and hung in twin braids across her shoulders. Her eyes were sad and heavy-lidded. Between prominent rounded cheekbones her nose lay rather flat, broadening and snubby at the tip. Her wide upper lip pouted. It was sharp-edged, puckering over a row of poor teeth—the soothing pucker of lips trying to ease an aching tooth or to hush a crying child. She had a soft little body, a back straight as honesty itself, and the small hands and feet of an Indian.

6   Sophie's English was good enough, but when Frank, her husband, was there she became dumb as a plate.

7   "Why won't you talk before Frank, Sophie?"

8   "Frank he learn school English. Me, no. Frank laugh my English words."

9   When we were alone she chattered to me like a sparrow.

10   In May, when the village was white with cherry blossom and the blue water or Burrard Inlet crept almost to Sophie's door— just a streak of grey sand and a plank walk between—and when Vancouver city was more beautiful to look at across the water than to be in—it was then I loved to take the ferry to the North Shore and to Sophie's.

11   Behind the village stood mountains topped by the grand old "Lions," twin peaks, very white and blue. The nearer mountains were every shade of young foliage, tender grey-green, getting greener and greener till, when they were close, you saw that the village grass outgreened them all. Hens strutted their broods,

papooses and pups and kittens rolled everywhere—it was good indeed to spend a day on the Reserve in spring.

Sophie and I went to see her babies' graves first. Sophie took   12
her best plaid skirt, the one that had three rows of velvet ribbon round the hem, from a nail on the wall, and bound a yellow silk handkerchief round her head. No matter what the weather, she always wore her great shawl, clamping it down with her arms, the fringe trickling over her fingers. Sophie wore her shoes when she walked with me, if she remembered.

Across the water we could see the city. The Indian Reserve was   13
a different world—no hurry, no business.

We walked over the twisty, up-and-down road to the cemetery.   14
Casamin, Tommy, George, Rosie, Maria, Emily, and all the rest were there under a tangle of vines. We rambled, seeking out Sophie's graves. Some had little wooden crosses, some had stones. Two babies lay outside the cemetery fence: they had not faced life long enough for baptism.

"See! Me got stone for Rosie now."   15

"It looks very nice. It must have cost lots of money, Sophie."   16

"Grave man make cheap for me. He say, 'You got lots, lots stone   17
from me, Sophie. Maybe bymby you get some more died baby, then you want more stone. So I make cheap for you.' "

Sophie's kitchen was crammed with excited women. They had   18
come to see Sophie's brand-new twins. Sophie was on a mattress beside the cook stove. The twin girls were in small basket papoose cradles, woven by Sophie herself. The babies were wrapped in cotton wool which made their dark little faces look darker; they were laced into their baskets and stuck up at the edge of Sophie's mattress beside the kitchen stove. Their brown, wrinkled faces were like potatoes baked in their jackets, their hands no bigger than brown spiders.

They were thrilling, those very, very tiny babies. Everybody was   19
excited over them. I sat down on the floor close to Sophie.

"Sophie, if the baby was a girl it was to have my name. There   20
are two babies and I have only one name. What are we going to do about it?"

"The biggest and the best is yours," said Sophie.   21

My Em'ly lived three months. Sophie's Maria lived three weeks.   22
I bought Em'ly's tombstone. Sophie bought Maria's.

Sophie's "mad" rampaged inside her like a lion roaring in the   23
breast of a dove.

"Look see," she said, holding a red and yellow handkerchief,   24 caught together at the corners and chinking with broken glass and bits of plaster of Paris. "Bad boy bloke my grave flower! Cost five dollar one, and now boy all bloke fo' me. Bad, bad boy! You come talk me fo' p'liceman?"

25   At the City Hall she spread the handkerchief on the table and held half a plaster of Paris lily and a dove's tail up to the eyes of the law, while I talked.

26   "My mad fo' boy bloke my plitty glave flower," she said, forgetting, in her fury, to be shy of the "English words."

27   The big man of the law was kind. He said, "It's too bad, Sophie. What do you want me to do about it?"

28   "You make boy buy more this plitty kind for my glave."

29   "The boy has no money but I can make his old grandmother pay a little every week."

30   Sophie looked long at the broken pieces and shook her head.

31   "That ole, ole woman got no money." Sophie's anger was dying, soothed by sympathy like a child, the woman in her tender towards old Granny. "My bloke no matter for ole woman," said Sophie, gathering up the pieces. "You scold boy big, Policeman? No make glanny pay."

32   "I sure will, Sophie."

33   There was a black skirt spread over the top of the packing case in the centre of Sophie's room. On it stood the small white coffin. A lighted candle was at the head, another at the foot. The little dead girl in the coffin held a doll in her arms. It had hardly been out of them since I had taken it to her a week before. The glassy eyes of the doll stared out of the coffin, up past the closed eyelids of the child.

34   Though Sophie had been through this nineteen times before, the twentieth time was no easier. Her two friends, Susan and Sara, were there by the coffin, crying for her.

35   The outer door opened and a half dozen women came in, their shawls drawn low across their foreheads, their faces grim. They stepped over to the coffin and looked in. Then they sat around it on the floor and began to cry, first with baby whimpers, softly, then louder, louder still—with violence and strong howling: torrents of tears burst from their eyes and rolled down their cheeks. Sophie and Sara and Susan did it too. It sounded horrible—like tortured dogs.

36   Suddenly they stopped. Sophie went to the bucket and got water in a tin basin. She took a towel in her hand and went to each of the guests in turn holding the basin while they washed their faces and dried them on the towel. Then the women all went out except

Sophie, Sara and Susan. This crying had gone on at intervals for three days—ever since the child had died. Sophie was worn out. There had been too all the long weeks of Rosie's tubercular° dying to go through.

"Sophie, couldn't you lie down and rest?"   37

She shook her head. "Nobody sleep in Injun house till dead   38
people go to cemet'ry."

The beds had all been taken away.   39

"When is the funeral?"   40

"I dunno. Pliest go Vancouver. He not come two more day.   41
'Spose I gots lots money he come quick. No hully up, except fo'
money."

She laid her hand on the corner of the little coffin.   42

"See! Coffin-man think box fo' Injun baby no matter."   43

The seams of the cheap little coffin had burst.   44

Sophie's other neighbour, Susan, produced and buried babies   45
almost as fast as Sophie herself. The two women laughed for each
other and cried for each other. With babies on their backs and
baskets on their arms they crossed over on the ferry to Vancouver
and sold their baskets from door to door. When they came to my
studio they rested and drank tea with me. My parrot, sheep dog,
the white rats, and the totem pole pictures all interested them. "An'
you got Injun flowers too," said Susan.

"Indian flowers?"   46

She pointed to ferns and wild things I had brought in from the   47
woods.

Sophie's house was shut up. There was a chain and padlock on   48
the gate. I went to Susan.

"Where is Sophie?"   49

"Sophie in sick house. Got sick eye."   50

I went to the hospital. The little Indian ward had four beds. I   51
took ice cream and the nurse divided it into four portions.

A homesick little Indian girl cried in the bed in one corner, an   52
old woman grumbled in another. In a third there was a young
mother with a baby, and in the fourth bed was Sophie.

There were flowers. The room was bright. It seemed to me that   53
the four brown faces on the four white pillows should be happier
and far more comfortable here than lying on mattresses on the hard
floors in the village, with all the family muddle going on about them.

"How nice it is here, Sophie."   54

"Not much good of hospital, Em'ly."   55

"Oh! What is the matter with it?"   56

"Bad bed."   57

58   "What is wrong with the beds?"

59   "Move, move, all time shake. 'Spose me move, bed move too."

60   She rolled herself to show me how the springs worked. "Me ole'-fashioned, Em'ly. Me like kitchen floor fo' sick."

61   Susan and Sophie were in my kitchen, rocking their sorrows back and forth and alternately wagging their heads and giggling with shut eyes at some small joke.

62   "You go live Victoria now, Em'ly," wailed Sophie, "and we never see those babies, never!"

63   Neither woman had a baby on her back these days. But each had a little new grave in the cemetery. I had told them about a friend's twin babies. I went to the telephone.

64   "Mrs. Dingle, you said I might bring Sophie to see the twins?"

65   "Surely, any time," came the ready reply.

66   "Come, Sophie and Susan, we can go and see the babies now."

67   The mothers of all those little cemetery mounds stood looking and looking at the thriving white babies, kicking and sprawling on their bed. The women said, "Oh my! Oh my!" over and over.

68   Susan's hand crept from beneath her shawl to touch a baby's leg. Sophie's hand shot out and slapped Susan's.

69   The mother of the babies said, "It's all right, Susan; you may touch my baby."

70   Sophie's eyes burned Susan for daring to do what she so longed to do herself. She folded her hands resolutely under her shawl and whispered to me:

71   "Nice ladies don' touch, Em'ly."

EMILY CARR

Emily Carr (1871–1945) was born in Victoria, B.C., and studied painting in the United States, England, and France. Until the 1930s, she created fine paintings of West Coast landscapes and Indian culture. Later in her life, she turned to writing; her books include *Klee Wyck* (1941), which won the Governor General's Award, and *The House of All Sorts* (1944).

Paragraph

Words and Meanings

1	appraise:	assess the value of
	trade-straightedness:	honesty in an exchange of goods or favours
36	tubercular:	suffering from tuberculosis, a serious and highly infectious lung disease

Structure and Strategy

1. In narration and description, one of the writer's challenges is to select only those details that are relevant to the overall purpose and that contribute to the desired effect. Identify the significant details in paragraphs 1, 12, and 33, and show how they contribute to UNITY.
2. What is the IRONY in the last line of this essay? Identify other examples of irony in the piece and explain how they contribute to Carr's purpose.
3. "Sophie" tells a story through a series of scenes and exchanges of dialogue. Compare the effectiveness of this method of story-telling with that used by Carol Geddes, whose "Growing Up Native" relies on summary to convey the story.
4. The time order of events in "Sophie" is important to the effect. Is the sequence of events clear? Can you put the events in chronological order? What is lost by arranging the scenes chronologically?
5. The use of flashbacks requires the writer to pay especially careful attention to COHERENCE. Identify three or four of the devices Carr uses to achieve coherence in this piece. Consider language and content as well as the familiar transitional devices.

Content and Purpose

1. Does Carr use STEREOTYPING in this piece? Consider her use of DICTION and descriptive details as well as content in your answer.
2. Throughout "Sophie," the contrast between life lived by Indians on the reserve and life lived by whites in the city is both stated and implied. Find several examples of this contrast and summarize it in your own words.
3. "Sophie" narrates a tragic story: the loss of one woman's twenty-one children. What factors do you think are responsible for the deaths of Sophie's children during infancy and childhood?

Suggestions for Writing

1. Contrast Sophie's resignation to the circumstances of her sad life with Carol Geddes's active resistance to the racism and poverty she describes in "Growing Up Native."
2. In a library, find some reproductions of Emily Carr's paintings of West Coast Indian life. Describe one of the paintings to convey both its physical appearance and its emotional content to your reader.
3. After studying some of Carr's paintings, write an essay in which

you identify and develop some of the themes that are found both
in her paintings and in "Sophie."

Growing Up Native

CAROL GEDDES

1   remember it was cold. We were walking
through a swamp near our home in the Yukon bush. Maybe it was
fall and moose-hunting season. I don't know. I think I was about
four years old at the time. The muskeg° was too springy to walk on,
so people were taking turns carrying me—passing me from one set
of arms to another. The details about where we were are vague, but
the memory of those arms and the feeling of acceptance I had is one
of the most vivid memories of my childhood. It didn't matter who
was carrying me—there was security in every pair of arms. That
response to children is typical of the native community. It's the first
thing I think of when I cast my mind back to the Yukon bush, where
I was born and lived with my family.

2   I was six years old when we moved out of the bush, first to
Teslin, where I had a hint of the problems native people face, then
to Whitehorse, where there was unimaginable racism. Eventually I
moved to Ottawa and Montreal, where I further discovered that to
grow up native in Canada is to feel the sting of humiliation and the
boot of discrimination. But it is also to experience the enviable
security of an extended family and to learn to appreciate the richness
of the heritage and traditions of a culture most North Americans
have never been lucky enough to know. As a film-maker, I have
tried to explore these contradictions, and our triumph over them,
for the half-million aboriginals° who are part of the tide of swelling
independence of the First Nations today.

3   But I'm getting ahead of myself. If I'm to tell the story of what
it's like to grow up native in northern Canada, I have to go back to
the bush where I was born, because there's more to my story than the
hurtful stereotyping that depicts Indian people as drunken welfare
cases. Our area was known as 12-mile (it was 12 miles from another
tiny village). There were about 40 people living there—including 25
kids, eight of them my brothers and sisters—in a sort of family
compound. Each family had its own timber plank house for sleeping,

and there was one large common kitchen area with gravel on the ground and a tent frame over it. Everybody would go there and cook meals together. In summer, my grandmother always had a smudge fire going to smoke fish and tan moose hides. I can remember the cosy warmth of the fire, the smell of good food, and always having someone to talk to. We kids had built-in playmates and would spend hours running in the bush, picking berries, building rafts on the lake and playing in abandoned mink cages.

One of the people in my village tells a story about the day the   4
old lifestyle began to change. He had been away hunting in the bush for about a month. On his way back, he heard a strange sound coming from far away. He ran up to the crest of a hill, looked over the top of it and saw a bulldozer. He had never seen or heard of such a thing before and he couldn't imagine what it was. We didn't have magazines or newspapers in our village, and the people didn't know that the Alaska Highway was being built as a defence against a presumed Japanese invasion during the Second World War. That was the beginning of the end of the Teslin Tlingit people's way of life. From that moment on, nothing turned back to the way it was. Although there were employment opportunities for my father and uncles, who were young men at the time, the speed and force with which the Alaska Highway was rammed through the wilderness caused tremendous upheaval for Yukon native people.

It wasn't as though we'd never experienced change before. The   5
Tlingit Nation, which I belong to, arrived in the Yukon from the Alaskan coast around the turn of the century. They were the middle-men and women between the Russian traders and the Yukon inland Indians. The Tlingit gained power and prestige by trading European products such as metal goods and cloth for the rich and varied furs so much in fashion in Europe. The Tlingit controlled Yukon trading because they controlled the trading routes through the high mountain passes. When trading ceased to be an effective means of survival, my grandparents began raising wild mink in cages. Mink prices were really high before and during the war, but afterwards the prices went plunging down. So, although the mink pens were still there when I was a little girl, my father mainly worked on highway construction and hunted in the bush. The Yukon was then, and still is in some ways, in a transitional period—from living off the land to getting into a European wage-based economy.

As a young child, I didn't see the full extent of the upheaval. I   6
remember a lot of togetherness, a lot of happiness while we lived in the bush. There's a very strong sense of family in the native community, and a fondness for children, especially young children. Even today, it's like a special form of entertainment if someone brings a baby to visit. That sense of family is the one thing that

has survived all the incredible difficulties native people have had. Throughout a time of tremendous problems, the extended family system has somehow lasted, providing a strong circle for people to survive in. When parents were struggling with alcoholism or had to go away to find work, when one of the many epidemics swept through the community, or when a marriage broke up and one parent left, aunts, uncles and grandparents would try to fill those roles. It's been very important to me in terms of emotional support to be able to rely on my extended family. There are still times when such support keeps me going.

7   Life was much simpler when we lived in the bush. Although we were poor and wore the same clothes all year, we were warm enough and had plenty to eat. But even as a youngster, I began to be aware of some of the problems we would face later on. Travelling missionaries would come and impose themselves on us, for example. They'd sit at our campfire and read the Bible to us and lecture us about how we had to live a Christian life. I remember being very frightened by stories we heard about parents sending their kids away to live with white people who didn't have any children. We thought those people were mean and that if we were bad, we'd be sent away, too. Of course, that was when social workers were scooping up native children and adopting them out to white families in the south. The consequences were usually disastrous for the children who were taken away—alienation, alcoholism and suicide, among other things. I knew some of those kids. The survivors are still struggling to recover.

8   The residential schools were another source of misery for the kids. Although I didn't have to go, my brothers and sisters were there. They told stories about having their hair cut off in case they were carrying head lice, and of being forced to do hard chores without enough food to eat. They were told that the Indian culture was evil, that Indian people were bad, that their only hope was to be Christian. They had to stand up and say things like "I've found the Lord," when a teacher told them to speak. Sexual abuse was rampant in the residential school system.

9   By the time we moved to Whitehorse, I was excited about the idea of living in what I thought of as a big town. I'd had a taste of the outside world from books at school in Teslin (a town of 250 people), and I was tremendously curious about what life was like. I was hungry for experiences such as going to the circus. In fact, for a while, I was obsessed with stories and pictures about the circus, but then when I was 12 and saw my first one, I was put off by the condition and treatment of the animals.

10   Going to school in Whitehorse was a shock. The clash of native and white values was confusing and frightening. Let me tell you a

story. The older boys in our community were already accomplished hunters and fishermen, but since they had to trap beaver in the spring and hunt moose in the fall, and go out trapping in the winter as well, they missed a lot of school. We were all in one classroom and some of my very large teenage cousins had to sit squeezed into little desks. These guys couldn't read very well. We girls had been in school all along, so, of course, we were better readers. One day the teacher was trying to get one of the older boys to read. She was typical of the teachers at that time, insensitive and ignorant of cultural complexities. In an increasingly loud voice, she kept commanding him to "Read it, read it." He couldn't. He sat there completely still, but I could see that he was breaking into a sweat. The teacher then said, "Look, she can read it," and she pointed to me, indicating that I should stand up and read. For a young child to try to show up an older boy is wrong and totally contrary to native cultural values, so I refused. She told me to stand up and I did. My hands were trembling as I held my reader. She yelled at me to read and when I didn't she smashed her pointing stick on the desk to frighten me. In terror, I wet my pants. As I stood there fighting my tears of shame, she said I was disgusting and sent me home. I had to walk a long distance through the bush by myself to get home. I remember feeling this tremendous confusion, on top of my humiliation. We were always told the white teachers knew best, and so we had to do whatever they said at school. And yet I had a really strong sense of receiving mixed messages about what I was supposed to do in the community and what I was supposed to do at school.

Pretty soon I hated school. Moving to a predominately white 11 high school was even worse. We weren't allowed to join anything the white kids started. We were the butt of jokes because of our secondhand clothes and moose meat sandwiches. We were constantly being rejected. The prevailing attitude was that Indians were stupid. When it was time to make course choices in class—between typing and science, for example—they didn't even ask the native kids, they just put us all in typing. You get a really bad image of yourself in a situation like that. I bought into it. I thought we were awful. The whole experience was terribly undermining. Once, my grandmother gave me a pretty little pencil box. I walked into the classroom one day to find the word "squaw" carved on it. That night I burned it in the wood stove. I joined the tough crowd and by the time I was 15 years old, I was more likely to be leaning against the school smoking a cigarette than trying to join in. I was burned out from trying to join the system. The principal told my father there was no point in sending me back to school so, with a Grade 9 education, I started to work at a series of menial° jobs.

Seven years later something happened to me that would change 12 my life forever. I had moved to Ottawa with a man and was working as a waitress in a restaurant. One day, a friend invited me to her place for coffee. While I was there, she told me she was going to university in the fall and showed me her reading list. I'll never forget the minutes that followed. I was feeling vaguely envious of her and, once again, inferior. I remember taking the paper in my hand, seeing the books on it and realizing, Oh, my God, I've read these books! It hit me like a thunderclap. I was stunned that books I had read were being read in university. University was for white kids, not native kids. We were too stupid, we didn't have the kind of mind it took to do those things. My eyes moved down the list, and my heart started beating faster and faster as I suddenly realized I could go to university, too!

13 My partner at the time was a loving supportive man who helped me in every way. I applied to the university immediately as a mature student but when I had to write Grade 9 on the application, I was sure they'd turn me down. They didn't. I graduated five years later, earning a bachelor of arts in English and philosophy (with distinction). . . .

14 Today, there's a glimmer of hope that more of us native people will overcome the obstacles that have tripped us up ever since we began sharing this land. Some say our cultures are going through a renaissance. Maybe that's true. Certainly there's a renewed interest in native dancing, acting and singing, and in other cultural traditions. Even indigenous° forms of government are becoming strong again. But we can't forget that the majority of native people live in urban areas and continue to suffer from alcohol and drug abuse and the plagues of a people who have lost their culture and have become lost themselves. And the welfare system is the insidious° glue that holds together the machine of oppression of native people.

15 Too many non-native people have refused to try to understand the issues behind our land claims. They make complacent pronouncements such as "Go back to your bows and arrows and fish with spears if you want aboriginal rights. If not, give it up and assimilate into white Canadian culture." I don't agree with that. We need our culture, but there's no reason why we can't preserve it and have an automatic washing machine and a holiday in Mexico, as well.

16 The time has come for native people to make our own decisions. We need to have self-government. I have no illusions that it will be smooth sailing—there will be trial and error and further struggle. And if that means crawling before we can stand up and walk, so be it. We'll have to learn through experience.

17 While we're learning, we have a lot to teach and give to the world—a holistic° philosophy, a way of living with the earth, not

disposing of it. It is critical that we all learn from the elders that an individual is not more important than a forest; we know that we're here to live on and with the earth, not to subdue it.

18   The wheels are in motion for a revival, for change in the way native people are taking their place in Canada. I can see that we're equipped, we have the tools to do the work. We have an enormous number of smart, talented, moral Indian people. It's thrilling to be a part of this movement.

19   Someday, when I'm an elder, I'll tell the children the stories: about the bush, about the hard times, about the renaissance, and especially about the importance of knowing your place in your nation.

$$\boxed{}$$

CAROL GEDDES

Carol Geddes is an Indian from the Tlingit Nation in the Yukon. She has a graduate degree in communications from McGill University and has made several films, including *Doctor, Lawyer, Indian Chief*, a National Film Board production about the struggles of native women.

Words and Meanings

Paragraph

muskeg:	swamp, marshland	1
aboriginal:	original or earliest known inhabitants of a region	2
menial:	low-skilled	11
indigenous:	aboriginal, belonging to the First Nations	14
insidious:	treacherous	
holistic:	believing in the oneness, the interconnected- ness of the earth and all living things	17

Structure and Strategy

1. Geddes frequently uses ANECDOTES to convey or support her points. Look at paragraph 10. What does the anecdote in that paragraph tell you about the author? About her teacher? Find another anecdote in the essay that also illustrates the clash between two cultures.
2. What is the topic of paragraph 12?
3. What is the function of the concluding paragraph of this essay? How does it contribute to the UNITY of the piece? Why do you think it appears at the end rather than at the beginning of the essay?

Content and Purpose

1. The essay begins with one of the author's early childhood memories; it goes on to describe life in the remote bush culture. What is the dominant impression Geddes creates of life for children growing up in northern native communities? Contrast this way of life with that of children growing up in large urban centres.

2. Paragraphs 4 and 5 outline some of the changes in the native way of life that have taken place in this century. What were these changes? What caused them?

3. What were some of the negative influences that the dominant white culture had on native people both in the bush and in the cities of the North, as Geddes describes them?

4. What were the effects of school on the author? How did she overcome these effects?

5. What thematic connection is there between paragraph 1 and paragraph 17?

6. In Geddes's view, what does the non-native culture have to gain from native culture?

Suggestions for Writing

1. Discuss the effects of the educational system on students who do not come from the mainstream culture.

2. Explore the reasons for the growth of native militancy with respect to land claims, self-government, and cultural survival.

3. In the last few years, the media have brought to public awareness evidence that the residential schools for native children were, as Geddes describes them, "a source of misery." After researching the topic, explain how these schools failed the children they were supposed to serve, and why.

4. Compare and contrast the view of native culture presented in Geddes's essay with that depicted in Kevin Costner's film, *Dances with Wolves* (or with another contemporary film on the same theme), or with Emily Carr's picture of native life in "Sophie."

Deficits

MICHAEL IGNATIEFF

t begins the minute Dad leaves the house.   1
"Where is George?"   2
"He is out now, but he'll be back soon."   3
"That's wonderful," she says.   4
About three minutes later she'll look puzzled: "But George . . ."   5
"He's away at work, but he'll be back later."   6
"I see."   7
"And what are you doing here? I mean it's nice, but . . . "   8
"We'll do things together."   9
"I see."   10
Sometimes I try to count the number of times she asks me these   11
questions but I lose track.

I remember how it began, five or six years ago. She was 66 then.   12
She would leave a pot to boil on the stove. I would discover it and
find her tearing through the house, muttering, "My glasses, my
glasses, where the hell are my glasses?"

I took her to buy a chain so that she could wear her glasses   13
around her neck. She hated it because her mother used to wear *her*
glasses on a chain. As we drove home, she shook her fist at the
windscreen.

"I swore I'd never wear one of these damned things."   14

I date the beginning to the purchase of the chain, to the silence   15
that descended over her as I drove her home from the store.

The deficits, as the neurologists call them, are localized. She can   16
tell you what it felt like when the Model T Ford ran over her at the
school gates when she was a girl of seven. She can tell you what a
good-looking man her grandfather was. She can tell you what her
grandmother used to say, "A genteel° sufficiency will suffice°,"
when turning down another helping at dinner. She remembers the
Canadian summer nights when her father used to wrap her in a
blanket and take her out to the lake's edge to see the stars.

But she can't dice an onion. She can't set the table. She can't   17
play cards. Her grandson is five, and when they play pairs with his

animal cards, he knows where the second penguin will be. She just turns up cards at random.

18   He hits her because she can't remember anything, because she keeps telling him not to run around quite so much.

19   Then I punish him. I tell him he has to understand.

20   He goes down on the floor, kisses her feet, and promises not to hit her again.

21   She smiles at him, as if for the first time, and says, "Oh, your kiss is so full of sugar."

22   After a week with him, she looks puzzled and says, "He's a nice little boy. Where does he sleep? I mean, who does he belong to?"

23   "He's your grandson."

24   "I see." She looks away and puts her hand to her face.

25   My brother usually stays with her when Dad is out of town. Once or twice a year, it's my turn. I put her to bed at night. I hand her the pills—small green ones that are supposed to control her moods—and she swallows them. I help her out of her bra and slip, roll down her tights, and lift the nightie over her head. I get into the bed next to hers. Before she sleeps she picks up a Len Deighton and reads a few paragraphs, always the same paragraphs, at the place where she has folded down the page. When she falls asleep, I pick the book off her chest and I pull her down in the bed so that her head isn't leaning against the wall. Otherwise she wakes up with a crick in her neck.

26   Often when I wake in the night, I see her lying next to me, staring into the dark. She stares and then she wanders. I used to try to stop her, but now I let her go. She is trying to hold on to what is left. There is a method in this. She goes to the bathroom every time she wakes, no matter if it is five times a night. Up and down the stairs silently, in her bare feet, trying not to wake me. She turns the lights on and off. Smooths a child's sock and puts it on the bed. Sometimes she gets dressed, after a fashion, and sits on the down-stairs couch in the dark, clutching her handbag.

27   When we have guests to dinner, she sits beside me at the table, holding my hand, bent forward slightly to catch everything that is said. Her face lights up when people smile, when there is laughter. She doesn't say much any more; she is worried she will forget a name and we won't be able to help her in time. She doesn't want anything to show. The guests always say how well she does. Sometimes they say, "You'd never know, really." When I put her to bed afterward I can see the effort has left her so tired she barely knows her own name.

28   She could make it easier on herself. She could give up asking questions.

29   "Where we are now, is this our house?"

"Yes."   30
"Where is our house?"   31
"In France."   32
I tell her: "Hold my hand, I'm here. I'm your son."   33
"I know."   34

But she keeps asking where she is. The questions are her way   35
of trying to orient° herself, of refusing and resisting the future that
is being prepared for her.

She always loved to swim. When she dived into the water, she   36
never made a splash. I remember her lifting herself out of the pool,
as sleek as a seal in a black swimsuit, the water pearling off her back.
Now she says the water is too cold and taking off her clothes too
much of a bother. She paces up and down the poolside, watching
her grandson swim, stroking his towel with her hand, endlessly
smoothing out the wrinkles.

I bathe her when she wakes. Her body is white, soft, and with-   37
ered. I remember how, in the changing-huts, she would bend over
as she slipped out of her bathing suit. Her body was young. Now I
see her skeleton through her skin. When I wash her hair, I feel her
skull. I help her from the bath, dry her legs, swathe her in towels,
sit her on the edge of the bath and cut her nails: they are horny and
yellow. Her feet are gnarled°. She has walked a long way.

When I was as old as my son is now I used to sit beside her at   38
the bedroom mirror watching her apply hot depilatory° wax to her
legs and upper lip. She would pull her skirt up to her knees, stretch
her legs out on the dresser, and sip beer from the bottle, while
waiting for the wax to dry. "Have a sip," she would say. It tasted
bitter. She used to laugh at the faces I made. When the wax had set,
she would begin to peel it off, and curse and wince, and let me
collect the strips, with fine black hairs embedded in them. When it
was over, her legs were smooth, silky to touch.

Now I shave her. I soap her face and legs with my shaving   39
brush. She sits perfectly still; as my razor comes around her chin we
are as close as when I was a boy.

She never complains. When we walk up the hill behind the   40
house, I feel her going slower and slower, but she does not stop
until I do. If you ask her whether she is sad, she shakes her head.
But she did say once, "It's strange. It was supposed to be more fun
than this."

I try to imagine what the world is like for her. Memory is what   41
reconciles° us to the future. Because she has no past, her future
rushes toward her, a bat's wing brushing against her face in the
dark.

"I told you. George returns on Monday."   42
"Could you write that down?"   43

44   So I do. I write it down in large letters, and she folds it in her white cardigan pocket and pats it and says she feels much less worried.

45   In half an hour, she has the paper in her hand and is showing it to me.

46   "What do I do about this?"

47   "Nothing. It just tells you what is going to happen."

48   "But I didn't know anything of this."

49   "Now you do," I say and I take the paper away and tear it up.

50   It makes no sense to get angry at her, but I do.

51   She is afraid Dad will not come back. She is afraid she has been abandoned. She is afraid she will get lost and never be able to find her way home. Beneath the fears that have come with the forgetting, there lie anxieties for which she no longer has any names.

52   She paces the floor, waiting for lunch. When it is set before her, she downs it before anyone else, and then gets up to clear the plates.

53   "What's the hurry?" I ask her.

54   She is puzzled. "I don't know," she says. She is in a hurry, and she does not know why. She drinks whatever I put before her. The wine goes quickly.

55   "You'll enjoy it more if you sip it gently."

56   "What a good idea," she says and then empties the glass with a gulp.

57   I wish I knew the history of this anxiety. But I don't. All she will tell me is about being sprawled in the middle of Regent Street amid the blood and shop glass during an air raid, watching a mother sheltering a child, and thinking: I am alone.

58   In the middle of all of us, she remained alone. We didn't see it. She was the youngest girl in her family, the straggler in the pack, born cross-eyed till they straightened her eyes out with an operation. Her father was a teacher and she was dyslexic°, the one left behind.

59   In her wedding photo, she is wearing her white dress and holding her bouquet. They are side by side. Dad looks excited. Her eyes are wide open with alarm. Fear gleams from its hiding place. It was her secret and she kept it well hidden. When I was a child, I thought she was faultless, amusing, regal. My mother.

60   She thinks of it as a happy family, and it was. I remember them sitting on the couch together, singing along to Fats Waller records. She still remembers the crazy lyrics they used to sing:

There's no disputin'
That's Rasputin
The high-falutin loving man.

I don't know how she became so dependent on him, how she lost so many of the wishes she once had for herself, and how all her wishes came to be wishes for him.

She is afraid of his moods, his silences, his departures, and his   61 returns. He has become the weather of her life. But he never lets her down. He is the one who sits with her in the upstairs room, watching television, night after night, holding her hand.

People say: it's worse for you, she doesn't know what is happen-   62 ing. She used to say the same thing herself. Five years ago, when she began to forget little things, she knew what was in store, and she said to me once, "Don't worry. I'll make a cheerful old nut. It's you who'll have the hard time." But that is not true. She feels everything. She has had time to count up every loss. Every night, when she lies awake, she stares at desolation.

What is a person? That is what she makes you wonder. What   63 kind of a person are you if you only have your habits left? She can't remember her grandson's name, but she does remember to shake out her tights at night and she never lets a dish pass her by without trying to clean it, wipe it, clear it up, or put it away. The house is littered with dishes she is putting away in every conceivable cupboard. What kind of a person is this?

It runs in the family. Her mother had it. I remember going to   64 see her in the house with old carpets and dark furniture on Prince Arthur Avenue. The windows were covered with the tendrils of plants growing in enormous Atlas battery jars, and the parquet° floors shone with wax. She took down the giraffe, the water buffalo, and the leopard—carved in wood—that her father had brought back from Africa in the 1880s. She sat in a chair by the fire and silently watched me play with them. Then—and it seems only a week later— I came to have Sunday lunch with her and she was old and diminished and vacant, and when she looked at me she had no idea who I was.

I am afraid of getting it myself. I do ridiculous things: I stand   65 on my head every morning so that the blood will irrigate my brain; I compose suicide notes, always some variant of Captain Oates's: "I may be gone for some time." I never stop thinking about what it would be like for this thing to steal over me.

She has taught me something. There are moments when her   66 pacing ceases, when her hunted look is conjured° away by the stillness of dusk, when she sits in the garden, watching the sunlight stream through all the trees they planted together over 25 years in this place, and I see something pass over her face which might be serenity°.

And then she gets up and comes toward me looking for a glass   67 to wash, a napkin to pick up, a child's toy to rearrange.

I know how the story has to end. One day I return home to see   68 her and she puts out her hand and says: "How nice to meet you." She's always charming to strangers.

69   People say I'm already beginning to say my farewells. No, she is still here. I am not ready yet. Nor is she. She paces the floor, she still searches for what has been lost and can never be found again.

70   She wakes in the night and lies in the dark by my side. Her face, in profile, against the pillow has become like her mother's, the eye sockets deep in shadow, the cheeks furrowed° and drawn, the gaze ancient and disabused°. Everything she once knew is still inside her, trapped in the ruined circuits—how I was when I was little, how she was when I was a baby. But it is too late to ask her now. She turns and notices I am awake too. We lie side by side. The darkness is still. I want to say her name. She turns away from me and stares into the night. Her nightie is buttoned at the neck like a little girl's.

MICHAEL IGNATIEFF

Michael Ignatieff (b. 1947) is a Canadian writer and broadcaster. He won the Governor General's Award for *The Russian Album* in 1987. His other books include *A Just Measure of Pain* (1978) and *The Needs of Strangers* (1985). Ignatieff is the son of a distinguished Canadian diplomat, the late George Ignatieff.

Words and Meanings

Paragraph

16	genteel:	polite, well-bred
	suffice:	be enough, satisfy
35	orient:	find her bearings; figure out where she is in time and space
37	gnarled:	knobby, crooked
38	depilatory:	hair remover
41	reconciles:	makes us able to accept; resigns us
58	dyslexic:	having a reading disability
64	parquet:	wood floor laid out in square design
66	conjured:	made to disappear magically
	serenity:	inner peace
70	furrowed:	deeply wrinkled
	disabused:	undeceived, under no illusion

Structure and Strategy

1. Look up the word "deficits" in a medical dictionary and in a good general dictionary. What meanings of the word apply to Ignatieff's title?
2. Using both narration and description, Ignatieff describes the effects of Alzheimer's disease on its victims, and on those who care for them. What function does the opening dialogue (paragraphs 1 to 11) serve?
3. This essay contains several passages of dialogue. Each is included because it supports in some way Ignatieff's thesis. Consider how each of the following passages contributes to the purpose or intended effect of the essay: paragraphs 28 to 35; paragraphs 42 to 49; paragraphs 52 to 56.
4. Paragraphs 37 and 38 present the ironic contrast between Ignatieff's boyhood relationship with his mother and their current relationship. Identify the specific details that you think are most effective in conveying this contrast.
5. How does the author's own fear of contracting Alzheimer's disease affect the TONE of the essay?

Content and Purpose

1. The thesis of Ignatieff's essay is implied rather than explicitly stated. Sum up the thesis in a one-sentence thesis statement.
2. What was the initial reaction of the mother when the first signs of the disease appeared? Does she maintain this feeling as her confusion and loss of memory increase?
3. Ignatieff includes a number of poignant descriptive details: the toenails, the gnarled feet, the depilatory wax, the bath. Why does he include these intimate aspects of his mother's life and condition? What emotional effect do they have on the reader?
4. What is the fundamental irony underlying the relationship between mother and son? Reread paragraphs 25, 27, and 70 for clues.
5. What experiences in the mother's life may be responsible for the "fear [that] gleams from its hiding place" in her eyes?
6. Is Ignatieff comfortable with the task of caring for his mother? Identify specific passages in the essay that point to the writer's personal conflict.

Suggestions for Writing

1. Modelling your essay on the combination of descriptive and narrative techniques that Ignatieff uses in "Deficits," write a

paper on the physical and psychological impact of a serious illness on someone you know.

2. Using "Deficits" and "The Way of All Flesh" by Judy Stoffman as background material, write an essay explaining how society can and must enable older people to live in dignity, despite physical or mental handicaps.

3. Traditional societies like the Chinese respect and venerate the old, but progressive western societies increasingly see the aged as an unwelcome burden. Write an essay in which you identify and explain two or three significant reasons why our society excludes or rejects the elderly.

The Softball Was Always Hard

HARRY BRUCE

1   When I tell young softball players I played the game barehanded, they regard me warily°. Am I one of those geezers who's forever jawing about the fact that, in *his* day, you had to walk through six miles of snowdrifts just to get to school? Will I tediously lament the passing of the standing broad jump, and the glorious old days when the only football in the Maritimes was English rugger, when hockey was an outdoor art rather than indoor mayhem and, at decent yacht clubs, men were gentlemen and women were *personae non grata*°? No, but I will tell today's softball players that—with their fancy uniforms, batters' helmets, dugouts, manicured diamonds, guys to announce who's at bat over public-address systems and, above all, gloves for every fielder—the game they play is more tarted-up and sissy than the one I knew.

2   Softball bloomed in the Dirty Thirties because it was a game the most impoverished deadbeat could afford to play. For schools, it had the edge that soccer still has over North American football: it required no expensive equipment. It was the people's game in the worst of times. Unlike baseball, which calls for a field the size of a town, softball could flourish in one corner of a city park, on a vacant lot, in any schoolyard. The only gear you needed was a ball, a bat, a catcher's glove and mask, and a first baseman's glove, a floppy

affair which I knew as a "trapper." Two amiable° teams might even use the same gloves—two gloves for eighteen players.

In the Toronto grade school league of the Forties, gloves for all other players were outlawed. This meant that early in the season the hands of a boy shortstop felt as though a 300-lb. vice-principal had given him the strap. Any team that lasted long enough to reach the city finals, however, boasted little infielders with palms like saddle-leather. They learned to catch a line drive with both hands, not by snaring it with a glove big enough to hold a medicine ball°. They cushioned the ball by drawing back their cupped hands at the split-second of impact. They fielded sizzling grounders by turning sideways, dropping one knee to the ground, getting their whole bodies in front of the ball, then scooping it up, again with both small, bare hands.

A word about balls. The *New Columbia Encyclopedia* says, "Despite the name, the ball used is not soft," which may be the understatement of the tome's 3,052 pages. There were three kinds of softballs, and each was about as soft as anthracite°. The best was simply a big baseball, with seams that were pretty well flush with the horsehide cover. Then there was a solid rubber ball with fake seams. After a while, this ball did soften up, but on grounds it no longer hurt enough for competition, it was then retired for use only in practice. Then there was the "outseam" ball. Perhaps it was not a sadist who invented it. Perhaps it was merely someone who sought durability in lean times. But the outseam was a quarter-inch ridge of leather so hard that, when you fielded a rifling, spinning grounder, the ball felt as though its real function was to rip the skin off your palms. The outseam ball was a character-builder.

We had no uniforms, but if you reached the city finals team sweaters might magically emerge from some secret cache in the school basement. Certain coaches had the stern theory that even these were bad news, that boys would be so captivated by their own spiffy appearance they'd lose that vital concentration on the game itself, and commit errors. Some boys played in the only shoes they owned, scampers or black oxfords. Others had beaten-up sneakers and, on most teams, some wore short pants and some long. But these youngsters, gangs of ragamuffins by today's standards of sartorial° elegance in softball, played furiously competitive, heads-up ball.

If you played outside the school system, for a team sponsored by a camera shop, dairy, hardware store or greasy spoon, then you did get a sweater. You swaggered in it. You'd earned it. Not every kid was good enough to make a team with sweaters. They were advertisements of ability. Nowadays, of course, any kid with the money can buy an Expos' jacket or a Pirates' cap. They're merely advertisements of disposable income, much like the $25 million worth of gear that the chains of athletic-shoe stores expected to sell in Canada during recession-ridden 1982.

7   But as a celebrator of softball austerity°, I am a pipsqueak beside an eighty-year-old tycoon I know. As a boy in a Nova Scotia coal-mining town, he played cricket and street baseball with home-made bats and balls. To make a ball, boys hoarded string and wrapped it around a rock, or if they were lucky a small rubber ball. "We made very good balls," he said, "and we had just as much fun as kids have today with all their expensive stuff." In line with Canada's hoariest° hockey tradition, he added, "We used a piece of frozen manure for a puck. It worked just about as good." It wasn't as durable as rubber, but in those days there was no shortage of horse poop.

8   I once played with a home-made baseball myself. Indeed, I placed the order for its construction. In the summer of '46, when I turned twelve, my father exiled me from Toronto to spend two months at the Bruce homestead on a Nova Scotian shore. That shore, even now, is as sleepy a spot as you're ever likely to find. Not even most Nova Scotians know where it is. But in 1946, the community was not merely remote, it was an anachronism°. It hadn't changed much since Victoria had been queen, and to a kid from what he fancied as a bustling, modern metropolis, its empty beauty was at first desolating. This was the ultimate sticks, the boondocks with a vengeance, and I worked off my loneliness by playing catch with myself. Hour after hour, I hurled a Toronto tennis ball against a bluenose barn, catching it on the rebound.

9   Then I discovered potential ballplayers.

10   They lived on the farm next door. They were a big, cheerful family, and my knowing them then started my lifelong love affair with the neighborhood. As things are unfolding now, I'll end up there for good. Anyway, several of these farm kids—the oldest was a gentle man of fifteen who, with one paralysing hand, pinned me to a hayfield while I endured the sweet, excruciating humiliation of having his giggling, thirteen-year-old sister plant saliva on my face— were old enough to play a form of softball. Amazingly, however, they'd never played it, nor seen it. They'd never even heard the word.

11   I told the fifteen-year-old a softball bat was *this* long, and *this* thick at one end, and *this* thin at the other. He made one in half an hour. It wasn't exactly a Louisville Slugger but it had heft to it, and at the same time it was light enough to enable the smaller kids to take a good cut at the ball. What ball? My tennis ball had split. When I knowledgeably declared that the heart of a real baseball was cork, the fifteen-year-old took me down to the stony shore to negotiate with a character I've preserved in memory as "the Ball-maker." He

was a hermit who had just given up commercial fishing on his own. He would never again sail the small schooner he'd built, and she'd begun to rot where she lay, a few feet closer to Chedabucto Bay than the ramshackle hut where he somehow survived the seasons.

He was a "beach person," as surely as the salt-stunted spruce 12 were beach trees, and therefore disreputable. If he had known women they had not been church-going women. He was thin, stooped, gnarled, and smelled as though he'd been embalmed in brine, rum, tar, tobacco juice, his own sweat and sinister doings. There was something wrong with one of his eyes and some of his fingers, and though he may only have been as old as I am now (forty-eight), I thought he was ancient enough, and certainly evil enough, to have slit throats for Blackbeard.

The Ball-maker conversed with grunts, snarls, illogical silences, 13 and an accent so thick that, to me, it was a foreign language. But we struck a deal. He gave me a dime. If I would walk inland, following a brookside path through a forest of spruce and fir, and on past a sawmill to a general store, and if I would use the dime to buy him a plug of chewing tobacco and, further, if I would then take the tobacco to him . . . well, he would meanwhile sculpt a baseball-sized sphere of cork. And he did. He fashioned it from three pieces: a thick, round disc and two polar caps, all jammed together with a single spike. That ball was so flawless it was spooky. I can still see it and feel it in my hand, a brown globe so perfect I wondered if the Ball-maker was a warlock°.

Back at my friends' farm, we encased the cork in scratchy manila 14 twine till we had something bigger than a hardball but smaller than a softball. For bases, we dropped sweaters among the cowflaps in a pasture, and the lesson began. We would play the kind of teamless ball that's been known in a million schoolyards; as each batter went out, the fielders would all change positions to guarantee that every player got a crack at batting. As the ace from Toronto, I naturally led off. Trouble was, I adored the afternoon's first pitcher. It was she who'd kissed me in the hayfield.

She had hair like a blonde waterfall, eyes like dark chocolate, 15 and skin I ached to touch and smell. Whenever we wrestled, she won. I still dislike that adult sneer, "puppy love." A boy of twelve can love a girl of thirteen with agonizing power. To make matters worse, he hasn't a hope in hell of even understanding the emotion that's racking his skinny being, much less satisfying it. All he knows is that she obsesses him, he yearns for her, he must always appear fine in her eyes.

She had never pitched in her life so it surprised me when she 16 tossed her waterfall in the sunlight and floated the ball gently into the strike zone. Her first pitch. It crept towards me, letter-high. It could have been hanging there in front of me on a string from the sky, and I stepped into it with all the style I'd learned from a hundred Toronto afternoons. Thwack! A line drive so fast no one saw it, and down she went. She crumpled in a heap of blouse, skirt, hair and bare, beloved arms and legs. I had smacked her with the cursed, hairy ball square on her right eye. Her big brother got her sitting up, and we all huddled round her, with me bleating horrified apologies. She never cried. She managed a smile, got to her feet, and shakily went home.

17   When she turned up for our second game, she had the ugliest black eye I have ever seen on a child. To me, it was a beauty mark. She never blamed me for it. It became a bond, proof of a famous incident we'd shared. She was a tough, forgiving farm girl, and she and her brothers and sisters taught me something I'd not forget about the rough grace of the country folk down home. We played ball for weeks. We played till we pounded the ball to bits, till her eye was once more perfect, and summer was gone.

18   The car that drove me to the train station passed their farm. Sheets on the clothesline billowed in the usual southwesterly. With her brothers and sister, she was horsing around with their wolfish mutt. They stopped to watch the car moving along the dirt road, and then they all waved goodbye. I was glad they were too far away to see my face. I still lacked her control.

19   I have my own cabin on that shore now, and though most of those farmyard ballplayers of thirty-seven summers ago have moved away I still see one of them occasionally. He's a mere forty-six, and I like him now as I liked him then. Sometimes I walk along the gravel beach to a patch of grass, from which a footpath once led to a general store. The Ball-maker's shack is gone, but gray planks and ribs and rusty boat nails still endure the lashing of the salt wind that ceaselessly sweeps the bay. They're all that's left of his schooner. Wrecked by time, like bare-handed softball.

HARRY BRUCE

Harry Bruce, journalist and essayist, was born in Toronto. He has written for the country's leading magazines and newspapers. *Each Moment As It Flies* is a collection of articles and essays. Bruce now makes his home in Halifax.

Words and Meanings
Paragraph

1   warily: cautiously, suspiciously
     personae non grata: unwelcome or unacceptable people

amiable:	friendly	2
medicine ball:	large, heavy, leather-covered ball thrown for exercise	3
anthracite:	a kind of coal	4
sartorial:	tailoring or dressing	5
austerity:	simplicity, without excess or luxury	7
hoariest:	very old, white with age	
anachronism:	out of time, part of an earlier era	8
warlock:	male version of a witch, a sorcerer	13

Structure and Strategy

1. What is being described in paragraph 3? In paragraph 4? In paragraph 5? Underline the clear, descriptive details Bruce provides to help the reader visualize his subject.
2. What change in direction occurs in paragraph 8? What story is begun? Where does the climax of the narrative occur?
3. Why is paragraph 9 only one sentence long? What is its affect on the reader?
4. What senses does Bruce appeal to in his description of the Ball-maker in paragraphs 12 and 13?
5. The DICTION of this essay ranges from formal and elegiac (e.g., "endure the lashing of the salt wind that ceaselessly sweeps the bay") to country colloquial ("no shortage of horse poop"). Why has Bruce chosen this range of language? How does it affect the TONE of the essay?
6. In the final paragraph, what does Bruce describe as having vanished? Is his conclusion UNIFIED and effective? Why or why not?

Content and Purpose

1. How do the contrasts developed in paragraphs 1 and 2 support the THESIS of the essay?
2. Why is Bruce a "celebrator of softball austerity"? What does he think of today's players' reliance on team uniforms and costly equipment?
3. The narrative that makes up the second half of the essay is more than a sports story. How effective is Bruce's exploration of another important adolescent passion?
4. What differences between his young self and the rural Nova

Scotians does Bruce explore in the essay? How does he show his own changed attitude toward their lives and community?

Suggestions for Writing

1. Write a narration of your childhood participation in a favourite sport. Make sure that you include clear, sensory details that help your reader visualize the experience.
2. Do you agree with Bruce that adolescent love has an "agonizing power" over us? Write a paper that describes someone with whom you fell hopelessly in love as a young person and tell the story of your infatuation.

Why I Love Opera, and Find It Irresistibly Funny

GEORGE JONAS

1   My fascination with opera goes back to a Turkish lady called Fatime. More precisely, it goes back to a contest between my uncle's sense of balance and Fatime's abdominal muscle.

2   I should warn readers who expect a salacious° story that they will be disappointed. No lady's abdominal muscle held much interest for me at the time, perhaps because I was six years old. My parents had asked me to join them at a dinner party for Fatime, a retired diva°, who was visiting us with her husband. We often had operatic visitors, because my father (who had been a baritone at the Viennese Opera before giving himself up to the world of business) seemed to enjoy them, but Fatime's party was the first I was invited to attend.

3   As I remember it (later my mother and father were to dispute some details), the party began with Fatime standing against the wall in the blue salon. As a rule, my parents entertained only cultural guests in the blue salon. Business guests were usually herded into the dining hall, underneath Beethoven's deathmask, where the seating arrangements were more formal. But that night it was only

Fatime with her husband, along with my uncle and aunt, and maybe two or three other people. This was probably why I was allowed to take my meal with the guests, though of course I was served at a separate table.

Fatime spoke German fearlessly, albeit with an intriguing Turk-   4
ish flavor. Her rich alto was booming across the room. "Belly is rock, rock is belly," she declared, as if she were quoting Keats. "The voice is all belly. You say to me, a singer has the voice by the throat? I reply: Ha-ha! I show you."

Her glance fell on my unfortunate uncle. "I want that you push   5
me!" she commanded. "Not where you sit like mushroom, but standing on legs like real man."

I looked up from my plate. Clearly, the conversation was taking   6
an interesting turn. Fatime, her splendid abdominal muscle wrapped in a minimum of silk, was resting her back against the wall. "In belly," she instructed my uncle. "Not poke-poke-poke like chicken, but push! Make a ball with your, how you call them, fingers."

"With your fist, you know, there's a good man," suggested the   7
Freiherr von X., whose name I no longer recall, but who had the rare fortune to be married to Fatime. "I often do it at home. You won't get any peace until you push her."

"You push like chicken," Fatime said to her husband, not with-   8
out tenderness. "Maybe he push like man."

My uncle certainly had the bulk; what he may have lacked was   9
the heart. He was a manufacturer of red as well as yellow bricks, born as Geza Stiglitz, but by then the possessor of a much more melodious name. My father, a man with some capacity for mental cruelty, had nicknamed him "Stiglitz the Nimrod°" many years earlier, soon after learning that Uncle had joined a rather exclusive hunting club. This was not because my father objected to people shooting—or even to people named Stiglitz—but only because he objected to people named Stiglitz shooting for social reasons.

My uncle, who was strictly a social shooter, hesitated for a   10
second, then essayed° a tentative° push against the undulating silk. "Ha!" said Fatime derisively°. "My nanny-goat push more, when little girl in Anatolia. Push like you give birth to locomotive."

A suggestible man, my uncle paled. "Please, dear lady," he   11
whispered, "I'm quite heavy, I could hurt you by accident."

"Push!"   12

My uncle closed his eyes and began to push. He was pushing,   13
still cautiously at first, then in earnest. Finally, he was driving his fist into Fatime's abdomen hard enough for the carpet to begin sliding under his feet.

14   "Good, just hold table with free hand," Fatime advised him contemptuously. "Now I will sing you."

15   My father, who must have known what was coming, had already seated himself at the piano. The black Bechstein roared to life, and so did Fatime's abdominal muscle. "*Stride la vampa!*" she began ominously, in the accents of Verdi's gypsy lady, her famous rôle in Vienna and Milan. Frightened and hopelessly off balance, with the rug slowly slipping out from under his feet, my uncle was no longer in a position to withdraw his fist. "*Sinistra splende sui volti orribili,*" Fatime insisted, staring into the middle distance. "*La tetra fiamma che s'alza al ciel!*"

16   Picture, if you will, the situation from my point of view. I was not particularly backward for my age, but until then I had led a rather sheltered life. It was my first operatic dinner party, and I was anxious to make a good impression, but it was a challenging spectacle for a six-year-old. There was Stiglitz the Nimrod, as red in the face as any of his bricks, balancing his entire bulk upon the belly of a well-dressed Turkish lady, who by then was screaming "*Grido feroce di morte levasi!*" at the top of her lungs.

17   Any healthy boy could see that it was to be a race between the aria° and the heavy Persian rug, which was sliding as slowly but as inexorably° as a glacier from under my uncle's feet. Fatime, unperturbed°, looked quite ready to go the distance. My father would eventually explain that Uncle did have an outside chance, because Azucena's tale was not a long one by Verdi's standards. But my uncle, who had never been exposed to *Il Trovatore*, had no way of knowing that. His expression soon began showing that abandonment of all hope that the Italian travel writer Dante Alighieri° remarked upon in connection with one of his trips.

18   A brick manufacturer leaning at a 45-degree angle is not a dignified sight, and it doesn't help matters when he appears to be coaxing dark and powerful musical notes from the belly of a fat lady in silk. My behavior didn't help, either. The fact is, I pointed my finger at them and began turning purple.

19   Later my father called me an annoying child. It was not a supportive comment but it was not inaccurate. To say that I laughed would not begin to describe my reaction at the end of Azucena's lament. I howled. I hooted. I'm afraid I actually stomped my feet, while my poor Uncle slid slowly to the floor, still hinged, as it were, to Fatime's belly by one fist.

20   My musical education had commenced some years before this incident. My father believed that any civilized child should be able

to play Clementi's *Sonatina* by the age of four, but my disgraceful behavior at the dinner party convinced both of my parents that Herr Miller's piano lessons were insufficient. Opera especially, my father felt, had to be approached in a different light. "For example," he said to me, "ignorant people look at *Lohengrin*, and they say that you can't rely on German swans running exactly on schedule."

"Well, of course, any fool knows that you can't rely on German swans. The great Leo Schlezak discovered that at the Metropolitan in New York when they dragged his own swan offstage before he could mount it, causing him to step into the river. But it made no difference. Schlezak, a tenor of great dignity drunk or sober, simply asked '*Wann kommt der nächste Schwann?*'° as if he were at a train station in Berlin, and everybody knew that he was still Parsifal's son, damn it! You don't measure opera by puny° standards!"

Perhaps it should be noted that this phase in my life occurred in the spring of 1941. Though Hitler was already preparing for Operation Barbarossa, the Molotov-Ribbentrop° pact still held. Initially, the pact had deeply disturbed everyone in our liberal circles, except my father, who thought that it was a perfect treaty between two identical systems. "Isn't it logical for the Nazis to be allied with the Communists?" he kept consoling his suicidal friends. "Isn't it natural? The unnatural thing would be for the great democracies to be allied with either one of them."

As it turned out, my operatic education continued against the backdrop of just such an unnatural development. "So, Stalin is now a friend of Roosevelt's," my father offered, "yet some people find it incredible that Azucena should throw her own baby into the fire instead of the old count di Luna's. Well, Azucena was a simple gypsy, while Roosevelt, for instance, is a man of education. He is Felix Frankfurter's buddy. Yet, if you ask me, if Roosevelt doesn't watch out, he could end up throwing his baby into the fire by mistake, as easily as Azucena."

Opera does arouse a certain kind of enthusiasm in people, my father explained. He gave the example of an incident that had happened at the Budapest Opera, when Anna Medek performed there shortly after the turn of the century. The orchestra was conducted by the famous Toccani, and at the end of the first act a gentleman set up a rhythmic chant, shouting "Medek! Toccani!" over and over again. He obviously liked the performance, and he may have forgotten that in Hungarian the words he kept yelling amounted to a statement of his intention to defecate without delay. "Go, by all means," someone said to him at last. "But why must you announce it?"

25   My father likened the incident to the Nuremberg rallies. "You shouldn't stretch the parallel too far, of course," he cautioned, "but it's a fact that many people don't know what they are shouting when they get carried away."

26   Operas were absurd, but they were majestic; it was silly for people to criticize them in the name of reality, my father suggested, when reality was just as absurd and often devoid of any majesty. "I've known some modern realists," he mused, "who walked out of *Tosca* because of Scarpia's behavior in the second act. Well, perhaps Scarpia does act a little melodramatically—but then I've watched the selfsame realists sitting glued to the radio, listening to Mussolini speak."

27   Some years later—this is an aside—my father and I were watching a newsreel showing the bodies of Mussolini and his mistress hanging by the heels from a pole outside a gas station. "Scarpia?" I asked him. *Sotto voce*, but with the wicked smile of someone proved correct by history itself, my father sang his reply: "*E avanti a lui tremava tutta Roma!*"°

28   One could sympathize with Madame Tosca's curtain line: by 1945, indeed, it was hard to imagine all of Rome trembling before a charred side of beef, in trousers, hanging from a pole. However, in 1941 the curtain was still a long way from falling.

29   I continued my operatic education while the fall of Moscow seemed imminent° to many realists who considered operas absurd. My father was virtually alone in the view that Hitler would have had second thoughts about invading Russia if he had known, in addition to his favorite composer Wagner, the operas of Borodin. The German high command should have especially listened to Prince Igor's great baritone air, "*Oh dahtye, dahtye mnye svobodu,*" which gave some indication of how Russians might react to the idea of foreign, as opposed to domestic, servitude. My father immediately sang Igor's aria for me, in a comic version, of course. He accompanied himself on the black Bechstein, roaring with laughter, until my mother bade him stop.

30   Soon after our musical soirée°, my socially ambitious uncle Nimrod was taken to a labor camp called Bor, quite famous in its time, in Nazi-occupied Serbia. Fatime and the Freiherr von X. began holding séances as the best means of communicating with their only son, Martin, who had disappeared at the Russian front. Except for the *Götterdämmerung*, I don't remember hearing any opera. The music on the radio was mainly brass in those years. The Gestapo had discovered other uses for piano wire.

GEORGE JONAS

George Jonas (b. 1935) is a Hungarian-born playwright, poet, and radio producer as well as an author whose works include *By Persons Unknown* (1977) and *Vengeance* (1984).

Words and Meanings

Paragraph

salacious:	erotic, lewd	2
diva:	great female opera singer	
Nimrod:	the first biblical hero, a great hunter and the conqueror of the Babylonians	9
essayed:	tried	10
tentative:	hesitant, experimental	
derisively:	mockingly, scornfully	
aria:	song	17
inexorably:	incapable of being stopped	
unperturbed:	not in the least upset	
Dante Alighieri:	famous Italian poet (1265–1321), writer of *The Divine Comedy*, in which the inscription, "Abandon hope, all ye who enter here" appears above the gates of Hell	
"Wann kommt der nächste Schwann?":	"When is the next swan due?"	21
puny:	small, insignificant	
Molotov:	Russian Communist who served as foreign minister under Stalin from 1939 to 1949	22
Ribbentrop:	German foreign minister under Hitler	
"E avanti a lui tremava tutta Roma!":	"Before him all Rome trembled."	27
imminent:	about to happen	29
soirée:	evening party	30

Structure and Strategy

1. Jonas's use of descriptive details contributes much to the effectiveness of the opening narrative. Find three or four descriptive passages that you think are particularly effective. What senses does Jonas appeal to?
2. In the second half of this essay, Jonas draws parallels between his musical and his political education. Identify three or four specific examples of the relationship Jonas sees between opera and politics.

3. What is the TONE of the concluding paragraph and how does it contribute to the impact of that paragraph on the reader?

Content and Purpose

1. More than half of this essay is a story, narrated by Jonas, of an encounter between his uncle and a Turkish opera singer that occurred when Jonas was six years old. What took place during this strange pushing match?
2. In addition to the humorous narrative at the beginning, the essay includes several anecdotes that evoke laughter (see, for example, paragraphs 20 to 21 and 24). Is this the response to opera that we usually expect? What point is Jonas making?
3. In paragraph 22, Jonas establishes the date of the opening narrative, and with it, a serious theme. What was happening in Europe at this time? How does Jonas connect the historical events to the opera?
4. In paragraphs 25 and 26, what relationship does Jonas suggest exists between art, specifically opera, and the often brutal world of politics?
5. This is an essay rich in ALLUSION (see paragraphs 4, 9, and 17 as well as the references to opera). The final sentence contains an ominous allusion to Nazi brutality. How does this conclusion unify an essay that focuses on opera, music, and European politics in the middle years of this century?

Suggestions for Writing

1. Describe your response to a performance you saw as a child that affected you strongly: a play, a film, a ballet, a concert, an opera, or a circus, for example. Narrate the story of the event, and relate it to your feelings as an adult about that art form.
2. If you are an opera fan, write an essay explaining your fascination with an art form that is unfamiliar and even intimidating to many people.

Additional Suggestions for Writing

NARRATION

Write a narrative based on one of the following topics. The narration should support a generalization, or thesis, about the experience, and it should be based on personal experience.

1. An embarrassing experience in your life
2. An act of courage that affected other people (something you have done or seen someone else do)
3. The first day of a new activity (e.g., school, job, marriage)
4. The birth of a child into a family
5. An experience that led to success
6. An experience that led to failure
7. A journey that taught you something
8. A chance encounter that led to something important
9. A memorable experience in your life
10. "Bliss was it in that dawn to be alive./But to be young was very heaven!" (William Wordsworth)
11. "Never trust the artist. Trust the tale." (D.H. Lawrence)

DESCRIPTION

Using a variety of sensory details, write a description of one of the following. Your description may be objective—in other words, entirely factual. Or it may be subjective, creating a dominant impression based on feelings.

1. The ugliest or most beautiful person you have ever seen
2. Your closest friend
3. A family holiday
4. A place that fills you with peace
5. Your favourite restaurant
6. A dangerous spot that you've explored
7. A sporting event
8. An illness
9. One of your parents (or children)
10. A famous person whom you encountered face-to-face
11. A place at your school
12. The most spectacular scenery you've ever experienced
13. "In the misfortune of our best friends, we always find something which is not displeasing to us." (de la Rochefoucauld)
14. "Was this the face that launch'd a thousand ships?/And burnt the topless towers of Ilium?" (Christopher Marlowe)

Example:
Explaining with
Word Pictures

What? The Definition

If someone were to tell you that the Canadian music industry has made a major contribution to the third generation of rock 'n' roll, you would probably be puzzled—even if you think you really know the rock scene. However, your confusion would quickly evaporate if the speaker were to explain by using the kind of word pictures we call **examples**. For instance, Jeff Healey and Alannah Myles are two examples of contemporary Canadian rock artists who have a creative, professional approach. The idea of rock's "third generation" becomes clear if you think of Elvis Presley as the father of the first generation and of The Beatles as the leaders of the second generation. These recognizable examples make the opening statement understandable to anyone who knows even a little about the rock industry.

An *example* is something selected from a class of things and used to show the character of all of them. Examples may be briefly stated instances of people, places, ideas, or things: three examples of automobiles manufactured in Germany are BMW, Audi, and Mercedes-Benz. Examples may also be developed at greater length: an extended example is sometimes called an *illustration*—that is, it is a "word picture." Examples or illustrations are essential in effective writing because they enable the reader to visualize the concept you are explaining. Both are needed if you want to be clear—and, furthermore, they're interesting.

Why? The Purpose

Explaining a subject by offering examples of it is probably the simplest of the various strategies available to a writer. Example papers answer the question, "What are some significant examples of S?" By identifying and explaining a few significant examples of your subject, you ensure that your reader understands what you mean. The consequences of *not* including examples can be disastrous, especially when you are trying to explain a concept or principle.

Here's an example of what we mean: every student has, at one time or another, suffered through a course given by a Droner. He's the instructor who, whether lecturing on the mysteries of quantum theory, the intricacies of accounting, or the subtleties of the semicolon, drones on and on, oblivious to the snores of his slumbering students. Often, the Droner has his material down cold; he knows all about physics, balance sheets, or punctuation—in theory, or what we call the ABSTRACT. But the Droner is unable or unwilling to relate these concepts to experiences that we can all understand. He cannot make the abstract principles CONCRETE for his listeners. His lectures lack specific examples that the students can picture in their minds or relate to their past experience to help them understand the concept he is trying so insensitively to explain.

Abstract words refer to ideas or qualities that we can't experience through our physical senses: words such as *love, evil, truth, justice, success*. Abstractions should be used cautiously in writing. Too many of them produce fuzzy generalities that explain little. Does the statement "Everyone needs love" refer to the "love" of a tender parent-child relationship or that of a torrid back-seat passion? Unless "love" is made concrete by the addition of examples or illustrations, the statement remains unclear. Your reader may well understand it to mean something quite different from what you intended. Good writing is a careful blend of abstract and concrete, general statement and specific examples. Thus, one important function of examples is to explain an abstraction or generality by providing vivid, familiar word pictures.

Another function of examples is to support or back up a statement, particularly a statement of your opinion about something. In this case, the use of examples becomes a persuasive strategy. If, for instance, you wanted to convince your reader that job prospects for college and university graduates are improving, you could provide statistical examples of increased hiring by major industries. Perhaps you might assemble instances of recent recruitment drives on campus by companies such as Bell Canada, Alcan, and the Bank of Montreal. Again, you use examples to clarify ideas and help persuade your reader that your opinion is valid.

Thus, examples are valuable on two counts. First, they ground your abstract concepts in concrete reality that your reader can see and understand. Second, they lend substance and credibility to your THESIS, the point you are making in your paper. If you use examples well, you'll ensure that your words don't suffer the fate of the Droner's: lost to the ears of a snoring audience.

We expect to find vivid word pictures in good writing. Examples bring ideas to life, and, therefore, we find them not just in the kind of paper we've been discussing in this chapter, but in all kinds of writing. Writers of classification, process analysis, comparison, or any other rhetorical pattern often use examples to illustrate or emphasize important points. Judith Finlayson, for instance, uses examples to clarify ideas and interest the reader in her cause and effect essay, "Math's Multiple Choices."

How? The Technique

Examples may be chosen from several sources: personal experience, the experience of others, quotations, statistics, or facts you've discovered through research. Whatever kinds of examples you choose to use, organizing and developing your paper require careful thought. The overall thesis must be clear and the scope of the examples appropriate to the thesis.

Your thesis statement will probably look something like this:

> Some examples of S are a, b, c. . . .

Example: Three Canadian doctors who have made significant contributions to human welfare are Frederick Banting, Hans Selye, and Norman Bethune.

All you need to do now is develop each example in turn. At the end of this introduction, we've included a short essay based on this thesis statement so you can see what the finished product looks like.

Examples are an all-purpose tool on the writer's workbench. They make your general ideas specific, your thesis convincing, and your communication interesting. Using a good example or two is also a sure-fire way to liven up an introduction or conclusion. Examples reach out and grab the reader's attention.

Now that you're aware of the usefulness of examples in your writing, you should know the three "safety rules" to follow when selecting them:

1. Make sure each example is *representative* of your subject. Wayne Gretzky is not a "typical hockey player," nor is Montreal's Westmount your "average Canadian neighbourhood." The

examples you choose must be typical enough to represent fairly the group or the idea you are explaining.

2. Make sure all examples are *pertinent*. They must be relevant, significant, and acceptable to your audience as examples of the quality or idea they've been chosen to illustrate. For instance, most readers would recognize Donald Sutherland as a Canadian actor who is an international star. The same readers might not accept Kate Nelligan as an example of the same phenomenon, since it's debatable whether or not she is internationally renowned. And if you were to identify Madonna as your example, your whole paper would be called into question, since she's not even Canadian.

3. Make sure the range and number of your examples is *limited*. You're not writing the Sears catalogue, throwing in every colour and size in a jumbled and eventually overwhelming list. There is no set number of examples to include. How many you need depends on your purpose. The challenge is to be both selective and comprehensive, to include just enough examples to convey your idea clearly and forcefully.

Following the structural principles and the safety rules outlined here will ensure that your paper is soundly constructed and communicates exactly what you want it to, as the essay below demonstrates:

The Social Value of Education

Introduction ────▶ Most of us think of higher education as something we engage in because it will benefit us personally. We often overlook the fact that education does more than just develop the mind and spirit or prepare us for a career. The education we acquire for personal reasons also benefits the society in which we live, sometimes in surprising ways. Medical doctors, for example, are among our most highly educated citizens and are in a position to promote not only the health of their patients but also the well-being of our society. Three Canadian

Thesis statement (S plus three examples) ── medical doctors who have made significant contributions to human welfare are Frederick Banting, Hans Selye, and Norman Bethune.

Paragraph 2
develops first
example in
thesis statement

➤ Frederick Banting (1891–1941) was born in Alliston, Ontario, and educated at the University of Toronto. He served in the Army Medical Corps in World War I. During the early 1920s, he joined a team of biochemical researchers at the University of Toronto. Along with physiologist Charles Best, Banting discovered the internal secretion of the pancreas, which they named "insulin." An insufficient supply of insulin causes the disease known as diabetes. The discovery and production of insulin made it possible to control the disease, thus saving or prolonging the lives of countless diabetics. Banting's contribution to this momentous medical achievement won him the Nobel Prize for Medicine and Physiology in 1923.

Paragraph 3
develops second
example

➤ Hans Selye (1907–1983), a Vienna-born endocrinologist, was a physician who specialized in the study of the glands in the body that secrete hormones. After studying in Prague, Paris, and Rome, Selye joined the faculty of McGill University in 1932 and in 1945 became the first director of the Institute of Experimental Medicine and Surgery at the University of Montreal. Over the next three decades, Selye's research and publications made him the world's foremost expert on the effects of stress on the human body. Through his books and lectures, he popularized the notion that there are two kinds of stress. One, "eustress," is beneficial and leads to accomplishment and healing. The other, "distress," is the kind more familiar to us. It is destructive: it breaks down the body and leads to diseases such as high blood pressure, ulcers, mental illness, even cancer. Selye's work has thus contributed to our understanding of the effects of stress not only on the individual but also on society, since a general increase in frustration and anxiety may lead to an overall increase in the incidence of disease.

Paragraph 4 develops third example

Norman Bethune (1890–1939), who was born in Gravenhurst, Ontario, studied medicine in Toronto and in England. He had a strong social conscience and throughout his life used his medical knowledge and skill to relieve the suffering of the poor. After contracting tuberculosis in the 1920s, he moved to Quebec, where he experimented with various treatments of that disease. His research led to improvements in the technology and techniques of chest surgery. Meanwhile, Bethune's leftist political views prompted him to challenge the conservative Canadian medical establishment and eventually to join the Communist party. His political commitment led him in 1936 to fight in the Spanish Civil War. There he organized the first mobile blood-transfusion service, an innovation that saved thousands of lives. In 1938, Bethune's commitment to the anti-fascist cause took him to China, which was then defending itself against the Japanese invasion. In China he worked tirelessly to bring the benefits of modern medicine to a peasant people. Though Bethune died of blood poisoning after he had been in China only a year, his humanitarian efforts and devotion to the downtrodden made him a hero and enhanced the reputation of Canada among the Chinese people.

Conclusion

These three Canadian physicians are good examples of the social value of education. Whether a person is engaged in medicine or business, teaching or technology, the education he or she acquires helps others. Though our achievements may be less dramatic than those of Banting, Selye,

or Bethune, what we learn will inevitably
benefit not just ourselves but also the
people around us, and, by extension,
society as a whole.

The Cat in the Bag
and Other Absolutely
Untrue Tales from
Our Urban Mythology

IAN PEARSON

1   here are no step dancers° in David and
Karen Mills's living room. It is evening, but no mummers° peep
through the windows. Instead of sea chanteys, there is Duke Elling-
ton on the stereo. But, despite the appearances, this relatively normal dinner party in Ancaster, Ontario, is a treasure trove of folklore.
After a couple of rounds of drinks are served, the stories come forth,
and although shopping malls and automobiles have replaced castles
and carriages, they are truly the stuff of legend.

2   The conversation has turned to cats, and David, a 31-year-old
businessman, recounts with glee an incident that purportedly° happened in nearby Brantford to friends of his family: "Julie was getting
married in the summer. She and her mother were going out to one
of the malls on the edge of Brantford to buy some clothes at the last
minute. En route, they ran over a cat. They knocked on a number
of doors to try to find the owner of the cat, but no one was home.
They figured they couldn't leave this mangled cat in the middle of
the road so somehow they had to dispose of it. The only thing they
had in their car that they could put this cat in was an empty Creeds°
bag. They scraped the cat into the bag and put it into the trunk of
the car. Then they continued to the shopping centre, intending to
try again to find the owner on their way back home.

3   "They parked the car and, because it was a hot day, they decided
they couldn't leave the festering cat remains in the hot, steamy
trunk. So they put the bag on the roof of the car. They went into
the mall and when they finished shopping they went for a cup of

coffee in a restaurant that overlooked the parking lot. They could see the roofs of the cars and the Creeds bag perched on top of theirs. As they were looking out, a large grey Cadillac cruised by and stopped in front of their car. A well-dressed woman got out and ambled over slowly and grabbed the bag, jumped back into the car and drove away to another part of the parking lot.

"Julie and her mother thought this was pretty funny. But a few   4 minutes later, the woman walked into the restaurant and sat down in a booth near them. She ordered a coffee and then she peeked into the bag to see what she had acquired. She screamed and fell over backward in a dead faint. At that point, the waitress had a conniption° and called an ambulance. The woman didn't revive when she was given smelling salts and slapped in the face. The ambulance arrived and the attendant said there was no problem, that she had just fainted. They whisked her away on a stretcher. Just as they were leaving, the waitress grabbed the Creeds bag and said, 'Excuse me, she's left this behind.' So the last Julie and her mother saw of the dead cat was it straddling the woman's chest as she was being wheeled, unconscious, into the ambulance."

A fine tale, and David's listeners are amused and convinced. It   5 has strong narrative momentum. It has convincing detail. It has wonderful irony. And it's not true.

The dead cat in the Creeds bag is a classic example of an urban   6 legend. Like a rumor, an urban legend is presented as the truth, contains a large number of corroborating° facts and is set in the recent past. Unlike a rumor, it has a developed plot that often results in an ironic twist. The bare-bones information of a snake biting a customer in a store (in Vancouver, it's a furrier; in Montreal, it's a sporting goods store) is a rumor. If it is elaborated into the story of a friend of a neighbor who was rushed to hospital and now is slightly paralyzed because of the snakebite, it is becoming a legend. If the same story persists for a number of years (and the dead cat tale has been traced back to 1906), it has achieved legend status. Although they are generally believed to be true by the teller, the same tales are passed along by word of mouth simultaneously across North America—the state of the art of apocrypha° now.

In Salt Lake City, you can hear about the cat in the Creeds bag   7 down to its most minute details, with the prestigious Castleton's store substituted for Creeds and Cottonwood Mall stepping in for the Brantford mall. Or, a few years ago, you might have heard the late Harry Chapin tell a similar story on the *Tonight* show. The singer told how his aunt was trying to dispose of her beloved German shepherd, which had died late on a Sunday night. She stuffed the corpse into a suitcase to take over to Harry's place, being unable to spend a night near the dead dog. On the subway, a man helped her with her heavy load, and then bolted away with her suitcase.

8   That black sense of irony permeates most of the legends. If everything in the legends was true, you would be well advised to arm yourself before reading any further. Because at this very moment there is an axe murderer in the house who has finished off your children and is about to call you from the upstairs extension. (Don't console yourself that such telecommunications pyrotechnics° are impossible: urban legends aren't big on logic.) The bucket of fried chicken beside your armchair contains a fried rat and at the bottom of the bottle of cola you're drinking are the remains of a dead mouse. The kitchen is a mess of fur and blood, because one of your (now deceased) family members brought in Trixie the toy poodle from the rain and attempted to dry her off in your new microwave oven. At least your other pet, a baby alligator brought back from Florida, is thriving because you flushed it down the toilet and it now marauds° the sewers.

9   Don't even think about escape. The mint condition Mercedes that you just bought for $60 last week (from an estranged wife who was seeking revenge on her runaway husband) has just been filled in with concrete by a jealous cement-truck driver. Your previous car was stolen while you were vacationing in the south: unfortunately the corpse of your grandmother (who died on the holiday) was rolled up in a rug on the roof since you were trying to sneak her past customs. (That was an extremely frantic day—just before your car was stolen you had an ugly brush with an enraged toll booth operator who had just been left with a cadaver's° arm, a dollar bill pasted to the outstretched palm, by a carload of medical students.) And running down the road won't help because *out there* somewhere is the hitchhiker who vanished into *thin air* from the back seat of your car just after predicting that something awful would happen to you, yes, on this very date.

10   Brrrrr, pretty scary stuff, eh kids, as SCTV's Count Floyd would say (and Count Floyd used to be Eddie Haskell, no?). What is this demented° mythology that we carry around in our communal consciousness like some sort of metaphysical° rubber snake? It is simply the same process of human psychology that brought us *Grimm's Fairy Tales* and Paul Bunyan. The legends give expression to some of the innermost anxieties and concerns that persist in the face of social change. "As urban men and women, we pride ourselves on our sophistication and our lack of superstition," says Dr. Martin Laba, an assistant professor of communication at B.C.'s Simon Fraser University who specializes in mass media and popular culture studies. "But clearly the existence of these legends is a testimony to the

fact that the impulse for, and certainly the fascination with, the supernatural is still there."

The prevalence° of urban legends also attests to the endurance 11 of oral communication in the face of the overwhelming influence of mass media. Often, as in the case of Chapin's dead dog, the legends gain credibility and a wider audience through electronic and print media. "It's a relatively recent phenomenon that very much feeds off its relationship with the media," says Dr. Carole Carpenter, associate professor of humanities at Toronto's York University and a specialist in Canadian culture and folklore. "The urban belief tales rely on the media for their validity. You often hear, 'I heard it from someone who heard it on Johnny Carson.' "

Newspapers and films also play an important role in the trans- 12 mission of legends. "The mass media can both substantiate and be the source of legends," Laba says. "Those tiny items on the back pages of newspapers are often retold orally and get mixed up in the process. You're dealing with a process like the children's game Broken Telephone, where the original story is lost and then elaborated upon. The wonder of oral communication is that things change. There's also a degree of ambiguity between fantasy and reality. In Hitchcock's *Rear Window*, a guy chops up his wife and puts her in bags. That has now become an urban legend. Did it begin with Hitchcock or did he get it from another source? It's impossible to say. I suspect that it began with the film and has been elaborated into a legend through oral sources."

While the media generate legends, they can also be vexed by 13 apocryphal tales that are often reported to them as true incidents. Last winter, *Vancouver Sun* columnist Denny Boyd attempted to trace a story about a football player's wife who took pity on an apparently infirm old lady in Pacific Centre and submitted to her request to provide a ride home. The wife called her husband to warn him that she would be late for dinner. The husband was suspicious and called the police, who descended on the car to find the old lady was a little old man with a wig and a hatchet. Boyd could have saved his time by looking up the exact tale in *Heads You Lose and Other Apocryphal Tales*, a 1981 collection by Francis Greig.

Similarly, when a story was circulating at the same time about 14 three West Vancouver children being kidnapped in Disneyland, the *Sun* was besieged by callers wanting to know why the newspaper was suppressing the news. A call to a detective in Anaheim, California, revealed that legends about Disneyland kidnappings had been circulating for eight or nine years. Jan Harold Brunvand's groundbreaking 1981 study, *The Vanishing Hitchhiker: American Urban Legends and Their Meaning*, shows that the Disneyland legend is common across North America.

15   Of all media people, gossip columnists are probably the most frequent victims of urban legends. Gary Dunford of *The Toronto Sun* printed the cat-in-the-Creeds-bag tale as a real story four years ago. "Then over three years I heard the story three more times in three different restaurants," Dunford recalls. "And each time you hear the story, it's always somebody's best friend who swears they were there."

16   That power of testimony caught Dunford off guard on another occasion when he printed the story of the banana man of North York, Ontario. A Lothario° had been dancing at several singles bars from cocktail hour to 2 A.M. As he drove home to the suburbs, he was knocked out cold in a traffic accident. He was rushed to emergency, and when the nurses undressed the still-unconscious reveller, they discovered a banana strapped with rubber bands to his thigh. "I believed the story because the guy who called me said his girlfriend was the nurse on duty in the hospital the night it happened," Dunford explains. "Two years later I heard the same story, just like the first time, but from another hospital in Etobicoke. You have to ask, 'Is there an Etobicoke banana man or is this an urban legend?' "

17   Most definitely an urban legend and one, like many, with a meaning that is clear on first listening. The North York banana man tells us that dishonesty, especially when combined with profligate° habits, leads only to humiliation. The dead cat warns (from beyond the grave) that theft invariably leads to punishment, in this case involving the dreaded taboo of a dead body. The old man with the hatchet simply says don't pick up strangers. Other legends, such as the woman drying her poodle in the microwave, are more reflections of social or technological change. Says Carpenter: "The microwave legend is not so much a moral tale as a commentary on a social circumstance. It's not told by 35-year-olds to 11-year-olds to instruct them how to operate a microwave. The most prominent tellers are teenagers trying to shock each other."

18   Still, urban legends are not necessarily restricted to entertainment value or to any age group. As Laba explains: "We tend to think that mass culture has encroached upon and destroyed the oral tradition. It's not so. Narrative is fun and it always involves entertainment value. But you have to look at legend telling within the permanent and enduring quality of storytelling. It is a fundamental means of education and communication, even in our urban society."

19   The permanence and endurance of many urban legends become apparent when they are compared to older, traditional legends. One recent apocryphal tale is as contemporary as today's baseball standings, but it contains oral conventions that have resonated° for centuries. Two middle-aged women from Hamilton, Ontario,

embark on their first trip to New York City. Their friends have given them the direst warnings about crime in the Big Apple: if anyone accosts you, do exactly what they say and don't make any trouble. The women choose an expensive hotel, and on their first evening they are careful not to stray beyond the taxi and the Met°. After the opera, they return directly to the hotel, pleased that the evening has proceeded uneventfully. When the elevator stops at the mezzanine level, a tall black man leading a Doberman pinscher° by a leash enters. The women keep their eyes to themselves as the dog shakes nervously at the ascent of the elevator. Suddenly the black man yells, "Sit!" Instantly and obediently, the two women sit on the elevator floor. The man apologizes profusely as he gets off at the fourth floor.

The next morning the women, chastened but composed, seat 20
themselves in the hotel's main dining room. Immediately the hotel's best breakfast appears at their table.

"There must be some mistake," protests one woman. 21

"No, it's all taken care of," assures the waiter. "By that gentle- 22
man in the corner banquette."

The women peer over, and spy the black man who smiles and 23
nods. "Who is he?" asks the other woman.

"Madam, that is Mr. Reggie Jackson." 24

In another version, it is former football star Rosie Grier. Gary 25
Dunford has heard the same tale set in Toronto's Royal York Hotel when the New York Yankees were in town and claims to have also read it in the *New York Post*. And now that Jackson toils in California, another New York black celebrity will surely pinch hit for him in the legend. Still, the teller of this version of the tale in Toronto insists that it is true, that it happened to her good friend Helen's aunt. When asked for verification, she replied that she had lost track of her good friend Helen.

But more fascinating than the variations of the legend is the fact 26
that its modern dress is draped over the body of a traditional devil legend common in Quebec. "It's got all the classic elements of a supernatural legend," explains Laba. "In many Roman Catholic legends, there's always a warning at the beginning that prescribes an order of behavior. And then the devil appears and you know there's going to be a disruption. In a racist society, the devil is always portrayed as black—the prince of darkness—and he's often accompanied by the devil hound. So here, the guy of course *has* to be black and the dog *has* to be a Doberman. At the same time the story tends to parody° all that stuff. It's almost a joke because at the moment they sit down you see the absurdity of the warning and of the entire situation."

The sophistication of the Reggie Jackson legend is essential to 27 its credibility. As the stories are more frequently repeated and the phenomenon of urban legends becomes better known, new twists and details must be added to convince the listener (who, of course, is the next teller of the legend). Perhaps the best-known urban legend of all tells of alligators infesting the sewers of New York. (Thomas Pynchon helped spread the tale with an Alligator Patrol in his extravagant 1963 novel *V.*) There is a kernel of truth to the legend. The February 10, 1935, *New York Times* ran an article with a headline and deck° that is almost a complete legend in itself: "Alligator Found In Uptown Sewer—Youths Shoveling Snow Into Manhole See Animal Churning in Icy Water—SNARE IT AND DRAG IT OUT—Reptile Slain by Rescuers When It Gets Vicious—Whence It Came Is Mystery." But even if there were alligators in the New York sewers in the 1930s, the legend has been officially denied so many times since then that most people now know that it is not true. In some cases, it has become what folklorists call an "antilegend," in which the denial is spread by word of mouth: "Did you know that there really *aren't* any alligators in the sewers of New York?" In other cases, the legend rejuvenates° itself with new details. In the late 1960s, stories spread among students about "New York White" marijuana, which had sprouted from seeds flushed through toilets during drug raids and flourished in the lightless sewers.

28   At the same time that old legends are being renewed, new ones are nudging their way into parlance°. A Toronto lawyer tells a story he heard in the courts of a drunk driver who was stopped by the police on a major expressway. The driver had been concentrating on his driving and was amazed that he had been pulled over.

29   "What's the matter, officer?" he asked.

30   "Do you have *any* idea how fast you were going?" came the reply.

31   "Gee, maybe 70 miles an hour. I wasn't that much over the limit."

32   "You were going *17* miles an hour!"

33   A sailor in Owen Sound, Ontario, relates the same story with identical figures. Possibly it happened exactly as it is told. But that does not affect its legendary character. What matters is not its veracity but its word-of-mouth form of transmission: *My lawyer told me about this guy who . . .* or, *This friend of Arch's was blotto and. . . .* Inevitably, new details and variations will be added, just as inevitably as floppy disks, Michael Jackson, video games, Brian Mulroney and sushi will seep into their own legends. And in each one, the story will be as simple and eternal as Cinderella's, as the old world gives the new one the power to be born.

[   ]

IAN PEARSON

Ian Pearson, the journalist, was born in Edmonton in 1954 and is a graduate of the University of Toronto. His articles have appeared in such magazines as *Maclean's*, *Canadian Business*, *Toronto Life*, and *Saturday Night*. He is an editor of *Toronto*, a magazine published by the *Globe and Mail*.

Words and Meanings

Paragraph

step dancers:	traditional Scottish-Irish folk dancers	1
mummers:	masked folk actors	
purportedly:	said to be	2
Creeds	fashionable women's clothing store in Toronto, now closed	
conniption:	fit of hysteria	4
corroborating	supporting	6
apocrypha	stories believed to be true but actually false or doubtful	
pyrotechnics	brilliant display, like fireworks	8
marauds	preys upon, raids	
cadaver	corpse	9
demented	crazy, obsessed	10
metaphysical	philosophical, abstract	
prevalence	wide presence	11
Lothario	ridiculous lover	16
profligate	sexually indiscriminate, wasteful	17
resonated	vibrated	19
the Met	Metropolitan Opera, in New York City	
Doberman pinscher	a fashionable type of guard dog	
parody	mock, make ridiculous	26
deck	part of a newspaper headline	27
rejuvenate	make young again	
parlance	everyday speech	28

Structure and Strategy

1. What INTRODUCTORY strategy has the author used?
2. Why does the author give an example of an urban legend (paragraphs 2 to 5) before he tells the reader how an urban legend comes about?

3. Summarize the psychological basis for these grim urban legends (paragraph 10).
4. What is the effect of the direct quotations the author uses in paragraphs 10, 11, and 12?
5. How does the concluding paragraph contribute to the UNITY of the whole essay?

Content and Purpose

1. Why does the author call his examples urban legends rather than modern legends?
2. What is the implied thesis of this essay?
3. Why is the story of the cat in the bag ironic (paragraph 5)? Why does "the black sense of IRONY permeate most of the legends" (paragraph 8)?
4. Explain in your own words the first sentence of paragraph 11. Define the terms *oral communication* and *mass media*.
5. What functions do urban legends have in our culture?

Suggestion for Writing

In paragraph 6, Pearson defines an urban legend as a story that is "presented as the truth, contains a large number of corroborating facts and is set in the recent past." Write an essay in which you develop this definition using your own examples.

Odd Enders

LARRY ORENSTEIN

1   eath is never funny. It is cancer, heart failure, stroke, clogged arteries, pneumonia, emphysema, asthma, bronchitis, choking, drowning, car accident. It is mostly quiet, conventional and inevitable.

2   But, in the twilight area between Dryden's "Death in itself is nothing" and Kojak's "Dead is dumb," there are "other causes." A man who stumbles during his morning constitutional°, bites his tongue and dies of gangrene—as Allan Pinkerton, head of the U.S. detective agency bearing his name, did in 1884—is a man who is

checking out with a drum roll, a man who, in short, is joining the
Club of Odd Ends.

Membership in the club sometimes requires the assistance of a   3
sponsor. In 1977, a 36-year-old San Diego woman decided to murder
her 23-year-old husband, a U.S. Marine drill instructor, to collect
his $20,000 in life insurance. First, she baked him a blackberry pie
containing the venom sac of a tarantula. But he ate only a few pieces.
She then tried to (1) electrocute him in the shower, (2) poison him
with lye, (3) run him over with a car, (4) make him hallucinate while
driving by putting amphetamines in his beer, and (5) inject an air
bubble into his veins with a hypodermic needle. Finally, dispensing
with subtlety, she and an accomplice, a 26-year-old woman, beat
him over the head with a metal weight while he slept. This worked.

In 1978, a Parisian grocer stabbed his wife to death with a wedge   4
of parmesan cheese. In 1984, a New Zealand man killed his wife by
jabbing her repeatedly in the stomach with a frozen sausage.

In April, 1984, a 41-year-old Pennsylvania man was asphyxiated   5
after his 280-pound wife sat on his chest during an argument. Nine
months later, a 41-year-old Indiana woman beat her male companion to death by repeatedly dropping a bowling ball on his head
while he lay on the floor in front of a television set.

Last summer, a man in Sao Paulo, Brazil, caught his wife in bed   6
with her lover, and glued her hands to the man's penis. Doctors
separated the two, but the man died from toxic chemicals absorbed
through his skin. In Prague, a woman jumped out of a third-story
window after learning her husband had been unfaithful. She landed
on the husband, who was entering the building at that moment. He
died instantly; she survived.

A despondent° Los Angeles man put a gun to his head and   7
pulled the trigger. The bullet passed through his head, ricocheted
off a water heater and struck his female companion between the
eyes.

Some people, of course, discover the Club of Odd Ends on their   8
own and sign their membership cards with a flourish. An Italian
man set himself on fire, apparently had second thoughts and died
falling off a cliff trying to beat out the flames. Last fall, a 26-year-old
computer specialist died near Bristol apparently after tying one end
of a rope to a tree and the other around his neck, getting into his
car and driving off.

In 1971, a Shrewsbury man killed himself by drilling into his   9
skull eight times with an electric power drill. Sixteen years later, a
Chichester man who could no longer bear the pain from angina
killed himself by drilling a hole in his heart.

Some people become Odd Enders by accident. In 1947, an eccen-   10
tric U.S. recluse°, while carrying food to his equally reclusive brother,

tripped a burglar trap in his house and was crushed to death under bundles of old newspapers, three breadboxes, a sewing machine and a suitcase filled with metal. His brother starved to death.

11   In 1982, a 27-year-old man fired two shotgun blasts at a giant saguaro cactus in the desert near Phoenix. The shots caused a 23-foot section of the cactus to fall and crush him to death. That same year, an elderly Louisiana man with ailing kidneys was waving a gun at quarrelling relatives when it went off. The bullet severed a tube from his dialysis° machine, and he bled to death.

12   In 1983, the assistant manager of a topless night club in San Francisco was crushed to death between the ceiling and a trick piano rigged to rise 12 feet above the club's stage. When the club was opened in the morning, the man's 240-pound body was found draped over his naked, intoxicated girl friend, who survived apparently by kicking a switch to stop the cables hoisting the piano.

13   In November, 1985, a flight attendant with three months of experience survived the hijacking of an Egyptian airliner that left 60 people dead in Malta. She was killed seven months later when her plane crashed in a sandstorm near Cairo.

14   In April, an award-winning astronomer at the University of Arizona was crushed to death between a door and a 150-ton revolving telescope dome. In June, a man demonstrating electrical currents to his children in Orillia, Ont., was electrocuted when an experiment backfired. A California woman taking pictures of a glacier in Alaska was killed when a 1,000-pound chunk of ice broke free and fell on her.

15   A 22-year-old Peruvian woman died of septicemic° poisoning in June after the rusty padlock on the leather chastity belt that her jealous husband forced her to wear dug into her flesh and caused an infection.

16   In 1980, the 70-year-old mayor of a Maryland town who was checking a sewage-treatment plant slipped on a catwalk°, fell into a tank of human waste and drowned. In July, a retired barman in Northern Ireland was buried alive when he fell into a grave being dug for his brother.

17   The Club of Odd Ends, however, does not accept all applicants. A Brazilian public servant lost an arm last summer when he stuck it into a lion's cage "to test God's power." One night in 1982, an Ohio bachelor awoke, thought he saw a prowler at the foot of his bed, reached for his gun, fired into the darkness and shot himself in the penis.

18   Some people, of course, are destined to become Odd Enders no matter what they do. In May, a Louisiana lawyer stood in the stern

of his new boat, raised his hands skyward and said: "Here I am."
He was killed by a bolt of lightning.

LARRY ORENSTEIN

Larry Orenstein is an assistant foreign editor at the *Globe and Mail* and is a
member of the Crime Writers of Canada.

Words and Meanings

Paragraph

constitutional:	a brisk walk taken for healthy exercise	2
despondent:	feeling hopeless, depressed	7
recluse:	someone who lives in isolation, avoiding the company of others	10
dialysis machine:	machine used for patients with severe kidney disease; it removes waste products from the blood	11
septicemic poisoning:	bacterial infection of the blood	15
catwalk:	narrow bridge or scaffolding	16

Structure and Strategy

1. Why has Orenstein written this piece in such short paragraphs? Who are his intended readers?
2. Orenstein identifies people who suffer bizarre deaths as belonging to the "Club of Odd Ends." Into what three categories of membership does he group his examples? (See paragraphs 3, 8, and 10.)
3. In the introduction to this unit, we identify three "safety rules" to follow when selecting examples to support a thesis. Does Orenstein follow these rules? If not, which one(s) do you think "Odd Enders" violates?
4. "Odd Enders" contains many examples of situational IRONY, such as the example given in paragraph 2, where the head of a famous detective agency dies after biting his own tongue. Explain the irony of this example, and find at least three more examples of situational irony in the article.
5. How does the concluding paragraph contribute to the UNITY of the article?

Content and Purpose

1. What is the thesis of Orenstein's article? Can you state it in one sentence?
2. What was your reaction to "Odd Enders"? Do you think your response was what the author intended?

Suggestion for Writing

Some of the examples in "Odd Enders" are similar to stories found in tabloid newspapers such as the *National Enquirer*. Write a short essay explaining the appeal of these kinds of papers. Why do people enjoy reading about strange murders, film star scandals, aliens, and Elvis sightings?

They Also Wait Who Stand and Serve Themselves

ANDREW WARD

1   Anyone interested in the future of American commerce should take a drive sometime to my neighborhood gas station. Not that it is or ever was much of a place to visit. Even when I first moved here, five years ago, it was shabby and forlorn: not at all like the garden spots they used to feature in the commercials, where trim, manicured men with cultivated voices tipped their visors at your window and asked what they could do for you.

2   Sal, the owner, was a stocky man who wore undersized, popped-button shirts, sagging trousers, and oil-spattered work shoes with broken laces. "Gas stinks" was his motto, and every gallon he pumped into his customers' cars seemed to take something out of him. "Pumping gas is for morons," he liked to say, leaning indelibly against my rear window and watching the digits fly on the pump register. "One of these days I'm gonna dump this place on a Puerto Rican, move to Florida, and get into something nice, like hero sandwiches."

3   He had a nameless, walleyed° assistant who wore a studded denim jacket and, with his rag and squeegee, left a milky film on

my windshield as my tank was filling. There was a fume-crazed, patchy German shepherd, which Sal kept chained to the air pump, and if you followed Sal into his cluttered, overheated office next to the service bays, you ran a gauntlet° of hangers-on, many of them Sal's brothers and nephews, who spent their time debating the merits of the driving directions he gave the bewildered travelers who turned into his station for help.

"I don't know," one of them would say, pulling a bag of potato   4
chips off the snack rack, "I think I would have put 'em onto 91, gotten 'em off at Willow, and then—bango!—straight through to Hamden."

Sal guarded the rest room key jealously and handed it out with   5
reluctance, as if something in your request had betrayed some dismal aberration°. The rest room was accessible only through a little closet littered with tires, fan belts, and cases of oil cans. Inside, the bulb was busted and there were never any towels, so you had to dry your hands on toilet paper—if Sal wasn't out of toilet paper, too.

The soda machine never worked for anyone except Sal, who,   6
when complaints were lodged, would give it a contemptuous kick as he trudged by, dislodging warm cans of grape soda which, when their pop-tops were flipped, gave off a fine purple spray. There was, besides the snack rack in the office, a machine that dispensed peanuts on behalf of the Sons of Garibaldi. The metal shelves along the cinderblock wall were sparsely stocked with cans of cooling system cleaner, windshield de-icer, antifreeze, and boxed head lamps and oil filters. Over the battered yellow wiper case, below the Coca-Cola clock, and half hidden by a calendar from a janitorial supply concern, hung a little brass plaque from the oil company, awarded in recognition of Salvatore A. Castallano's ten-year business association.

I wish for the sake of nostalgia that I could say Sal was a crafts-   7
man, but I can't. I'm not even sure he was an honest man. I suspect that when business was slow he may have cheated me, but I never knew for sure because I don't know anything about cars. If I brought my Volvo in because it was behaving strangely, I knew that as far as Sal was concerned it could never be a simple matter of tightening a bolt or re-attaching a hose. "Jesus," he'd wearily exclaim after a look under the hood. "Mr. Ward, we got problems." I usually let it go at that and simply asked him when he thought he could have it repaired, because if I pressed him for details he would get all worked up. "Look, if you don't want to take my word for it, you can go someplace else. I mean, it's a free country, you know? You got spalding on your caps, which means your dexadrometer isn't charging, and pretty soon you're gonna have hairlines in your flushing

drums. You get hairlines in your flushing drums and you might as well forget it. You're driving junk."

8   I don't know what Sal's relationship was with the oil company. I suppose it was pretty distant. He was never what they call a "participating dealer." He never gave away steak knives or NFL tumblers or stuffed animals with his fill-ups, and never got around to taping company posters on his windows. The map rack was always empty, and the company emblem, which was supposed to rotate thirty feet above the station, had broken down long before I first laid eyes on it, and had frozen at an angle that made it hard to read from the highway.

9   If, outside of television, there was ever such a thing as an oil company service station inspector, he must have been appalled by the grudging service, the mad dog, the sepulchral° john. When there was supposed to have been an oil shortage a few years ago, Sal's was one of the first stations to run out of gas. And several months ago, during the holiday season, the company squeezed him out for good.

10   I don't know whether Sal is now happily sprinkling olive oil over salami subs somewhere along the Sun Belt. I only know that one bleak January afternoon I turned into his station to find him gone. At first, as I idled by the no-lead pump, I thought the station had been shut down completely. Plywood had been nailed over the service bays, Sal's name had been painted out above the office door, and all that was left of his dog was a length of chain dangling from the air pump's vacant mast.

11   But when I got out of the car I spotted someone sitting in the office with his boots up on the counter, and at last caught sight of the "Self-Service Only" signs posted by the pumps. Now, I've always striven for a degree of self-sufficiency. I fix my own leaky faucets and I never let the bellboy carry my bags. But I discovered as I squinted at the instructional sticker by the nozzle that there are limits to my desire for independence. Perhaps it was the bewilderment with which I approach anything having to do with the internal combustion engine; perhaps it was my conviction that fossil fuels are hazardous; perhaps it was the expectation of service, the sense of helplessness, that twenty years of oil company advertising had engendered°, but I didn't want to pump my own gas.

12   A mongrel rain began to fall upon the oil-slicked tarmac as I followed the directions spelled out next to the nozzle. But somehow I got them wrong. When I pulled the trigger on the nozzle, no gas gushed into my fuel tank, no digits flew on the gauge.

13   "Hey, buddy," a voice sounded out of a bell-shaped speaker overhead. "Flick the switch."

I turned toward the office and saw someone with Wild Bill   14
Hickok hair leaning over a microphone.

"Right. Thanks," I answered, and turned to find the switch.   15
There wasn't one. There was a bolt that looked a little like a switch,
but it wouldn't flick.

"The switch," the voice crackled in the rain. "Flick the switch."   16

I waved back as if I'd finally understood, but I still couldn't   17
figure out what he was talking about. In desperation, I stuck the
nozzle back into my fuel tank and pulled the trigger. Nothing.

In the office I could see that the man was now angrily pulling   18
on a slicker. "What the hell's the matter with you?" he asked,
storming by me. "All you gotta do is flick the switch."

"I couldn't find the switch," I told him.   19

"Well, what do you call this?" he wanted to know, pointing to   20
a little lever near the pump register.

"A lever," I told him.   21

"Christ," he muttered, flicking the little lever. The digits on the   22
register suddenly formed neat rows of zeros. "All right, it's set. Now
you can serve yourself," the long-haired man said, ducking back to
the office.

As the gas gushed into my fuel tank and the fumes rose to my   23
nostrils, I thought for a moment about my last visit to Sal's. It hadn't
been any picnic: Sal claimed to have found something wrong with
my punting brackets, the German shepherd snapped at my heels as
I walked by, and nobody had change for my ten. But the transaction°
had dimension to it: I picked up some tips about color antennas,
entered into the geographical debate in the office, and bought a can
of windshield wiper solvent (to fill the gap in my change). Sal's
station had been a dime a dozen, but it occurred to me, as the nozzle
began to balk and shudder in my hand, that gas stations of its kind
were going the way of the village smithy and the corner grocer.

I got a glob of grease on my glove as I hung the nozzle back on   24
the pump, and it took more than a minute to satisfy myself that I
had replaced the gas cap properly. I tried to whip up a feeling of
accomplishment as I headed for the office, but I could not forget
Sal's dictum: Pumping gas is for morons.

The door to the office was locked, but a sign directed me to a   25
stainless steel teller's drawer which had been installed in the plate
glass of the front window. I stood waiting for a while with my
money in hand, but the long-haired man sat inside with his back to
me, so at last I reached up and hesitantly knocked on the glass with
my glove.

The man didn't hear me or had decided, in retaliation° for our   26
semantic° disagreement, to ignore me for a while. I reached up to
knock again, but noticed that my glove had left a greasy smear on

the window. Ever my mother's son, I reflexively reached into my pocket for my handkerchief and was about to wipe the grease away when it hit me: at last the oil industry had me where it wanted me— standing in the rain and washing its windshield.

<hr>

ANDREW WARD

Andrew Ward was born in Chicago in 1946. His essays and short stories appear regularly in American magazines, and he has written a number of books of humour, including *Fits and Starts: The Posthumous Memoirs of Andrew Ward* and *Bits and Pieces*.

Words and Meanings

The title is an ALLUSION to a sonnet by John Milton, a seventeenth-century English poet, on the subject of his blindness and how it had altered the way in which the poet could serve God. The poem concludes with the line, "They also serve who only stand and wait."

Paragraph

3	walleyed:	having an opaque, whitish eye caused by injury or disease
	run a gauntlet:	run between rows of armed persons who strike the runner in passing; a form of punishment
5	aberration:	an abnormality
9	sepulchral:	like a sepulchre or tomb
11	engendered:	created
23	transaction:	business deal
26	retaliation:	response, revenge
	semantic:	concerned with the meanings of words

Structure and Strategy

1. What is Ward's thesis? Where does he state it?
2. What two ILLUSTRATIONS does Ward use to prove his point?
3. Identify some of the specific examples Ward uses to convey the impression that Sal's gas station is disorganized, decrepit, and run-down.
4. How does Ward achieve an effective TRANSITION between the description of Sal's old-style station and the new, self-service replacement?
5. What strategy does Ward use in his CONCLUSION (paragraph 26)?

How does the conclusion contribute to the UNITY of the essay as a whole?

Content and Purpose

1. What is the overall purpose of this essay? Is Ward's intent to contrast the "old" and "new" ways of operating a gas station, or does he use these examples to illustrate a larger point?
2. What is Ward's attitude toward Sal and the kind of business operation he represents? What is the purpose of including Sal's nonsensical diagnosis of what is wrong with Ward's Volvo (paragraph 7)?
3. Summarize in a sentence or two the main reason Ward prefers the old-style gas station to the new.

Suggestions for Writing

1. Using two extended examples, compare the small-town corner grocery store with the large supermarket, or the small neighbourhood clothing store with the large department store, or the small advertising agency with the large agency, or any small, owner-operated organization with a large organization. Be certain to use specific details within your extended examples.
2. Use two or three extended examples to prove (or disprove) the thesis that self-service operations are advantageous to the customer.

Good Old Us

WALTER STEWART

Williams Lake, British Columbia, 1966. An 1 Indian girl met some youths in a beverage room°, and they agreed to give her a lift to her aunt's place. Of course, they didn't take her to her aunt's; they took her to a garbage dump, where the three whites thought they would get a little free loving. Everybody knows about Indian girls.

Unfortunately, this girl didn't. She was found dead the next 2 morning, naked and dead by the roadside. The youths, all of good families, admitted that they had wrestled her around some, got fed up with her, and pitched her out of the car into the cold April night. She died of a broken neck, but they said she was alive when they last saw her. What they did wasn't right, maybe, but it wasn't murder, either. A white jury agreed; two of the youths were convicted of assault, and fined $200; the charge against the third was dismissed.

3   The House of Commons, Ottawa, 1938. Premier Maurice Duplessis of Quebec had brought in a law, the Padlock Law, that permitted the seizure and closing of any premises suspected of being used to propagate° communism. No proof was required, no defence was permitted, and "communism" was never defined. The law was used against all of Duplessis's political opponents. In Ottawa, J.S. Woodsworth, leader of the CCF, rose in his place in Parliament and, his voice shaking with emotion, declared, "Twice every day for six months the provincial police have carried out execution without judgment, dispossession° without due process of law; twenty times a month they have trampled on liberties as old as Magna Carta°." Woodsworth was shouted down. Ernest Lapointe, Minister of Justice, told him, "In spite of the fact that the words are so unpleasant to the honourable member for Winnipeg North Centre, I do desire to say that the reign of law must continue in this country, that peace and order must prevail."

4   Outside Vancouver, 1887. A mob of whites, disturbed that indentured° Chinese coolie labourers had taken jobs in the mines that God meant white men to have, rushed the Chinese camp and drove the workers out into the January night. There was a twenty-foot cliff behind the camp, and the coolies were driven over it; you could hear them going plump, plump, plump, into the freezing sea.

5   Toronto, 1945. E.B. Jolliffe, provincial leader of the CCF, charged that the Ontario Provincial Police were being used as political spies by the Conservative government, that a special squad was gathering private information for Premier George Drew, and that this information was being used to harass Liberals and CCFers. Jolliffe said the OPP was acting as a private "Gestapo°"—an emotive° word for that time. He had an impressive amount of evidence, including the testimony of Alvin Rowe, an OPP officer who had worked on the secret squad and who had come to Jolliffe because, he said, he was being used as a political spy, and didn't like it. A royal commission was called to inquire into Jolliffe's charges, but its terms of reference were so narrow that it was barred from conducting a real investigation. Then Alvin Rowe was killed in a plane crash; Jolliffe's party was badly punished at the polls.

6   Sydney, Nova Scotia, 1971. The Sydney police went on strike for higher wages. They had barely left their posts when gangs of toughs took over the town and began drag-racing up and down the

main street. Fights, looting, then a general riot broke out; the town was in a state bordering on anarchy° until the strike was settled.

Near Seven Oaks, Manitoba, 1816. A disagreement arose 7 between fur traders of the North West Company and settlers brought in by Lord Selkirk to found a permanent community. So the company arranged to have the settlement attacked, and twenty people were murdered. When Selkirk tried to exact justice, he was blocked by the political manoeuvrings of his opponents, defeated in court, and eventually driven into near bankruptcy.

Near Wymark, Saskatchewan, 1967. A man who had complained 8 that the RCMP was slow in acting on his earlier charges that he was being harassed by obscene telephone calls was working in his pasture. An RCMP car pulled up, two constables piled out, and he was taken away and held for forty days, under the Saskatchewan Mental Health Act, without ever being charged, or convicted, or even told what he had done wrong.

During the forty days he was subjected to shock treatments and 9 drug therapy and then, one day, he was turned loose as suddenly as he had been locked up.

Montreal, 1949. A university professor's house blew up, and his 10 wife and daughter were killed, while he was injured. He was clapped into jail and held for three months under the provincial Coroner's Act. Police had discovered that he had a mistress some time previously, and they assumed, without a shred of proof, that he had blown up his own house. He was not charged; he was simply held, while the press seethed with stories of his infidelity°, his callousness°, his savagery. Eventually, it turned out that the house had been destroyed by a natural gas explosion. He was released.

Toronto, 1974. An American sociologist, a controversial figure 11 alleged to hold strong and wrong views on the subject of race, had been invited to speak at the University of Toronto. A group of left-wing students and teachers decreed that he was an inappropriate speaker; they stormed the lectern°, staged a minor riot, and drove the sociologist away. His speech was never made. Months later, two students were suspended for their part in the affair; it can be argued that freedom of speech remains suspended at the university.

I am in favour of smugness°, to a point; it rounds the figure, 12 deepens the dimples, and aids the digestive process. I believe, too, that Canadians have a certain amount to be smug about; by and large, we have been a reasonable and prosperous people; by and large, we have avoided mass murder, organized tyranny, and the more public forms of corruption. However, since 1972, since Water-gate, smugness has become a national religion, a national disease. Nothing that has happened on the North American continent since our side sacked Washington in 1814 has given Canadians such unalloyed° pleasure as Watergate. While the Americans wallow in guilt and self-doubt, we bubble with joy and self-righteousness. Thank God, we say, for our British traditions and innate° Canadian decency. There may be rot and racism, inequity and injustice, among those fractious°, rebellious Yankees, but not in Canada.

13   Well, we have never had anything quite like Watergate, but that is a claim we share with most nations of the world. We have, however, had major political corruption involving our highest figures— remember Sir John A. and the Pacific Scandal, remember the McGreevy brothers, remember the Beauharnois Scandal, remember the Ontario Highways Scandal?—and we have had extensive cover-ups, political dirty tricks, payoffs, and—God knows—thousands of examples of the abuse of power.

14   A major difference between us and the Americans—besides the size, the pervasiveness, the sheer bloody-mindedness of Water-gate—is our diffidence°. Except for the Pacific Scandal (after all, that was a long time ago), Canadian outbursts of corruption, venality°, brutality, racism, and oppression have gone largely unrecorded. It's not that we don't want to hear about such subjects—we do—but we don't want to hear them when they happen in Canada. During the spring of 1975, Canadians flocked to their theatres to see an American film about authoritarianism in the U.S., called *Hearts and Minds*. At the same time, they stayed away in droves from a Cana-dian film about authoritarianism in Canada, called *Les Ordres*. There are some things we would rather not know.

15   We view ourselves as a superior people, a sober, peaceable people, a people of extraordinarily decent instincts and firmly entrenched liberties, and we reject any contrary evidence. Thus, when our federal government comes along, as it did in October 1970°, and throws 435 people into jail without charge or trial, when it makes it a crime ever to have belonged to a political organization that was legal five minutes before the law was passed, we are not shocked or upset; we applaud. If the government chooses to estab-lish retroactive crime, our reaction is not to say that our civil liberties are in jeopardy°, but that the government must have powerful reasons, secret reasons, reasons that remain secret to this day, to act so arbitrarily°. Indeed, some officers of the Canadian Civil Liberties Association give their approval—although the Association itself does not. Because we know we are decent, reasonable people, because our government would never do anything really wrong, really suppressive, whatever is done must, of necessity, be reason-able and right. Indeed, some Canadians are still half-expecting the government to produce secret reasons, one of these days, that will

explain the whole thing satisfactorily (just as some of us still wait around on Easter morn for a bunny to drop off a clutch of eggs).

One of the problems we face as a nation, perhaps in greater measure than other nations, is that we are held captive by the myth of the reasonable citizen. The Canadian as we see him, the Canadian in the mind of God, is a man who never gives into extremism; he is a patient man (who shuns violence), a neighbourly man (who spurns racism), a democratic man (who supports free speech, civil liberties, and honesty in politics). He is, in short, all the things your average wild-eyed, gun-toting, bigoted, loud-mouthed, venal°, aggressive, tyrannical° bastard of an American is not. What is more, his history has made him the gentle citizen he is today. There have been blots on the copybook°—things like the Winnipeg General Strike, the Regina Riot, the incarceration° of Japanese Canadians during World War II—but these are minor slips, casually recorded or missed entirely in our history of ourselves.   16

Enough. Canadians, as a people, are no better and no worse than anyone else. We were slavers in the eighteenth and early nineteenth centuries, and our treatment of minorities, from Indians to Jehovah's Witnesses, is only marginally different from that of the Americans. We have staged some of the bigger and more bloody-minded riots on the continent, from the Bytown Riots of the 1840s ("Them Bytown days was fightin' days") to the Kenora race riots of 1974. We have not only passed, but applauded, viciously repressive legislation, and our gun laws, to take only one minor example of wrong-headed self-congratulation, are in fact looser and dumber than those in most U.S. states.   17

WALTER STEWART

Walter Stewart (b. 1931) is a journalist and teacher whose works include *Strike!* (1971), *But Not in Canada!* (1976), and *Canadian Newspapers: The Inside Story* (1980).

Words and Meanings

Paragraph

beverage room:	bar, saloon	1
propagate:	spread	3
dispossession:	the wrongful seizure of someone's property	
Magna Carta:	the "great charter" of English civil liberties, issued by King John in 1215	
indentured:	enslaved	4

5   Gestapo: German secret police during Nazi regime
     emotive: provoking strong feelings

6   anarchy: state of lawlessness; chaos

10   infidelity: unfaithfulness, disloyalty
     callousness: lack of feelings

11   lectern: a speaker's stand; podium

12   smugness: feeling of being very satisfied with oneself
     unalloyed: pure, unmixed
     innate: in-born, natural
     fractious: tending to fight, be unruly

14   diffidence: lack of self-confidence
     venality: corruption, the taking of bribes

15   October 1970:   date the Trudeau government implemented the
                               War Measures Act
     jeopardy: danger
     arbitrarily: without consultation

16   venal: corrupt, bribable
     tyrannical: dictatorial, oppressive
     blots on the copybook: errors, faults, inconsistencies
     incarceration: internment, imprisonment

In a contemporary Canadian encyclopedia, look up the following references:

13   Pacific Scandals,
        McGreevy Brothers,
        Beauharnois Scandal,
        Ontario Highways
        Scandal

15   War Measures Act

16   Winnipeg General Strike,
        Regina Riots

17   Bytown Riots, Kenora
        race riots

Structure and Strategy

1. Stewart begins his essay by citing nine incidents in eleven para-
    graphs. The incidents, which span the period from 1816 to 1974,
    are not arranged chronologically. What do these examples have
    in common? When does the reader begin to sense the
    connection?
2. Why does Stewart preface each example with the place and
    date? What point is he making? What would be the effect of
    arranging these examples in chronological order?

3. In paragraph 12, the structure and the tone of the essay change. What is the function of the second half of the essay (paragraphs 12 to 17)? What connection is there between the two halves of the essay?
4. What is the TONE of paragraphs 1, 2, and 4? Of paragraphs 3, 5, and 11? Identify three or four sentences that you think most clearly reveal Stewart's attitude toward his subject.
5. Paragraphs 1 and 2 depend for their effect, in part, on Stewart's use of STEREOTYPING. Explain how he uses this technique to create an emotional impact on his readers. Consider Stewart's use of DICTION in your answer.
6. Paragraph 15 ends with a SIMILE. What is its function and what effect does it have on the reader?

Content and Purpose

1. Sum up the argument of this essay in a single thesis statement. (You might find it useful to review paragraphs 15 and 16 first.)
2. Stewart draws a major contrast between Canadians and Americans in this essay. What specific characteristics are contrasted? Why does Stewart think Canadians are "smug"? Do you agree with him?
3. What point is Stewart making by his reference to the imposition of the War Measures Act and its aftermath (paragraph 15)?
4. Does "Good Old Us" portray Canadians as morally superior, inferior, or similar to the people of other nations? Is this how we normally think of ourselves?
5. Read Neil Bissoondath's " 'I'm Not Racist But . . .' " and compare his view of stereotyping with Stewart's.

Suggestions for Writing

1. Write an essay presenting the opposite side of Stewart's argument. Cite examples of Canadian tolerance, reasonableness, peacefulness, and generosity.
2. Using as background material some or all of the essays by Michele Landsberg, Rick Groen, Barry Callaghan, and William Thorsell, write an essay contrasting three aspects of American and Canadian culture. Be sure to support your points with examples, some (but not all) of which should be quoted from your sources.
3. Contrast Stewart's view of racism and stereotyping in Canada with Bissoondath's in " 'I'm Not Racist But . . .'."

Canadian Wry

BARRY CALLAGHAN

1   hese are strange times. I live in a country that's a hotbed of rest, where crafty lawyers argue that the holocaust° was a hoax, serious men believe they have no cash in their pockets because the poor are hoarding money, and malevolent° men, now that Pierre Trudeau is gone, want me to explain Canada.

2   Well, the first thing is this: we Canadians are never what we appear to be. Deception, sometimes self-deception, is our genius. We appear to be boring, but in fact, we're zany and make no sense at all.

3   For example, like everyone else, we have our secret police, but what other people in the world would dress up their secret cops in scarlet coats and have them ride around on horses wagging their lances at the wind, calling covert action a musical ride? What other country's serious ideologues on the radical left would call themselves the Waffle° so that absolutely no one would take them seriously? What other country could dissolve into a duality after a twelve-minute skirmish two hundred years ago on a ratty field outside Quebec City and make both inept generals who got themselves killed into heroes? And what of our national heroine—Laura Secord—our Paul Revere in drag? The fact is, that craggy face we all know from school books and chocolate boxes, is not Laura Secord at all. It's a deception, the portrait was posed for by a grandniece and was painted over a portrait of Premier George Ross. My God, George Ross in drag. In fact, the whole land as it lies on the map is a deception: huge, bigger than the United States, but almost empty because the mass of the few million folk cling to the border by their finger nails, as if the 49th parallel were a window ledge on America, on the world.

4   So, that world on the other side of the window likes to think we're boring, likes to think we win more bronze medals than anyone else on the face of the earth. We love people to think we're boring. We've raised being boring to a wacky art form. And why? Because it pays off.

5   Take William Lyon Mackenzie King, our prime minister through the war, and so it seemed, for all time until Pierre Trudeau came

along and seemed to be prime minister for all time. King held power longer than any other Western politician in this century. How did such a pudgy, mundane little man do it? The truth is, he did it deliberately. He was shrewd and self-effacing, and he told one of his friends that he made every speech as boring as possible because then no one would ever remember what he said and hold it against him. Twenty-two years in power, droning on and on over the airwaves, and meanwhile, he was as crazy as a loon.

He talked to his dead mother, consulted his dog, sought signs   6
from F.D.R.° in his shaving cream in the mirror, did missionary work with local street hookers, and built his own little backyard temple from the stone remnants of old Parliament buildings. He was a choice one, *fol dol di die do*, but not so rare: after all, we're the only people anywhere who ever took the radical right-wing Social Credit economics of Ezra Pound so seriously that we've elected several Social Credit governments, and still do, in British Columbia—where the first premier's name was W.A.C. Bennett—and if such wacky right-wingers are not in power, then radical socialists are. Out East, cuddly Joey Smallwood° bossed his own fiefdom in Newfoundland for a couple of decades in a way that would have made Huey Long° green with envy. Mounties were his private strike-breaking police. And what can anyone make of our seesawing in Ottawa—from a prairie populist prime minister, John Diefenbaker, who wanted to "green" the Arctic, to the lisping internationalist, Lester Pearson who—it's true—won the Nobel Peace Prize, but it's a good thing he never had to go to war, because on the one day the Red Phone rang in his office, he couldn't find it, followed by the ascetic and acerbic Trudeau who took a flower child in tow to the marriage chamber and somehow "arranged" that two of his children actually be born on Christmas day, except his wife then ran away with all the Rolling Stones.

But wackiness is a rolling stone that gathers no moss, so now   7
we have God's smooth little fixer, Brian Mulroney, bogman and bagman from Quebec. As for Quebec . . . well, not even the French from France understand the québécois, who, when they cry *vierge, hostie, ciboire, tabernacle*°, seem to be chanting tidbits from the catechism. In fact, they are cursing along the lines, in English, of *hot shit, suck this, my sweet ass*. The scatological is hidden inside the sacramental.

Who knows this? Do they want anyone to know? Not necessar-   8
ily: who else in the world can walk up to you and, as far as he's concerned, call you a suckhole to your face and smile as you cross yourself in accord, believing yourself blessed? Clever, we're clever as we cling to the ledge of the world. And this is not just a matter of politicians cakewalking in secret. No! The determination to present a

flat face to the world crankles through our high-tone culture, too. No one but a Canadian would have carried on like Glenn Gould, the silver bullet among interpreters of Bach and Beethoven, and a great natural showman—wrapped in his scarf, playing with his winter mittens on, always seated on a dilapidated chair as if it were the abyss—the toast of the concert halls, and what did he do? Dismissed it all as vaudeville, as irrelevant as the appendix, and refused to ever play in public again, a recluse tinkling to no one but machines in closed recording studios, a powerful presence, a studied absence.

9   So, what's the advantage of all this dodging, all this disdain for the glitter, let alone the glitz, of stardom? Well, we have—for all our lust for law and order—a remarkable freedom. In the United States, they suffer through a House Un-American Activities Committee° because they not only know who they're supposed to be, but insist on it. Such a committee in Canada would be laughable. We still refuse to agree on what the words to our national anthem are. We don't know who we are and don't want to. That way we don't have to be anybody's anything. In fact, we can pretend to be everybody else, and if we make a mistake, *they* take the rap.

10   Our largest corporations got very rich during the Vietnam war, and several are getting rich right now in South Africa and South and Central America, but when's the last time you saw or heard of an anti-Canadian demonstration in the streets of Santiago? We're so clean we squeak, the sound of the sullen mouse beside the lumbering elephant. Haw! The Americans are our whipping boys, and if they think about us at all it's to assure us that we're lucky to be among them.

11   And actually, we are: not so much lucky, but among them. We're insidious infiltrators inside their system. Do you know—do they know—that nearly fifty per cent of their major television reporters around the world and commentators at home are Canadian? It's true. Every night we tell millions of Americans how to see the world, how to see their wars and their movie stars and heroes and bums, their dreams achieved and broken. And if Americans ever laugh at their own insanity, Canadians control the scripts. On the loneliest night of the American week, the television program *Saturday Night Live* is a joke conceived and produced by Canadians.

12   As such, the archetypal Canadian is invisible—a no one who is everyone from nowhere, like Rich Little . . . the most skilled impersonator in America. Having no voice of his own, he has everyone else's—male or female—and he "does" them, as they say, perfectly. People in Las Vegas and the folk in the White House prefer him to the real thing. In half an hour they get John Wayne talking to Nixon, Sylvester Stallone to Ronnie Reagan. What would Charlie McCarthy

have been without Edgar Bergen, that boring deadpan man, the perfect Canadian?

You see, you pick up a few tricks, clinging to the ledge of the   13
world. You learn how to amiably draw no attention to yourself while having your own way. Canadians could be the world's greatest secret agents. Who knows? Remembering our man in Iran, perhaps we are. After all, Ken Taylor° told the world that to get the Americans out of Iran, he "disguised them as Canadians."

Anyway, if we fool the world, we also outfox ourselves. Margaret   14
Atwood, the poet, once said our national mental illness is paranoid schizophrenia. That's too grim, too American. Our so-called paranoia is really nostalgia for a future we know we can never have, and the so-called schizophrenia is really the sound of two sensibilities acutely aware of each other as they rattle around inside one skull.

Sound and fury behind a bland face. But it was that global   15
villager, Marshall McLuhan° (what a perfect Canadian stance—the secret conservative adored by a New York advertising world he abhorred), who came close to the point when he said that English Canada leapt directly from the eighteenth century into the twentieth century, skipping the romantic assertion of self so central to the nineteenth century. True enough, for we've got a lot of poor lost Loyalists° dragging a bogus Toryism° and a collection of coronation china around in a child's wagon in English Canada, while Quebec— as counter culture to the nation—lives in the self-aggrandizing nineteenth as if it were an *arrondissement*°, dreaming of an independent national orbit, knowing such a state can never be.

To live in Canada, illusion and delusion are so necessary that   16
the "quick change artist" is commonplace, whether it's a change of hats or loyalties. We stand astride life, you see, as if it were a seesaw, balancing, waiting. The prime minister who was the master of this balancing act was Wilfrid Laurier (who of course had a "secret" mistress everyone, including his wife, knew about), and he said, "The twentieth century shall be the century of Canada." Among those who think that California is still a dream, such an idea brings hoots of derision, but he was right—that is, if Samuel Beckett° has touched any chord in the contemporary heart. We are two cultures in Canada, like the two tramps by the side of the road, watching in amazement as the Pozzos° and Luckys° of this world pass through our lives, and we wait. Bland-faced, we wait, and wait, and shrug and make sly jokes and probes—as McLuhan would have it. Trudeau's most characteristic gesture, after completing a comic pirouette behind some august person like the Queen, was a shrug. Everything may be up to date in Kansas City, but you can't get any more contemporary than that shrug.

And lest you think that this gift for deception behind the mask   17 of boredom is only a flash in the fullness of callow youth, we carry it to the grave. I know that one of the world's favorite humorists is Stephen Leacock, master of the comic light touch, with a tinge of blackness around the edges, a little like a requiem mass card. Our own secret agent of small town laughter. But did you know how he went to his grave? It was, you see, the tradition in his family to be buried in a plain, good old Canadian pine box, but he'd bought a huge oak and brass-handled job and six burly men carried it to the plot not knowing—no one knew—that he'd had himself cremated and was only a little glass bottle of ashes cradled in a satin puff inside the box.

18   Oh, wait till we really get to know our new prime minister, Mulroney, for we have only heard, so far, the sound of melting chocolate. When it comes to the temper of our times—the smooth capacity to touch an audience's heart by saying absolutely nothing several sweet times over—he makes Ronnie Reagan look awkward. He's as slick as analgesic balm in Gilead°. He's a genius, a master of mindless phrase, mindfully wrought. And he can do it in two languages, too, with ease.

19   It's already the accepted wisdom that Mulroney will be in power a long time. Already, no one can remember anything he's said. Shrewd and self-effacing. Then, after he's gone, we'll all discover he was a total secret wacko, with a fetish for changing clothes three and four times a day—not an astringent intellectual but something of a mystic—a man in search of the perfect press . . . just a typical Canadian on a musical ride. Trudeau, you see, was not so special. He just went out to lunch in foreign capitals and wore, instead of a bronze medal, a rose in his lapel.

20   P.S. My favorite Trivial Pursuit question is this: *Who invented Trivial Pursuit?* The answer, of course, is two Canadians, but nobody, not even masters of the game, can remember their names.

BARRY CALLAGHAN

Barry Callaghan, short-story writer, journalist, and editor, was born in Toronto in 1937. He teaches at Atkinson College, York University, Toronto, where he edits the quarterly magazine *Exile*. Callaghan originally wrote "Canadian Wry" for *Punch*, a British humour magazine.

Words and Meanings

Paragraph

1   holocaust: the attempted extermination of the Jews by the
                                    Nazis during World War II

malevolent:	evil-minded, spiteful, mischievous
Waffle:	ultrasocialist and nationalist group within the NDP in the 1960s [3]
F.D.R.:	Franklin Delano Roosevelt, U.S. president (1933–45) [6]
Joey Smallwood:	first premier of Newfoundland (1949–72)
Huey Long:	demagogue and governor of Louisiana (1928–35)
vierge, hostie, ciboire, tabernacle:	French religious references used as swear words in Quebec [7]
House Un-American Activities Committee:	U.S. Senate committee obsessed with Communist subversion in the 1950s [9]
Kenneth Taylor:	Canadian ambassador to Iran (1977–80) [13]
Marshall McLuhan:	theorist of the media, originator of the phrase "the global village" [15]
Loyalists:	Anglo-Americans loyal to Britain who left the United States in protest against the Revolution to settle in Ontario and the Maritimes
Toryism:	doctrine of the Progressive Conservative (Tory) party
arrondissement:	French word for a district
Samuel Beckett:	playwright, author of *Waiting for Godot* [16]
Pozzo and Lucky:	two characters in *Waiting for Godot*
balm in Gilead:	Old Testament reference to comfort, consolation, or cure [18]

Structure and Strategy

1. Look at the structure of paragraph 1. Is it an effective INTRODUCTION?
2. What is the function of paragraph 2?
3. What is the TOPIC of paragraph 3? How is the topic developed?
4. In paragraph 4, Callaghan poses a question and answers it, very briefly. What is the function of paragraphs 5 and 6?
5. Paragraph 11 provides a TRANSITION to Callaghan's point about Canadians' unique role as "infiltrators." Which paragraphs illustrate this role?
6. The CONCLUSION of this essay suggests some reasons for and provides more examples of Canadian "wackiness" disguised as blandness. Identify the concluding paragraphs. Are they effective?

Content and Purpose

1. What TONE does Callaghan adopt in this essay? Is it appropriate to his purpose? Why or why not?
2. Why does Callaghan think Canadians are deceptive? How does he think we benefit from this deceptiveness?
3. What is the price Callaghan says we pay for our deceptiveness, for being "closet wackos"?
4. Find two or three places in which Callaghan speaks of Canadians as "clinging to the ledge." Why do you think he chose this metaphor to describe the Canadian condition?
5. What is Callaghan's view of Canadian history? Do you think this view is accurate or has he twisted the facts?

Suggestions for Writing

1. Write a paper in which you provide examples of what you define as "the Canadian character."
2. Write a paper illustrating three or four differences between Canadians and Americans, or between Maritimers and Westerners, or between two other groups that suggest a similar contrast.

Mankind's Better Moments

BARBARA TUCHMAN

1   n this troubled world of ours, pessimism seems to have won the day. But we would do well to recall some of the positive and even admirable capacities of the human race. We hear very little of them lately.

2   Ours is not a time of self-esteem or self-confidence as was, for instance, the 19th Century, whose self-esteem may be seen oozing from its portraits. Victorians, especially the men, pictured themselves as erect, noble and splendidly handsome. Our self-image looks more like Woody Allen or a character from Samuel Beckett. Amid a mass of worldwide troubles and a poor record for the 20th Century, we see our species—with cause—as functioning very badly, as blunderers when not knaves, as violent, ignoble°, corrupt,

inept, incapable of mastering the forces that threaten us, weakly subject to our worst instincts; in short, decadent.

The catalogue is familiar and valid but it is growing tiresome. A study of history reminds one that mankind has its ups and downs and during the ups has accomplished many brave and beautiful things, exerted stupendous endeavors°, explored and conquered oceans and wildernesses, achieved marvels of beauty in the creative arts and marvels of science and social progress, loved liberty with a passion that throughout history has led men to fight and die for it over and over again, pursued knowledge, exercised reason, enjoyed laughter and pleasures, played games with zest, shown courage, heroism, altruism, honor and decency; experienced love, known comfort, contentment, and, occasionally, happiness. All these qualities have been part of human experience and if they have not had as important notice as the negatives nor exerted as wide and persistent an influence as the evils we do, they nevertheless deserve attention, for they currently are all but forgotten.   3

Among the great endeavors, we have in our time carried men to the moon and brought them back safely—surely one of the most remarkable achievements in history. Some may disapprove of the effort as unproductive, as too costly, and a wrong choice of priorities in relation to greater needs, all of which may be true but does not, as I see it, diminish the achievement. If you look carefully, all positives have a negative underside, sometimes more, sometimes less, and not all admirable endeavors have admirable motives.   4

Great endeavor requires vision and some kind of compelling impulse, as in the case of the Gothic cathedrals of the Middle Ages. The architectural explosion that produced this multitude of soaring vaults, arched, ribbed, pierced with jeweled light, studded with thousands of figures of the stone-carvers' art, represents in size, splendor and numbers one of the great, permanent artistic achievements of human hands.   5

What accounts for it? Not religious fervor alone. Although a cathedral was the diocesan seat° of a bishop, the decision to build did not come from the Catholic Church alone, which by itself could not finance the operation, but from the whole community. Only the common will shared by nobles, merchants, guilds, artisans, and commissioners in general could command the resources and labor to sustain such an undertaking. Each group contributed donations, especially the magnates of commerce who felt relieved thereby from the guilt of money-making. Collections were made from the public in towns and countryside, and indulgences° granted in return for gifts. Voluntary work programs involved all classes. "Who has ever seen or heard tell in times past," wrote an observer, "that powerful princes of the world, that men brought up in honors and wealth,   6 that nobles —men and women—have bent their haughty necks to the harness of carts and like beasts of burden have dragged to the abode of Christ these wagons loaded with wines, grains, oil, stones, timber and all that is necessary for the construction of the church?"

7   The higher and lighter grew the buildings and slenderer the columns, the more new expedients° and techniques had to be devised to hold them up. Buttresses° flew like angels' wings against the exterior. It was a period of innovation and audacity. In a single century, from 1170 to 1260, 600 cathedrals and major churches were built in France alone. In England in that period, the cathedral of Salisbury with the tallest spire in the country was completed in thirty-eight years. The spire of Freiburg in Germany was constructed entirely of filigree° in stone as if spun by some supernatural spider. In the Sainte Chapelle in Paris the fifteen miraculous windows swallow the walls; they have become the whole.

8   Explanations of the extraordinary burst that produced the cathedrals are several. Art historians will tell you that it was the invention of the ribbed vault, permitting subdivision, independence of parts, replacement of solid walls by columns, multiplication of windows and all the extrapolations° that followed. But this does not explain the energies that took hold of and developed the rib. Religious historians say these were the product of an age of faith that believed that with God's favor anything was possible. In fact, it was not a period of untroubled faith but of heresies° and Inquisition°. Rather, one can only say that conditions were right. Social order under monarchy and the towns was replacing the anarchy° of the barons so that existence was no longer merely a struggle to stay alive but allowed a surplus of goods and energies and greater opportunity for mutual effort. Banking and commerce were producing capital, roads making possible wheeled transport, universities nourishing ideas and communication. It was one of history's high tides, an age of vigor, confidence and forces converging to quicken the blood.

9   Even when the general tide was low, a particular group of doers could emerge in exploits that still inspire awe. What of the founding of our own country? We take the Mayflower for granted, yet think of the boldness, the enterprise°, the determined independence, the sheer grit it took to leave the known and set out across the sea for the unknown where no houses or food, no stores, no cleared land, no crops or livestock, none of the equipment or settlement of organized living awaited.

10   Equally bold was the enterprise of the French in the northern forests who throughout the 17th Century explored and opened the land from the St. Lawrence to the Mississippi, from the Great Lakes to the Gulf of Mexico. They came not for liberty like the Pilgrims, but for gain and dominion, and rarely in history have men willingly

embraced such hardship, such daunting adventure and persisted with tenacity and endurance.

Happily, man has a capacity for pleasure too, and in contriving   11 ways to entertain and amuse himself, has created brilliance and delight. Pageants, carnivals, festivals, fireworks, music, dancing and drama, parties and picnics, sports and games, the comic spirit and its gift of laughter, all the range of enjoyment from grand ceremonial to the quiet solitude of a day's fishing has helped to balance the world's infelicity°. Homo ludens, man at play, is surely as significant a figure as man at war or at work. No matter what else is happening, the newspapers today give more space to the sports pages than to any other single activity. (I do not cite this as necessarily admirable, merely indicative.) In human activity the invention of the ball may be said to rank with the invention of the wheel. Imagine America without baseball, Europe without soccer, England without cricket, the Italians without bocci, China without ping pong, and tennis for no one.

But mankind's most enduring achievement is art. At its best, it   12 reveals the nobility that coexists in human nature along with flaws and evils, and the beauty and truth it can perceive. Whether in music or architecture, literature, painting or sculpture, art opens our eyes and ears and feelings to something beyond ourselves, something we cannot experience without the artist's vision and the genius of his craft. The placing of Greek temples like the Temple of Poseidon on the promontory at Sunion outlined against the piercing blue of the Aegean Sea, Poseidon's home; the majesty of Michelangelo's sculptured figures in stone; Shakespeare's command of language and knowledge of the human soul; the intricate order of Bach, the enchantment of Mozart; the purity of Chinese monochrome pottery with the lovely names—celadon, oxblood, peach blossom, claire de lune; the exuberance of Tiepolo's ceiling where, without the picture frames to limit movement, a whole world in exquisitely beautiful colors lives and moves in the sky; the prose and poetry of all the writers from Homer to Cervantes to Jane Austen and John Keats to Dostoevsky and Chekov—who made all these things? We—our species—did.

If we have lost beauty and elegance in the modern world, we   13 have gained much, through science and technology and democratic pressures in the material well-being of the masses. The change in the lives of, and society's attitude toward, the working class marks the great divide between the modern world and the old regime.

It is true, of course, that the underside of the scientific progress   14 is prominent and dark. The weaponry of war in its ever-widening capacity to kill is an obvious negative, and who is prepared to state with confidence that the overall effect of the automobile, airplane, telephone, television, and computer has been on balance beneficent°?

15   Pursuit of knowledge for its own sake has been a more certain good. There was a springtime in the 18th Century when, through knowledge and reason, everything seemed possible; when reason was expected to break through religious dogma like the sun breaking through fog, and man armed with knowledge and reason would be able at last to control his own fate and construct a good society. The theory that because it exists, this is the best of all possible worlds, spread outward from Leibniz; the word "optimism" was used for the first time in 1737.

16   What a burst of intellectual energies shook these decades! In the 20 years, 1735–55, Linnaeus named and classified all of known botany; Buffon systematized Natural History in 36 volumes; the American, John Bartram, scoured the wilderness for plants to send to correspondents in Europe; Voltaire, Montesquieu and Hume investigated the nature of man and the moral foundations of law and society; Benjamin Franklin demonstrated electricity from lightning; Dr. Johnson by himself compiled the first dictionary of the English language; Diderot and the Encyclopedists of France undertook to present all knowledge in enlightened terms; the secret of making porcelain having just previously been discovered in Europe through intensive experiments, its manufacture in a thousand forms flourished at Meissen and Dresden; clearing for the Place de la Concorde, to be the most majestic in Europe, was begun in Paris, and the fantastic cascades of Caserta constructed for the Bourbons of Naples; 150 newspapers and journals circulated in England; Henry Fielding wrote *Tom Jones*; Thomas Jefferson was born; Tiepolo painted his gorgeous masterpiece, the Four Continents, on the archducal ceilings at Wurzburg; Chardin, no less supreme, painted his gentle and affectionate domestic scenes; Hogarth, seeing a different creature in the species, exposed the underside in all its ribaldry° and squalor. It was an age of enthusiasm: At the first London performance of Handel's Messiah in 1743, George II was so carried away by the Hallelujah Chorus that he rose to his feet, causing the whole audience to stand with him. A custom was thereby established, still sometimes followed by Messiah audiences.

17   If the twenty-year period is stretched by another ten, it includes the reverberatory° voice of Rousseau's "Social Contract," Beccaria's groundbreaking study on "Crime and Punishment," Gibbon's beginning of the "Decline and Fall," and despite the Lisbon earthquake and Voltaire's "Candide," the admission of "optimism" into the Dictionnaire de l'Académie Française.

18   Although the Enlightenment may have overestimated the power of reason to guide human conduct, it nevertheless opened

to men and women a more humane view of their fellow passengers. Slowly the harshest habits gave way to reform—in treatment of the insane, reduction of death penalties, mitigation° of the fierce laws against debtors and poachers, and in the passionately fought cause for abolition of slave trade. The humanitarian movement was not charity, which always carries an overtone of being done in the donor's interest, but a more disinterested benevolence—altruism, that is to say, motivated by conscience. Through recent unpleasant experiences, we have learned to expect ambition, greed or corruption to reveal itself behind every public act, but it is not invariably so. Human beings do possess better impulses, and occasionally act upon them, even in the 20th Century. Occupied Denmark, during World War II, outraged by Nazi orders for deportation of its Jewish fellow citizens, summoned the courage of defiance and transformed itself into a united underground railway to smuggle virtually all 8,000 Danish Jews out to Sweden. Far away and unconnected, a village in southern France, Le Chamben-sur-Lignon, devoted itself to rescuing Jews and other victims of the Nazis at the risk of the inhabitants' own lives and freedom. "Saving lives became a hobby of the people of Le Chamben," said one of them. The larger record of the time was admittedly collaboration°, passive or active. We cannot reckon on the better impulses predominating in the world; only that they will always appear.

The strongest of these in history, summoner of the best in men, has been zeal for liberty. Time after time, in some spot somewhere on the globe, people have risen in what Swinburne called the "divine right of insurrection"—to overthrow despots, repel alien conquerors, achieve independence—and so it will be until the day power ceases to corrupt, which, I think, is not a near expectation.   19

The phenomenon continues today in various forms, by Algerians, Irish, Vietnamese, peoples of Africa and the Middle East. Seen at close quarters and more often than not manipulated by outsiders, contemporary movements seem less pure and heroic than those polished by history's gloss, for instance the Scots of the Middle Ages against the English, the Swiss against the Hapsburgs, Joan of Arc arousing a dispirited people against the occupier, the Albanian Scanderbeg against the Turks, the American colonies against the mother country.   20

So far I have considered qualities of the group rather than of the individual, except for art which is always a product of the single spirit. Happiness too is a matter of individual capacity. It springs up here or there, haphazard, random, without origin or explanation. It resists study, laughs at sociology, flourishes, vanishes, reappears somewhere else. Take Izaak Walton, author of *The Compleat Angler*, that guide to contentment as well as fishing of which Charles Lamb   21 said, "It would sweeten any man's temper at any time to read it." Although Walton lived in distracted times of revolution and regicide°, though he adhered to the losing side in the Civil War, though he lost in their infancy all seven children by his first wife and the eldest son of his second marriage, though he was twice a widower, his misfortunes could not sour an essentially buoyant° nature. "He passes through turmoil," in the words of a biographer, "ever accompanied by content."

22   Walton's secret was friendship. Born to a yeoman° family and apprenticed in youth as an ironmonger, he managed to gain an education and through sweetness of disposition and a cheerful religious faith, became a friend on equal terms of various learned clergymen and poets whose lives he wrote and works he prefaced. John Donne, vicar of the parish in Chancery Lane where Walton worked, was his mentor and his friend. Others were Archbishop Sheldon of Canterbury, George Morley, Bishop of Winchester, Richard Hooker, Sir Henry Wotton, George Herbert, Michael Drayton and the Royalist, Charles Cotton.

23   *The Compleat Angler*, published when the author was 60, glows in the sunshine of his character. In it are humor and piety°, grave advice on the idiosyncracies° of fish and the niceties° of landing them, delight in nature and in music. Walton saw five editions reprinted in his lifetime while innumerable later editions secured him immortality. The surviving son by his second wife became a clergyman; the surviving daughter married one and gave her father a home among grandchildren. He wrote his last work, a life of his friend Robert Sanderson, at eighty-five and died at ninety after being celebrated in verse by one of his circle as a "happy old man" whose life "showed how to compass true felicity." Let us think of him when we grumble.

24   Is anything to be learned from my survey? I raise the question only because most people want history to teach them lessons, which I believe it can do, although I am less sure we can use them when needed. I gathered these examples not to teach but merely to remind people in a despondent° era that the good in mankind operates even if the bad secures more attention. I am aware that selecting out the better moments does not result in a realistic picture. Turn them over and there is likely to be a darker side, as when Project Apollo, our journey to the moon, was authorized because its glamor could obtain subsidies for rocket and missile development that otherwise might not have been forthcoming. That is the way things are.

25   It is a paradox° of our time that never have so many people been so relatively well off and never has society been more troubled. Yet I suspect that humanity's virtues have not vanished, although the experiences of our century seem to suggest they are in abeyance°.

A century that took shape in the disillusion that followed the enormous effort and hopes of World War I, that saw revolution in Russia congeal into the same tyranny it overthrew, saw a supposedly civilized nation revert under the Nazis into organized and unparalleled savagery, saw the craven appeasement by the democracies, is understandably suspicious of human nature. A literary historian, Van Wyck Brooks, discussing the 1920s and '30s, spoke of "an eschatological° despair of the world." Whereas Whitman and Emerson, he wrote, "had been impressed by the worth and good sense of the people, writers of the new time" were struck by their lusts, cupidity° and violence, and had come to dislike their fellow men. The same theme reappeared a few months ago when a drama critic, Walter Kerr, described a mother in a play who had a problem with her two "pitilessly contemptuous" children. The problem was that "she wants them to be happy and they don't want to be." They prefer to freak out or watch horrors on television. In essence, this is our epoch. It keeps turning to look on Sodom and Gomorrah°; it has no view of the Delectable Mountains°.

_____

BARBARA TUCHMAN

Barbara Tuchman, the well-known historian, was born in 1919 in New York and died in 1989. She is the author of numerous best-selling histories, including *The Guns of August*, *A Distant Mirror*, and *The Proud Tower*.

Words and Meanings

Paragraph

ignoble:	dishonourable, unworthy	2
endeavors:	strenuous efforts, attempts	3
diocesan seat:	church's diocese or bishop's district	6
indulgence:	an absolution formally excusing one from punishment for a sin	
expedients:	means to an end	7
buttresses:	structural supports	
filigree:	delicate lacework	
extrapolations:	developments, conjectures	8
heresies:	false religious doctrines	
Inquisition:	religious trials often ending in torture	
anarchy:	social chaos	
enterprise:	initiative, endeavour	9
infelicity:	unhappiness	11

14	beneficent:	positive, good
16	ribaldry:	indecency
17	reverberatory:	echoing
18	mitigation:	lessening
	collaboration:	working together, often with the enemy
21	regicide:	killing a king
	buoyant:	cheerful, optimistic
22	yeoman:	worker, small landowner
23	piety:	religious devotion
	idiosyncracies:	individual characteristics or oddities
	niceties:	polite acts
24	despondent:	dejected, downcast, not optimistic
25	paradox:	seeming contradiction
	abeyance:	dormancy, not in use
	eschatological:	concerned with last things: death, judgment, heaven and hell
	cupidity:	greed
	Sodom and Gomorrah:	cities in the Old Testament punished by God for their wickedness
	the Delectable Mountains:	desired goal in *Pilgrim's Progress*; as close as humans can get to heaven on earth

Structure and Strategy

1. What is the function of the first two paragraphs of this essay? Why are they so short?
2. Identify the thesis statement in paragraph 3. How does it differ from a thesis statement that you might write for an essay of example?
3. What is the topic sentence of paragraph 12, and how does Tuchman develop that topic sentence?
4. If paragraphs 16 and 17 deal with intellectual discoveries, what does paragraph 18 deal with? Why does Tuchman use these discoveries as a prelude to paragraph 18?
5. How does Tuchman effectively conclude her essay in paragraphs 24 and 25? What is the purpose of the reference to Walter Kerr at the end of the essay?

Content and Purpose

1. What is Tuchman's purpose in this essay? Do you think she has been successful or unsuccessful? Give reasons for your opinion.

2. In an essay titled "Mankind's Better Moments," why does Tuchman make the contrast she does in paragraphs 9 and 10?
3. Summarize the reasons why Tuchman considers art to be "mankind's most enduring achievement" (see paragraph 12).
4. Why does Tuchman consider Izaak Walton to be a hero? (See paragraphs 21 and 22.)
5. Tuchman was a historian. What does she believe a knowledge of history can do, and what are its limitations? (See paragraph 24.) Do you agree or disagree?

Suggestions for Writing

1. Are you optimistic or pessimistic about the human condition as we approach the end of the twentieth century? Write a brief essay defending your point of view and include two or three well-chosen illustrations to support your thesis.
2. In paragraphs 19 and 20, Tuchman declares that the strongest of humanity's better impulses has been "the zest for liberty," and she gives a number of examples of groups who have fought for liberty. However, she mentions only two individuals: Joan of Arc and Scanderbeg. Is there any individual who fought for liberty on a small or large scale whom you particularly admire? If so, write a brief essay of example explaining three of his or her accomplishments.

Additional Suggestions for Writing: Example

Choose one of the topics below and write a thesis statement based on it. Expand your thesis statement into an essay by selecting specific examples from your own experience, current events, or your studies to develop the main points.

1. Fast food is becoming a gastronomic way of life.
2. A person is not always what he or she appears to be.
3. Recent ecological disasters show how little we care for the environment that sustains us.
4. Popular tourist attractions share certain characteristics.
5. Television commercials reveal some significant characteristics of our culture.
6. A good novel is a wonderful way to escape from everyday cares.
7. Choosing a spouse is easy if one knows what to look for.
8. "Good fences make good neighbours." (Robert Frost)
9. Faith is a source of strength in one's personal life.
10. "Religion is the opiate of the people." (Karl Marx)
11. Through travel, we learn about ourselves as well as about other people.
12. A good teacher is concerned for students' personal well-being as well as for their intellectual development.
13. Clothing styles reveal personality.
14. Films aimed at those between 15 and 22 share certain characteristics.
15. "The love of money is the root of all evil." (I Timothy 6:10)
16. "Money is indeed the most important thing in the world; and all sound and successful personal and national morality should have this fact for its basis." (George Bernard Shaw)
17. "Manners are more important than laws." (Edmund Burke)
18. "Feeling godless, what we have done is made technology God." (Woody Allen)
19. "Power corrupts. Absolute power corrupts absolutely." (Lord Acton)
20. "To blame others for our misfortune shows a lack of education; to blame ourselves shows the beginning of education; to blame no one shows a complete education." (Epictetus)

Process Analysis: Explaining "How"

What? The Definition

The next time you find yourself sitting in a dentist's waiting room, pick up a copy of one of the women's magazines—*Chatelaine, Good Housekeeping*, or *Ladies' Home Journal*, for instance. In the table of contents, you'll find a wealth of articles that are examples of process analysis: "Lose Ten Pounds in Ten Days," "Bake the Ultimate Chocolate Cheesecake," or "Raising the Perfect Child." Many of the articles in men's magazines are no different in form, only in content. Their readers learn how to choose a sports car, make a killing in the stock market, tie a Windsor knot, or meet the perfect mate. Across the land, bookstores abound with manuals on fitness, beauty, computer programming, weight control, financial planning, sexuality, and gourmet cooking. These examples of writing, all intended to teach us how to do something, attest to our interest in self-improvement and our fascination with figuring out how something is done. **Process analysis** is the kind of writing that explains how the various steps of a procedure lead to its successful accomplishment.

Why? The Purpose

Process analysis is used for two different purposes that lead to two different kinds of papers or reports. The first kind is the strictly "how-to" paper that gives the reader directions to follow. A **directional process analysis** answers one of two questions:
1. How do you do S?
2. How do you make S?

Students often need to write a directional process analysis on exams or in assignments. For example, how do you debug a COBOL program? How does a paramedic file an accident report? What are the essential steps in assembling a hydraulic valve? In directional process analysis, you are writing for the do-it-yourselfer. You must make the instructions clear so that your readers can follow along, step by step. Directions that are vague or incomplete will infuriate them. Remember the Christmas you spent struggling to assemble your supercharged, battery-operated UltraZapMobile? Remember the hopelessly confusing directions provided: "Insert Tab Square B2 firmly into Slot 5A3 while simultaneously sliding the grommet-blaster into the rotating webfork . . ."? No mere mortal could possibly comprehend such GOBBLEDYGOOK.

The second kind of process analysis, on the other hand, answers these questions:

1. How does S work?
2. How does S occur?
3. How is S done?

These questions lead to **informational process analysis**. Its purpose is to explain to your reader how something is, or was, accomplished. Your readers simply want to be informed about the subject; they don't necessarily want to do the task themselves. Jessica Mitford's "Behind the Formaldehyde Curtain" is a fascinating example of informational process analysis. The subject is a process about which everyone should be informed, but few would care to try out at home. Topics such as how the greenhouse effect is developing, how Newfoundland entered Confederation, how a cell divides, how a corporate merger occurs, or how the Alberta Badlands were formed would all require the writer to produce informational process analyses.

How? The Technique

Writing a process analysis that will direct or inform your readers rather than confuse or infuriate them is not difficult if you follow these six steps:

1. Think through the whole process carefully and write down, in order, an outline of all the steps involved. If you are describing a complex process, break down each step in the sequence into substeps and group them CHRONOLOGICALLY.
2. Now write your thesis statement. Here's the formula for a thesis statement for a *directional* paper:

> To do S, you first a, then b, and finally c.

Example: To fail your year in the grand style, you must antagonize your teachers, disdain your studies, and cheat on your work.

The thesis statement for an *informational* paper also identifies the steps or stages of the process you are explaining:

> S consists of a, b, c. . . .

Example: The speech process consists of four phases: breathing, phonation, resonation, and articulation.

3. Check to be sure you have included any preparatory steps or special equipment the reader should know about before beginning, as in this example: "Make sure you have your pliers, screwdriver, table saw, and bandages handy."

4. Define any specialized or technical terms that may be unfamiliar to your reader. If you need to use words like "phonation," "resonation," or "articulation"—as we did in the example above—you must explain clearly what the terms mean. Underline the mystery words in your outline, so you'll remember to define them as you write the paper. (See Unit Seven for instructions on how to write simple sentence definitions.)

5. Write your first draft. Be sure to use TRANSITIONS, or time-markers, to indicate the progression through the steps or stages. A variety of transitional words and phrases will help smooth your reader's path through your explanation of the process, as these examples illustrate:

   "*First*, assemble your tools. . . ."

   "*Next*, the legal assistant must. . . ."

   "*After* the Conservative regime was defeated, . . ."

   "The sound is *then* shaped by the tongue, lips, and teeth. . . ."

   "*Finally*, Brascan's takeover of Genstar was approved by the shareholders. . . ."

6. Revise your draft carefully. What may seem like a simple procedure to you, since you know it so well, can bewilder someone who knows little about it. Ask a friend to read through your process analysis. If it's as clear to her as it is to you, you're done—congratulations! If it isn't clear to her, back to the drawing board. Clarify any steps that caused confusion and revise until

the whole paper is both clear and interesting to whoever reads it.

The essay below, written with tongue firmly in cheek, illustrates the form and development of a directional process paper:

Flunking with Style

Introduction (challenges widely held opinion)

People often remark that succeeding in school takes plenty of hard work. The remark implies that failure is a product of general idleness and zero motivation. This is an opinion I'd like to challenge. My long and checkered past in numerous educational institutions has taught me that to fail grandly, to fail extravagantly, to go down in truly blazing splendour, requires effort and imagination.

Thesis statement

To fail your year in the grand style, you must antagonize your teachers, disdain your studies, and cheat on your work. Keep the following guidelines in mind.

First step (developed by example)

The first step, antagonizing your teachers, isn't difficult if you keep in mind what it is that teachers like: intelligent, interested, even enthusiastic faces in front row centre. Show that you're bored before the class begins by slouching in a desk at the back of the room. Wear your Walkman, and don't forget to turn up the volume when that teacher starts to talk. Carry on running conversations with your seatmates. Aim an occasional snort or snicker in the teacher's direction when she's putting a complex point on the board. Above all, never volunteer an answer and respond sullenly with an "I dunno" if the teacher has the nerve to ask you a question. Before long, you'll have that teacher bouncing chalk stubs off your head. Once you've earned the loathing of all your instructors, you'll be well on your way to a truly memorable failure.

Second step (note the enumerated transitions) ⟶ The second step, disdaining your studies, is easy to master; they're probably B-O-R-I-N-G anyway. First, don't buy your books until close to midterm and keep them in their original condition; don't open, read, or note anything in them. Better yet, don't buy your texts at all. Second, never attempt to take notes in class. Third, stop going to class completely, but have lots of creative excuses for missed assignments: "My friend's aunt died;" "My gerbil's in a coma;" "My boyfriend was in another car wreck;" "My dog ate the lab report;" "I've got mono." You can bet your teachers will be really amused by these old stand-bys. By now, you are well on your way to disaster.

Third step (more examples)

The third step, cheating, will deliver the *coup de grâce* to your academic career. Should an instructor be so sadistic as to assign a research paper, just copy something out of a book that the librarian will be happy to find for you. Your instructor will be astonished at the difference between the book's polished, professional prose and your usual halting scrawls; you're guaranteed a zero. During your exams, sit at the back and crane your neck to read your classmate's paper. Roll up your shirt-sleeves to reveal the answers you've tattooed all over your forearms. Ask to be excused three or four times during the test so you can consult the notes you've stashed in the hall or the washroom. Be bold! Dig out your old wood-burning kit and emblazon cheat notes on the desk. If you want to ensure not just failure but actual expulsion, send in a ringer—a look-alike to write the exam for you!

Conclusion (issues a challenge)

If you follow these guidelines, you will be guaranteed to flunk your year. Actively courting failure with verve, with flair, and with a sense of drama will not only ensure your status as an academic washout but will also immortalize you in the memories of teachers and class-mates alike. The challenge is yours! Become a legend—pick up the torch and fall with it!

Baked Beans

PIERRE BERTON

1   ow we come to my famous (or infamous°) formula for Klondike° baked beans, the one that disturbed so many people because of its complexity. Well, winter is coming on and these beans will be needed, no matter how complex they seem to be. There is nothing quite like them. They are guaranteed to melt the frostiest heart, bring warmth to the palest cheeks, satisfy the most gnawing hunger, and rekindle the spark of hope in the coldest breast.

2   The Klondikers carried baked beans frozen solid in their packs and, when the trail grew weary and the stomach cried out for succour°, they would chop pieces off with a knife and gnaw at them as they plunged onward. For beans carry a warmth locked within them, and when the human fire burns low, they act as hot coals to send the blood coursing through the veins.

3   My beans are more exotic than the 1898 variety, and they are not meant to be eaten frozen, but the principle is exactly the same.

4   I warn you that this is a lengthy task, so fortify° yourself in any of the several ways known to cooks the world over. Step One is the simplest: simply take the quantity of navy beans that you require and soak them overnight in cold water.

5   The next morning, early, Step Two begins: simmer these soaked beans very lightly. Put them over a low heat and throw in a couple of crushed bay leaves, a handful of finely chopped parsley, some crushed garlic, oregano, thyme, chili powder, cloves, and salt. The idea here is to get the beans soft and to impregnate them with a basic flavour.

6   Let them simmer gently for an hour or two while you go over to the butcher's for some salt pork. Have him cut the pork—or good

side bacon will do as well—into large cubes or chunks, the size of marshmallows. Get lots of pork; the makers of tinned beans skimp on the stuff, but we don't have to. There's nothing quite so good as pork or bacon cooked to a soft succulence in a frothing mass of beans and molasses.

You can tell if your beans are soft enough by picking a couple   7 out of the pot and blowing on them. If the skins break, you're ready for Step Three. Turn off the heat and drain away the liquid, but for heaven's sake don't throw it away. It is nectar. What you don't use in the finished dish you can always save as soup stock.

Pour the drained beans in a big earthenware casserole and   8 throw in the salt pork. I often serve beans at a party along with a good smoked ham; if you do this throw some of the ham fat in with the beans. Pour it right out of the pan, if you like.

Now we are into Step Three, and it is here that the boys are   9 separated from the men, and the men from the women. Take a few cups of the liquid you poured from the beans and put it in a pot to simmer. Chop up some tomatoes and throw them in the pot with a few shots of chili sauce and a tin of tomato paste. Chop several onions, half of them very fine, so they'll disappear in the brew, and half in chunks, and throw them in. Green onion tops, chopped up, go well, too, if you can get them.

Now season this mixture, tasting carefully as you go, with dry   10 mustard, freshly ground black pepper, Worcestershire sauce, crushed garlic, celery seed, a few squirts of tabasco, and some monosodium glutamate.

When it tastes pungent° and hot (remember that the pungency   11 will be cut by the beans) stir in a large quantity of molasses. Most people don't put in enough molasses, and yet this is the essence of all good baked bean dishes. For there comes a critical moment when the sweetness of the molasses is wedded to the sharpness of the vegetables and herbs, and it is this subtle flavour, baked indelibly into the beans and mingling with the pork fat, that brings a sparkle to the eyes.

Now pour this bubbling and fragrant syrup over the pot of pork   12 and beans. Put a lid on the pot and bake the beans for several hours in a 250 degree oven. They should bake for at least six hours, but you can bake them much longer if you want. The longer they bake, the better they taste. This gives you time to work up an appetite, shovelling snow, chopping logs for the fire and so on.

About half-way through the baking, pull out the pot and taste   13 the beans. *Taste*, I said! Don't eat them all up—they're nowhere near done. But at this point you ought to check the bouquet°. Is it right? Are they too sweet or not sweet enough? Do they need more liquid? Don't let them get too dry.

14   Fix them up and put them back in for some more baking. One hour before they're ready you perform another important rite. Pour a cup of good sherry over them. Not cooking sherry—but the kind you drink yourself.

15   Do I see a small bird-like woman in the back row rise and denounce me for spreading debauchery and intoxication through the land? Control yourself, madam. I give you my bond that before this dish is done the alcoholic content of that fortified wine will have vanished, leaving only its delicate flavour behind, fused inseparably with a dish which supplies its own intoxication.

16   Now take some bacon strips and cover the entire top of the beans. Fifteen minutes before serving, take the lid off the pot so the bacon crispens into a thick crust.

17   By now you should be close to starvation, for the beans are meant to be devoured only when the tortured stomach pleads for sustenance°. Call in your friends. Get some fresh bread with a hard crust. Tear open these loaves and rip out the soft insides. Now open the steaming pot, plunge a ladle through the bacon crust, spoon the bubbling brown beans, the soft globes of pork, and all the attendant juices, into the containers of bread.

18   Notice that the pork is sweet to the tooth, that the beans while still firm and round are infused with a delirious flavour, and that the simmering sauce is maddening to the palate.

19   Provide the company with mugs of steaming coffee. Now as you tear ravenously at the bread and feel the piping hot beans begin to woo your taste buds, accept the homage° of your friends, for you have earned it. And, as your tired muscles lose their tensions, and the beans begin to come out of your ears, and the day passes into history, give thanks to your Maker for putting beans on this earth and giving men the wit° to bake them as they deserve.

PIERRE BERTON

Pierre Berton, the author and media personality, was born in 1920 in Dawson City, Yukon Territory. He is well known for his television appearances and for his best-selling books: *Klondike*, *The National Dream*, and *Vimy*, to name a few.

Words and Meanings

Paragraph

1   infamous: notorious, scandalous

Klondike:	a region in the southwestern part of the Yukon that includes the Klondike River and its tributaries; scene of the Klondike Gold Rush of 1896.	
succour:	relief	2
fortify:	strengthen	4
pungent:	spicy, stimulating	11
bouquet:	aroma produced by cooking spices	13
sustenance:	food	17
homage:	worship	19
wit:	intelligence	

Structure and Strategy

1. List, in order, the steps to follow to produce Berton's dish.
2. Identify the words and phrases Berton uses to establish TRANSITION and create COHERENCE.
3. Consider the TONE of the last two paragraphs. Do you think Berton's conclusion is effective? Why or why not?

Content and Purpose

1. Why does Berton introduce his essay by justifying his recipe for baked beans? See paragraphs 1 to 4.
2. Why does Berton choose words such as "exotic" and "nectar" to describe such a simple and ordinary dish as baked beans?
3. In several places, Berton makes an association between baked beans and the gold that men sought in the Klondike. For example: "For beans carry a warmth locked within them, and when the human fire burns low, they act as hot coals to send the blood coursing through the veins." Why does Berton make this association?

Suggestion for Writing

Do you have a special recipe that you feel satisfies both the stomach and the spirit? Write the directions for this recipe in chronological order. In your conclusion, explain why you think this dish is food for the soul as well as the body.

A Fugitive° Pleasure: Perfume in the 18th Century

MEREDITH CHILTON

1   o recall the ephemeral° pleasures of the privileged in the 18th century is to invoke the Rococo° period, marked by its frivolity, lightness, and hedonism. The art of Boucher offers intimate glimpses of nymphs and shepherdesses. There were water gardens and chinoiserie° pavilions, the fleeting delights of taking tea alfresco°, witty conversations and flirtation in the salon° or the boudoir°, the refinement of charm and elegance of manner, and of course, the elusive scent of perfume. . . .

2   Perfume [was] an intrinsic part of fashionable life. It was used in a wide variety of products, one of the most popular of which was perfumed gloves, a conceit° introduced during the 16th century. *Neroli*, a scent made from bitter-orange blossoms, named for the Duchess of Neroli, was the favored fragrance for gloves of the period. A prohibitive tax on hides, introduced in the 1760s, devastated the industry, which was centered in Grasse and Montpellier. Many *gantiers-parfumeurs*, or perfumed-glove makers, moved to Paris to become simply perfumers. . . .

3   Perfume was also an important ingredient in cosmetics and hairdressing. Upon rising, the lady of fashion would attend to her toilette°. "The role of a young Beauty is much more serious than you can imagine. Nothing is more important than what happens at her toilette in the morning," wrote Montesquieu. First a foundation called plâtre, or plaster, was applied. It often consisted of fine white clay, ground pearls, honey, and gum. In spite of criticism from the medical profession, many recipes called for powdered white lead. It was combined with pomade, a thick paste similar to modern cold cream made from a mixture of pure white lard and essential oils of violets, jasmine, or lilies-of-the-valley. This foundation was then carefully applied to the skin to conceal wrinkles.

4   Rouge came next. A typical recipe for Carmin rouge involved pulverizing a mixture of talc and cochineal, and then stirring in olive

oil and gum. Rosewater was then added before the rouge was transferred to small pots. It was applied to the face with a small brush or a spherical suede tampon.

Finally, beauty spots were applied. These were small pieces of   5
black fabric, cut in a variety of fanciful shapes such as hearts and crescent moons, which were stuck onto the face with gum. The placing of patches was an art in itself and involved much discussion at the dressing table. While dressing, a lady might be joined in her boudoir by her paramour°, friends, and relatives, as well as by tradesmen, musicians, and hairdressers. Advice would be given on the position of a curl or the placing of a beauty spot. Each location of a beauty spot on the face had a name and a significant meaning. Thus a lady might inform everyone of her moods and intentions by wearing "the discreet," "the passionate," or "the coquette°. . . . "

After dressing and the application of cosmetics came the arrang-   6
ing of the hair. Wigs had been introduced by Louis XIII and were initially worn only by men, who sported cascading curls of brown or black human hair or horsehair in the latter years of the 17th century. Under Louis XVI the fashion changed and extraordinarily elaborate wigs were worn by both men and women. Ladies' wigs became so extreme that hairdressers were obliged to use small ladders to arrange the topmost curls. Wigs were usually powdered either gray or white. The powder was made of talc, a soft mineral that was ground, purified, and sometimes supplemented with china clay or starch. It was sifted through silk screens and scented with essential oils. The most popular perfume for wigs in the 18th century was orris root, which smelt slightly of violets. Powder would be applied to a lightly pomaded wig in a "powder room." Ladies and gentlemen would protect their clothes with large dust cloths, and hold cone-shaped masks over their faces to prevent the powder from settling on their make-up.

This elaborate toilette required several hours of preparation in   7
the boudoir. Most ladies of fashion never appeared in public before noon. . . .

Perfumes were used not only in the boudoir but also in the   8
drawing room. Pot-pourri was made from dried flowers, such as roses, orange blossoms, lavender, myrtle, oakmoss, and orris root, layered with salt and left to macerate in the sun for several days. It was then placed in porcelain containers vented with airholes. . . .

Rooms were also scented with perfumed pastilles° that were   9
burnt to release their aromatic smoke. At Louis XV's court, these were called *oiselets de Chypre*, or little birds of Cyprus, a curious name of unknown origin. The pastilles were formed by hand by rolling gum mixed with laudanum, storax, cloves, sandalwood, camphor, aloes, and sugar of valerian. They were lit like candles and placed

inside small vented porcelain figures or special containers. At Meissen, oriental figures were made with pierced ears and open mouths for the perfumed smoke to escape. . . .

10   Perhaps the most frivolous and extravagant use of perfume is recounted in a story based upon a malicious rumor spread by the Marquis d'Argenson, one of Mme de Pompadour°'s most outspoken opponents. In 1750, he accused Louis XV's mistress of a "scandalous extravagance," by her squandering of 800,000 livres on Vincennes porcelain flowers.

11   Vincennes had become famous for naturalistic porcelain flowers: they formed a substantial part of the factory's production in the early days. In 1748, 45 women were employed solely to create flowers. These were made of porcelain, assembled petal by petal, and were either fitted onto painted stems, or onto wire ones wrapped in green silk.

12   The story gradually evolved from the Marquis's rumor. Apparently Mme de Pompadour planted a winter garden filled with thousands of these artificial porcelain flowers, at her Château de Bellevue, near Paris. Each flower was said to have been perfumed correctly; roses were scented with rosewater, carnations with carnations, lilies with lilies-of-the-valley—all this just to amuse the king at a time when most of the population was impoverished. Only recently has Mme de Pompadour been exonerated° in this matter. Careful scrutiny of the records of her purchases revealed that the king's mistress purchased only 24 vases embellished with 88 flowering porcelain plants in 1750. She spent 32,696 livres at Vincennes that year, far less than the rumored 800,000 livres. For his calumny°, the unwise Marquis d'Argenson lost his ministerial position. Mme de Pompadour remains, nonetheless, the most conspicuous patron of precious perfumes and delicate porcelain of her age.

13   And after all, who would not agree with Cowley when he wrote:

Who that has reason, and his smell,
Would not among the roses and jasmine dwell,
Rather than all his spirits choke
With exhalations of dirt and smoke?

[ ]

MEREDITH CHILTON

Meredith Chilton (b. 1953) is the curator of the George R. Gardiner Museum of Ceramic Art, an institution affiliated with the Royal Ontario Museum in Toronto.

Words and Meanings

Paragraph

fugitive:	brief, short-lived	
ephemeral:	short-lived, fleeting	1
Rococo:	early eighteenth century style characterized by highly ornate decoration	
chinoiserie:	style characterized by use of Chinese images and motifs	
alfresco:	outside, in the open air	
salon:	reception room, usually used for formal occasions	
boudoir:	lady's bedroom, often used for informal entertainments	
conceit:	a frivolous fashion	2
toilette:	the process of grooming, dressing, and adorning oneself	3
paramour:	lover	5
coquette:	flirtatious woman	
pastilles:	small rolls or tablets of perfumed paste	9
Mme de Pompadour:	infamous mistress of Louis XV	10
exonerated:	cleared from blame	12
calumny:	slander, false statement	

Structure and Strategy

1. What TRANSITIONS does Chilton use in paragraphs 3 to 5 to achieve COHERENCE in this process analysis?
2. What shift in focus occurs in paragraph 8? How does Chilton accomplish the transition smoothly?
3. Summarize in your own words the ANECDOTE that concludes the essay. Is the conclusion effective? Why or why not?

Content and Purpose

1. Why do you think Chilton has given her essay the title, "A Fugitive Pleasure"?
2. What process is described in this essay? Is it directional or informational? Identify the steps involved in a lady of fashion's toilette.
3. To what social group did the people described in this essay belong? What kind of lives did they lead? Were they typical of the time?

Suggestions for Writing

1. Write a process analysis describing the preparations you might undertake if you were going to a wedding or other formal occasion. Describe each of the steps in order, and be sure to include specific details that appeal to the readers' senses, as Chilton has done in "A Fugitive Pleasure."
2. Fashions change, as Chilton's essay illustrates, but the human instinct to enhance our appearance has remained constant throughout the centuries. Write an essay in which you explain why people take such pains to groom and adorn themselves in the fashion of their time.

Desperation Writing

PETER ELBOW

1   I know I am not alone in my recurring twinges of panic that I won't be able to write something when I need to, I won't be able to produce coherent° speech or thought. And that lingering doubt is a great hindrance° to writing. It's a constant fog or static that clouds the mind. I never got out of its clutches till I discovered that it was possible to write something— not something great or pleasing but at least something usable, workable—when my mind is out of commission. The trick is that you have to do all your cooking out on the table: your mind is incapable of doing any inside. It means using symbols and pieces of paper not as a crutch but as a wheel chair.

2   The first thing is to admit your condition: because of some mood or event or whatever, your mind is incapable of anything that could be called thought. It can put out a babbling kind of speech utterance, it can put a simple feeling, perception, or sort-of-thought into understandable (though terrible) words. But it is incapable of considering anything in relation to anything else. The moment you try to hold that thought or feeling up against some other to see the relationship, you simply lose the picture—you get nothing but buzzing lines or waving colors.

3   So admit this. Avoid anything more than one feeling, perception, or thought. Simply write as much as possible. Try simply to

steer your mind in the direction or general vicinity of the thing you are trying to write about and start writing and keep writing.

Just write and keep writing. (Probably best to write on only one   4
side of the paper in case you should want to cut parts out with scissors—but you probably won't.) Just write and keep writing. It will probably come in waves. After a flurry°, stop and take a brief rest. But don't stop too long. Don't think about what you are writing or what you have written or else you will overload the circuit again. Keep writing as though you are drugged or drunk. Keep doing this till you feel you have a lot of material that might be useful; or, if necessary, till you can't stand it any more—even if you doubt that there's anything useful there.

Then take a pad of little pieces of paper—or perhaps 3×5 5
cards—and simply start at the beginning of what you were writing, and as you read over what you wrote, every time you come to any thought, feeling, perception, or image that could be gathered up into one sentence or one assertion°, do so and write it by itself on a little sheet of paper. In short, you are trying to turn, say, ten or twenty pages of wandering mush into twenty or thirty hard little crab apples. Sometimes there won't be many on a page. But if it seems to you that there are none on a page, you are making a serious error—the same serious error that put you in this comatose° state to start with. You are mistaking lousy, stupid, second-rate, wrong, childish, foolish, worthless ideas for no ideas at all. Your job is not to pick out *good* ideas but to pick out ideas. As long as you were conscious, your words will be full of things that could be called feelings, utterances, ideas—things that can be squeezed into one simple sentence. This is your job. Don't ask for too much.

After you have done this, take those little slips or cards, read   6
through them a number of times—not struggling with them, simply wandering and mulling through them; perhaps shifting them around and looking through them in various sequences. In a sense these are cards you are playing solitaire with, and the rules of this particular game permit shuffling the unused pile.

The goal of this procedure with the cards is to get them to   7
distribute themselves in two or three or ten or fifteen different piles on your desk. You can get them to do this almost by themselves if you simply keep reading through them in different orders; certain cards will begin to feel like they go with other cards. I emphasize this passive, thoughtless mode because I want to talk about desperation writing in its pure state. In practice, almost invariably at some point in the procedure, your sanity begins to return. It is often at this point. You actually are moved to have thoughts or—and the difference between active and passive is crucial here—to *exert* thought; to hold

two cards together and *build* or *assert* a relationship. It is a matter of bringing energy to bear.

8   So you may start to be able to do something active with these cards, and begin actually to think. But if not, just allow the cards to find their own piles with each other by feel, by drift, by intuition, by mindlessness.

9   You have now engaged in the two main activities that will permit you to get something cooked out on the table rather than in your brain: writing out into messy words, summing up into single assertions, and even sensing relationships between assertions. You can simply continue to deploy these two activities.

10   If, for example, after that first round of writing, assertion-making, and pile-making, your piles feel as though they are useful and satisfactory for what you are writing—paragraphs or sections or trains of thought—then you can carry on from there. See if you can gather each pile up into a single assertion. When you can, then put the subsidiary° assertions of that pile into their best order to fit with that single unifying one. If you *can't* get the pile into one assertion, then take the pile as the basis for doing some more writing out into words. In the course of this writing, you may produce for yourself the single unifying assertion you were looking for; or you may have to go through the cycle of turning the writing into assertions and piles and so forth. Perhaps more than once. The pile may turn out to want to be two or more piles itself; or it may want to become part of a pile you already have. This is natural. This kind of meshing into one configuration, then coming apart, then coming together and meshing into a different configuration°—this is growing and cooking. It makes a terrible mess, but if you can't do it in your head, you have to put up with a cluttered desk and a lot of confusion.

11   If, on the other hand, all that writing *didn't* have useful material in it, it means that your writing wasn't loose, drifting, quirky, jerky, associative enough. This time try especially to let things simply remind you of things that are seemingly crazy or unrelated. Follow these odd associations. Make as many metaphors as you can—be as nutty as possible—and explore the metaphors themselves—open them out. You may have all your energy tied up in some area of your experience that you are leaving out. Don't refrain from writing about whatever else is on your mind: how you feel at the moment, what you are losing your mind over, randomness that intrudes itself on your consciousness, the pattern on the wallpaper, what those people you see out the window have on their minds—though keep coming back to the whateveritis you are supposed to be writing about. Treat it, in short, like ten-minute writing exercises. Your best perceptions and thoughts are always going to be tied up in whatever

is really occupying you, and that is also where your energy is. You may end up writing a love poem—or a hate poem—in one of those little piles while the other piles will finally turn into a lab report on data processing or whatever you have to write about. But you couldn't, in your present state of having your head shot off, have written that report without also writing the poem. And the report will have some of the juice of the poem in it and vice versa.

$$\boxed{}$$

PETER ELBOW

Peter Elbow (b. 1935) is an influential teacher of writing in the United States. His works include *Writing without Teachers* (1973) and *Writing with Power* (1981).

Words and Meanings

Paragraph

coherent:	see COHERENCE in the List of Useful Terms	1
hindrance:	something that gets in the way	
flurry:	short, intense burst of activity	4
assertion:	statement, sentence that is to be proved	5
comatose:	in a deep sleep, incapable of moving	
subsidiary:	subordinate, supporting	10
configuration:	combination of parts into a whole	

Subject and Structure

1. For whom is Elbow writing this essay? Who is his AUDIENCE?
2. Throughout the essay, Elbow speaks directly to his readers, addressing them as "you." What is the effect of this technique? How would the essay be different if it had been written in the third person? Try rewriting paragraph 2 in the third person to see the difference (e.g., "The first thing writers must do is to admit their condition. . . .").
3. Identify the main steps into which Elbow breaks down the process of "desperation writing."
4. What is the function of paragraph 9? How does it help the reader follow the process?
5. Elbow recommends that desperate writers should "make as many metaphors as [they] can . . . and explore the metaphors themselves." Identify three metaphors Elbow uses in this essay. (See paragraphs 1, 4, and 6. For a definition of metaphor, see FIGURES OF SPEECH.) Are they effective? Why?

Content and Purpose

1. How does the author describe the confusion that clouds the minds of people when they know they have to write something, but feel blocked? Do you ever have this feeling, and if so, how do you deal with it?
2. What kind of advice does Elbow provide to help people get something, anything, on paper? What does the "desperate writer" then do with the material that is generated?
3. In paragraph 9, Elbow describes the "two main activities" that will eventually lead to coherent writing. Is there any similarity between the strategies he recommends and the organizational strategies for writing a thesis statement that this text recommends?
4. Paragraph 11 deals with the "drifting, quirky, jerky, associative" writing that the desperate writer produces. What is the relationship between this tapping of the unconscious mind and the conscious mind's shaping of the material into coherent writing?

Suggestions for Writing

1. "A man may write at any time, if he will set himself doggedly to it," wrote Samuel Johnson in 1750. Explain the process that you go through when faced with a writing assignment.
2. Write a brief process analysis outlining how you approach a necessary task that you do not want to do; for example, filing your income tax return, cleaning the house, going to the laundromat, studying for a final exam.

The Way of All Flesh:

The Worm Is at Work in Us All

JUDY STOFFMAN

1   When a man of 25 is told that aging is inexorable°, inevitable, universal, he will nod somewhat impatiently at being told something so obvious. In fact, he has little idea of the meaning of the words. It has nothing to do with him. Why should

it? He has had no tangible evidence yet that his body, as the poet Rilke said, enfolds old age and death as the fruit enfolds a stone.

The earliest deposits of fat in the aorta, the trunk artery carrying blood away from the heart, occur in the eighth year of life, but who can peer into his own aorta at this first sign of approaching debility°? The young man has seen old people but he secretly believes himself to be the exception on whom the curse will never fall. "Never will the skin of my neck hang loose. My grip will never weaken. I will stand tall and walk with long strides as long as I live." The young girl scarcely pays attention to her clothes; she scorns makeup. Her confidence in her body is boundless; smooth skin and a flat stomach will compensate, she knows, for any lapses in fashion or grooming. She stays up all night, as careless of her energy as of her looks, believing both will last forever.

In our early 20s, the lung capacity, the rapidity of motor responses and physical endurance are at their peak. This is the athlete's finest hour. Cindy Nicholas of Toronto was 19 when she first swam the English Channel in both directions. The tennis star Bjorn Borg was 23 when he triumphed this year at Wimbledon for the fourth time.

It is not only *athletic* prowess° that is at its height between 20 and 30. James Boswell, writing in his journal in 1763 after he had finally won the favors of the actress Louisa, has left us this happy description of the sexual prowess of a 23-year-old: "I was in full flow of health and my bounding blood beat quick in high alarms. Five times was I fairly lost in supreme rapture. Louisa was madly fond of me; she declared I was a prodigy°, and asked me if this was extraordinary in human nature. I said twice as much might be, but this was not, although in my own mind I was somewhat proud of my performance."

In our early 30s we are dumbfounded to discover the first grey hair at the temples. We pull out the strange filament and look at it closely, trying to grasp its meaning. It means simply that the pigment has disappeared from the hair shaft, never to return. It means also— but this thought we push away—that in 20 years or so we'll relinquish° our identity as a blonde or a redhead. By 57, one out of four people is completely grey. Of all the changes wrought by time this is the most harmless, except to our vanity.

In this decade one also begins to notice the loss of upper register hearing, that is, the responsiveness to high frequency tones, but not all the changes are for the worse, not yet. Women don't reach their sexual prime until about 38, because their sexual response is learned rather than innate. The hand grip of both sexes increases in strength until 35, and intellectual powers are never stronger than at that age. There is a sense in the 30s of hitting your stride, of coming into your own. When Sigmund Freud was 38 an older colleague, Josef Breuer, wrote: "Freud's intellect is soaring at its highest. I gaze after him as a hen at a hawk."

7   Gail Sheehy in her book *Passages* calls the interval between 35 and 45 the Deadline Decade. It is the time we begin to sense danger. The body continually flashes us signals that time is running out. We must perform our quaint deeds, keep our promises, get on with our allotted tasks.

8   Signal: The woman attempts to become pregnant at 40 and finds she cannot. Though she menstruates each month, menstruation being merely the shedding of the inner lining of the womb, she may not be ovulating regularly.

9   Signal: Both men and women discover that, although they have not changed their eating habits over the years, they are much heavier than formerly. The man is paunchy around the waist; the woman no longer has those slim thighs and slender arms. A 120-pound woman needs 2,000 calories daily to maintain her weight when she is 25, 1,700 to maintain the same weight at 45, and only 1,500 calories at 65. A 170-pound man needs 3,100 calories daily at 25, 300 fewer a day at 45 and 450 calories fewer still at 65. This decreasing calorie need signals that the body consumes its fuel ever more slowly; the cellular fires are damped and our sense of energy diminishes.

10   In his mid-40s the man notices he can no longer run up the stairs three at a time. He is more easily winded and his joints are not as flexible as they once were. The strength of his hands has declined somewhat. The man feels humiliated: "I will not let this happen to me. I will turn back the tide and master my body." He starts going to the gym, playing squash, lifting weights. He takes up jogging. Though he may find it neither easy nor pleasant, terror drives him past pain. A regular exercise program can retard some of the symptoms of aging by improving the circulation and increasing the lung capacity, thereby raising our stamina and energy level, but no amount of exercise will make a 48-year-old 26 again. Take John Keeley of Mystic, Connecticut. In 1957, when he was 26, he won the Boston marathon with a time of 2:20. This year he is fit and 48 and says he is as fiercely competitive as ever, yet it took him almost 30 minutes longer to run the same marathon.

11   In the middle of the fourth decade, the man whose eyesight has always been good will pick up a book and notice that he is holding it farther from his face than usual. The condition is presbyopia, a loss of the flexibility of the lens which makes adjustment from distant to near vision increasingly difficult. It's harder now to zoom in for a closeup. It also takes longer for the eyes to recover from glare; between 16 and 90, recovery time from exposure to glare is doubled every 13 years.

In our 50s, we notice that food is less and less tasty; our taste   12
buds are starting to lose their acuity°. The aged Queen Victoria was
wont to complain that strawberries were not as sweet as when she
was a girl.

Little is known about the causes of aging. We do not know if we are   13
born with a biochemical messenger programmed to keep the cells
and tissues alive, a messenger that eventually gets lost, or if there is
a 'death hormone,' absent from birth but later secreted by the thy-
mus or by the mysterious pineal gland, or if, perhaps, aging results
from a fatal flaw in the body's immunity system. The belief that the
body is a machine whose parts wear out is erroneous, for the
machine does not have the body's capacity for self-repair.

"A man is as old as his arteries," observed Sir William Osler.   14
From the 50s on, there's a progressive hardening and narrowing of
the arteries due to the gradual lifelong accumulation of calcium and
fats along the arterial walls. Arteriosclerosis eventually affects the
majority of the population in the affluent countries of the West.
Lucky the man or woman who, through a combination of good
genes and good nutrition, can escape it, for it is the most evil change
of all. As the flow of blood carrying oxygen and nutrients to the
muscles, the brain, the kidneys and other organs diminishes, these
organs begin to starve. Although all aging organs lose weight, there
is less shrinkage of organs such as the liver and kidneys, the cells of
which regenerate, than there is shrinkage of the brain and the
muscles, the cells of which, once lost, are lost forever.

For the woman it is now an ordeal to be asked her age. There   15
is a fine tracery of lines around her eyes, a furrow in her brow even
when she smiles. The bloom is off her cheeks. Around the age of 50
she will buy her last box of sanitary pads. The body's production of
estrogen and progesterone which govern menstruation (and also
help to protect her from heart attack and the effects of stress) will
have ceased almost completely. She may suffer palpitations°, suddenly break into a sweat; her moods may shift abruptly. She looks in
the mirror and asks, "Am I still a woman?" Eventually she becomes
reconciled to her new self and even acknowledges its advantages:
no more fears about pregnancy. "In any case," she laughs, "I still
have not bad legs."

The man, too, will undergo a change. One night in his early 50s   16
he has some trouble achieving a complete erection, and his powers
of recovery are not what they once were. Whereas at 20 he was
ready to make love again less than half an hour after doing so, it
may now take two hours or more; he was not previously aware that
his level of testosterone, the male hormone, has been gradually
declining since the age of 20. He may develop headaches, be unable

to sleep, become anxious about his performance, anticipate failure and so bring on what is called secondary impotence—impotence of psychological rather than physical origin. According to Masters and Johnson, 25 percent of all men are impotent by 65 and 50 percent by 75, yet this cannot be called an inevitable feature of aging. A loving, undemanding partner and a sense of confidence can do wonders. "The susceptibility° of the human male to the power of suggestion with regard to his sexual prowess," observe Masters and Johnson, "is almost unbelievable."

17   After the menopause, the woman ages more rapidly. Her bones start to lose calcium, becoming brittle and porous. The walls of the vagina become thinner and drier; sexual intercourse now may be painful unless her partner is slow and gentle. The sweat glands begin to atrophy° and the sebaceous glands that lubricate the skin decline; the complexion becomes thinner and drier and wrinkles appear around the mouth. The skin, which in youth varies from about one-fiftieth of an inch on the eyelids to about a third of an inch on the palms and the soles of the feet, loses 50 percent of its thickness between the ages of 20 and 80. The woman no longer buys sleeveless dresses and avoids shorts. The girl who once disdained cosmetics is now a woman whose dressing table is covered with lotions, night creams and makeup.

18   Perhaps no one has written about the sensation of nearing 60 with more brutal honesty than the French novelist Simone de Beauvoir: "While I was able to look at my face without displeasure, I gave it no thought. I loathe my appearance now: the eyebrows slipping down toward the eyes, the bags underneath, the excessive fullness of the cheeks and the air of sadness around the mouth that wrinkles always bring. . . . Death is no longer a brutal event in the far distance; it haunts my sleep."

19   In his early 60s the man's calves are shrunken, his muscles stringy looking. The legs of the woman, too, are no longer shapely. Both start to lose their sense of smell and both lose most of the hair in the pubic area and the underarms. Hair, however, may make its appearance in new places, such as the woman's chin. Liver spots appear on the hands, the arms, the face; they are made of coagulated melanin, the coloring matter of the skin. The acid secretions of the stomach decrease, making digestion slow and more difficult.

20   Halfway through the 60s comes compulsory retirement for most men and working women, forcing upon the superannuated worker the realization that society now views him as useless and unproductive. The man who formerly gave orders to a staff of 20 now finds himself underfoot as his wife attempts to clean the house or get the shopping done. The woman fares a little better since there is a continuity in her pattern of performing a myriad of essential house-

hold tasks. Now they must both set new goals or see themselves wither mentally. The unsinkable American journalist I.F. Stone, when he retired in 1971 from editing *I.F. Stone's Weekly*, began to teach himself Greek and is now reading Plato in the original. When Somerset Maugham read that the Roman senator Cato the Elder learned Greek when he was 80, he remarked: "Old age is ready to undertake tasks that youth shirked° because they would take too long."

However active we are, the fact of old age can no longer be   21 evaded from about 65 onward. Not everyone is as strong minded about this as de Beauvoir. When she made public in her memoirs her horror at her own deterioration, her readers were scandalized. She received hundreds of letters telling her that there is no such thing as old age, that some are just younger than others. Repeatedly she heard the hollow reassurance, "You're as young as you feel." But she considers this a lie. Our subjective reality, our inner sense of self, is not the only reality. There is also an objective reality, how we are seen by society. We receive our revelation of old age from others. The woman whose figure is still trim may sense that a man is following her in the street; drawing abreast, the man catches sight of her face—and hurries on. The man of 68 may be told by a younger woman to whom he is attracted: "You remind me of my father."

Madame de Sévigné, the 17th-century French writer, struggled   22 to rid herself of the illusion of perpetual youth. At 63 she wrote: "I have been dragged to this inevitable point where old age must be undergone: I see it there before me; I have reached it; and I should at least like so to arrange matters that I do not move on, that I do not travel further along this path of the infirmities, pains, losses of memory and the disfigurement. But I hear a voice saying: 'You must go along, whatever you may say; or indeed if you will not then you must die, which is an extremity from which nature recoils.' "

Now the man and the woman have their 70th birthday party.   23 It is a sad affair because so many of their friends are missing, felled by strokes, heart attacks or cancers. Now the hands of the clock begin to race. The skeleton continues to degenerate from loss of calcium. The spine becomes compressed and there is a slight stoop nothing can prevent. Inches are lost from one's height. The joints may become thickened and creaking; in the morning the woman can't seem to get moving until she's had a hot bath. She has osteoarthritis. This, like the other age-related diseases, arteriosclerosis and diabetes, can and should be treated, but it can never be cured. The nails, particularly the toenails, become thick and lifeless because the circulation in the lower limbs is now poor. The man has difficulty learning new things because of the progressive loss of neurons from the brain. The woman goes to the store and forgets what she has come to buy. The two old people are often constipated because the involuntary muscles are weaker now. To make it worse, their children are always saying, "Sit down, rest, take it easy." Their digestive tract would be toned up if they went for a long walk or even a swim, although they feel a little foolish in bathing suits.

24   In his late 70s, the man develops glaucoma, pressure in the eyeball caused by the failure of aqueous humour° to drain away; this can now be treated with a steroid related to cortisone. The lenses in the eyes of the woman may thicken and become fibrous, blurring her vision. She has cataracts, but artificial lenses can now be implanted using cryosurgery°. There is no reason to lose one's sight just as there's no reason to lose one's teeth; regular, lifelong dental care can prevent tooth loss. What can't be prevented is the yellowing of teeth, brought about by the shrinking of the living chamber within the tooth which supplies the outer enamel with moisture.

25   Between 75 and 85 the body loses most of its subcutaneous fat. On her 80th birthday the woman's granddaughter embraces her and marvels: "How thin and frail and shrunken she is! Could this narrow, bony chest be the same warm, firm bosom to which she clasped me as a child?" Her children urge her to eat but she has no enjoyment of food now. Her mouth secretes little saliva, so she has difficulty tasting and swallowing. The loss of fat and shrinking muscles in the 80s diminish the body's capacity for homeostasis, that is, righting any physiological imbalance. The old man, if he is cold, can barely shiver (shivering serves to restore body heat). If he lives long enough, the man will have an enlarged prostate which causes the urinary stream to slow to a trickle. The man and the woman probably both wear hearing aids now; without a hearing aid, they hear vowels clearly but not consonants; if someone says "fat," they think they've heard the word "that."

26   At 80, the speed of nerve impulses is 10 percent less than it was at 25, the kidney filtration rate is down by 30 percent, the pumping efficiency of the heart is only 60 percent of what it was, and the maximum breathing capacity, 40 percent.

27   The old couple is fortunate in still being able to express physically the love they've built up over a lifetime. The old man may be capable of an erection once or twice a week (Charlie Chaplin fathered the last of his children when he was 81), but he rarely has the urge to climax. When he does, he sometimes has the sensation of seepage rather than a triumphant explosion. Old people who say they are relieved that they are now free of the torments of sexual desire are usually the ones who found sex a troublesome function all their lives; those who found joy and renewal in the act will cling to their libido°. Many older writers and artists have expressed the

conviction that continued sexuality is linked to continued creativity: "There was a time when I was cruelly tormented, indeed obsessed by desire," wrote the novelist André Gide at the age of 73, "and I prayed, 'Oh let the moment come when my subjugated° flesh will allow me to give myself entirely to. . . . ' But to what? To art? To pure thought? To God? How ignorant I was! How mad! It was the same as believing that the flame would burn brighter in a lamp with no oil left. Even today it is my carnal self that feeds the flame, and now I pray that I may retain carnal desire until I die."

Aging, says an American gerontologist°, "is not a simple slope which   28 everyone slides down at the same speed; it is a flight of irregular stairs down which some journey more quickly than others." Now we arrive at the bottom of the stairs. The old man and the old woman whose progress we have been tracing will die either of a cancer (usually of the lungs, bowel or intestines) or of a stroke, a heart attack or in consequence of a fall. The man slips in the bathroom and breaks his thigh bone. But worse than the fracture is the enforced bed rest in the hospital which will probably bring on bed sores, infections, further weakening of the muscles and finally, what Osler called "an old man's best friend": pneumonia. At 25 we have so much vitality that if a little is sapped by illness, there is still plenty left over. At 85 a little is all we have.

And then the light goes out.

The sheet is pulled over the face.

In the last book of Marcel Proust's remarkable work *Remembrance of*   29 *Things Past*, the narrator, returning after a long absence from Paris, attends a party of his friends throughout which he has the impression of being at a masked ball: "I did not understand why I could not immediately recognize the master of the house, and the guests, who seemed to have made themselves up, in a way that completely changed their appearance. The Prince had rigged himself up with a white beard and what looked like leaden soles which made his feet drag heavily. A name was mentioned to me and I was dumbfounded at the thought that it applied to the blonde waltzing girl I had once known and to the stout, white haired lady now walking just in front of me. We did not see our own appearance, but each like a facing mirror, saw the other's." The narrator is overcome by a simple but powerful truth: the old are not a different species. "It is out of young men who last long enough," wrote Proust, "that life makes its old men."

The wrinkled old man who lies with the sheet over his face was   30 once the young man who vowed, "My grip will never weaken. I will walk with long strides and stand tall as long as I live." The young man who believed himself to be the exception.

| |

JUDY STOFFMAN

Translator and journalist Judy Stoffman was born in Budapest, Hungary, in 1957, grew up in Vancouver, then studied in England and France. She is an editor of *Canadian Living* magazine.

Words and Meanings

Paragraph

1	inexorable:	relentless, unstoppable
2	debility:	weakness
4	prowess:	courage, skill
	prodigy:	person capable of extraordinary achievement
5	relinquish:	give up
12	acuity:	sharpness
15	palpitations:	irregular heartbeats
16	susceptibility:	sensitiveness, impressibility
17	atrophy:	wither
20	shirked:	neglected
24	aqueous humour:	fluid in the interior chamber of the eyeball
	cryosurgery:	surgical technique involving freezing of the tissues
27	libido:	sexual desire
	subjugated:	conquered, subdued
28	gerontologist:	expert on aging

Structure and Strategy

1. How does the first paragraph reinforce the title and subtitle of this essay?
2. Into how many stages does Stoffman divide the aging process? Identify the paragraphs that describe each stage.
3. Why do you think Stoffman uses so many direct quotations in an essay on the subject of aging? Select two of these direct quotations and explain why they are particularly effective.
4. How does the last paragraph unify or bring together the whole

essay? Why do you think Stoffman ends her essay with a sentence fragment?

Content and Purpose

1. The title of this essay is a biblical ALLUSION ("I am going the way of all the earth. . . ." 1 Kings 2:2). Why do you think Stoffman chose this title?
2. What is "the worm" referred to in the subtitle?
3. Summarize the changes, both internal and external, that occur during one's fifties (paragraphs 12 to 17).
4. On his eightieth birthday, Morley Callaghan, the celebrated Canadian novelist, declared that "everyone wants to live to be 80, but no one wants to *be* 80." Do you think Stoffman would agree or disagree with Callaghan?
5. As a result of the new Charter of Rights in Canada, many vigorous 65-year-olds are challenging the principle of compulsory retirement. Do you agree or disagree that workers should be required to retire at 65? Why?

Suggestions for Writing

1. Write a directional process essay explaining how to enjoy old age.
2. Write a directional process essay explaining how to put off the aging process for as long as possible.

Behind the Formaldehyde° Curtain

JESSICA MITFORD

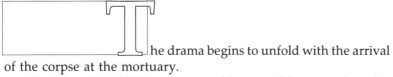

he drama begins to unfold with the arrival   1
of the corpse at the mortuary.

Alas, poor Yorick°! How surprised he would be to see how his   2
counterpart of today is whisked off to a funeral parlor and is in short
order sprayed, sliced, pierced, pickled, trussed, trimmed, creamed,
waxed, painted, rouged and neatly dressed—transformed from a

common corpse into a Beautiful Memory Picture. This process is known in the trade as embalming and restorative art, and is so universally employed in the United States and Canada that the funeral director does it routinely, without consulting corpse or kin. He regards as eccentric those few who are hardy enough to suggest that it might be dispensed with. Yet no law requires embalming, no religious doctrine commends it, nor is it dictated by considerations of health, sanitation, or even of personal daintiness. In no part of the world but in Northern America is it widely used. The purpose of embalming is to make the corpse presentable for viewing in a suitably costly container; and here too the funeral director routinely, without first consulting the family, prepares the body for public display.

3   Is all this legal? The processes to which a dead body may be subjected are after all to some extent circumscribed by law. In most states, for instance, the signature of next of kin must be obtained before an autopsy may be performed, before the deceased may be cremated, before the body may be turned over to a medical school for research purposes; or such provision must be made in the decedent's° will. In the case of embalming, no such permission is required nor is it ever sought. A textbook, *The Principles and Practices of Embalming*, comments on this: "There is some question regarding the legality of much that is done within the preparation room." The author points out that it would be most unusual for a responsible member of a bereaved family to instruct the mortician, in so many words, to "*embalm*" the body of a deceased relative. The very term "embalming" is so seldom used that the mortician must rely upon custom in the matter. The author concludes that unless the family specifies otherwise, the act of entrusting the body to the care of a funeral establishment carries with it an implied permission to go ahead and embalm.

4   Embalming is indeed a most extraordinary procedure, and one must wonder at the docility° of Americans who each year pay hundreds of millions of dollars for its perpetuation, blissfully ignorant of what it is all about, what is done, how it is done. Not one in ten thousand has any idea of what actually takes place. Books on the subject are extremely hard to come by. They are not to be found in most libraries or bookshops.

5   In an era when huge television audiences watch surgical operations in the comfort of their living rooms, when, thanks to the animated cartoon, the geography of the digestive system has become familiar territory even to the nursery school set, in a land where the satisfaction of curiosity about almost all matters is a national pastime, the secrecy surrounding embalming can, surely, hardly be attributed to the inherent gruesomeness of the subject. Custom in this regard

has within this century suffered a complete reversal. In the early days of American embalming, when it was performed in the home of the deceased, it was almost mandatory° for some relative to stay by the embalmer's side and witness the procedure. Today, family members who might wish to be in attendance would certainly be dissuaded° by the funeral director. All others, except apprentices, are excluded by law from the preparation room.

A close look at what does actually take place may explain in large measure the undertaker's intractable reticence° concerning a procedure that has become his major *raison d'être*. Is it possible he fears that public information about embalming might lead patrons to wonder if they really want this service? If the funeral men are loath to discuss the subject outside the trade, the reader may, understandably, be equally loath to go on reading at this point. For those who have the stomach for it, let us part the formaldehyde curtain. . . .   6

The body is first laid out in the undertaker's morgue—or rather, Mr. Jones is reposing in the preparation room—to be readied to bid the world farewell.   7

The preparation room in any of the better funeral establishments has the tiled and sterile look of a surgery, and indeed the embalmer-restorative artist who does his chores there is beginning to adopt the term "dermasurgeon" (appropriately corrupted by some mortician-writers as "demi-surgeon") to describe his calling. His equipment, consisting of scalpels, scissors, augers, forceps, clamps, needles, pumps, tubes, bowls and basins, is crudely imitative of the surgeon's, as is his technique, acquired in a nine- or twelve-month post-high-school course in an embalming school. He is supplied by an advanced chemical industry with a bewildering array of fluids, sprays, pastes, oils, powders, creams, to fix or soften tissue, shrink or distend it as needed, dry it here, restore the moisture there. There are cosmetics, waxes and paints to fill and cover features, even plaster of Paris to replace entire limbs. There are ingenious aids to prop and stabilize the cadaver: a Vari-Pose Head Rest, the Edwards Arm and Hand Positioner, the Repose Block (to support the shoulders during the embalming), and the Throop Foot Positioner, which resembles an old-fashioned stocks°.   8

Mr. John H. Eckels, president of the Eckels College of Mortuary Science, thus describes the first part of the embalming procedure: "In the hands of a skilled practitioner, this work may be done in a comparatively short time and without mutilating the body other than by slight incision—so slight that it scarcely would cause serious inconvenience if made upon a living person. It is necessary to remove the blood, and doing this not only helps in the disinfecting, but removes the principal cause of disfigurements due to discoloration."   9

10   Another textbook discusses the all-important time element: "The earlier this is done, the better, for every hour that elapses between death and embalming will add to the problems and complications encountered. . . . " Just how soon should one get going on the embalming? The author tells us, "On the basis of such scanty information made available to this profession through its rudimentary and haphazard system of technical research, we must conclude that the best results are to be obtained if the subject is embalmed before life is completely extinct—that is, before cellular death has occurred. In the average case, this would mean within an hour after somatic° death." For those who feel that there is something a little rudimentary°, not to say haphazard, about this advice, a comforting thought is offered by another writer. Speaking of fears entertained in early days of premature burial, he points out, "One of the effects of embalming by chemical injection, however, has been to dispel fears of live burial." How true; once the blood is removed, chances of live burial are indeed remote.

11   To return to Mr. Jones, the blood is drained out through the veins and replaced by embalming fluid pumped in through the arteries. As noted in *The Principles and Practices of Embalming*, "every operator has a favorite injection and drainage point—a fact which becomes a handicap only if he fails or refuses to forsake his favorites when conditions demand it." Typical favorites are the carotid artery, femoral artery, jugular vein, subclavian vein. There are various choices of embalming fluid. If Flextone is used, it will produce a "mild, flexible rigidity. The skin retains a velvety softness, the tissues are rubbery and pliable. Ideal for women and children." It may be blended with B. and G. Products Company's Lyf-Lyk tint, which is guaranteed to reproduce "nature's own skin texture . . . the velvety appearance of living tissue." Suntone comes in three separate tints: Suntan; Special Cosmetic Tint, a pink shade "especially indicated for young female subjects"; and Regular Cosmetic Tint, moderately pink.

12   About three to six gallons of a dyed and perfumed solution of formaldehyde, glycerin, borax, phenol, alcohol and water is soon circulating through Mr. Jones, whose mouth has been sewn together with a "needle directed upward between the upper lip and gum and brought out through the left nostril," with the corners raised slightly "for a more pleasant expression." If he should be bucktoothed, his teeth are cleaned with Bon Ami and coated with colorless nail polish. His eyes, meanwhile, are closed with flesh-tinted eye caps and eye cement.

13   The next step is to have at Mr. Jones with a thing called a trocar. This is a long, hollow needle attached to a tube. It is jabbed into the abdomen, poked around the entrails and chest cavity, the contents

of which are pumped out and replaced with "cavity fluid." This done, and the hole in the abdomen sewn up, Mr. Jones's face is heavily creamed (to protect the skin from burns which may be caused by leakage of the chemicals), and he is covered with a sheet and left unmolested for a while. But not for long—there is more, much more, in store for him. He has been embalmed, but not yet restored, and the best time to start the restorative work is eight to ten hours after embalming, when the tissues have become firm and dry.

The object of all this attention to the corpse, it must be remem-   14
bered, is to make it presentable for viewing in an attitude of healthy repose. "Our customs require the presentation of our dead in the semblance of normality . . . unmarred by the ravages of illness, disease or mutilation," says Mr. J. Sheridan Mayer in his *Restorative Art*. This is rather a large order since few people die in the full bloom of health, unravaged by illness and unmarked by some disfigurement. The funeral industry is equal to the challenge: "In some cases the gruesome appearance of a mutilated or disease-ridden subject may be quite discouraging. The task of restoration may seem impossible and shake the confidence of the embalmer. This is the time for intestinal fortitude° and determination. Once the formative work is begun and affected tissues are cleaned or removed, all doubts of success vanish. It is surprising and gratifying to discover the results which may be obtained."

The embalmer, having allowed an appropriate interval to elapse,   15
returns to the attack, but now he brings into play the skill and equipment of sculptor and cosmetician. Is a hand missing? Casting one in plaster of Paris is a simple matter. "For replacement purposes, only a cast of the back of the hand is necessary; this is within the ability of the average operator and is quite adequate." If a lip or two, a nose or an ear should be missing, the embalmer has at hand a variety of restorative waxes with which to model replacements. Pores and skin texture are simulated by stippling with a little brush, and over this cosmetics are laid on. Head off? Decapitation cases are rather routinely handled. Ragged edges are trimmed, and head joined to torso with a series of splints, wires and sutures. It is a good idea to have a little something at the neck—a scarf or a high collar— when time for viewing comes. Swollen mouth? Cut out tissue as needed from inside the lips. If too much is removed, the surface contour can easily be restored by padding with cotton. Swollen necks and cheeks are reduced by removing tissue through vertical incisions made down each side of the neck. "When the deceased is casketed, the pillow will hide the suture incisions . . . as an extra precaution against leakage, the suture may be painted with liquid sealer."

16   The opposite condition is more likely to present itself—that of emaciation. His hypodermic syringe now loaded with massage cream, the embalmer seeks out and fills the hollowed and sunken areas by injection. In this procedure the backs of the hands and fingers and the under-chin area should not be neglected.

17   Positioning the lips is a problem that recurrently challenges the ingenuity of the embalmer. Closed too tightly, they tend to give a stern, even disapproving expression. Ideally, embalmers feel, the lips should give the impression of being ever so slightly parted, the upper lip protruding slightly for a more youthful appearance. This takes some engineering, however, as the lips tend to drift apart. Lip drift can sometimes be remedied by pushing one or two straight pins through the inner margin of the lower lip and then inserting them between the two front upper teeth. If Mr. Jones happens to have no teeth, the pins can just as easily be anchored in his Armstrong Face Former and Denture Replacer. Another method to maintain lip closure is to dislocate the lower jaw, which is then held in its new position by a wire run through holes which have been drilled through the upper and lower jaws at the midline. As the French are fond of saying, *il faut souffrir pour être belle°.*

18   If Mr. Jones has died of jaundice, the embalming fluid will very likely turn him green. Does this deter the embalmer? Not if he has intestinal fortitude. Masking pastes and cosmetics are heavily laid on, burial garments and casket interiors are color-correlated with particular care, and Jones is displayed beneath rose-colored lights. Friends will say "How *well* he looks." Death by carbon monoxide, on the other hand, can be rather a good thing from the embalmer's viewpoint: "One advantage is the fact that this type of discoloration is an exaggerated form of a natural pink coloration." This is nice because the healthy glow is already present and needs but little attention.

19   The patching and filling completed, Mr. Jones is now shaved, washed and dressed. Cream-based cosmetic, available in pink, flesh, suntan, brunette and blond, is applied to his hands and face, his hair is shampooed and combed (and, in the case of Mrs. Jones, set), his hands manicured. For the horny-handed son of toil° special care must be taken; cream should be applied to remove ingrained grime, and the nails cleaned. "If he were not in the habit of having them manicured in life, trimming and shaping is advised for better appearance—never questioned by kin."

20   Jones is now ready for casketing (this is the present participle of the verb "to casket"). In this operation his right shoulder should be depressed slightly "to turn the body a bit to the right and soften the appearance of lying flat on the back." Positioning the hands is a matter of importance, and special rubber positioning blocks may

be used. The hands should be cupped slightly for a more lifelike, relaxed appearance. Proper placement of the body requires a delicate sense of balance. It should lie as high as possible in the casket, yet not so high that the lid, when lowered, will hit the nose. On the other hand, we are cautioned, placing the body too low "creates the impression that the body is in a box."

Jones is next wheeled into the appointed slumber room where 21 a few last touches may be added—his favorite pipe placed in his hand or, if he was a great reader, a book propped into position. (In the case of little Master Jones a Teddy bear may be clutched.) Here he will hold open house for a few days, visiting hours 10 A.M. to 9 P.M.

All now being in readiness, the funeral director calls a staff 22 conference to make sure that each assistant knows his precise duties. Mr. Wilber Kriege writes: "This makes your staff feel that they are a part of the team, with a definite assignment that must be properly carried out if the whole plan is to succeed. You never heard of a football coach who failed to talk to his entire team before they go on the field. They have drilled on the plays they are to execute for hours and days, and yet the successful coach knows the importance of making even the bench-warming third-string substitute feel that he is important if the game is to be won." The winning of *this* game is predicated upon glass-smooth handling of the logistics°. The funeral director has notified the pallbearers whose names were furnished by the family, has arranged for the presence of clergyman, organist, and soloist, has provided transportation for everybody, has organized and listed the flowers sent by friends. In *Psychology of Funeral Service* Mr. Edward A. Martin points out: "He may not always do as much as the family thinks he is doing, but it is his helpful guidance that they appreciate in knowing they are proceeding as they should. . . . The important thing is how well his services can be used to make the family believe they are giving unlimited expression to their own sentiment."

The religious service may be held in a church or in the chapel 23 of the funeral home; the funeral director vastly prefers the latter arrangement, for not only is it more convenient for him but it affords him the opportunity to show off his beautiful facilities to the gathered mourners. After the clergyman has had his say, the mourners queue up to file past the casket for a last look at the deceased. The family is *never* asked whether they want an open-casket ceremony; in the absence of their instruction to the contrary, this is taken for granted. Consequently well over 90 per cent of all American funerals feature the open casket—a custom unknown in other parts of the world. Foreigners are astonished by it. An English woman living in San Francisco described her reaction in a letter to the writer:

> I myself have attended only one funeral here—that of an elderly fellow worker of mine. After the service I could not understand why everyone was walking towards the coffin (sorry, I mean casket), but thought I had better follow the crowd. It shook me rigid to get there and find the casket open and poor old Oscar lying there in his brown tweed suit, wearing a suntan makeup and just the wrong shade of lipstick. If I had not been extremely fond of the old boy, I have a horrible feeling that I might have giggled. Then and there I decided that I could never face another American funeral—even dead.

24   The casket (which has been resting throughout the service on a Classic Beauty Ultra Metal Casket Bier) is now transferred by a hydraulically operated device called Porto-Lift to a balloon-tired, Glide Easy casket carriage which will wheel it to yet another conveyance, the Cadillac Funeral Coach. This may be lavender, cream, light green—anything but black. Interiors, of course, are color-correlated, "for the man who cannot stop short of perfection."

25   At graveside, the casket is lowered into the earth. This office, once the prerogative° of friends of the deceased, is now performed by a patented mechanical lowering device. A "Lifetime Green" artificial grass mat is at the ready to conceal the sere° earth, and overhead, to conceal the sky, is a portable Steril Chapel Tent ("resists the intense heat and humidity of summer and the terrific storms of winter . . . available in Silver Grey, Rose or Evergreen"). Now is the time for the ritual scattering of earth over the coffin, as the solemn words "earth to earth, ashes to ashes, dust to dust" are pronounced by the officiating cleric. This can today be accomplished "with a mere flick of the wrist with the Gordon Leak-Proof Earth Dispenser. No grasping of a handful of dirt, no soiled fingers. Simple, dignified, beautiful, reverent! The modern way!" The Gordon Earth Dispenser (at $5) is of nickel-plated brass construction. It is not only "attractive to the eye and long wearing"; it is also "one of the 'tools' for building better public relations" if presented as "an appropriate noncommercial gift" to the clergyman. It is shaped something like a saltshaker.

26   Untouched by human hand, the coffin and the earth are now united.

27   It is in the function of directing the participants through this maze of gadgetry that the funeral director has assigned to himself his relatively new role of "grief therapist." He has relieved the family of every detail, he has revamped° the corpse to look like a living doll, he has arranged for it to nap for a few days in a slumber room, he has put on a well-oiled performance in which the concept

of *death* has played no part whatsoever—unless it was inconsiderately mentioned by the clergyman who conducted the religious service. He has done everything in his power to make the funeral a real pleasure for everybody concerned. He and his team have given their all to score an upset victory over death.

JESSICA MITFORD

Essayist Jessica Mitford was born to a prominent family at Batsford mansion, England, in 1917, and settled in the United States in 1939. Mitford began her writing career in the 1950s; among her best known works are *Hons and Rebels*, *The Trial of Dr. Spock*, and *Kind and Unusual Punishment*.

Words and Meanings

Paragraph

formaldehyde:	chemical used to embalm bodies	
Alas, poor Yorick:	famous line from Shakespeare's *Hamlet*, addressed to a skull	2
decedent:	dead person	3
docility:	lamblike trust and willingness	4
mandatory:	necessary	5
dissuaded:	persuaded against	
intractable reticence:	unwillingness to discuss	6
stocks:	wooden shackles used to punish offenders	8
somatic:	bodily	10
rudimentary:	basic	
intestinal fortitude:	"guts," courage	14
il faut souffrir pour être belle:	French for "you have to suffer to be beautiful"	17
horny-handed son of toil:	cliché for a labourer	19
logistics:	arrangements	22
prerogative:	privilege	25
sere:	dry	
revamped:	altered	27

Structure and Strategy

1. Consider the title and first paragraph of this essay. What ANALOGY is introduced? How does the analogy help establish Mitford's TONE?
2. Look at the last paragraph. How is the analogy introduced in paragraph 1 reinforced in the conclusion? What words specifically contribute to the analogy?
3. The process of preparing a corpse for burial involves two main procedures: embalming and restoration. Identify the paragraphs in which Mitford explains these two procedures.
4. Identify the substeps that make up the final stage in the burial process (paragraphs 20 to 25).

Content and Purpose

1. In paragraphs 2 and 8, without saying so directly, how does Mitford imply that she disapproves of embalming? Can you find other examples of her implied disapproval?
2. What medical justification for embalming is offered in paragraph 10? How does Mitford undercut this argument?
3. Why does Mitford refer to the corpse as "Mr. Jones"?
4. What reason does Mitford suggest is behind the "secrecy surrounding embalming"? If the details of the procedure were common knowledge, what do you think the effect would be on the mortuary business?
5. What was your reaction to Mitford's essay? Do you think your response was what the author intended?

Suggestions for Writing

1. Mitford's essay explains the funeral director's job as a process. Write a process analysis explaining a job or task with which you are familiar.
2. Research another means of disposing of the dead, such as cremation (burning a dead body) or cryonics (freezing a dead, diseased body in the hope of restoring it to life when a cure has been found). Write an informational process paper explaining it.
3. Write an informational process analysis explaining the ceremony or ritual behaviour associated with the birth of a baby, a child's birthday, or the initiation of a child into the religious community (such as a bar mitzvah or confirmation).

Additional Suggestions for Writing: Process Analysis

I. Choose one of the topics below and develop it into an informational process analysis.
    1. How a computer (or any other mechanical device) works
    2. How a child is born
    3. How a particular rock group, sports personality, or political figure appeals to the crowd
    4. How a bill is passed in parliament
    5. How a company plans the marketing of a new product
    6. How a particular chemical reaction takes place
    7. How alcohol (or any other drug) affects the body
    8. How microwaves cook food
    9. How learning takes place
    10. How a particular process in nature occurs: for example, how coral forms, a spider spins a web, salmon spawn, lightning happens, or a snowflake forms
II. Choose one of the topics below and develop it into a directional process analysis.
    1. How to buy (or sell) something: a used car, a house, a piece of sports equipment, a stereo system, junk
    2. How to perform a particular life-saving technique: for example, mouth-to-mouth resuscitation or the Heimlich manoeuvre
    3. How to play roulette, blackjack, poker, or some other game of chance
    4. How to get attention
    5. How to prepare for a job interview
    6. How to choose a mate (or roommate, friend, or pet)
    7. How to make or build something: for example, beer, a kite, a radio transmitter, bread
    8. How to survive English (or any other subject you are studying)
    9. How to get your own way
    10. How to talk your way out of a traffic ticket, a failing grade, a date, a conversation with a bore, a threatened punishment, or keeping a promise

U N I T

Division and Classification: Explaining Parts and Kinds

What? The Definition

In **analysis**, we separate something into its parts in order to determine their essential features and study their relationship to each other. A research chemist, for example, analyzes a substance by breaking it down into its component elements. We speak of trying to "analyze someone's motives" in an effort to understand what prompts a person to behave in a certain way. Some people undergo years of psychoanalysis in an attempt to identify and explore their unconscious mental processes. In Unit Three, we used the term *process analysis* to describe a writing pattern in which the subject is divided into steps or stages: the steps involved in baking beans or in embalming a body, for instance. In Unit Six, we will look at subjects that are analyzed in terms of their causes or effects, an organizational pattern called *causal analysis*. The subjects of this unit, **division** and **classification**, are also forms of analysis.

The various kinds of analysis all involve dividing or sorting— breaking a complex whole into its parts or categories.

In the rhetorical pattern called *division*, a single subject is divided into its component parts. For example, a Big Mac consists of two all-beef patties, special sauce, pickles, cheese, lettuce, and onions on a sesame seed bun. A newspaper can be divided into its various sections: news, sports, features, entertainment, and classified ads. In one of the reading selections that follows, Martin Luther King, Jr., divides a "complete life" into three dimensions: length, breadth, and height. In division, the subject is always a single entity: one hamburger, one newspaper, or one life. The writer's task is to identify and explain the parts that make up the whole.

In *classification*, on the other hand, the subject is a whole group of things, and the writer's task is to sort the group into classes or categories on the basis of some shared characteristic. For example, fast-food hamburgers can be classified according to the chains that serve them: McDonald's, Wendy's, Harvey's, and Burger King. Then the writer would explain the distinctive features of the burgers in each category. Newspapers can be classified into tabloids like the *Toronto Sun*, which aim for a working-class audience; broad-based, general circulation papers like the *Toronto Star*, which aim for a middle-class audience; and upscale, business-oriented papers like the *Globe and Mail*, which appeal to professional, upper-middle-class readers. Singles could be classified into the kinds of dates they represent: divine, dull, or disastrous.

Classification is a familiar strategy. It is used so often that there is even an old joke that relies on popular knowledge of the technique for its point: "There are two kinds of people in the world—those who sort the world into two kinds of people and those who don't."

Why? The Purpose

Division and classification are methods by which we can isolate, separate, and sort things. They are essential ways of making sense out of the world around us. Both strategies appeal to the reader's need for order in the way information is presented.

A *division paper* usually answers one of two questions:

1.   What are the component parts of S?
2.   What are the important characteristics or features of S?

Once you have reduced the subject to its constituent parts, you can examine each part in turn to discover its distinctive features and its function within the whole. Division can be used to explore and clarify many kinds of subjects. You can analyze an organization (a college, for instance), a geographical location (such as the city of Winnipeg), a musical group (perhaps a rock band), an idea (equal pay for work of equal value), or a part of the body (such as the heart), by dividing it into its parts.

Classification, as we've seen, is a sorting mechanism. It is the pattern to choose when you find yourself writing a paper that answers the question, "What are the main kinds or types of S?"

Classification is useful when you need to examine a group of similar things with meaningful differences between them. You could classify colleges: CEGEPs in Quebec, CAATs in Ontario, and university-transfer institutions in British Columbia. You could classify people: various kinds of musicians or actors or athletes, for example. In one of the essays in this unit, Max Eastman classifies all the people of the world into two types: practical and poetic. Ideas (such as economic theories), places (such as resorts, slums, amusement parks), and events (such as golf tournaments, weddings, elections) can all be sorted into kinds and explained in terms that your readers will find informative, useful, and even—when appropriate— entertaining.

Division and classification are used to give shape and order to the welter of information that surrounds us. In the business world, for example, papers and reports are too often a hodgepodge of data or opinion that fails to provide the reader with an orderly explanation of the subject. Dividing or classifying the material organizes it into logically related units that the reader can grasp and understand.

Besides giving form and focus to shapeless chunks of information, division and classification are useful for evaluation purposes. A real estate company might divide a city into its residential areas so that prospective home buyers can choose where they want to live. Consumers' magazines classify different kinds of dishwashers, stereo turntables, automobiles, or dandruff shampoos, in order to recommend which brand is the best buy. Whether the writer's purpose is to organize a mass of data or to evaluate the relative merits of several items or ideas, division and classification can help to ensure a clear, coherent piece of communication.

How? The Technique

Writing a good *division paper* involves three steps: clarifying the principle of division, identifying the appropriate components of the subject, and constructing a clear thesis statement.

Most subjects can be divided in a number of different ways. For instance, you could divide a college into its physical areas: classrooms, offices, cafeteria, recreational facilities, and plant services. Or you could divide a college into its human components: faculty, students, administrators, and support staff. How you choose to divide something will determine the parts that you analyze and the relationship between those parts that you explore. Choose your dividing principle carefully, keeping your audience in mind: what specific aspects of your subject do you want your readers to know more about?

Second, decide whether your division is to be *exhaustive* (that is, to include *all* the component parts of the subject) or *representative* (to include *a few* of the major component parts). Sometimes, the nature of your subject determines which approach you will take: if there are only two or three component parts, for example, it makes good sense to include them all. But if there are a dozen or more, a carefully chosen representative sampling will give your readers the information they require without trying their patience in the process.

Third, include a thesis statement that maps out the scope and arrangement of your paper. It will probably look something like this:

> The component parts of S are a, b, c, and d.

Example: Blood is made up of plasma, red cells, white cells, and platelets.
On the other hand, it may read like this:

> The significant characteristics of S are a, b, and c.

Example: A good business letter is one that is concise, clear, and courteous.

Classification papers involve similar steps. To begin with, make sure your classification is both complete and logical. For instance, classifying the Romance languages (those descended from Latin since 800 A.D.) into French, Italian, and Portuguese would be incomplete because there are many more Romance languages than these three. However, if your purpose were to classify the Romance languages most frequently spoken in Canada today, the list above would be complete.

Your classification will be logical as long as your categories do not overlap: they must all be different from each other. To test your classification for logical soundness, check to be sure no example can be included under more than one category. For instance, if you were to classify your favourite kinds of movies into the categories of science fiction, comedy, and war films, where would you put *Catch-22*, a comic film about war, or *Star Wars*?

Of course, a classification paper must be based on a clear thesis statement:

> The kinds (or categories) of S are a, b, c, and d.

Example: Most teachers fit into one of three categories: Bumblers, Martinets, and Pros.

Division and classification are useful rhetorical strategies by themselves, but they can be used together effectively, too. In "What I Have Lived For," for example, Bertrand Russell divides his life's purpose, his reason for living, into what he calls "three passions": the longing for love, the search for knowledge, and pity for the suffering of mankind. Then he classifies his search for knowledge into the three kinds of knowledge he sought: the social sciences, the natural sciences, and mathematics.

Whether you choose to apply them separately or together, division and classification are two of the most useful strategies you can use to explain a complex subject to your readers. They can help you create order out of chaos in many different situations. Both strategies have practical and professional applications. Division is used on the job in organizational analyses, cost breakdowns, and technical reports. Classification is frequently the logical pattern on which performance appraisals, market projections, or product assessments are based. The ability to analyze through division and classification is obviously a useful skill for any writer to acquire.

The sample essay below is a paper that classifies into three categories a subject dear to the hearts of all students: teachers.

Bumblers, Martinets, and Pros

Introduction
(uses quotations) →

The playwright George Bernard Shaw provided us with the memorable definition, "Those who can, do. Those who can't, teach." The film director Woody Allen took the definition one step farther, "Those who can't teach, teach gym." At one time or another, most of us have suffered these truisms. We've all encountered teachers who fit Shaw's definition, as well as some who manage to do their jobs successfully, even cheerfully. Overall, most teachers fit into

Thesis statement → one of three categories: Bumblers, Martinets, and Pros.

First category
(developed with
descriptive
details)

Every student gets a Bumbler at least once. She's the teacher who trips over the doorjamb as she makes her first entrance. She looks permanently flustered, can't find her lesson plan, and dithers as she scrambles through her mess of books and papers. The Bumbler can't handle the simplest educational technologies: chalk self-destructs in her fingers, overhead projectors blow up at her touch, and filmstrips snap if she so much as looks in their direction. Organization isn't Ms. Bumbler's strong point, either. She drifts off in mid-sentence, eyes focused dreamily out the window. Students can easily derail her with off-topic questions. She'll forget to collect assignments or to give the test that everyone has studied for. The Bumbler is an amiable sort, but her mind is on a perpetual slow boat to nowhere. Students can learn in her class, but only if they are willing to take a great deal of initiative.

Second category (note the definition of an unfamiliar term)

Martinet was the name of a seventeenth-century French general who invented a particularly nasty system of military drill. Thus, the word itself has come to mean a strict disciplinarian, a stickler for the rules, a tough "drill sergeant." As a teacher, the Martinet is an uptight, rigid authoritarian who sends shivers down students' spines. He rarely smiles, certainly not during the first month. His voice is harsh, biting, and he specializes in the barbed response and the humiliating putdown. His classes unfold in a precise and boring manner. Each minute is accounted for, as he scouts the room for any disruptive or slumbering captives to be brought to heel. He tolerates no searching questions or interesting digressions. His assignments are lengthy and tedious; his tests are notoriously fearsome. Instead of the critical inquiry into ideas, rote learning takes place in the Martinet's classroom. And it takes place at the expense of the patience and self-esteem of his students.

Third category (note the implied contrast to the previous two categories)

➤ Every once in a while, a student is blessed with the teacher who can be described as a Professional. The Pro is characterized by a genuine liking and respect for students and is motivated by enthusiasm for the subject matter. This teacher is organized enough to present lessons clearly, but not so hidebound as to cut off questions or the occasional excursion along an interesting sideroad of learning. The Pro's classroom is relaxed, friendly, yet stimulating enough to keep students concentrating on the task at hand. Assignments are designed to enhance learning; tests are rigorous but fair. Landing in the Pro's class is a stroke of luck. Such a teacher is a gift, for the Pro imparts the desire and ability to learn to the students he or she encounters.

Conclusion
(asks a rhetorical question)

These characterizations of the Bumbler, the Martinet, and the Pro are, of course, extreme portraits of some of the worst and best qualities a teacher can possess. Indeed, some teachers, in Jekyll-and-Hyde fashion, display characteristics of two or more types, sometimes in a single class period! In an ideal world and a perfect course, the student would be given a choice of instructors. Who would opt for a Bumbler or a Martinet, given the chance to sign up for a Pro?

What I Have Lived For

BERTRAND RUSSELL

1   Three passions, simple but overwhelmingly strong, have governed my life: the longing for love, the search for

"What I Have Lived For" from *The Autobiography of Bertrand Russell*. Copyright 1967. Reprinted with the permission of The Bertrand Russell House, George Allen, and Unwin Limited.

knowledge, and unbearable pity for the suffering of mankind. These passions, like great winds, have blown me hither and thither, in a wayward° course, over a deep ocean of anguish, reaching to the very verge° of despair.

I have sought love, first, because it brings ecstasy°—ecstasy so   2
great that I would often have sacrificed all the rest of life for a few hours of this joy. I have sought it, next, because it relieves loneliness—that terrible loneliness in which one shivering consciousness looks over the rim of the world into the cold unfathomable lifeless abyss°. I have sought it, finally, because in the union of love I have seen, in a mystic miniature, the prefiguring° vision of the heaven that saints and poets have imagined. This is what I sought, and though it might seem too good for human life, this is what—at last—I have found.

With equal passion I have sought knowledge. I have wished to   3
understand the hearts of men. I have wished to know why the stars shine. And I have tried to apprehend the Pythagorean° power by which number holds sway above the flux°. A little of this, but not much, I have achieved.

Love and knowledge, so far as they were possible, led upward   4
toward the heavens. But always pity brought me back to earth. Echoes of cries of pain reverberate° in my heart. Children in famine, victims tortured by oppressors, helpless old people a hated burden to their sons, and the whole world of loneliness, poverty, and pain make a mockery of what human life should be. I long to alleviate° the evil, but I cannot, and I too suffer.

This has been my life. I have found it worth living, and would   5
gladly live it again if the chance were offered me.

┌─────────────────────┐
│   │
│   │
└─────────────────────┘

BERTRAND RUSSELL

Bertrand Russell (1872–1970), the philosopher, mathematician, and social reformer, was awarded the Nobel Prize for Literature in 1950. His progressive views on the liberalization of sexual attitudes and the role of women led to his dismissal from the University of California at Los Angeles in the 1920s. Russell was a leading pacifist and proponent of nuclear disarmament. Among his many books are *Principia Mathematica*, *Why I Am Not a Christian*, and *History of Western Philosophy*.

Words and Meanings
Paragraph

wayward:	unpredictable, wandering	1
verge:	edge, brink	

2   ecstasy: supreme joy
    abyss: bottomless pit, hell
    prefiguring: picturing to oneself beforehand

3   Pythagorean: relating to the Greek philosopher Pythagoras
                                and his theory that through mathematics one
                                could understand the relationship between all
                                things and the principle of harmony in the
                                universe
    flux: continual motion, change

4   reverberate: echo
    alleviate: relieve, lessen

Structure and Strategy

1. Identify Russell's thesis statement and the topic sentences of paragraphs 2, 3, and 4.
2. How does the structure of the second sentence in paragraph 1 reinforce its meaning?
3. The number three is the basis for the structure of Russell's essay. Three is an ancient symbol for unity and completeness and for the human life cycle: birth, life, death. Find as many examples as you can of Russell's effective use of three's. (Look at paragraph and sentence structure as well as content.)
4. What is the function of the first sentence of paragraph 4?
5. How does Russell's concluding paragraph contribute to the UNITY of the essay?
6. Refer to the introduction to this chapter and show how paragraph 1 sets up a division essay and how paragraph 5 is actually a classification.
7. Analyze the order in which Russell explains his three passions. Do you think the order is chronological, logical, climactic, or random? Does the order reflect the relative importance or value that Russell ascribes to each passion? How?

Content and Purpose

1. Love, to Bertrand Russell, means more than physical passion. What else does he include in his meaning of love (paragraph 2)?
2. What are the three kinds of knowledge Russell has spent his life seeking?
3. Which of Russell's three "passions" has he been least successful in achieving? Why?

Suggestions for Writing

1. What goals have you set for yourself for the next ten years? Write a short paper in which you identify and explain two or three of your goals.
2. In what ways are you different from other people? Write a short paper in which you identify and explain some of the qualities and characteristics that make you a unique human being.
3. Imagine that you are 75 years old. Write a short paper explaining what you have lived for.

Practical and Poetic People

MAX EASTMAN

A simple experiment will distinguish two   1
types of human nature. Gather a throng of people and pour them into a ferry-boat. By the time the boat has swung into the river you will find that a certain proportion have taken the trouble to climb upstairs, in order to be out on deck and see what is to be seen as they cross over. The rest have settled indoors, to think what they will do upon reaching the other side, or perhaps lose themselves in apathy° or tobacco smoke. But leaving out those apathetic, or addicted to a single enjoyment, we may divide all the alert passengers on the boat into two classes—those who are interested in crossing the river, and those who are merely interested in getting across. And we may divide all the people on the earth, or all the moods of people, in the same way. Some of them are chiefly occupied with attaining ends, and some with receiving experiences. The distinction of the two will be more marked when we name the first kind practical, and the second poetic, for common knowledge recognizes that a person poetic or in a poetic mood is impractical, and a practical person is intolerant of poetry.

We can see the force of this intolerance too, and how deeply it   2
is justified, if we make clear to our minds just what it means to be practical, and what a great thing it is. It means to be controlled in your doings by the consideration of ends yet unattained. The practi-

"Practical and Poetic People." Reprinted with permission of Charles Scribner's Sons, an imprint of Macmillan Publishing, from *Enjoyment of Poetry* by Max Eastman. Copyright 1939 by Charles Scribner's Sons.

cal man is never distracted by things, or aspects of things, which have no bearing on his purpose, but, ever seizing the significant, he moves with a single mind and a single emotion toward the goal. And even when the goal is achieved you will hardly see him pause to rejoice in it; he is already on his way to another achievement. For that is the irony of his nature. His joy is not in any conquest or destination, but his joy is in going toward it. To which joy he adds the pleasure of being praised as a practical man, and a man who will arrive.

3   In a more usual sense, perhaps, a practical man is a man occupied with attaining certain ends that people consider important. He must stick pretty close to the business of feeding and preserving life. Nourishment and shelter, money-making, maintaining respectability, and if possible a family—these are the things that give its common meaning to the word "practical." An acute regard for such features of the scenery, and the universe, as contribute or can be made to contribute to these ends, and a systematic neglect of all other features, are the traits of mind which this word popularly suggests. And it is because of the vital importance of these things to almost all people that the word "practical" is a eulogy°, and is able to be so scornful of the word "poetic."

4   "It is an earnest thing to be alive in this world. With competition, with war, with disease and poverty and oppression, misfortune and death on-coming, who but fools will give serious attention to what is not significant to the business?"

5   "Yes—but what is the *use* of being alive in the world, if life is so oppressive in its moral character that we must always be busy getting somewhere, and never simply realizing where we are? What were the value of your eternal achieving, if we were not here on our holiday to appreciate, among other things, some of the things you have achieved?"

6   Thus, if we could discover a purely poetic and a purely practical person, might they reason together. But we can discover nothing so satisfactory to our definitions, and therefore let us conclude the discussion of the difference between them. It has led us to our own end—a clearer understanding of the nature of poetic people, and of all people when they are in a poetic mood. They are lovers of the qualities of things. They are not engaged, as the learned say that all life is, in becoming adjusted to an environment, but they are engaged in becoming acquainted with it. They are possessed by the impulse to realize, an impulse as deep, and arbitrary, and unexplained as that "will to live" which lies at the bottom of all the explanations. It seems but the manifestation°, indeed, of that will

itself in a concrete and positive form. It is a wish to experience life and the world. That is the essence of the poetic temper.

```
┌─────────────────────────┐
│                         │
└─────────────────────────┘
```

MAX EASTMAN

Max Eastman (1883–1969) was a poet, philosopher, and social critic who taught at Columbia University. Co-founder and editor of various socialist periodicals and an editor of Karl Marx's works, Eastman is best known for his social criticism, including such works as *The Literary Mind: Its Place in an Age of Science* and *The End of Socialism in Russia*.

Words and Meanings

Paragraph

apathy:	indifference, lack of interest	1
eulogy:	praise, positive expression	3
manifestation:	demonstration, display	6

Structure and Strategy

1. Eastman introduces his thesis with an ANALOGY. Why? How does it help the reader to understand his point?
2. What method of development does Eastman use in paragraphs 2 and 3? What is the function of these two paragraphs?
3. What unusual method does Eastman use to develop paragraphs 4 and 5? Why?
4. Where does Eastman explain what he means by the "poetic" personality? Why does he devote comparatively little space to this topic?

Content and Purpose

1. In paragraph 1, Eastman regards "a person . . . in a poetic mood as impractical, and a practical person as intolerant of poetry." Do you agree?
2. Which sort of person does Eastman prefer—the practical or the poetic? How do you know?
3. On the basis of Eastman's classification, would you describe yourself as a "practical" or a "poetic" person? Why?

Suggestions for Writing

1. Write a short paper in which you classify the members of a familiar group such as parents, police officers, friends, salespersons, bosses, or car drivers.

2. Write a short paper in which you explore some of the relation-
    ships in your life. How many different roles do you play? Explain
    three or four of the several roles or identities you have.

Life in the Stopwatch Lane

AMY WILLARD CROSS

1   ⌐￢f time is money, the rates have skyrock-
eted and you probably can't afford it. North Americans are suffering
a dramatic time shortage since demand greatly exceeds supply. In
fact, a recent survey revealed that people lost about 10 hours of
leisure per week between 1973 and 1987. Maybe you were too busy
to notice.

2   Losing that leisure leaves a piddling 16.6 hours to do whatever
you want, free of work, dish-washing or car-pooling. In television
time, that equals a season of 13 "thirtysomething" episodes, plus
$3^1/_2$ re-runs. Hardly enough time to write an autobiography or carry
on an affair.

3   How has replacing free time with more billable hours affected
society? It has created a new demographic group: the Busy Class—
who usurped° the Leisure Class. Easy to recognize, members of the
Busy Class constantly cry to anyone listening, "I'm *soooooo* busy."
So busy they can't call their mother or find change for a panhandler.
Masters of doing two things at once, they eke° the most out of time.
They dictate while driving, talk while calculating, entertain guests
while nursing, watch the news while pumping iron. Even business
melts into socializing—people earn their daily bread while they
break it.

4   In fact, the Busies must make lots of bread to maintain themselves in the standard of busy-ness to which they've become accustomed. To do that, they need special, expensive stuff. Stuff like call
waiting, which lets them talk to two people at once. Stuff like two-
faced watches, so they can do business in two time zones at once.
Neither frenzied executives nor hurried housewives dare leave the
house without their "book"—leather-bound appointment calendars
thick as bestsellers. Forget hi-fi's or racing cars, the new talismans° of

overachievers also work: coffee-makers that brew by alarm; remote-controlled ignitions; or car faxes. Yet, despite all these time-efficient devices, few people have time to spare.

That scarcity has changed how we measure time. Now it's being   5
scientifically dissected into smaller and smaller pieces. Thanks to digital clocks, we know when it's 5:30 (and calculate we'll be home in three hours, eight minutes). These days lawyers can reason in 1/10th of an hour increments; they bill every six minutes. This to-the-minute precision proves time's escalating° value.

Time was, before the advent of car phones and digital clocks,   6
we scheduled two kinds of time: time-off and work hours. Not any more. Just as the Inuit label the infinite varieties of snow, the Busy Class has identified myriad° subtleties of free time and named them. Here are some textbook examples of the new faces of time:

Quality time: For those working against the clock, the quality   7
of time spent with loved ones supposedly compensates° for quantity. This handy concept absolves° guilt as quickly as rosary counting. So careerist couples dine à deux once a fortnight. Parents bond by reading kids a story after nanny [has] fed and bathed them. When pressed for time, nobody wastes it by fighting about bad breath or unmade beds. People who spend quality time with each other view their relationships through rose-colored glasses. And knowing they've created perfect personal lives lets the Busy Class work even harder—guilt-free.

Travel time: With an allowance of 16.6 hours of fun, the Busy   8
Class watches time expenditures carefully. Just [as] businesses do while making bids, normal people calculate travel time for leisure activities. If two tram rides away, a friendly squash game loses out. One time-efficient woman even formulated a mathematical theorem: fun per mile quotient. Before accepting any social invitation, she adds up travel costs, figures out the time spent laughing, drinking and eating. If the latter exceeds the former, she accepts. It doesn't matter who asks.

Downtime: Borrowed from the world of heavy equipment and   9
sleek computers, downtime is a professional-sounding word meaning the damned thing broke, wait around until it's fixed. Translated into real life, downtime counts as neither work nor play, but a maddening no-man's-land where *nothing* happens! Like lining up for the ski-lift, or commuting without a car phone, or waiting a while for the mechanic's diagnosis. Beware: people who keep track of their downtime probably indulge in less than 16 hours of leisure.

Family time: In addition to 60-hour weeks, aerobics and dinner   10
parties, some people make time for their children. When asked to brunch, a young couple will reply, "We're sorry but that's our family time." A variant of quality time, it's Sunday afternoon between lunch

and the Disney Hour when nannies frequent Filipino restaurants. In an effort to entertain their children without exposure to sex and violence, the family attends craft fairs, animated matinees or tree-tapping demonstrations. There, they converge with masses of family units spending time alone with the kids. After a noisy, sticky afternoon, parents gladly punch the clock come Monday.

11   Quiet time: Overwhelmed by their schedules, some people try to recapture the magic of childhood when they watched clouds for hours on end. Sophisticated grown-ups have rediscovered the quiet time of kindergarten days. They unplug the phone (not the answering machine), clutch a book and try not to think about work. But without teachers to enforce it, quiet doesn't last. The clock ticks too loudly. As a computer fanatic said, after being entertained at 16 megahertz, sitting still to watch a sunset pales by comparison.

12   As it continues to increase in value, time will surely divide into even smaller units. And people will share only the tiniest amounts with each other. Hey, brother, can you spare a minute? Got a second? A nanosecond?

```



```

AMY WILLARD CROSS

Amy Willard Cross (b. 1960) has written articles and essays for U.S. and Canadian magazines and is a regular contributor to the *Globe and Mail*.

Words and Meanings

Paragraph

3	usurped:	took over from
	eke:	make the most of; squeeze
4	talismans:	objects that bring good luck or that ward off evil
5	escalating:	increasing
6	myriad:	a vast number
7	compensates:	makes up for
	absolves:	sets us free from

Structure and Strategy

1. What is the TONE of this piece? Identify three or four particularly effective examples that contribute to the tone.
2. Study the DICTION in paragraph 1. How do the words Cross has chosen reinforce the view that "time is money"?
3. How has Cross arranged her points: are they in chronological,

logical, climactic, or random order? Could they be rearranged without affecting the meaning or the impact of the article?

4. Cross uses many examples to develop her notion of the "Busy Class." Why do you think she calculates leisure hours in "television time" (paragraph 2)? What do the examples in paragraphs 3 and 4 tell us about the Busy Class?

5. How does the concluding paragraph develop the "time is money" thesis introduced in paragraph 1?

Content and Purpose

1. What is the literal meaning of the title of this article, and what does the title imply?

2. Write a thesis statement that summarizes in a single sentence the subject and main points of this article.

3. What characteristics do members of the Busy Class have in common?

4. In paragraph 8, Cross describes how "careerist couples" create their "perfect personal lives." How does the reader view the lives these hyper-busy people create for themselves?

5. What are the implications for society of our dividing time into ever-smaller units? What is Cross warning us of in paragraph 12?

Suggestion for Writing

How do you spend your time? Write a classification essay that explains the categories into which you divide your time each week.

Closing the Gap

LINDA FLOWER

The goal of the writer is to create a momen- 1
tary common ground between the reader and the writer. You want the reader to share your knowledge and your attitude toward that knowledge. Even if the reader eventually disagrees, you want him or her to be able for the moment to *see things as you see them*. A good piece of writing closes the gap between you and the reader.

The first step in closing that gap is to gauge the distance between 2

"Closing the Gap," an excerpt from *Problem-Solving Strategies for Writing* by Linda Flower. Copyright 1981. Reprinted with the permission of Harcourt Brace Jovanovich.

the two of you. Imagine, for example, that you are a student writing your parents, who have always lived in New York City, about a wilderness survival expedition you want to go on over spring break. Sometimes obvious differences such as age or background will be important, but the critical differences for writers usually fall into three areas: the reader's *knowledge* about the topic, his or her *attitude* toward it, and his or her personal or professional *needs*. Because these differences often exist, good writers do more than simply express their meaning; they pinpoint the critical differences between themselves and their reader and design their writing to reduce those differences. Let us look at these three areas in more detail.

3   [Knowledge] is usually the easiest difference to handle. What does your reader need to know? What are the main ideas you hope to teach? Does your reader have enough background knowledge to really understand you? If not, what would he or she have to learn?

4   When we say a person has knowledge, we usually refer to his conscious awareness of explicit facts and clearly defined concepts. This kind of knowledge can be easily written down or told to someone else. However, much of what we "know" is not held in this formal, explicit way. Instead it is held as an attitude or image—as a loose cluster of associations. For instance, my image of lakes includes associations many people would have, including fishing, water skiing, stalled outboards, and lots of kids catching night crawlers with flashlights. However, the most salient° or powerful parts of my image, which strongly color my whole attitude toward lakes, are thoughts of cloudy skies, long rainy days, and feeling generally cold and damp. By contrast, one of my best friends has a very different cluster of associations: to him a lake means sun, swimming, sailing, and happily sitting on the end of a dock. Needless to say, our differing images cause us to react quite differently to a proposal that we visit a lake. Likewise, one reason people often find it difficult to discuss religion and politics is that terms such as "capitalism" conjure up radically different images.

5   As you can see, a reader's image of a subject is often the source of attitudes and feelings that are unexpected and, at times, impervious° to mere facts. A simple statement that seems quite persuasive to you, such as "Lake Wampago would be a great place to locate the new music camp," could have little impact on your reader if he or she simply doesn't visualize a lake as a "great place." In fact, many people accept uncritically any statement that fits in with their own attitudes—and reject, just as uncritically, anything that does not.

6   Whether your purpose is to persuade or simply to present your perspective, it helps to know the image and attitudes that your

reader already holds. The more these differ from your own, the more you will have to do to make him or her *see* what you mean. When writers discover a large gap between their own knowledge and attitudes and those of the reader, they usually try to change the reader in some way. Needs, however, are different. When you analyze a reader's needs, it is so that you, the writer, can adapt to him. If you ask a friend majoring in biology how to keep your fish tank from clouding, you don't want to hear a textbook recitation on the life processes of algae. You expect the friend to adapt his or her knowledge and tell you exactly how to solve your problem.

The ability to adapt your knowledge to the needs of the reader is often crucial to your success as a writer. This is especially true in writing done on a job. For example, as producer of a public affairs program for a television station, eighty percent of your time may be taken up planning the details of new shows, contacting guests, and scheduling the taping sessions. But when you write a program proposal to the station director, your job is to show how the program will fit into the cost guidelines, the FCC° requirements for relevance, and the overall programming plan for the station. When you write that report your role in the organization changes from producer to proposal writer. Why? Because your reader needs that information in order to make a decision. He may be *interested* in your scheduling problems and the specific content of the shows, but he *reads* your report because of his own needs as station director of that organization. He has to act.

In college, where the reader is also a teacher, the reader's needs are a little less concrete but just as important. Most papers are assigned as a way to teach something. So the real purpose of a paper may be for you to make connections between two historical periods, to discover for yourself the principle behind a laboratory experiment, or to develop and support your own interpretation of a novel. A good college paper doesn't just rehash the facts; it demonstrates what your reader, as a teacher, needs to know—that you are learning the thinking skills his or her course is trying to teach.

Effective writers are not simply expressing what they know, like the student madly filling up an examination bluebook. Instead they are *using* their knowledge: reorganizing, maybe even rethinking their ideas to meet the demands of an assignment or the needs of their reader.

Sometimes it is also necessary to decide who is your primary audience as opposed to your secondary audience. Both may read your paper, but the primary audience is the reader you most want to teach, influence, or convince. When this is the case, you will want to design the paper so the primary reader can easily find what he or she needs.

```

```

LINDA FLOWER

Author of numerous articles on the process of writing, Linda Flower is a professor of English at Carnegie-Mellon University. "Closing the Gap" is excerpted from her well-known text, *Problem-Solving Strategies for Writing*, first published in 1981.

Paragraph
Words and Meanings

4   salient: prominent, most noticeable

5   impervious: resistant, not responsive to

8   FCC: Federal Communications Commission (regulates broadcasting in the United States)

Structure and Strategy

1. What is the THESIS of "Closing the Gap"? Where does Flower state it most clearly?
2. What is Flower's definition of "knowledge"? Of "attitude"?
3. How does Flower establish TRANSITIONS between one main idea and the next? (See paragraphs 4 and 7.)
4. What is the function of the examples introduced in paragraphs 4, 7, and 8? Are they effective—that is, do they help "close the gap" between you and the author?

Content and Purpose

1. What is, or should be, the goal of a writer, according to Flower? Does this excerpt from her book fulfil that goal?
2. Which of the three potential differences between writer and reader is least developed in the essay? Why does Flower devote so little space to this potential "gap"?
3. How does the essay distinguish between primary and secondary audiences? Who is Flower's primary audience?

Suggestions for Writing

1. Select an essay from this book that you think has effectively closed the gap between writer and reader. Write a short paper analyzing how the essay you have chosen successfully reaches its audience in terms of their knowledge, attitudes, and needs.

2. Peter Elbow's "Desperation Writing" is a process analysis whose
   goal is to help student writers be more effective. Compare and
   contrast some of the strategies he and Flower recommend for
   writing good papers.

I Want a Wife

JUDY SYFERS

I belong to that classification of people
known as wives. I am A Wife. And, not altogether incidentally, I am
a mother.

Not too long ago a male friend of mine appeared on the scene
fresh from a recent divorce. He had one child, who is, of course,
with his ex-wife. He is looking for another wife. As I thought about
him while I was ironing one evening, it suddenly occurred to me
that I, too, would like to have a wife. Why do I want a wife?

I would like to go back to school so that I can become economically independent, support myself, and, if need be, support those
dependent upon me. I want a wife who will work and send me to
school. And while I am going to school I want a wife to take care of
my children. I want a wife to keep track of the children's doctor and
dentist appointments. And to keep track of mine, too. I want a wife
to make sure my children eat properly and are kept clean. I want a
wife who will wash the children's clothes and keep them mended.
I want a wife who is a good nurturant° attendant to my children,
who arranges for their schooling, makes sure that they have an
adequate social life with their peers, takes them to the park, the zoo,
etc. I want a wife who takes care of the children when they are sick,
a wife who arranges to be around when the children need special
care, because, of course, I cannot miss classes at school. My wife
must arrange to lose time at work and not lose the job. It may mean
a small cut in my wife's income from time to time, but I guess I can
tolerate that. Needless to say, my wife will arrange and pay for the
care of the children while my wife is working.

I want a wife who will take care of *my* physical needs. I want a
wife who will keep my house clean. A wife who will pick up after
my children, a wife who will pick up after me. I want a wife who
will keep my clothes clean, ironed, mended, replaced when need

be, and who will see to it that my personal things are kept in their proper place so that I can find what I need the minute I need it. I want a wife who cooks the meals, a wife who is a *good* cook. I want a wife who will plan the menus, do the necessary grocery shopping, prepare the meals, serve them pleasantly, and then do the cleaning up while I do my studying. I want a wife who will care for me when I am sick and sympathize with my pain and loss of time from school. I want a wife to go along when our family takes a vacation so that someone can continue to care for me and my children when I need a rest and change of scene.

5   I want a wife who will not bother me with rambling complaints about a wife's duties. But I want a wife who will listen to me when I feel the need to explain a rather difficult point I have come across in my course of studies. And I want a wife who will type my papers for me when I have written them.

6   I want a wife who will take care of the details of my social life. When my wife and I are invited out by my friends, I want a wife who will take care of the babysitting arrangements. When I meet people at school that I like and want to entertain, I want a wife who will have the house clean, will prepare a special meal, serve it to me and my friends, and not interrupt when I talk about things that interest me and my friends. I want a wife who will have arranged that the children are fed and ready for bed before my guests arrive so that the children do not bother us. I want a wife who takes care of the needs of my guests so that they feel comfortable, who makes sure that they have an ashtray, that they are passed the hors d'oeuvres, that they are offered a second helping of the food, that their wine glasses are replenished° when necessary, that their coffee is served to them as they like it. And I want a wife who knows that sometimes I need a night out by myself.

7   I want a wife who is sensitive to my sexual needs, a wife who makes love passionately and eagerly when I feel like it, a wife who makes sure that I am satisfied. And, of course, I want a wife who will not demand sexual attention when I am not in the mood for it. I want a wife who assumes the complete responsibility for birth control, because I do not want more children. I want a wife who will remain sexually faithful to me so that I do not have to clutter up my intellectual life with jealousies. And I want a wife who understands that *my* sexual needs may entail more than strict adherence° to monogamy°. I must, after all, be able to relate to people as fully as possible.

8   If, by chance, I find another person more suitable as a wife than the wife I already have, I want the liberty to replace my present wife with another one. Naturally, I will expect a fresh, new life; my

wife will take the children and be solely responsible for them so that I am left free.

When I am through with school and have a job, I want my wife   9 to quit working and remain at home so that my wife can more fully and completely take care of a wife's duties.

My God, who *wouldn't* want a wife?   10

```
┌─────────────────────────┐
│                         │
│                         │
└─────────────────────────┘
```

JUDY SYFERS

Judy Syfers (b. 1937) is a writer, feminist, and activist who has published numerous articles on topics such as union organizing, abortion, and women's role in society.

Words and Meanings

Paragraph

nurturant:	providing care, food, and training	3
replenished:	filled	6
adherence:	constancy, sticking to	7
monogamy:	custom of marrying, being faithful to only one mate	

Structure and Strategy

1. What is the function of the first two paragraphs? What TONE do they establish?
2. Into what main functions does Syfers divide the role of a wife? Identify the paragraph(s) that focus on each. Then write a thesis statement for this essay.
3. Why does Syfers never use the pronouns "she" or "her" to refer to a wife? Is the frequent repetition of the word "wife" awkward? Or does it serve a particular purpose?
4. What is the effect of having so many sentences begin with the words, "I want"?

Content and Purpose

1. What is Syfers's attitude to the roles traditionally assigned to men and to women in our society? Identify two or three passages that clearly convey her feelings.
2. Consider the degree to which Syfers's portrayal of male and female roles is an accurate reflection of our society's expectations. Who or what is responsible for these expectations?
3. Can you identify any contradictions between the duties that "a

wife" would be required to perform and the actions of "the husband" who benefits from her care?

4. What would be the effect of this essay if it had been written by a man? How would the readers respond?

Suggestions for Writing

1. Write an essay organized, like Syfers's, on the principle of division. Your first paragraph should contain the sentence, "I want a husband."
2. Write an essay in which you classify types of wives or husbands (or mothers, or fathers, or children).
3. In a short paper, identify and explain the differences in spousal (or parental) roles between your parents' generation and the family you have (or plan to have).

The Dimensions of a Complete Life

MARTIN LUTHER KING, JR.

1   Many, many centuries ago, out on a lonely, obscure island called Patmos°, a man by the name of John° caught a vision of the new Jerusalem descending out of heaven from God. One of the greatest glories of this new city of God that John saw was its completeness. It was not partial and one-sided, but it was complete in all three of its dimensions. And so, in describing the city in the twenty-first chapter of the book of Revelation, John says this: "The length and the breadth and the height of it are equal." In other words, this new city of God, this city of ideal humanity, is not an unbalanced entity but it is complete on all sides.

2   Now John is saying something quite significant here. For so many of us the book of Revelation° is a very difficult book, puzzling to decode. We look upon it as something of a great enigma° wrapped in mystery. And certainly if we accept the book of Revelation as a record of actual historical occurrences it is a difficult book, shrouded with impenetrable mysteries. But if we will look beneath the peculiar jargon of its author and the prevailing apocalyptic° symbolism, we will find in this book many eternal truths which continue to chal-

lenge us. One such truth is that of this text. What John is really saying is this: that life as it should be and life at its best is the life that is complete on all sides.

There are three dimensions of any complete life to which we   3
can fitly give the words of this text: length, breadth, and height. The length of life as we shall think of it here is not its duration or its longevity, but it is the push of a life forward to achieve its personal ends and ambitions. It is the inward concern for one's own welfare. The breadth of life is the outward concern for the welfare of others. The height of life is the upward reach for God.

These are the three dimensions of life, and without the three   4
being correlated, working harmoniously together, life is incomplete. Life is something of a great triangle. At one angle stands the individual person, at the other angle stand other persons, and at the top stands the Supreme, Infinite Person, God. These three must meet in every individual life if that life is to be complete.

Now let us notice first the length of life. I have said that this is   5
the dimension of life in which the individual is concerned with developing his inner powers. It is that dimension of life in which the individual pursues personal ends and ambitions. This is perhaps the selfish dimension of life, and there is such a thing as moral and rational self-interest. If one is not concerned about himself he cannot be totally concerned about other selves.

Some years ago a learned rabbi, the late Joshua Liebman, wrote   6
a book entitled *Peace of Mind*. He has a chapter in the book entitled "Love Thyself Properly." In this chapter he says in substance that it is impossible to love other selves adequately unless you love your own self properly. Many people have been plunged into the abyss° of emotional fatalism° because they did not love themselves properly. So every individual has a responsibility to be concerned about himself enough to discover what he is made for. After he discovers his calling he should set out to do it with all of the strength and power in his being. He should do it as if God Almighty called him at this particular moment in history to do it. He should seek to do his job so well that the living, the dead, or the unborn could not do it better. No matter how small one thinks his life's work is in terms of the norms of the world and the so-called big jobs, he must realize that it has cosmic significance if he is serving humanity and doing the will of God.

To carry this to one extreme, if it falls your lot to be a street-   7
sweeper, sweep streets as Raphael painted pictures, sweep streets as Michelangelo carved marble, sweep streets as Beethoven composed music, sweep streets as Shakespeare wrote poetry. Sweep streets so well that all the hosts of heaven and earth will have to pause and

say, "Here lived a great street-sweeper who swept his job well." In the words of Douglas Mallock:

If you can't be a highway, just be a trail;
If you can't be the sun, be a star,
For it isn't by size that you win or you fail—
Be the best of whatever you are.

When you do this, you have mastered the first dimension of life—the length of life.

8   But don't stop here; it is dangerous to stop here. There are some people who never get beyond this first dimension. They are brilliant people; often they do an excellent job in developing their inner powers; but they live as if nobody else lived in the world but themselves. There is nothing more tragic than to find an individual bogged down in the length of life, devoid of the breadth.

9   The breadth of life is that dimension of life in which we are concerned about others. An individual has not started living until he can rise above the narrow confines of his individualistic concerns to the broader concerns of all humanity.

10   You remember one day a man came to Jesus and he raised some significant questions. Finally he got around to the question, "Who is my neighbor?" This could easily have been a very abstract question left in mid-air. But Jesus immediately pulled that question out of mid-air and placed it on a dangerous curve between Jerusalem and Jericho. He talked about a certain man who fell among thieves. Three men passed; two of them on the other side. And finally another man came and helped the injured man on the ground. He is known to us as the good Samaritan. Jesus says in substance that this is a great man. He was great because he could project the "I" into the "thou."

11   So often we say that the priest and the Levite were in a big hurry to get to some ecclesiastical meeting and so they did not have time. They were concerned about that. I would rather think of it another way. I can well imagine that they were quite afraid. You see, the Jericho road is a dangerous road, and the same thing that happened to the man who was robbed and beaten could have happened to them. So I imagine the first question that the priest and the Levite asked was this: "If I stop to help this man, what will happen to me?" Then the good Samaritan came by, and by the very nature of his concern reversed the question: "If I do not stop to help this man, what will happen to him?" And so this man was great because he had the mental equipment for a dangerous altruism°. He was great because he could surround the length of his life with the breadth of life. He was great not only because he had ascended to

certain heights of economic security, but because he could conde-scend° to the depths of human need.

All this has a great deal of bearing in our situation in the world 12
today. So often racial groups are concerned about the length of life, their economic privileged position, their social status. So often nations of the world are concerned about the length of life, perpetu-ating their nationalistic concerns, and their economic ends. May it not be that the problem in the world today is that individuals as well as nations have been overly concerned with the length of life, devoid of the breadth? But there is still something to remind us that we are interdependent°, that we are all involved in a single process, that we are all somehow caught in an inescapable network of mutu-ality. Therefore whatever affects one directly affects all indirectly.

As long as there is poverty in the world I can never be rich, even 13
if I have a billion dollars. As long as diseases are rampant and millions of people in this world cannot expect to live more than twenty-eight or thirty years, I can never be totally healthy even if I just got a good check-up at Mayo Clinic. I can never be what I ought to be until you are what you ought to be. This is the way our world is made. No individual or nation can stand out boasting of being independent. We are interdependent. So John Donne placed it in graphic terms when he affirmed, "No man is an island entire of itself. Every man is a piece of the continent, a part of the main." Then he goes on to say, "Any man's death diminishes me because I am involved in mankind, and therefore never send to know for whom the bell tolls; it tolls for thee." When we discover this, we master the second dimension of life.

Finally, there is a third dimension. Some people never get 14
beyond the first two dimensions of life. They master the first two. They develop their inner powers; they love humanity, but they stop right here. They end up with the feeling that man is the end of all things and that humanity is God. Philosophically or theologically, many of them would call themselves humanists°. They seek to live life without a sky. They find themselves bogged down on the hori-zontal plane without being integrated on the vertical plane. But if we are to live the complete life we must reach up and discover God. H.G. Wells was right: "The man who is not religious begins at nowhere and ends at nothing." Religion is like a mighty wind that breaks down doors and makes that possible and even easy which seems difficult and impossible.

In our modern world it is easy for us to forget this. We so often 15
find ourselves unconsciously neglecting this third dimension of life. Not that we go up and say, "Good-by, God, we are going to leave you now." But we become so involved in the things of this world that we are unconsciously carried away by the rushing tide of mate-

rialism° which leaves us treading in the confused waters of secularism°. We find ourselves living in what Professor Sorokin of Harvard called a sensate° civilization, believing that only those things which we can see and touch and to which we can apply our five senses have existence.

16   Something should remind us once more that the great things in this universe are things that we never see. You walk out at night and look up at the beautiful stars as they bedeck the heavens like swinging lanterns of eternity, and you think you can see all. Oh, no. You can never see the law of gravitation that holds them there. You walk around this vast campus and you probably have a great esthetic experience as I have had walking about and looking at the beautiful buildings, and you think you see all. Oh, no. You can never see the mind of the architect who drew the blueprint. You can never see the love and the faith and the hope of the individuals who made it so. You look at me and you think you see Martin Luther King. You don't see Martin Luther King; you see my body, but, you must understand, my body can't think, my body can't reason. You don't see the me that makes me me. You can never see my personality.

17   In a real sense everything that we see is a shadow cast by that which we do not see. Plato° was right: "The visible is a shadow cast by the invisible." And so God is still around. All of our new knowledge, all of our new developments, cannot diminish his being one iota°. These new advances have banished God neither from the microcosmic compass of the atom nor from the vast, unfathomable ranges of interstellar space. The more we learn about this universe, the more mysterious and awesome it becomes. God is still here.

18   So I say to you, seek God and discover him and make him a power in your life. Without him all of our efforts turn to ashes and our sunrises into darkest nights. Without him, life is a meaningless drama with the decisive scenes missing. But with him we are able to rise from the fatigue of despair to the buoyancy of hope. With him we are able to rise from the midnight of desperation to the daybreak of joy. St. Augustine was right—we were made for God and we will be restless until we find rest in him.

19   Love yourself, if that means rational, healthy, and moral self-interest. You are commanded to do that. That is the length of life. Love your neighbor as you love yourself. You are commanded to do that. That is the breadth of life. But never forget that there is a first and even greater commandment, "Love the Lord thy God with all thy heart and all thy soul and all thy mind." This is the height of life. And when you do this you live the complete life.

20   Thank God for John who, centuries ago, caught a vision of the new Jerusalem. God grant that those of us who still walk the road of life will catch this vision and decide to move forward to that city

of complete life in which the length and the breadth and the height are equal.

```
┌─────────────────┐
│                 │
└─────────────────┘
```

MARTIN LUTHER KING, JR.

Dr. Martin Luther King, Jr. (1929–1968), the American civil rights leader, was a Baptist minister who advocated racial equality and non-violent resistance against discriminatory laws and practices. He was awarded the Nobel Prize for Peace in 1964. In 1968, he was assassinated in Memphis, Tennessee.

Words and Meanings

Paragraph

John of Patmos:	Christian saint, author of the book of Revelation	1
the book of Revelation:	last book of the New Testament, concerned with the end of the world and other mysteries	2
enigma:	puzzle, mystery	
apocalyptic:	concerned with the Apocalypse, the last day	
abyss:	bottomless pit, hell	6
fatalism:	belief that a predetermined fate rules our lives	
altruism:	selfless concern for others	11
condescend:	stoop, bend down to	
interdependent:	dependent on each other	12
humanists:	people interested in human nature and concerns	14
materialism:	concern only for the goods of this world	15
secularism:	social and non-religious concern for the world	
sensate:	perceived by the senses	
Plato:	ancient Greek philosopher, idealist	17
iota:	smallest particle	

Structure and Strategy

1. What ANALOGY are paragraphs 1 and 2 based on? What analogy is introduced in paragraph 4?
2. Identify King's thesis statement. What question of division does it answer? (See the introduction to this unit.)
3. What is the function of paragraph 3? How does King begin to develop his three points in this paragraph?
4. Identify the paragraphs that develop each of the three dimensions of life. In what ORDER has King arranged his points?

5. How does paragraph 8 contribute to COHERENCE? Paragraphs 9 and 14?
6. Paragraphs 19 and 20 form the conclusion of this piece. What is the function of paragraph 20? How does it round off or conclude the essay effectively?
7. Writers and speakers often use PARALLEL STRUCTURE to emphasize key ideas. King's thesis statement is, of course, an example of parallelism, but there are other examples. Identify parallel structures in paragraphs 7 and 18. What do they emphasize? How effective are they? (Hint: read the paragraphs aloud.)

Content and Purpose

1. King originally wrote "Dimensions" as a speech. As you read through the piece, what clues can you find that indicate it was designed to be heard rather than read?
2. King regards the length of life as "selfish," but, nevertheless, the basis of the other dimensions of life. How does King convince the reader that this "selfishness" is a positive rather than a negative quality?
3. What is a parable? What is the purpose of the parable in paragraphs 11 and 12?
4. King's purpose in this piece is to demonstrate that the complete life is one in which the personal, social, and spiritual dimensions are integrated. Study King's development of one of these dimensions and show how he has carefully selected his examples to reinforce his thesis.

Suggestions for Writing

1. Write an essay of division in which you analyze your own vision of the complete life. What will bring you happiness and satisfaction?
2. Though it lasted only 39 years, King's own life fulfilled the dimensions of a "complete life." After doing some research, write a short paper describing his accomplishments.
3. Think of someone you know or have read about and write a paper explaining how that person's life satisfies King's criteria for completeness.

Additional Suggestions for Writing: Division and Classification

Use division or classification, whichever is appropriate, to analyze one of the topics below into its component parts, or characteristics, or kinds. Write a thesis statement based on your analysis and then develop it into a detailed, interesting essay.

part-time jobs
marriages
films
pop singers
role-playing games
popular novels
radio stations
TV game shows
families
dreams
college students
cameras

advice
morality
friendship
an unforgettable event
parenting
a winning team
a short story, poem, or play
shopping malls
a religious or social ritual (such as a
   wedding, funeral, bar mitzvah,
   birthday celebration)

U N I T

Comparison and Contrast: Explaining Similarities and Differences

What? The Definition

Why does a person choose to go to college rather than find a full-time job? How does that same person choose between attending Douglas College and B.C. Institute of Technology in Vancouver, or between Laurentian University and the Haileybury School of Mines in Sudbury? Which Canadian hockey team deserves the title of dynasty: the Toronto Maple Leafs or the Montreal Canadiens? Who will be remembered as the better prime minister: Pierre Trudeau or Brian Mulroney? What's for lunch: chicken wings and potato skins, or a plate of nachos and a wet burrito? Every day of our lives, we are called upon to make choices, to evaluate alternatives. Sometimes, as in the "what's-for-lunch?" question, the decision may have few consequences (other than indigestion). But sometimes our decisions have far-reaching effects, as in the college-or-job dilemma. Fortunately, our minds quite naturally work in a way that helps us to assess the options and to choose between the alternatives.

First, we consider what the two subjects we are comparing have in common; in other words, how are they alike? The Leafs and the Canadiens both skate, shoot, and occasionally score, and both teams have illustrious pasts. Then we consider how the two teams are different; in other words, what distinguishes one from the other? Montreal has good scouting, consistent coaching, and solid ownership. The Leafs? Well, perhaps the less said, the better.

Pointing out similarities is called **comparing**; pointing out differences is called **contrasting**. When we assess both similarities and differences, we are engaging in **comparison and contrast**. Often, however, people use the term "comparison" to mean comparing, or contrasting, or both. In this chapter, we will use *comparison* to cover all three approaches.

Why? The Purpose

Comparison is a natural mental process; it's something we do, consciously or unconsciously, all the time. In writing, we use comparison to answer these questions:

1. What are the main similarities between S_1 and S_2?
2. What are the main differences between S_1 and S_2?
3. What are the main similarities and differences between S_1 and S_2?

Using such a pattern in written communication can be useful in several ways. First, an essay or report structured to compare various items can be highly informative. It can explain two subjects clearly by putting them alongside each other. Second, a comparison paper can evaluate as well as inform. It can assess the relative merits of two subjects and provide reasons on which a reader can base a judgment, or reasons to explain the writer's preference for one item over the other.

In school, you use the comparison pattern for both purposes: to *inform* and to *evaluate*. An exam may ask, "What similarities and differences are there between analog and digital computers?" A research paper, on the other hand, may require you to focus on the parallels and divergences between health-insurance plans in Ontario and Alberta, while a test question may take the comparison a step further by requiring you to evaluate the merits of the two health-care plans. Your field placement, for instance, may require a judgment as to the overall competence of two engineering firms. Each case calls for a *comparison*. It serves as the structural principle of your exam answer, your paper, or your report.

How? The Technique

Organizing a paper according to the principle of comparison isn't difficult if you approach the task by asking three questions. First: are the two items really comparable? Second: what are the terms of comparison? Third: what is the most appropriate pattern of organization to use?

Comparing Wayne Gretzky to Dolly Parton has, at first glance, at least comic potential. It's true they are both highly paid entertainers. But there is no sustained or significant basis for drawing a comparison between them because their talents are just too different. The writer of a comparison, then, must be sure that a meaningful similarity exists between the two subjects. They must have something *significant* in common. For instance, Wayne Gretzky could be compared in an interesting manner to another hockey legend like Bobby Orr. Dolly Parton would best be compared to another high-camp vamp of the silver screen—Mae West, perhaps—or another country singer such as k.d. lang.

After deciding that your two subjects are comparable in a meaningful way, you should then carefully consider the terms of the comparison. If, for instance, you were asked to assess two engineering firms, it would make little sense to compare the management structure and computer systems of one firm to the washrooms and cafeteria food of the other. Resemblances and differences must be assessed in the same terms or categories. Your report should be organized to assess both firms in identical terms: management structure, computer systems, and employee facilities, for example.

Your final step is to decide on an appropriate structure for your comparison. There are two effective patterns to choose from: subject-by-subject and point-by-point. Like pineapples, comparison papers can be processed into *chunks* or *slices*. (Pineapples also come crushed, but this form is precisely what you're trying to avoid.)

Structuring a comparison according to the *chunk* pattern involves separating the two subjects and discussing each one separately, under the headings or categories you've chosen to consider. If you were asked, for example, to compare the novel and film versions of Mordecai Richler's *The Apprenticeship of Duddy Kravitz*, you might decide to focus your analysis on the characters, the setting, and the plot of the two versions. You would first discuss the novel in terms of these three points, then you would do the same for the film. Here is a sample chunk outline for such an essay:

Paragraph 1   Introduction and thesis statement
Paragraph 2   S₁ Novel
                        a. characters in the novel

b. setting of the novel

c. plot of the novel

Paragraph 3 S_2 Film

a. characters in the film

b. setting of the film

c. plot of the film

Paragraph 4   Conclusion summarizing the similarities and differences and possibly stating your preference

The chunk pattern does not rule out a discussion of the two subjects in the same paragraph. In this example, particularly in your analysis of the film, some mention of the novel might be necessary. However, the overall structure of the chunk comparison should communicate the essentials about Subject 1, then communicate the essentials about Subject 2.

The chunk style works best with fairly short papers (essay questions on exams, for instance) where the reader does not have to remember many intricate details about Subject 1 while trying to assimilate the details of Subject 2.

Structuring a comparison according to the *slice* pattern involves setting out the terms or categories of comparison, then discussing both subjects under each category heading. The *Duddy Kravitz* essay structured in slices could communicate the same information as the chunked paper, yet its shape and outline would be quite different:

Paragraph 1   Introduction and thesis statement

Paragraph 2   Characters

S_1 in the novel

S_2 in the film

Paragraph 3   Setting

S_1 in the novel

S_2 in the film

Paragraph 4   Plot

S_1 in the novel

S_2 in the film

Paragraph 5   Conclusion with, perhaps, a statement of your preference

The slice pattern makes the resemblances and differences between the two subjects more readily apparent to the reader. It's the type of structure that is ideally suited to longer reports and papers, where the terms of comparison are complex and demand high reader recall.

Because comparing and contrasting is a natural human thought process, organizing written communication in this pattern is not very difficult. It does, however, require clear thinking and preparation. Before you even begin to write, you need to study the subjects themselves, decide on the terms of comparison, and choose the appropriate structure.

A good thesis statement is essential to a well-written comparison paper (as it is, indeed, to any piece of writing). Because comparison involves considering two different items in terms of several aspects, writing the thesis statement presents an interesting challenge.

Here are three models for you to choose from in drafting thesis statements for comparison papers.

> S_1 and S_2 can be compared in terms of a, b, and c.

Example: Trudeau and Mulroney can be compared in terms of their power bases, religious backgrounds, and family ties.

> S_1 and S_2 can be contrasted in terms of a, b, and c.

Example: College and university can be contrasted in terms of cost, instruction, and orientation.

> Although S_1 and S_2 are different in terms of a, b, and c, they are alike in terms of d.

Example: Although Canada and Scotland are different in terms of size, geography, and culture, they are alike in terms of their relationship with their southern neighbours.

Be prepared to spend time shaping and perfecting your thesis statement. The effort you invest at this stage will pay off by providing a solid framework on which you can construct and then communicate what it is you want to say.

Here is a comparison essay that illustrates the slice pattern of organization, based on the second example above.

College or University?

Introduction
(makes use of
a contrast)

In the United States, the word "college" is used to designate all formal education that takes place after high school. Whether people attend a local two-year junior college or a university as re-

Thesis statement ⟶

First point (developed with examples and statistics)

Second point (again, note the well-chosen examples)

nowned as Harvard, they are described as "going to college." In Canada, however, the word "college" is contrasted with the word "university." Here, "going to college" denotes a different educational experience from that of "going to university." The college experience and the university experience in Canada can be contrasted in terms of cost, instruction, and orientation.

A college education is less costly than a university education, partly because it takes less time to complete. For instance, a student can complete an engineering technology program at most community colleges in three years; the technician's program takes only two. An engineering degree from a university requires an investment of four years, or in some cases even five, if the particular institution offers a co-op program. Each extra year in school costs the student money in lost wages as well as in living expenses and tuition. Tuition is, of course, another reason for the difference in cost. By and large, university fees are about three times as high as those of a college. Although statistics indicate that the average university graduate earns, over a lifetime, approximately twice as much as the average college graduate, going to university costs considerably more than going to a community college.

The methods of instruction are different at university and college. At many universities, especially in the first two years, students attend large lecture classes for their introductory courses. They may participate in smaller seminar groups led by graduate students, yet the fundamentals of the undergraduate curriculum, whether in mathematics, psychology, or literature, are often presented in classes containing hundreds of people. Colleges offer a more "hands-on" approach and smaller-group interaction between students and instructors. Students who require psychology to complete a correctional worker program, for instance, will probably find themselves in a small class in which dialogue between students and teacher is encouraged.

The transition here connects the first and second points to the third point — the topic of this paragraph

➤ The above example points to the third and most important difference between university and college: their orientation toward career learning. Though professional studies—those aimed at a particular career—may be part of a university education, the curriculum is largely based on theoretical learning—learning for its own sake. Often a student must complete postgraduate work in order to qualify for a particular profession, such as law, teaching, or medicine. Universities aim at providing students with a background in arts, sciences, and languages in addition to their chosen discipline. Colleges, on the other hand, are usually oriented toward providing a career education that will prepare students for jobs in such fields as data processing, recreation leadership, or fashion design. Hence, while there is an element of general education in most college programs, much of the learning is practical and job-specific.

Conclusion (restates the thesis in different words)

Canadian students interested in post-secondary education thus have an important choice to make. After considering the differences in time and cost and weighing the advantages of the broader academic study offered by a university as opposed to the more career-specific training provided by a college, they can decide which kind of

institution best suits their needs, apti-
tudes, and goals.

Two Talk-Show Kings and a Tale of Two Countries

RICK GROEN

sk who reigns as the king of the talk show   1
in the United States, and no one will pause: Johnny Carson. Ask
who holds the same title in Canada, and the pause may be longer,
but the consensus will be just as strong: Peter Gzowski. Carson and
Gzowski, Gzowski and Carson—somehow even the names sound
dissonant°, the one pure white-bread, the other a dark loaf of consonants. But let's stop and examine. If the Meech debate is just another
(albeit intense) chapter in our interrogative saga—aren't we always
wondering Whither Canada?, Why Canada?, Who Canada?—perhaps a comparative peek at these media icons° may offer us a small
identifying clue. This, then, is not just a story of two talk *meisters*°,
it's a tale of two countries.

First, the similarities—there are more than you might think. Both   2
men have developed strong public personalities, carefully nurtured
and curiously alike. Sharing a small-town heritage (Lincoln in
Nebraska, Galt in Ontario), they exude the same kind of boyish
charm, a mix of ingenuous° wonder and old-fashioned virtue spiced
with a likeable dab of nervous idiosyncracy°—a slight tic for one, a
mild stammer for the other.

It's a cultivated personality that allows them to forge an intimate   3
rapport° with their audience. Yet with intimacy comes responsibility,
because each man is a national figure in more than mere celebrity;
he is seen by others (maybe even by himself) to embody the very
soul of his country—a heavier burden here than there.

Which brings us to the differences. To grasp them is to glimpse   4
the distinction not only between the men but also between the
national characters they've come to embody. The list is long, and
speaks quietly for itself.

One weaves his intimate magic in the flamboyant° medium of   5 commercial television, the other in the earnest° medium of public radio. One is based on the coast, the other in the centre. One works at night (The Tonight Show) and comes into our bedroom, the other works in the morning (Morningside) and comes into our kitchen.

6   One spends a lot of time talking to celebrities and actors; the other spends a lot of time talking to the Canadian version of celebrities and actors: journalists and politicians. One strives mainly to entertain, but is mighty proud of those moments when he happens to inform (an interview with Carl Sagan); the other strives mainly to inform, but is mighty proud of those moments when he happens to entertain (a chat with the best darn fiddler in Acadia).

7   One has guests, who, if they appear frequently enough, become "guest-hosts"; the other has visitors, who, if they visit frequently enough, become "friends of Morningside." One rigorously° draws his guests from the two poles of his country—New York and L.A.; the other rigorously draws his visitors from every region of his country and every part of the world.

8   One occasionally talks to "just plain folks" from the heartland, who, being plain, must be freakish—the fat lady from Peoria with the planet's biggest ball of yarn; the other regularly talks to just plain folks from the regions, who, being plain, must be wise—the socially-perceptive fishermen from Inuvik.

9   One is anti-intellectual, a comedian first and a talker second; the other is cerebral°, a writer first and a talker second. One is filthy rich and has books written about him; the other is not filthy rich and writes books himself, sometimes about himself, sometimes about the show. (The latter, essentially transcriptions of selected interviews, are a unique hybrid—not quite literature, not quite radio. "Readio," perhaps.)

10   One is insular°, the other isn't. One has a chortling toadie for a sidekick, the other doesn't. One is called Johnny, the other is not called Petie. One airs repeats and titles them The Best Of Carson; the other airs repeats and titles them The Best Of Morningside. One is known to almost everyone in Canada; the other is known to almost no one in the United States.

11   Carson and Gzowski, Gzowski and Carson, *vive la différence.* The other would make an honest stab at pronouncing that phrase properly; the one wouldn't bother.

RICK GROEN

Rick Groen (b. 1947) has a Master's degree in English literature from the University of Toronto and is a critic for the Arts section of the *Globe and Mail.*

Words and Meanings

Paragraph

dissonant:	clashing, not in harmony	1
icon:	image (usually an object of worship)	
meister:	master practitioner	
ingenuous:	straightforward, honest, naïve	2
idiosyncracy:	peculiarity of character, quirk	
rapport:	relationship, bond	3
flamboyant:	highly colourful, attention-getting	5
earnest:	serious, sincere	
rigorously:	strictly, deliberately	7
cerebral:	intellectual	9
insular:	narrow, limited	10

Structure and Strategy

1. Is this essay organized according to the "chunk" or the "slice" method? (See the introduction to this unit.) Why do you think the author chose this pattern of organization for this piece?
2. Groen uses PARALLELISM and repetition to reinforce the contrast between Carson ("the one") and Gzowski ("the other"). Given the pattern the author establishes in paragraphs 5 through 10, what makes paragraph 11 a particularly effective conclusion?
3. What METAPHOR does the author use in paragraph 1? How is it effective in communicating the difference between both the two talk-show hosts and their two countries?

Content and Purpose

1. Groen's essay does not contain an explicit thesis statement. Can you summarize its content in a single sentence?
2. In comparing and contrasting Carson and Gzowski, Groen creates a larger contrast. Besides the two talk-show hosts, what differences is he exploring in the article?
3. Identify three of the similarities that the author develops between Carson and Gzowski and their respective countries.
4. The contrasts identified between Carson and Gzowski include differences in medium, geographical base, audience, and guests (see paragraphs 5 and 6). But the author also points to

a significant difference in purpose. What is this difference between Carson's and Gzowski's goals?

5. Paragraph 8 points out that the two talk-show hosts deal very differently with the "just plain folks" who occasionally appear on their shows. What is the author suggesting about the two men? What is he suggesting this difference says about their countries' cultures?

6. What contrasts between Canada and the United States does the author identify in paragraphs 9 through 11?

Suggestions for Writing

1. Compare and/or contrast two examples of American and Canadian media: television shows, movies, or magazines. Do Canadians always copy American formulas, or do they add something of their own?

2. Read Peter Gzowski's "People and Their Machines and Vice Versa" and listen to a few interviews on his CBC radio show, "Morningside." Then write a short essay describing Gzowski's character. What makes him a "typical Canadian"?

People and Their Machines and Vice Versa

PETER GZOWSKI

1   If I have remembered my own history correctly, it is exactly thirty years ago this week that I arrived in Timmins, Ontario, to begin my life as a newspaperman. Almost every day for those thirty years, I have opened my working procedures the same way. I have cranked a piece of paper into my typewriter, banged out what newspapermen call a slug at the top of the page, usually followed, for reasons I don't know but by a habit I can't break, by the page number typed four or five times, and started pounding away with as many fingers as seemed to fit. Like most old newspapermen, I am as fast as a Gatling gun° at my machine, and almost as noisy. I make mistakes—which is like saying Wayne

Gretzky gets scoring points—but I strike them out: xxxxxxx or, if I'm really flying, mnmnmnmnmnmn, *m* with the right forefinger, *n* with the left. Afterward, I go over what I've done with the heaviest pencil I can find, changing a word here, a phrase there. I cross out some more, with a bold, black stroke and a flourishing delete sign. I add. Sometimes I make what one of my editors called chicken tracks from the place I had the first thought out into the margin. Out there, I create anew. I scribble up into the bare space at the top, up by the stammering page numbers, and on good days, when my juices are flowing and the ghost of Maxwell Perkins° is looking over my shoulder, I carry on from there, turning the page under my pencil, down the outer edges, filling the bottom and off, off into virgin territories, leaving my inky spoor° behind me. When I am pleased with what I have done, or when the chicken tracks get too dense to follow, I put a new page in the typewriter and start again. This is not the way anyone taught me to work. But it is the way I have done things. It has served me through five books, more magazine articles than you could shake an art director's ruler at and enough newspaper pieces to line the cage of every eagle that ever flew.

But no more. I am a word-processor man now, or trying to   2 become one. I made the change at the end of this summer. The words I am reading to you now first appeared to my eye etched in green on a dark screen. Or, rather, some *version* of the words I am reading to you now so appeared. "Green," for instance, was "gereen," or perhaps "jereen," until I danced my cursor around the screen (the "screeen?") and obliterated the extra *e*. "Etched," too, is probably the wrong word. The process by which these words appear is too sophisticated for my manually operated mind, and I no more understand it than I understand what really happens when I turn on the ignition of my car. All I know, in fact, are two things: one, I can do it. If I take my time, and think my way through such delicate differences as that between the "control" key and the shift lock, and resist the urge to hit the space bar (which makes sense to me) and instead hit a simultaneous "control" and *d* (which doesn't) when I want to move my little cursor over one notch, I can, however painstakingly, make the words come out in prose. That's one. Two is that I hate doing it. Over the years, the relationship I have built up with my various manuals° is an emotional one. I pound them and they respond, as the Steinway° responded to Glenn Gould. I knew I was working because I could hear it, and the measure of what I had accomplished in a working day was often the pile of out-takes that grew in my wastepaper basket, like tailings at a mine. Now, I work silently. I wrote what you are hearing now while my daughter slept in the next room. This was convenient for Alison, but it did not seem to me to be what I have always done for a living.

It neither sounded nor felt like *writing*. God, it seems to me, no more meant words to appear in fluorescent electronic letters than he meant pool tables to be pink, or golf balls orange.

☐

PETER GZOWSKI

Peter Gzowski, broadcaster and journalist, was born in Toronto in 1934 but was raised in Galt, Ont. He is the regular host of the CBC radio program "Morningside" and the author or editor of numerous books, including *Spring Tonic* and *The Game of Our Lives*, a study of hockey.

Words and Meanings

Paragraph

1　Gatling gun:　　　　　early form of machine gun
　Maxwell Perkins:　　　well-known New York book editor
　spoor:　　　　　　　　track or scent of an animal

2　manuals:　　　　　　　manually operated (non-electric) typewriters
　Steinway:　　　　　　　make of concert piano

Structure and Strategy

1. First review the different patterns for comparison and contrast thesis statements in the introduction to this unit and then write a thesis statement for Gzowski's essay.
2. Has Gzowski used the *slice* or *chunk* method to organize his essay?
3. What effective ALLUSIONS and FIGURES OF SPEECH has Gzowski used in paragraph 1?
4. How has Gzowski achieved TRANSITION between paragraphs 1 and 2? Why is the first sentence of paragraph 2 so short?
5. How does the contrast in DICTION in paragraphs 1 and 2 help reinforce Gzowski's thesis?
6. Gzowski uses two particularly effective comparisons in paragraph 2. What are they, and why are they appropriate to convey his attitude toward writing?

Content and Purpose

1. What are the implications of the title? How does the title prepare the reader for Gzowski's thesis?
2. What is the essential difference, according to Gzowski, between composing at a typewriter and composing on a word processor?
3. Why does Gzowski make the following revelation about himself and his method of writing: "This is not the way anyone taught

me to work. But it is the way I have done things. It has served me through five books. . . ."? Is he just bragging, or does the statement communicate something the reader needs to know?

Suggestions for Writing

1. Write thesis statements comparing and/or contrasting the following: two cars, two sports, two fashion designers, two celebrities, two political leaders, two teachers.
2. Compare and/or contrast an old and a new way of performing a task with which you are familiar, such as playing a game, operating a machine, raising a child, or preparing a meal.

If You Drop a Stone . . .

HUGH MACLENNAN

If you drop a stone into the ocean the impact is as great as if you drop it into a farmer's pond. The difference is that the ocean doesn't seem to care. It swallows the stone and rolls on. But the pond, if the stone is large enough, breaks into waves and ripples that cover its surface and are audible in every cranny along its banks.

So it is with life in a metropolis and life in a small town. It takes a colossal event to affect a city. After the bombing of Hamburg in which eighty thousand people were killed, the city was functioning within a few days. Grief did not paralyse it because, to the survivors, most of the casualties were people they had never met. But a single murder can convulse a small town for the reason that in such a community people care who lives and who dies. They care because they know each other. All knowledge is relative to our capacity to grasp its details, and no matter what the communists and industrial organizers may say, no man can think humanly if he thinks in terms of masses. In the small town, and not in the metropolis, human life is understood in fundamental terms.

Because I grew up in a smallish town, this idea struck me with the force of a shock the first time I saw a play in London about

London life. I marvelled how any audience could believe in it. Apparently, I thought, Londoners don't know each other and the playwright has taken advantage of their ignorance. A play as superficial as this, I said to myself when I left the theatre, could never succeed in Halifax.

4   My youthful reaction was naïve°, but it was not stupid. I did not know then, as I have learned since, that practically no creative ideas have ever originated in a megalopolis°. The prelude° to creation, as every parent knows, is intimacy. I had come straight to London from an intimate town, and what we knew about each other in that town could have kept a Balzac° supplied with material for life. Small-town gossip may be notorious, but by no means all of it is malicious°. It has one virtue which its metropolitan imitators, the newspapers, cannot claim. Most of it has personal significance for the people who listen to it.

5   We knew in our town, for example, and we knew in detail, how our wealthiest citizens had made their money. Although we did not know a neurosis° from a psychosis°, we understood, and made allowances for, the family conditions which caused one man to be aggressive and another subservient, one woman to be charming and another to be a shrew°. We had a sixth sense which the more intelligent city-dwellers lack—a sense of time. We knew that a family, like Rome, is not built in a day.

6   We would look at one family and remember hearing about the grandfather, now dead, who used to sit in his galluses° on a stool outside the livery stable chewing a straw and occasionally reaching up with the thumb of his left hand to scratch his head. It had been a matter of interested speculation whether he scratched because he was nervous or because he was lousy°. The father, still with us, was a middle-aged man doing fairly well in a hardware business. He never scratched his head, but it was noticed that he had a curious habit of stopping suddenly while walking down the street to lift the right leg of his trousers and scratch the back of his calf. As the hardware merchant was certainly not lousy, this gesture was assumed to be hereditary; as such, it cleared the grandfather's reputation from all suspicion of uncleanliness. The merchant's son raised the family one notch higher. He went to college, did well, and now was laying the foundations of a solid career in the administration in Ottawa. Perhaps he might even rise to cabinet rank and make us all proud, for rumour had it that the Prime Minister's eye was on him. Incidentally, he was never seen to scratch himself at all.

7   This kind of small-town knowledge may seem petty, but the sum of it is vast. Through a multitude of intimate details people come to know the best and the worst about each other, and concealment of

character is impossible over a lifetime. A ruthless° or a cunning° man can ride roughshod° over his neighbours and cop° most of the money in the place. In every small town there are always a few who try this, and at least one who succeeds. They make bad bargains, for they spend the rest of their days knowing exactly what their neighbours think and say about them. In the small town, since everyone knows the sins of everyone else, each man must live as best he can with the knowledge that his faults and weaknesses are part of the lore of the whole community. That is what I mean by saying that in a small town people know life as it really is. That is why Halifax or Peterborough has a better chance of producing a Balzac than London or New York, and why a little place like Bermuda, where the stakes are really high, could produce a second Shakespeare if some Bermudian had the genius and the nerve to write as Shakespeare did.

But for the past two hundred years the small towns have failed 8 in what should be their mission, which is the illumination of life. Only to a very small extent has their unrivalled knowledge of life been used for artistic purposes. They have given the world nearly all its famous writers and artists, but the moment their gifted children are ready to produce they are compelled to leave home and emigrate to the city. "Appearances must be maintained," a small-town friend said to me not long ago; "otherwise life couldn't go on." But to maintain appearances is the one thing no creative artist can ever do. If he tries, his work shows as much liveliness and veracity° as the average obituary column. So, for freedom's sake, he moves to the big city and there he tends to stay. That is why for the past two hundred years art has always been associated in people's minds with the life of the metropolis.

But the metropolis—London, Paris, New York, Rome—does not 9 nurture° art. It merely gives the immigrant artist or writer freedom to paint or write as he pleases. And it exacts a bitter price for this freedom, the loss of the small-town intimacy from which all life-knowledge derives. That is why so many writers over the past two hundred years have done their best work before they were forty. In their early years in the big city, they availed themselves of the freedom it offered to be themselves. They wrote, generally, of the life they had lived in their native regions. But as they grew older they inevitably consumed their vital material, and in middle age they tended to run dry. The metropolis which was now their home failed to provide them with the life-giving material they required.

The very freedom the big city grants is based on a kind of 10 indifference to the individual, an indifference that springs from ignorance. The city has no real gossip. In the city a man is a name or a career, a unit in a factory or the occupant of an office desk.

There is no universal folk-memory of the grandfather who scratched his head or the son who hoisted his trouser to scratch the back of his leg. The emotional upheavals which shatter families are swallowed up by the city as the ocean swallowed the *Titanic*, and to the onlooking artist they seem almost as meaningless as traffic accidents because he cannot possibly know, much less feel, the forces which caused them.

11   When modern writers attempt to use metropolitan life as the material for tragedy their work is usually cold and dry. This has been especially notable in the English-speaking centres of London and New York. It is true that Dickens was a Londoner; it is equally true that he saw only the surface of things. As for New York, in the whole of American literature not a single great book has been based on its life.

12   How could it be? In New York, who cares who commits suicide? The crowds massed in the street to see if the stranger will jump from the skyscraper window are not interested in the man, because they do not know him. They are interested only in the spectacle. In New York, who cares who cheats whom? Or who survives through endurance? Or who, by a denial of himself, wins spiritual greatness? This does not imply that New York is less noble than a small town. It merely implies that in terms of art it is too large for any individual artist to handle.

13   Far different was the situation in the days when no cities were immense and a few small or medium-sized towns were the life-centres of a whole people. Ancient Athens at the height of her glory had a voting list somewhat smaller than that of modern Halifax. But she had a spirit which Halifax and all modern smallish towns entirely lack—she preferred excitement to caution and greatness to respectability. She invented tragic and comic drama, the art of history, and the democratic method of government. All these stupendous inventions arose out of her own experience. The characters in her great comedies were living Athenian citizens, and when Socrates° was satirized in *The Clouds* by Aristophanes he rose in the theatre so that everyone would know that he was enjoying the play, too. Plato's° *Republic* had its origin in a dinner party which assembled after a late-afternoon walk just as casually as Joe Smith gets together his cronies for a poker game by the simple expedient of walking the length of the main street from the barber shop to the Maple Leaf Hotel.

14   It has always been the same—without intimacy, there can be no creation. Republican Rome was a relatively small town. Florence, Genoa, Venice, and Pisa, in the days of their glory, were about a quarter the size of Ottawa. In Shakespeare's London everyone who mattered knew everyone else, and we can be pretty certain that the

characters who live in Shakespeare's plays were modelled on people the playwright knew personally or had heard about from the intimate gossip of others who did.

But these wonderful small towns had one thing in common   15 besides the intimate knowledge of life which all small towns share. It never occurred to them that their knowledge should be repressed° "in order that life might go on." There was no conspiracy of silence when it came to writing books and plays. The citizens were not afraid of gossip. In such communities a man like Mackenzie King could never have become Prime Minister, nor would a generation of public servants have admired his theory that a leader should veil his thoughts in the stuffiest language possible lest the public become sufficiently interested to make an effort to find out what he was talking about.

It seems to me, thinking along these lines, that the cultural   16 future of Canada is opposed only by fear of what the neighbours will say. For Canada, by and large, is still a nation of small towns. Toronto, for all its sprawling size, has a small-town psychology. So, when it comes down to it, does Montreal; in this city we still have a great deal of the intimate small-town knowledge of life which New York and London lack. It has made us shrewder than we realize. We know, for example, that our present material prosperity does not mean, in itself, that we are a great country. We know intuitively° that we will become great only when we translate our force and knowledge into spiritual and artistic terms. Then, and only then, will it matter to mankind whether Canada has existed or not.

```
┌─────────────────────┐
│                     │
│                     │
└─────────────────────┘
```

HUGH MACLENNAN

Hugh MacLennan (1907–1990), the essayist and novelist, was born in Glace Bay, N.S. He won five Governor General's awards for his writing. Among his many publications are *Barometer Rising, Return of the Sphinx, The Watch that Ends the Night, The Rivers of Canada,* and *Voices in Time.*

Words and Meanings

Paragraph

naïve:	unsophisticated, inexperienced	4
megalopolis:	huge city	
prelude:	condition that precedes, or comes before	
Balzac:	Honoré de Balzac, great nineteenth-century French novelist	
malicious:	evil-minded, harmful	

5	neurosis:	an emotional disorder; anxiety
	psychosis:	a serious mental illness
	shrew:	nagging, scolding woman
6	galluses:	suspenders
	lousy:	infested with lice (plural of louse)
7	ruthless:	without pity
	cunning:	shrewd, clever
	ride roughshod over:	show no consideration for
	cop:	grab (slang)
8	veracity:	truthfulness
9	nurture:	nourish, provide environment in which something can grow
13	Socrates:	ancient Greek philosopher
	Plato:	ancient Greek philosopher, student of Socrates
15	repressed:	silenced, not expressed
16	intuitively:	instinctively, without thinking about it

Structure and Strategy

1. With what ANALOGY does MacLennan introduce his subject?
2. What is the topic sentence of paragraph 2, and how does Mac-Lennan use a contrast to develop it?
3. Where does MacLennan state his thesis?
4. Has MacLennan used the *chunk* or *slice* method of organizing his material? (See the introduction to this unit.)
5. What is the function of paragraphs 5, 6, and 7? What point do they develop?
6. What concluding strategy does MacLennan use in paragraph 16? Is it effective?

Content and Purpose

1. MacLennan believes that "practically no creative ideas have ever originated in a megalopolis." Do you agree? Or can you cite examples to disprove his thesis?
2. Why does MacLennan feel that small-town dwellers develop "a sense of time" that city dwellers lack?
3. What are the reasons underlying MacLennan's belief that the big cities have failed to produce great art?
4. According to MacLennan, is Canada likely to produce great artists? Why or why not?

Suggestions for Writing

1. Write a short paper using the *chunk* method of organization (see
    the introduction to this unit) in which you compare high school
    and college. You may want to adapt some of MacLennan's ideas:
    think of the high school as a small town and college as a big
    city.
2. Write a paper, using either the *chunk* or the *slice* method of
    organization, that compares two different ways of life: rural and
    urban, single and married; living with and without children, or
    with and without a strong religious belief.

Love and Lust

HENRY FAIRLIE

Lust is not interested in its partners, but   1
only in the gratification of its own craving: not even in the satisfaction of our whole natures, but in the appeasement merely of an
appetite which we are unable to subdue. It is therefore a form of
self-subjection; in fact of self-emptying. The sign it wears is: "This
property is vacant." Anyone may take possession of it for a while.
Lustful people may think that they can choose a partner at will for
sexual gratification. But they do not really choose; they accept what
is available. Lust accepts any partner for a momentary service; anyone may squat in its groin.

Love has meaning only insofar as it includes the idea of its   2
continuance. Even what we rather glibly° call a love affair, if it comes
to an end, may continue as a memory that is pleasing in our lives,
and we can still renew the sense of privilege and reward of having
been allowed to know someone with such intimacy and sharing.
But Lust dies at the next dawn and, when it returns in the evening,
to search where it may, it is with its own past erased. Love wants
to enjoy in other ways the human being whom it has enjoyed
in bed. But in the morning Lust is always furtive. It dresses as
mechanically as it undressed, and heads straight for the door, to
return to its own solitude. Like all the sins, it makes us solitary. It is
a self-abdication° at the very heart of one's own being, of our need
and ability to give and receive.

3   Love is involvement as well as continuance; but Lust will not get involved. This is one of the forms in which we may see it today. If people now engage in indiscriminate° and short-lived relationships more than in the past, it is not really for some exquisite sexual pleasure that is thus gained, but because they refuse to become involved and to meet the demands that love makes. They are asking for little more than servicing, such as they might get at a gas station. The fact that it may go to bed with a lot of people is less its offense than the fact that it goes to bed with people for whom it does not care. The characteristic of the "singles" today is not the sexual freedom they supposedly enjoy, but the fact that this freedom is a deception. They are free with only a fraction of their natures. The full array of human emotions is hardly involved. The "singles bar" does not have an obnoxious° odor because its clients, before the night is over, may hop into bed with someone whom they have just met, but because they do not even consider that, beyond the morning, either of them may care for the other. As they have made deserts of themselves, so they make deserts of their beds. This is the sin of Lust: just as it dries up human beings, so it dries up human relationships. The word that comes to mind, when one thinks of it, is that it is parched. Everyone in a "singles bar" seems to have lost moisture, and this is peculiarly the accomplishment of Lust, to make the flesh seem parched, to deprive it of all real dewiness, shrivelling it to no more than a husk.

┌─────────────────────────┐
│   │
└─────────────────────────┘

HENRY FAIRLIE

Henry Fairlie, political correspondent and writer, was born in England in 1924 and has lived in the United States since 1966. He has contributed to *Punch*, the *New Statesman*, and *The New Yorker*. His books include *The Spoiled Child of the Western World* and *The Seven Deadly Sins Today*.

Words and Meanings

Paragraph

2	glibly:	smoothly, thoughtlessly
	self-abdication:	renunciation, rejection
3	indiscriminate:	promiscuous
	obnoxious:	unpleasant, foul

Structure and Strategy

1.   Has Fairlie structured his essay in *chunks* or in *slices*? (See the introduction to this unit.)

2. What words does Fairlie choose to show how repugnant lust is? Find some examples of the effective use of DICTION in paragraph 1.
3. How does Fairlie's use of PERSONIFICATION contribute to the effect of his essay?
4. How does Fairlie effectively conclude his essay? (See ANALOGY.)

Content and Purpose

1. What are the major differences between love and lust that Fairlie identifies?
2. Why does Fairlie regard lust as selfish?
3. Later in the essay from which "Love and Lust" has been excerpted, Fairlie writes:

> The managers of our society much prefer that we are infatuated with our sexuality than that we look long and steadily at what they contrive from day to day. . . . They have discovered that, now that religion has been displaced, sex can be made the opiate of the masses. When the entire society is at last tranquilly preoccupied in the morbid practices of onanism, they will know that there is nothing more for them to do but rule forever over the dead.

What does he mean by "opiate of the masses"? Where does the phrase come from? Do you agree with Fairlie that the commercialization of sex manipulates us? What examples can you cite to support your point of view?

Suggestion for Writing

Write a paper of four or five paragraphs in which you explain the similarities and differences between any two abstract qualities—such as optimism and pessimism; generosity and selfishness; conservatism and liberalism; bravery and cowardice; honesty and dishonesty; professionalism and amateurism; or innocence and guilt.

Erotica and Pornography:

A Clear and Present Difference

GLORIA STEINEM

1   uman beings are the only animals that experience the same sex drive at times when we can—and cannot— conceive.

2   Just as we developed uniquely human capacities for language, planning, memory, and invention along our evolutionary path, we also developed sexuality as a form of expression; a way of communicating that is separable from our need for sex as a way of perpetuating ourselves. For humans alone, sexuality can be and often is primarily a way of bonding, of giving and receiving pleasure, bridging differentness, discovering sameness, and communicating emotion.

3   We developed this and other human gifts through our ability to change our environment, adapt physically, and in the long run, to affect our own evolution. But as an emotional result of this spiraling path away from other animals, we seem to alternate between periods of exploring our unique abilities to forge new boundaries, and feelings of loneliness in the unknown that we ourselves have created; a fear that sometimes sends us back to the comfort of the animal world by encouraging us to exaggerate our sameness.

4   The separation of "play" from "work," for instance, is a problem only in the human world. So is the difference between art and nature, or an intellectual accomplishment and a physical one. As a result, we celebrate play, art, and invention as leaps into the unknown; but any imbalance can send us back to nostalgia° for our primate° past and the conviction that the basics of work, nature, and physical labor are somehow more worthwhile or even moral.

5   In the same way, we have explored our sexuality as separable from conception: a pleasurable, empathetic° bridge to strangers of the same species. We have even invented contraception—a skill that has probably existed in some form since our ancestors figured out

the process of birth—in order to extend this uniquely human difference. Yet we also have times of atavistic° suspicion that sex is not complete—or even legal or intended-by-god—if it cannot end in conception.

No wonder the concepts of "erotica" and "pornography" can   6
be so crucially different, and yet so confused. Both assume that sexuality can be separated from conception, and therefore can be used to carry a personal message. That's a major reason why, even in our current culture, both may be called equally "shocking" or legally "obscene," a word whose Latin derivative means "dirty, containing filth." This gross condemnation of all sexuality that isn't harnessed to childbirth and marriage has been increased by the current backlash against women's progress. Out of fear that the whole patriarchal structure° might be upset if women really had the autonomous° power to decide our reproductive futures (that is, if we controlled the most basic means of production), right-wing groups are not only denouncing prochoice abortion literature as "pornographic," but are trying to stop the sending of all contraceptive information through the mails by invoking obscenity laws. In fact, Phyllis Schlafly° recently denounced the entire Women's Movement as "obscene."

Not surprisingly, this religious, visceral° backlash has a secular°,   7
intellectual counterpart that relies heavily on applying the "natural" behavior of the animal world to humans. That is questionable in itself, but these Lionel Tiger°-ish studies make their political purpose even more clear in the particular animals they select and the habits they choose to emphasize. The message is that females should accept their "destiny" of being sexually dependent and devote themselves to bearing and rearing their young.

Defending against such reaction in turn leads to another tempta   8
tion: to merely reverse the terms, and declare that *all* nonprocreative° sex is good. In fact, however, this human activity can be as constructive or destructive, moral or immoral, as any other. Sex as communication can send messages as different as life and death; even the origins of "erotica" and "pornography" reflect that fact. After all, "erotica" is rooted in *eros* or passionate love, and thus in the idea of positive choice, free will, the yearning for a particular person. (Interestingly, the definition of erotica leaves open the question of gender.) "Pornography" begins with a root meaning "prostitution" or "female captives," thus letting us know that the subject is not mutual love, or love at all, but domination and violence against women. (Though, of course, homosexual pornography may imitate this violence by putting a man in the "feminine" role of victim.) It ends with a root meaning "writing about" or "description of" which puts still more distance between subject and object, and replaces

a spontaneous yearning for closeness with objectification and a voyeur°.

9   The difference is clear in the words. It becomes even more so by example.

10   Look at any photo or film of people making love; really making love. The images may be diverse, but there is usually a sensuality and touch and warmth, an acceptance of bodies and nerve endings. There is always a spontaneous sense of people who are there because they *want* to be, out of shared pleasure.

11   Now look at any depiction of sex in which there is clear force, or an unequal power that spells coercion°. It may be very blatant°, with weapons of torture or bondage, wounds and bruises, some clear humiliation, or an adult's sexual power being used over a child. It may be much more subtle: a physical attitude of conqueror and victim, the use of race or class difference to imply the same thing, perhaps a very unequal nudity, with one person exposed and vulnerable while the other is clothed. In either case, there is no sense of equal choice or equal power.

12   The first is erotic: a mutually pleasurable, sexual expression between people who have enough power to be there by positive choice. It may or may not strike a sense-memory in the viewer, or be creative enough to make the unknown seem real; but it doesn't require us to identify with a conqueror or a victim. It is truly sensuous, and may give us a contagion of pleasure.

13   The second is pornographic: its message is violence, dominance, and conquest. It is sex being used to reinforce some inequality, or to create one, or to tell us the lie that pain and humiliation (ours or someone else's) are really the same as pleasure. If we are to feel anything, we must identify with conqueror or victim. That means we can only experience pleasure through the adoption of some degree of sadism° or masochism°. It also means that we may feel diminished by the role of conqueror, or enraged, humiliated, and vengeful by sharing identity with the victim.

14   Perhaps one could simply say that erotica is about sexuality, but pornography is about power and sex-as-weapon—in the same way we have come to understand that rape is about violence, and not really about sexuality at all.

15   Yes, it's true that there are women who have been forced by violent families and dominating men to confuse love with pain, so much so that they have become masochists. (A fact that in no way excuses those who administer such pain.) But the truth is that, for most women—and for men with enough humanity to imagine themselves into the predicament of women—true pornography could serve as aversion therapy for sex.

16   Of course, there will always be personal differences about what

is and is not erotic, and there may be cultural differences for a long time to come. Many women feel that sex makes them vulnerable and therefore may continue to need more sense of personal connection and safety before allowing any erotic feelings. We now find competence and expertise erotic in men, but that may pass as we develop those qualities in ourselves. Men, on the other hand, may continue to feel less vulnerable, and therefore more open to such potential danger as sex with strangers. As some men replace the need for submission from childlike women with the pleasure of cooperation from equals, they may find a partner's competence to be erotic, too.

Such group changes plus individual differences will continue   17
to be reflected in sexual love between people of the same gender, as well as between women and men. The point is not to dictate sameness, but to discover ourselves and each other through sexuality that is an exploring, pleasurable, empathetic part of our lives; a human sexuality that is unchained both from unwanted pregnancies and from violence.

But that is a hope, not a reality. At the moment, fear of change   18
is increasing both the indiscriminate repression of all nonprocreative sex in the religious and "conservative" male world, and the pornographic vengeance against women's sexuality in the secular world of "liberal" or "radical" men. It's almost futuristic to debate what is and is not truly erotic, when many women are again being forced into compulsory motherhood, and the number of pornographic murders, tortures, and woman-hating images are on the increase in both popular culture and real life.

It's a familiar division: wife or whore, "good" woman who is   19
constantly vulnerable to pregnancy or "bad" woman who is unprotected from violence. *Both* roles would be upset if we were to control our own sexuality. And that's exactly what we must do.

In spite of all our atavistic suspicions and training for the "natu-   20
ral" role of motherhood, we took up the complicated battle for reproductive freedom. Our bodies had borne the health burden of endless births and poor abortions, and we had a greater motive for separating sexuality and conception.

Now we have to take up the equally complex burden of explain-   21
ing that all nonprocreative sex is *not* alike. We have a motive: our right to a uniquely human sexuality, and sometimes even to survival. As it is, our bodies have too rarely been enough our own to develop erotica in our own lives, much less in art and literature. And our bodies have too often been the objects of pornography and the woman-hating, violent practice that it preaches. Consider also our spirits that break a little each time we see ourselves in chains or full labial display for the conquering male viewer, bruised or on our

knees, screaming a real or pretended pain to delight the sadist, pretending to enjoy what we don't enjoy, to be blind to the images of our sisters that really haunt us—humiliated often enough ourselves by the truly obscene idea that sex and the domination of women must be combined.

22   Sexuality *is* human, free, separate—and so are we.

23   But until we untangle the lethal° confusion of sex with violence, there will be more pornography and less erotica. There will be little murders in our beds—and very little love.

┌─────────────────────────┐
│   │
└─────────────────────────┘

GLORIA STEINEM

Gloria Steinem, the American journalist and feminist, was born in 1934 in Toledo, Ohio. She was co-founder in New York of the feminist magazine *Ms.* and is the author of numerous essays, including her now-famous piece on becoming a Playboy bunny.

Words and Meanings

Paragraph

4	nostalgia:	yearning for earlier times
	primate:	highest order of animals, including monkeys and man
5	empathetic:	having ability to share deeply the thoughts, feelings, and attitudes of others
	atavistic:	reversion to earlier, more primitive behaviour
6	patriarchal structure:	social system governed by males
	autonomous:	self-governing, independent
	Phyllis Schlafly:	conservative opponent of Equal Rights Amendment in the United States
7	visceral:	bodily
	secular	non-religious
	Lionel Tiger	Montreal-born anthropologist who writes about the animality of man
8	nonprocreative:	not leading to conception and childbirth
	voyeur:	someone who gets sexual gratification by watching others
11	coercion:	force
	blatant:	obvious, offensive; unsubtle
13	sadism:	deriving pleasure through inflicting pain on others

masochism:	deriving pleasure through inflicting pain on oneself	
lethal:	causing death	23

Structure and Strategy

1. What is the function of paragraphs 1 to 5? What contrast is established in these paragraphs that serves as a basis for the whole essay?
2. Why are paragraphs 1, 9, and 22 so short? What function do they serve?
3. What is the function of paragraph 8? How does it contribute to the reader's understanding of the contrast between erotica and pornography?
4. How does Steinem structure her contrast in paragraphs 10 to 13?
5. In paragraph 12, the word "contagion" is a lapse of DICTION. Can you substitute a word that would be more consistent with the tone of the paragraph?
6. Steinem's shifts in point of view are worth studying. Why, for example, does she change from third person ("they") to first person ("we") in the middle of paragraph 16? Who are the "we" referred to in paragraphs 2 to 5? Who are the "we" in paragraphs 16 to 21? Is the change in meaning purposeful and effective, or does it lead to confusion?

Content and Purpose

1. What is Steinem's overall purpose? Summarize her thesis in your own words.
2. What link does Steinem identify between pornography and rape?
3. What is Steinem's attitude to homosexuality? How does she defend her view?
4. What attitude toward men does Steinem reveal in paragraph 15?
5. How does Steinem account for the current conservative back-lash against free sexual expression and even abortion?
6. Why does Steinem believe women must reject their traditional roles of wife and whore? What role must they adopt instead?
7. The meaning of paragraphs 22 and 23 depends in part on whom the "we" refers to: either to all men and women, or to women alone. How does the reader's understanding of the conclusion depend on the interpretation of the "we"?

Suggestions for Writing

1. Use your dictionary to check the etymologies of one of the following pairs of words, then compare them, using the *chunk* method of organization: philanthropy and philosophy; virility and virtue; character and charisma.

2. Compare two men's views on feminism. You could choose one man who is opposed to it and one man who supports a more powerful role for women in society. Alternatively, you could compare the views of two men who belong to different generations.

3. Compare Fairlie's concept of lust in "Love and Lust" with Steinem's concept of pornography. Or compare Fairlie's concept of love with Steinem's concept of erotica.

Additional Suggestions for Writing:
Comparison and Contrast

Write a comparison and/or contrast paper based on one of the topics below. Make sure that your thesis statement clarifies the basis of your comparison or contrast, then develop it by providing sufficient and relevant examples and details.

1. People's lifestyles often reveal their personal philosophies. Choose two people of your acquaintance whose ways of life reveal very different attitudes.
2. Compare and/or contrast living in Canada with living in another country. (Be sure to limit this topic to a few specific characteristics before you begin to write.)
3. Compare and/or contrast two sports, teams, or players.
4. Compare and/or contrast men and women as consumers (or voters, or employees, or supervisors, etc.).
5. Compare and/or contrast the appearance, mood, or appeal of a specific place in the summer and in the winter: your home town, a secret hideaway, a neighbourhood park, a favourite hangout.
6. Compare and/or contrast two artists with whose work you are familiar: two painters, poets, film directors, musicians, or actors.
7. Contrast your present career goals with those you dreamed of having as a child. How do you account for the differences between the two sets of goals?
8. Choose an issue and contrast the way a typical Progressive Conservative and a typical New Democrat would respond to it: free trade, gay rights, equal pay for work of equal value, fully subsidized day-care.
9. Contrast the way in which you and your parents view a particular issue: premarital sex, post-secondary education, family life, careers for women.
10. "Love is a gambling table on which women recklessly throw dollars and men carefully place pennies." (Richard Needham)

6

Cause and Effect: Explaining "Why"

What? The Definition

Until about 500 years ago, human beings observed the sky, watched the sun come up and the sun go down, and remarked on the comfortable regularity of the sun's journey around our planet. Not until a Polish astronomer named Copernicus doubted the validity of this earth-centred view of the universe did people begin to see that the predictability of the sun had a completely different *cause*: it was we who were going around it! The *effects* of the Copernican theory were momentous. Its publication in 1543 caused much controversy and spurred the study of astronomy and mathematics. Less than a hundred years later, a scientist named Galileo almost lost his life at the hands of conservative religious authorities for supporting the Copernican theory. Ultimately, we earthlings had to cease viewing ourselves as the centre of all existence, and this shift has had profound consequences for religion and science, philosophy and art.

The Copernican theory is an example of the search for causes as well as the attempt to understand effects. Identifying reasons and consequences is one of the ways we try to make sense of the flow of events around us. Asking "Why?" is a fundamental human impulse—just ask the parent of any two-year-old. Finding out "What happened then?" is also part of our natural human curiosity. **Cause and effect**, sometimes called **causal analysis**, is a rhetorical pattern based on these instincts: the writer explains the reasons for something, such as an event or decision, or analyzes its consequences. Sometimes, a writer attempts to do both, which is necessarily a longer, more complex process. Taking one direction, either cause *or* effect, is usually sufficient in a paper.

Why? The Purpose

Causal analysis answers one of two questions:

1. What are the causes of S?
2. What are the effects or consequences of S?

To write a good causal analysis, you must be honest and objective in your investigation. You must analyze complex ideas carefully in order to sort out the *remote*—more distant, not immediately apparent—causes or effects and the *immediate*—direct, readily apparent—causes or effects. Don't be the prisoner of old prejudices in your causal reasoning. For instance, concluding that the reason for a strike is the workers' greed and laziness, without exploring the motives behind their demands or investigating possible management errors, is irresponsible reasoning: it will lead to an ineffective causal analysis that will convince no one.

Oversimplification is another pitfall in writing cause and effect. To claim, for example, that the increase in juvenile crime is caused by "all the violence on TV" or that women's wages are lower than men's because "men are plotting to keep women down" is an unsubstantiated simplification of complex issues. Such statements contribute nothing to your reader's understanding of causes and effects.

Similarly, you should recognize that an event can be triggered by a complex variety of things. Sometimes, it is necessary to focus on several immediate reasons, while omitting what may be remote causes. For example, if you were asked to identify the causes of a social trend such as the increased consumption of light alcoholic beverages rather than hard liquor, you might have enough space to write only about the concern for fitness and the increasing awareness of the dangers of drunk driving, leaving aside the historical and demographic causes that could not be adequately explained in a short paper. Selecting your focus and scope, then, is very important when you are writing cause and effect.

A common error in causal analysis is assuming that one event that happened to occur before another is the cause of the second event. For example, you walked under a ladder yesterday morning, and that is why you got a speeding ticket in the afternoon. Mistaking coincidence for causation is called the *post hoc* error (from the Latin *post hoc ergo propter hoc*—"after this, therefore because of this"), and it is bad reasoning.

How? The Technique

After looking at some of the problems involved in sorting through cause and effect relationships, you can see that a manageable topic and a clear thesis are essential in any causal analysis. For instance, it would be impossible to explain the causes of all serious eating disorders in a 500-word paper. However, you could adequately explain why a particular person is anorexic. Similarly, you could, after some investigation, describe the effects of anorexia on the patient or on her family. In other words, limit your topic to one you can explore thoroughly. Avoid the unwieldy "Effects of Nuclear Radiation" and choose instead the more manageable "Effects of the Chernobyl Nuclear Reactor Meltdown." The more specific your topic, the more manageable it will be for you and, since you'll be able to support it with specific details, the more interesting it will be for your reader.

Once you have decided on your topic, spend some time shaping your thesis statement. The causes or effects you wish to explain usually become the main points in your thesis statement and outline. In a short paper, each main point can be developed in a paragraph. Your thesis statement may be patterned after one of these models:

> The causes of S are a, b, and c.

Example: The principal causes of failure in college are lack of basic skills, lack of study skills, and lack of motivation.

> There are three effects of S: a, b, and c.

Example: There are three consequences of minor league hockey violence: brutal playing styles, injured children, and angry parents.

To explain both causes and effects is a challenging task in a paper or report. If you choose to analyze both cause and effect in a single paper, be sure that your topic is narrow enough to enable you to develop your points adequately. In this kind of essay, to attempt too much is practically to guarantee confusing, if not overwhelming, your reader.

The final point to keep in mind when writing causal analysis is that your assertions must be fully supported. If you are trying to convince your reader that A causes B or that the inevitable effect of X is Y, you must supply compelling proof. This back-up material may take the form of statistical data, facts gleaned from research, "expert witness" quotations, or well-chosen examples. Don't rely on your audience's indulgence or intelligence; the logic of your identification of causes and effects must be apparent to the reader. Illustrate your causal analysis with sufficient—and interesting—supporting data and examples.

An example of a simple causal analysis follows:

Why Do They Fail?

Introduction (gets attention with a startling statistic)

Statistics show that most people who begin high school finish. Some drop out, of course, but approximately three-quarters earn a diploma. At the post-secondary level, however, fewer than two-thirds of the students complete their program of study. Why do so many college and university students drop out? Knowing the factors that prevent students from completing their post-secondary programs may prove crucial to you regardless of whether you are presently a college student or thinking of becoming one.

Thesis statement

Most educators agree that the principal causes of failure are lack of basic skills, lack of study skills, and lack of motivation.

First point (developed with facts and examples)

A firm grasp of basic skills—what are termed the three Rs: reading, writing, and arithmetic—is a must for college or university work. Not only are texts and research material more difficult to understand than they were in high school, but also the quantity of required reading is greater. The ability to express oneself clearly in standard written English is essential; garbled essays, ungrammatical reports, or poorly spelled and punctuated papers will be routinely failed by instructors, regardless of the ideas the writer may think he is expressing. Similarly, mathematical skills are essential to a student's success in many post-secondary programs. Business, science, technology, and some applied arts programs

**Second point
(note continuing
contrast between
high school and
college experience)**

**Third point
(developed by
division)**

require sound computational skills. Post-secondary students who lack these basic skills often find little remedial help available and little instructor tolerance for poor work; hence, they fall behind and drop out.

Occasionally students come to college equipped with the 3Rs but lacking the study skills necessary for success. Time management is critical; keeping up with course work when classes meet only once or twice a week is often a challenge for those accustomed to the high school routine. Students must know how to take notes from texts and lectures because college instructors, unlike high school teachers, rarely provide notes. Basically, good study skills in college or university mean taking responsibility for one's own learning. Going to class, reading and reviewing material, and preparing for assignments and tests are all up to the student. Few instructors will hound or cajole their students into learning as teachers may have done in high school.

Lack of motivation is also a major cause of failure. Even with good basic skills, a student who doesn't really *want* to be in college, who doesn't possess the necessary drive to do the work, may fail. School must be a priority in the student's life. For instance, if a student works 30 hours a week in a demanding job that she finds more interesting and rewarding than school, it is almost inevitable that her school work will suffer. To be successful, the student must also have a firm commitment to the career for which the college program is preparation. Finally, the successful student is someone with genuine intellectual curiosity. Without the will to learn as well as to succeed, a student is unlikely to complete a post-secondary education.

Conclusion
(points out
additional benefits)

Basic skills, study skills, and motivation: all are essential to success in college. Students who possess all three will not automatically achieve straight As, but they are on the right road to a degree or diploma. And—an important side benefit—those students will have mastered the traits that will make them as successful in their careers as they have been in school.

Math's Multiple Choices

JUDITH FINLAYSON

The world has been transformed in the past twenty years. Geared to microchips, floppy disks, and video display terminals, today's society demands a higher degree of mathematical skill than ever before. But, sadly and even dangerously misinformed about the realities of the working world, many teenaged girls across the country are repeating their mothers' mistake, a mistake that has propelled the majority of Canadian working women into low-paying, dead-end jobs. In high school, they are dropping out of science and math.

Today, a background in math is required for most high-paying technical jobs in fields such as computer technology and microelectronics, as well as for many apparently unrelated professions such as law, interior design, and urban planning. Some companies require Grade 12 math for all entry-level positions, even for caretaking jobs.

The need for mathematical competence has been heightened not only by the extraordinary technological change of the past two decades, but by social change as well. Women have entered the work force in unprecedented numbers. They can also expect to stay there—from 25 to 45 years, even if they choose to marry and have children as well as a job outside the home. And they should anticipate° changing careers at least twice during that time.

As Donna Stewart, educational co-ordinator for WomenSkills,

a Vancouver organization devoted to education and research on women's work, warns: "Whole fields of work are shrinking or disappearing entirely. We export enormous amounts of work to countries where labour is cheap, or we give it to machines. One result is that greater levels of competence are required, even for low-level jobs."

5   It's not surprising that a research report published in 1987 by the Economic Council of Canada stressed the value of flexibility in today's workplace. Not only are better-educated and highly skilled women more likely to benefit from technical change, but the report also concluded that their adjustment may be dependent upon how successfully they enter nontraditional occupations. It is important to note, however, that both higher education and nontraditional work are increasingly linked with competence in math.

6   Consider, for instance, that a minimum of high-school math is often required for entrance to university courses such as nursing, teaching, and law. It is also mandatory° for many social-science courses such as psychology and sociology, as well as for admission to a substantial number of community college courses. The problem is, female students tend to drop math and sciences as they progress through high school. This fact has led educators to conclude that math is an "invisible filter" denying females entry into the growth-related industries of the future.

7   Math and science avoidance in females is generally acknowledged as a serious issue, but unfortunately there are no national statistics that document the full extent of the problem. Research by the Toronto Board of Education, however, shows that even at the introductory level, the ratio of students in computer science courses is two-thirds male to one-third female. By Grade 13, approximately two-thirds of girls in Toronto schools have dropped out of maths and sciences.

8   "I'm still seeing the Cinderella myth at work," says Arlene Day, a resource teacher for equality in education with the Manitoba Teacher's Society. "Even though they see their mothers working outside the home because the family needs the money, girls are refusing to believe that the same thing will happen to them. They're still aiming for clerical jobs. Most are not even acquiring the computer skills that are necessary to be successful at office work." And her view is echoed in *What Will Tomorrow Bring?*, a 1985 Canadian Advisory Council on the Status of Women report that concluded, "adolescent girls still see their lives in very traditional and romanticized terms."

9   Statistics confirm that the majority of women (almost 60 percent) hold clerical and service-sector jobs, which are generally low paid, offer little potential for advancement, and may be in danger of becoming obsolete°. Although women have made serious inroads

into some male-dominated professions, such as business, medicine, and law, they are still segregated outside the more scientific fields, such as engineering and computer science. According to Statistics Canada, at the university level, the majority of women remain concentrated in the traditional fields of study, such as education, nursing, and the humanities. The pattern also holds true for community colleges, where most women continue to study secretarial science, community and social services, nursing, education, and the arts.

"To some extent, women have succumbed° to the myths about   10
women's work," comments Donna Stewart. "They want to be helpers and to work with people. They may be avoiding nontraditional jobs and careers that require a sound basis in math because they haven't seen the human context° to these jobs. Social service agencies need to balance their books. And no one builds bridges alone. You're part of a team."

Women who avoid math may be ignoring more than the human   11
context of working with numbers. Mathematical training has been linked with high salaries and job security in fields that have been targeted for future growth. Engineering technology, a profession that is 92 percent male, is one example of this trend. Two years after graduating from community college, an engineering student can expect to earn $20 000 a year. Perhaps more importantly, engineering technologists who reach the senior level will likely make more than $30 000 and, if they rise in management, they can earn up to $50 000 annually.

Compare these salaries to those in a female-dominated field.   12
Ninety-nine percent of secretaries are female. Not only is their average salary just $14 100 two years after graduation from community college, but according to a 1983 Labour Canada report, even those who reach senior levels earn on average under $20 000.

This kind of wage discrepancy° alarms educators who see girls   13
avoiding math. "Nowadays, a math and science background is necessary for most of the higher-paying jobs," says Linda McClelland, a science teacher at Crescent Heights High School in Calgary. "And girls are losing out on these credentials at the same time that more and more women are entering the work force. In addition, there is a rising number of women supporting families on their own who really need to earn a decent wage."

Tasoula Berggren, an instructor of calculus and linear algebra at   14
Simon Fraser University in Burnaby, British Columbia, points to at least 82 careers for which math education is a prerequisite. Last November, she organized what she hopes will become an annual conference, Women Do Math, for girls in Grades 9 and 10 and their parents. Four students from each of 85 Vancouver schools were invited. "I thought we would get 100 people," Berggren recalls,

"and 300 registered, with many more schools asking to bring more students."

15   Berggren designed the conference not only to introduce girls to women professionals but to provide an introduction to basic mathematical concepts. "Once they see the application of calculus— how a formula can give them the volume of a lake—they find it exciting. They say, 'This is great, I'm enjoying math!' "

16   She stresses the necessity of constant parental encouragement, something that Myra Novogrodsky, co-ordinator of women's labour studies at the Toronto Board of Education, observes does not come naturally. She is conducting a new program designed to make parents of Grade 7 and 8 girls aware of the importance of math and science education to their daughters' futures.

17   "I usually begin the workshops with a true-or-false quiz designed to test awareness," she says. "I've discovered that a lot of people haven't thought much about the implications of social change. They still think that most girls will live in a nuclear family and be secondary wage earners, if they work outside the home at all."

18   One result of this misconception° is that many parents have lower career expectations for their daughters than for their sons. Their attitude is reinforced by negative role modelling, which can include apparently innocuous° statements such as "Women don't have a head for figures" or "Her mother can't balance a cheque-book." These stereotypes can seriously undermine the confidence of girls who may have an interest in technical subjects or nontraditional work.

19   "By Grade 10, I knew I was mechanically oriented, but people said that physics was too hard for me and I believed them," recalls Heather Bears, who is currently studying electronics technology at Red River Community College in Winnipeg. As a result, after graduating from high school, she spent two unsatisfactory years in the work force doing odd clerical or child-care jobs. Career counsel-ling finally revealed her scientific aptitude and motivated her to return to high school as an adult student. Not only did she make up her physics courses, but she earned straight A's.

20   Today, as a second-year electronics student, she still feels the negative effects of gender roles. "When I entered the course there were only two other girls and approximately 100 guys. There was a real sense that we were bucking the system and it was scary. At its most basic, I'm only five-foot-two and most of the male students are in the six-foot range."

21   Although Bears admits that it is difficult being a pioneer—"some teachers pick on us and others favour us"—the satisfaction of doing what she finds fulfilling is worth the price. "If I had one piece of

advice for girls in high school, it would be, 'Don't be afraid to enter a man's world.' I believed people who said I couldn't do it because I was a girl, and that's what held me back."

Mary Elizabeth Morris, a math teacher at Castle Frank High   22
School in Toronto, believes that the "my mother/my self syndrome" can also influence a girl's career expectations. "A woman who does low-level work could undermine her daughter's success because she might not convey the sense that work can be a rewarding experience," she says. "If her mother is a poor role model in terms of job satisfaction, a girl may cling to the Cinderella myth because she doesn't see work outside the home as desirable."

Studies such as *What Will Tomorrow Bring?* show that profes-   23
sional mothers tend to be positive role models for their daughters. But mothers who don't work outside the home can also encourage their daughters to develop an interest in traditionally male domains by organizing scientifically oriented excursions, such as a visit to a science museum, or by doing traditionally masculine tasks.

"We live on a farm, so my mother is a real handyman," says   24
Robin Chant, a Grade 12 student at MacGregor Collegiate Institute in MacGregor, Manitoba, who excels at maths and sciences. "I think one of the reasons I do well in math is because, like her, I enjoy figuring things out."

Chant was the only girl in her physics class last year and there   25
is only one other girl in this year's math class, compared to nine boys. "Most of my girlfriends have dropped math because they think it's too hard," she says. "They all want traditional jobs as secretaries and day-care workers. They plan to get married and have kids. I'm different because I really want to have a career."

Myra Novogrodsky believes that if mothers are to help their   26
daughters overcome their negative outlook toward math, they must become aware of and overcome their own negative feelings. If parents "suffered" through math class themselves, they may convey their anxiety and inadvertently undermine their children's performance. Equally important are the role models that girls receive outside the home.

"It's hard for girls to accept the message that they can have high   27
career aspirations and study maths and sciences if they don't see any other women doing it," says Linda McClelland. "We need more female math and science teachers as role models, as well as more women in nontraditional careers."

All the women math and science teachers interviewed for this   28
article strongly agreed. Moreover, those who kept statistics on the ratio of males to females in their classes reported that the fact that a woman was teaching the subjects had a positive effect on girls.

"In the past there was usually only one female student in senior-   29 level physics," recalls Shelagh Pryke, who teaches all the physics classes at Kwalikum Secondary School in Qualicum Beach, B.C. "Now as many as 42 percent of my students are girls, and I know the fact that I'm a woman who is married with a family has played a role in this change. The girls see that it's socially acceptable to be a woman who is interested in science."

30   Lydia Picucha, a math and science teacher at Mount Elizabeth Junior and Senior Secondary School in Kitimat, B.C., shares this point of view. "I've been teaching here for seven years and I know my female students relate to the idea of a woman who enjoys her work and takes her career seriously. As a result, most of my female students—about 70 percent—have continued with science into Grade 11, when girls normally start dropping out."

31   The lack of female teachers as role models is complicated by the way maths and sciences are taught in schools. Mathematics, for example, may alienate girls because it is typically taught in a masculine style. John Clark, co-ordinator of mathematics at the Toronto Board of Education, says, "Math is usually presented as a search for the right answer rather than as a process of enquiry. Some sociologists believe that females have a more collaborative° style. They want to work by consensus and talk with other people."

32   Whether or not there is any inherent difference between the male and female aptitude for mathematics remains a hotly debated issue. However, there is no doubt that the way girls are socialized undermines whatever natural ability they might have. For example, the kinds of throwing, jumping, and mechanically oriented play that boys engage in actually prepares them for an understanding of maths and sciences.

33   Consider the game of baseball. Most boys catch balls better than most girls simply because by constantly playing ball sports they have learned how to estimate where the ball will land and, therefore, how to position their hands. What is less obvious is that this skill requires an understanding of the relationship between distance, force, and velocity that serves them well once they begin to study physics.

34   At the Institute of Child Study, a school that operates in conjunction with the University of Toronto's Faculty of Education, teacher Robin Ethier confirms that there is a division of play along gender lines by the time the children arrive at kindergarten. "The boys choose blocks and sand to build large spaces, whereas the girls prefer small paper projects," she says. "The few girls who prefer large motor-skill projects really stand out. They are identified as tomboys."

35   Even so, Anne Cassidy, the Grade 5 teacher at the school, says she is not aware of a gender difference in her students' approach to

maths and sciences. To some extent, she believes the school's emphasis on intuitive and personalized learning has helped minimize the difference. Classes are small and teachers strongly encourage children to learn through their own activities. For example, to teach the law of averages, she might ask her class to count up the pennies all seven grades collected for UNICEF over Hallowe'en. When she asks her students to work out approximately how much each grade collected, they soon realize that to get an average they must divide the total number of pennies by the number of classes. In the end, they discover the mathematical formula all on their own.

This kind of hands-on learning validates the children's own observations about the world. It also reinforces their sense of themselves as autonomous° problem solvers, a skill linked with success in math. Parents can play an important role in helping their children develop this problem-solving ability by transforming daily activities into informal lessons in maths and sciences. Children should be encouraged to play mathematically oriented games such as backgammon and chess. Cooking is an excellent activity for teaching fractions as well as the principles of chemistry. Similarly, carpentry teaches measurement and spatial concepts, and comparing sizes and prices at the supermarket can turn even shopping into a learning experience. 36

"People make the mistake of trying to introduce new math concepts with paper and pencil," according to Dr. Ada Schermann, principal of the Institute of Child Study. "Start with a game or a fun activity such as cooking, gardening, or playing a mathematically based card game like 21. Then children don't think they're being taught, and the learning comes naturally." 37

Girls' poor problem-solving abilities have been linked to the fact that they are not usually encouraged to assert themselves as individuals. So perhaps it's not surprising that they begin to retreat from maths and sciences during their teenage years. During this period their willingness to consider a non-traditional career also wanes. 38

It must be the responsibility of parents and teachers to erase the myth that an interest in math makes a girl "different" or "unfeminine." From pre-school to high school, maths and sciences should be as natural and nonthreatening subjects of study as English or history. Without a solid grounding in these subjects, the doors of opportunity will slam shut for yet another generation of young women—and, unfortunately, unemployment figures are the numbers *everyone* understands. 39

JUDITH FINLAYSON

Judith Finlayson (b. 1941) was born in Burlington, Iowa, and graduated from Harvard. She is a Toronto-based writer, researcher, and journalist whose books include *Whose Money Is it Anyway? The Showdown on Pensions* (1988).

Words and Meanings

Paragraph

3	anticipate:	expect
6	mandatory:	required
9	obsolete:	no longer in existence
10	succumbed: context:	given in to setting, surroundings
13	discrepancy:	difference, variance
18	misconception: innocuous:	mistaken belief innocent, harmless
31	collaborative:	working in combination with others
36	autonomous:	independent

Subject and Structure

1. Identify the introductory and concluding strategies Finlayson employs in this essay. Are they effective?
2. Finlayson frequently uses the technique of making a point, then quoting an expert source to support it. Identify three examples of this technique that you think make a particularly strong impact on the reader. Why are they so effective?
3. This essay presents three factors that strongly influence the way girls respond to math and science: parents, schools, and the teaching process itself. Identify the paragraphs that focus on each of these factors. What points does Finlayson make about these influences?
4. In paragraphs 14 to 17, Finlayson presents some solutions to the dilemma of math avoidance among young girls. What are they?
5. Where does the essay provide ILLUSTRATIONS of learning activities parents can undertake to increase their children's interest and success in math and science?
6. What is the function of paragraphs 11 and 12? What is Finlayson's purpose in including them?

Content and Purpose

1. What are the "multiple choices" referred to in the title?
2. In paragraph 1, Finlayson explains a specific effect. What is it? How is it related to the overall purpose of the essay?
3. Paragraphs 2 and 3 explore two reasons why women should study math and science in high school and college. What are these reasons?
4. In paragraph 9, Finlayson identifies what could be described as a female employment ghetto. Why are women drawn to these careers rather than to careers in traditionally male-dominated professions?
5. What is the "Cinderella myth" that Finlayson refers to in paragraph 22?
6. Do you find Finlayson's causal analysis convincing? Why or why not?

Suggestions for Writing

1. Write a short essay in which you analyze the causes that prompted you to stay with (or abandon) the study of math and science in high school.
2. In paragraphs 11 and 12, Finlayson provides salary statistics for careers that are traditionally dominated by men and by women. Are her figures dated? Research the issue by finding out what college graduates earn after completing programs in these fields, and write a short paper contrasting the rewards of typically "male" and typically "female" jobs.

Reflections on My Brother's Murder

DAVID FINN

Several months ago, my brother, Herbert 1
Finn, a prominent civil rights lawyer from Phoenix, Arizona, was shot and killed while visiting my family in New York. We had been to the opera—Herbert, his wife, my wife, my sister, my daughter, and I—and the six of us drove to the quiet residential neighborhood

"Reflections on My Brother's Murder" by David Finn. Copyright 1980. Reprinted with the permission of *Saturday Review* magazine.

of Riverdale, where my daughter lives. I left the car for a few minutes to take her to her apartment. While I was gone, several young black men held up the rest of the family, taking pocketbooks from my wife and sister and grabbing my brother's wallet as he took out his money for them. Although no one is quite sure what happened, we think my brother reached out to retrieve the credit cards in his wallet because he was planning to leave the next day on a trip to Egypt and Israel. One impatient robber fired a single .22-caliber bullet, and all of them fled. A moment later I arrived on the scene to find the women screaming and my brother dead.

2   All that night I repeated four words— *I can't believe it*—so often that they must be imprinted on my brain. The murder took place just after midnight, and we finished with the police interrogation at 5:30 the next morning. My wife and I had a couple of drinks to try to calm our nerves, but the alcohol didn't work. I couldn't stop myself from shivering (although I wasn't cold) and repeating the four words endlessly. In desperation, I took a pad from the drawer next to my bed and wrote "I can't believe it" 26 times, as if writing it out would serve as a cathartic° for disbelief. But it was no help. I truly could *not* believe it. I went on repeating the words to myself all through the next day as I sat with my wife, sister, and sister-in-law in three different police stations, going through hundreds of mug shots and answering questions posed by various teams of detectives. While I could not absorb the reality of what had happened, neither could I get the sight of it—the sight of my brother slumped in the back seat—out of my mind.

3   About two weeks later, four suspects were arrested. Their ages were 19, 17, 17, and 15. Newspaper accounts stated that three of them came from middle-class homes in Mt. Vernon, New York.

4   Two of the youths confessed. The story they told deepened the crease of incredulity° in my brain. It went something like this: One boy borrowed his mother's car to go to a high-school dance. He changed his mind and instead picked up three friends, drove to a pizzeria, then to a disco, and finally went for a ride in Riverdale. As they were cruising, the four boys thought of sticking up an ice-cream store, but by the time they got there it was closed. Later, they passed our car, saw the people in it, and thought it looked like an interesting target. They pulled into a driveway, and three of them said they'd check our car and be right back. The fourth boy waited, listening to his car radio. A minute later he heard a noise and the three ran back screaming, "Get out of here, get out of here." As they sped away, one of the boys kept asking another, "Why did you do it? Why did you shoot him?" "I had to," he answered and then said reassuringly, "Don't worry about it." They argued for a while. Finally, one of them distributed $44 to each of the others. "You

shot [this guy] for less than $200? That's stupid," one of the boys remarked. "Don't worry," the murderer insisted.

As told by the two who confessed, the casualness of the whole   5
incident—taking my brother's life to get some money for fun—makes the tragedy all the more unbearable. It was apparently just a matter of going after easy pickings and striking down a victim who might have been trying to hold out. It was like swatting a fly. That was all there was to it.

In the months that followed, the shock waves of what we initially   6
took to be a private nightmare radiated farther than any of us could have imagined. People from all over the world called and wrote to give some expression to the pain they felt. I could almost hear the whispers echoing in the atmosphere as anybody who had the slightest connection to us passed the story on. What dumbfounded° acquaintances was the senselessness, the chilling irony, of Herbert's death. Dying from an illness is no better than dying from a robber's bullet, but we learn to accept death from disease as fate, while murder threatens to undermine the assumption that man can control societal forces.

A friend who served for many years as Chief of Police in the Bronx,   7
Anthony Bouza, has likened the unchecked spread of crime to a cancer that will destroy our society unless we attack its cause—poverty and unemployment. People who can't speak the language, can't get jobs, and can't find decent places to live are excluded from society. They come to feel that robbing and killing are the only ways they can survive. Desperation, Chief Bouza believes, overwhelms morality and the law. What is worse, he says, is the more recent development. As the poor increasingly resort to their desperate solutions, more fortunate youths adopt the same measures to accomplish their own ends. Robbing and killing fill the emptiness caused, not by hunger, but by boredom and a lack of purpose in their lives. The cancer that begins in the burned-out buildings of our cities metastasizes° to the rest of society.

A number of people, reacting to my brother's death, are seeking   8
cures for the disease Bouza describes. Some say they will work for stricter gun-control laws. Others want tougher sentences for convicted criminals. Still others want to reinstate the death penalty. And some want to work for a stronger and better equipped police force. But it seems to me that these efforts, many of which are clearly necessary, are unlikely to rid us of the cancer; they treat the symptoms, not the disease. The cancer itself can be arrested, I believe, only if we minister to° its root cause. We must stop the decay in our cities and the deterioration of our values. We must have faith in our own power to cure the disease and the determination to exercise that power.

The shock of my brother's death has in itself given rise to some   9
innovative° ideas that illustrate the kind of determination called for.

While talking about Herbert's death, for example, a friend who heads an influential foundation raised the question of relating education to work opportunities. He proposed an unusual plan for a pilot project: If a small group of underprivileged students would promise to finish their college education, he would arrange jobs for them in advance, guaranteeing them positions on graduation. The companies for which they would work would pay only half their salaries, and his foundation would pay the rest. If the project succeeds, he would encourage other foundations to do the same thing for thousands of young people. His idea could be the small beginning of a major accomplishment.

10   My brother's death was cruel, inhuman, personally devastating; but I do not want to believe it was futile°. Taking initiatives° to cope with the disease rather than despairing at its ravages° is the only sane response to our tragedy. If we who have been subjected to such horrors can show the world that we have not lost our faith, if out of our pain we can help to awaken the forces within our society that are capable of curing the disease, his death and the deaths of other martyrs° of the streets will not have been in vain.

thesis

DAVID FINN

David Finn, a painter, photographer, and writer, was born in 1921 in the United States. His work has been exhibited in several galleries and museums in New York and his writings have appeared in *Saturday Review* and other publications.

Words and Meanings

Paragraph

2	cathartic:	purging, cleansing
4	incredulity:	unwillingness or inability to believe
6	dumbfounded:	astonished; left speechless
7	metastasizes:	spreads cancer cells from one part of the body to another
8	minister to:	tend to; treat
9	innovative:	new, experimental
10	futile:	useless
	initiatives:	fresh starts
	ravages:	destructive effects
	martyrs:	people who are killed for their beliefs

Structure and Strategy

1. In what ORDER are the ideas of paragraphs 2 to 3 arranged? What is the effect on the reader?
2. How does Finn create the effect of immediacy in paragraph 4?
3. What ANALOGY is introduced in paragraph 7?
4. Why did Finn write this essay in the first person, using the pronouns "I" and "we"? How would the effect have been different if he had written this piece in the third person?

Content and Purpose

1. According to Finn, what are the causes of crime among the poor? Among the more affluent?
2. Do you agree with Finn that the death of a loved one from disease is easier to bear than death caused by murder?
3. Why does Finn reject the solutions to crime that other well-meaning people have proposed? (See paragraph 8.)
4. Finn wrote this essay several months after his brother's death, describing it as "inhuman," but he never mentions the very human desire for vengeance. Why do you think he chose not to include the idea in his essay, even if he himself might have wanted to seek revenge?

Suggestions for Writing

1. Have you or has a member of your family been affected by a serious crime? Identify and explain the effects the crime had on the victim and/or his or her family.
2. Write a short paper explaining why so many teenagers commit "petty crimes" such as shoplifting or joy-riding.

O Rotten Gotham°— Sliding Down into the Behavioral Sink

TOM WOLFE

 just spent two days with Edward T. Hall,   1

"O Rotten Gotham—Sliding Down into the Behavioral Sink" from *The Pump House Gang* by Tom Wolfe. Copyright 1968 by Tom Wolfe. Reprinted by permission of Farrar, Straus and Giroux, Inc.

an anthropologist, watching thousands of my fellow New Yorkers short-circuiting themselves into hot little twitching death balls with jolts of their own adrenalin. Dr. Hall says it is overcrowding that does it. Overcrowding gets the adrenalin going, and the adrenalin gets them queer, autistic°, sadistic°, barren, batty, sloppy, hot-in-the-pants, chancred-on-the-flankers°, leering, puling°, numb—the usual in New York, in other words, and God knows what else. Dr. Hall has the theory that overcrowding has already thrown New York into a state of behavioral sink. Behavioral sink is a term from ethology, which is the study of how animals relate to their environment. Among animals, the sink winds up with a "population collapse" or "massive die-off." O rotten Gotham.

2   It got to be easy to look at New Yorkers as animals, especially looking down from some place like a balcony at Grand Central° at the rush hour Friday afternoon. The floor was filled with the poor white humans, running around, dodging, blinking their eyes, making a sound like a pen full of starlings or rats or something.

3   "Listen to them skid," says Dr. Hall.

4   He was right. The poor old etiolate° animals were out there skidding on their rubber soles. You could hear it once he pointed it out. They stop short to keep from hitting somebody or because they are disoriented and they suddenly stop and look around, and they skid on their rubber-soled shoes, and a screech goes up. They pour out onto the floor down the escalators from the Pan-Am Building, from 42nd Street, from Lexington Avenue, up out of subways, down into subways, railroad trains, up into helicopters—

5   "You can also hear the helicopters all the way down here," says Dr. Hall. The sound of the helicopters using the roof of the Pan-Am Building nearly fifty stories up beats right through. "If it weren't for this ceiling"—he is referring to the very high ceiling in Grand Central—"this place would be unbearable with this kind of crowding. And yet they'll probably never 'waste' space like this again."

6   They screech! And the adrenal glands in all those poor white animals enlarge, micrometer by micrometer, to the size of cantaloupes. Dr. Hall pulls a Minox camera out of a holster he has on his belt and starts shooting away at the human scurry°. The Sink!

7   Dr. Hall has the Minox up to his eye—he is a slender man, calm, 52 years old, young-looking, an anthropologist who has worked with Navajos, Hopis, Spanish-Americans, Negroes, Trukese. He was the most important anthropologist in the government during the crucial years of the foreign aid program, the 1950's. He directed both the Point Four training program and the Human Relations Area Files. He wrote *The Silent Language* and *The Hidden Dimension*, two books that are picking up the kind of "underground" following his friend Marshall McLuhan° started picking up about five years ago.

He teaches at the Illinois Institute of Technology, lives with his wife, Mildred, in a high-ceilinged town house on one of the last great residential streets in downtown Chicago, Astor Street; he has a grown son and daughter, loves good food, good wine, the relaxed, civilized life—but comes to New York with a Minox at his eye to record!—perfect—The Sink.

We really got down in there by walking down into the Lexing- 8 ton Avenue line subway stop under Grand Central. We inhaled those nice big fluffy fumes of human sweat, urine, effluvia°, and sebaceous secretions°. One old female human was already stroked out on the upper level, on a stretcher, with two policemen standing by. The other humans barely looked at her. They rushed into line. They bellied each other, haunch to paunch, down the stairs. Human heads shone through the gratings. The species North European tried to create bubbles of space around themselves, about a foot and a half in diameter—

"See, he's reacting against the line," says Dr. Hall.   9

—but the species Mediterranean presses on in. The hell with 10 bubbles of space. The species North European resents that, this male human behind him presses forward toward the booth . . . *breathing* on him, he's disgusted, he pulls out of the line entirely, the species Mediterranean resents him for resenting it, and neither of them realizes what the hell they are getting irritable about exactly. And in all of them the old adrenals grow another micrometer.

Dr. Hall whips out the Minox. Too perfect! The bottom of The 11 Sink.

It is the sheer overcrowding, such as occurs in the business 12 sections of Manhattan five days a week and in Harlem, Bedford-Stuyvesant, southeast Bronx every day—sheer overcrowding is converting New Yorkers into animals in a sink pen. Dr. Hall's argument runs as follows: all animals, including birds, seem to have a built-in inherited requirement to have a certain amount of territory, space, to lead their lives in. Even if they have all the food they need, and there are no predatory animals threatening them, they cannot tolerate crowding beyond a certain point. No more than two hundred wild Norway rats can survive on a quarter acre of ground, for example, even when they are given all the food they can eat. They just die off.

But why? To find out, ethologists have run experiments on all 13 sorts of animals, from stickleback crabs to Sika deer. In one major experiment, an ethologist named John Calhoun put some domesticated white Norway rats in a pen with four sections to it, connected by ramps. Calhoun knew from previous experiments that the rats tend to split up into groups of ten to twelve and that the pen, therefore, would hold forty to forty-eight rats comfortably, assuming they formed four equal groups. He allowed them to reproduce until there were eighty rats, balanced between male and female, but did not let it get any more crowded. He kept them supplied with plenty of food, water, and nesting materials. In other words, all their more obvious needs were taken care of. A less obvious need—space—was not. To the human eye, the pen did not even look especially crowded. But to the rats, it was crowded beyond endurance.

14   The entire colony was soon plunged into a profound behavioral sink. "The sink," said Calhoun, "is the outcome of any behavioral process that collects animals together in unusually great numbers. The unhealthy connotations of the term are not accidental: a behavioral sink does act to aggravate all forms of pathology° that can be found within a group."

15   For a start, long before the rat population reached eighty, a status hierarchy° had developed in the pen. Two dominant male rats took over the two end sections, acquired harems of eight to ten females each, and forced the rest of the rats into the two middle pens. All the overcrowding took place in the middle pens. That was where the "sink" hit. The aristocrat rats at the end grew bigger, sleeker, healthier, and more secure the whole time.

16   In The Sink, meanwhile, nest building, courting, sex behavior, reproduction, social organization, health—all of it went to pieces. Normally, Norway rats have a mating ritual in which the male chases the female, the female ducks down into a burrow and sticks her head up to watch the male. He performs a little dance outside the burrow, then she comes out, and he mounts her, usually for a few seconds. When The Sink set in, however, no more than three males—the dominant males in the middle sections—kept up the old customs. The rest tried everything from satyrism° to homosexuality or else gave up on sex altogether. Some of the subordinate males spent all their time chasing females. Three or four might chase one female at the same time, and instead of stopping at the burrow entrance for the ritual, they would charge right in. Once mounted, they would hold on for minutes instead of the usual seconds.

17   Homosexuality rose sharply. So did bisexuality. Some males would mount anything—males, females, babies, senescent° rats, anything. Still other males dropped sexual activity altogether, wouldn't fight and, in fact, would hardly move except when the other rats slept. Occasionally, a female from the aristocrat rats' harems would come over the ramps and into the middle sections to sample life in The Sink. When she had had enough, she would run back up the ramp. Sink males would give chase up to the top of the ramp, which is to say, to the very edge of the aristocratic preserve. But one glance from one of the king rats would stop them cold and they would return to The Sink.

The slumming females from the harems had their adventures   18
and then returned to a placid, healthy life. Females in The Sink,
however, were ravaged°, physically and psychologically. Pregnant
rats had trouble continuing pregnancy. The rate of miscarriages
increased significantly, and females started dying from tumors and
other disorders of the mammary glands, sex organs, uterus, ovaries,
and Fallopian tubes. Typically, their kidneys, livers, and adrenals
were also enlarged or diseased or showed other signs associated
with stress.

Child-rearing became totally disorganized. The females lost the   19
interest or the stamina to build nests and did not keep them up if
they did build them. In the general filth and confusion, they would
not put themselves out to save offspring they were momentarily
separated from. Frantic, even sadistic competition among the males
was going on all around them and rendering their lives chaotic. The
males began unprovoked and senseless assaults upon one another,
often in the form of tail-biting. Ordinarily, rats will suppress this
kind of behavior when it crops up. In The Sink, male rats gave up
all policing and just looked out for themselves. The "pecking order"
among males in The Sink was never stable. Normally, male rats set
up a three-class structure. Under the pressure of overcrowding,
however, they broke up into all sorts of unstable subclasses, cliques,
packs—and constantly pushed, probed, explored, tested one another's power. Anyone was fair game, except for the aristocrats in the
end pens.

Calhoun kept the population down to eighty, so that the next   20
stage, "population collapse" or "massive die-off," did not occur.
But the autopsies showed that the pattern—as in the diseases among
the female rats—was already there.

The classic study of die-off was John J. Christian's study of Sika   21
deer on James Island in the Chesapeake Bay, west of Cambridge,
Maryland. Four or five of the deer had been released on the island,
which was 280 acres and uninhabited, in 1916. By 1955 they had
bred freely into a herd of 280 to 300. The population density was
only about one deer per acre at this point, but Christian knew that
this was already too high for the Sikas' inborn space requirements,
and something would give before long. For two years the number
of deer remained 280 to 300. But suddenly, in 1958, over half the
deer died; 161 carcasses were recovered. In 1959 more deer died and
the population steadied at about 80.

In two years, two-thirds of the herd had died. Why? It was not   22
starvation. In fact, all the deer collected were in excellent condition,
with well-developed muscles, shining coats, and fat deposits
between the muscles. In practically all the deer, however, the adrenal glands had enlarged by 50 percent. Christian concluded that the

die-off was due to "shock following severe metabolic disturbance, probably as a result of prolonged adrenocortical hyperactivity. . . . There was no evidence of infection, starvation, or other obvious cause to explain the mass mortality." In other words, the constant stress of overpopulation, plus the normal stress of the cold of the winter, had kept the adrenalin flowing so constantly in the deer that their systems were depleted of blood sugar and they died of shock.

23   Well, the white humans are still skidding and darting across the floor of Grand Central. Dr. Hall listens a moment longer to the skidding and the darting noises, and then says, "You know, I've been on commuter trains here after everyone has been through one of these rushes, and I'll tell you, there is enough acid flowing in the stomachs in every car to dissolve the rails underneath."

24   Just a little invisible acid bath for the linings to round off the day. The ulcers the acids cause, of course, are the one disease people have already been taught to associate with the stress of city life. But overcrowding, as Dr. Hall sees it, raises a lot more hell with the body than just ulcers. In everyday life in New York—just the usual, getting to work, working in massively congested areas like 42nd Street between Fifth Avenue and Lexington, especially now that the Pan-Am Building is set in there, working in cubicles such as those in the editorial offices at Time-Life, Inc., which Dr. Hall cites as typical of New York's poor handling of space, working in cubicles with low ceilings and, often, no access to a window, while construction crews all over Manhattan drive everybody up the Masonite wall with air-pressure generators with noises up to the boil-a-brain decibel level, then rushing to get home, piling into subways and trains, fighting for time and for space, the usual day in New York—the whole now-normal thing keeps shooting jolts of adrenalin into the body, breaking down the body's defenses and winding up with the work-a-daddy human animal stroked out at the breakfast table with his head apoplexed° like a cauliflower out of his $6.95 semi-spread Pima-cotton shirt, and nosed over into a plate of No-Kloresto egg substitute, signing off with the black thrombosis, cancer, kidney, liver, or stomach failure, and the adrenals ooze to a halt, the size of eggplants in July.

25   One of the people whose work Dr. Hall is interested in on this score is Rene Dubos at the Rockefeller Institute. Dubos's work indicates that specific organisms, such as the tuberculosis bacillus or a pneumonia virus, can seldom be considered "the cause" of a disease. The germ or virus, apparently, has to work in combination with other things that have already broken the body down in some way—such as the old adrenal hyperactivity. Dr. Hall would like to see some autopsy studies made to record the size of adrenal glands

in New York, especially of people crowded into slums and people who go through the full rush-hour-work-rush-hour cycle every day. He is afraid that until there is some clinical, statistical data on how overcrowding actually ravages the human body, no one will be willing to do anything about it. Even in so obvious a thing as air pollution, the pattern is familiar. Until people can actually see the smoke or smell the sulphur or feel the sting in their eyes, politicians will not get excited about it, even though it is well known that many of the lethal substances polluting the air are invisible and odorless. For one thing, most politicians are like the aristocrat rats. They are insulated from The Sink by practically sultanic buffers—limousines, chauffeurs, secretaries, aides-de-camp, doormen, shuttered houses, high-floor apartments. They almost never ride subways, fight rush hours, much less live in the slums or work in the Pan-Am Building.

[ ]

TOM WOLFE

Tom Wolfe, the American journalist and author, was born in 1931 in Richmond, Virginia. One of the best-known writers of New Journalism, he is the author of such books as *The Electric Kool-Aid Acid Test*, *The Right Stuff*, and *The Bonfire of the Vanities*.

Words and Meanings

Paragraph

Gotham:	humorous reference to New York	
autistic:	self-absorbed	1
sadistic:	deriving pleasure from the pain of others	
chancred-on-the-flankers:	slang expression for genital infection	
puling:	crying weakly, whining	
Grand Central:	major train and subway station in New York	2
etiolate:	pale as a result of being deprived of sun	4
scurry:	run with short, quick steps, like mice	6
Marshall McLuhan:	Canadian-born philosopher of the media	7
effluvia:	exhaled odours	8
sebaceous secretions:	substances produced by skin glands	
pathology:	disease	14
status hierarchy:	order based on rank, social position	15
satyrism:	uncontrollable sexual appetite in males	16

17	senescent	aged
18	ravaged:	devastated, ruined
24	apoplexed:	having suffered an internal rupture as a result of a stroke

Structure and Strategy

1. Where and why does Wolfe use definition in paragraph 2?
2. How does Wolfe create feelings of disgust and even horror in paragraphs 8 to 10? Consider both DICTION and SYNTAX.
3. What is the function of paragraph 14? Could it be omitted without affecting the reader's understanding?
4. With what specific ANALOGY does Wolfe conclude his essay? How does the last sentence of paragraph 19 prepare us for the conclusion?
5. The DICTION, TONE, and STYLE of this essay are distinctive. Contrast the restrained, scientific language of paragraphs 21 and 22 with the vocabulary and style of paragraph 24. Find other examples of Wolfe's unique personal prose style. What is the overall effect of this style on the reader?

Content and Purpose

1. What is the thesis of this essay?
2. Wolfe constructs an elaborate ANALOGY to support his thesis. What is the analogy and how does it help to make his point clear?
3. What or who is the "species North European" and the "species Mediterranean" (paragraph 10)? What is the difference between them? Can you account for this difference?
4. Summarize anthropologist Edward Hall's explanation of behavioural sinks.
5. In the last paragraph of this essay, Wolfe suggests that while there is no single *cause* of the behavioural sinks urban dwellers live in, there is an identifiable, assignable *responsibility*. Whom does he blame for the existence of behavioural sinks, and why?

Suggestions for Writing

1. Think of a situation that leads to overcrowding: registration line-ups, rush-hour traffic, jam-packed buses or subways, or the crowds at a game, for example. Write a short paper describing the effects of this overcrowding on the people who must endure it.
2. After doing some research, write an essay explaining the causes

of a particular scientific effect, such as the "greenhouse effect";
use Hall's description of the behavioural sink as your model.

Canadians: What Do They Want?

MARGARET ATWOOD

Last month, during a poetry reading, I tried   1
out a short prose poem called "How to Like Men." It began by
suggesting that one start with the feet. Unfortunately, the question
of jackboots° soon arose, and things went on from there. After the
reading I had a conversation with a young man who thought I had
been unfair to men. He wanted men to be liked totally, not just from
the heels to the knees, and not just as individuals but as a group;
and he thought it negative and inegalitarian° of me to have alluded°
to war and rape. I pointed out that as far as any of us knew these
were two activities not widely engaged in by women, but he was
still upset. "We're both in this together," he protested. I admitted
that this was so; but could he, maybe, see that our relative positions
might be a little different.

This is the conversation one has with Americans, even, uh,   2
good Americans, when the dinner-table conversation veers round to
Canadian-American relations. "We're in this together," they like to
say, especially when it comes to continental energy reserves. How
do you *explain* to them, as delicately as possible, why they are not
categorically° beloved? It gets like the old Lifebuoy ads: even their
best friends won't tell them. And Canadians are supposed to be their
best friends, right? Members of the family?

Well, sort of. Across the river from Michigan, so near and yet so 3
far, there I was at the age of eight, reading *their* Donald Duck comic
books (originated however by one of *ours*; yes, Walt Disney's parents
were Canadian) and coming at the end to Popsicle Pete, who promised me the earth if only I would save wrappers, but took it all away
from me again with a single asterisk: Offer Good Only in the United
States. Some cynical members of the world community may be
forgiven for thinking that the same asterisk is there, in invisible ink,
on the Constitution° and the Bill of Rights°.

4   But quibbles° like that aside, and good will assumed, how does one go about liking Americans? Where does one begin? Or, to put it another way, why did the Canadian women lock themselves in the john during a '70s "international" feminist conference being held in Toronto? Because the American sisters were being "imperialist°," that's why.

5   But then, it's always a little naïve° of Canadians to expect that Americans, of whatever political stamp, should stop being imperious. How can they? The fact is that the United States is an empire and Canada is to it as Gaul° was to Rome.

6   It's hard to explain to Americans what it feels like to be a Canadian. Pessimists among us would say that one has to translate the experience into their own terms and that this is necessary because Americans are incapable of thinking in any other terms—and this in itself is part of the problem. (Witness all those draft dodgers who went into culture shock when they discovered to their horror that Toronto was not Syracuse.)

7   Here is a translation: Picture a Mexico with a population ten times larger than that of the United States. That would put it at about two billion. Now suppose that the official American language is Spanish, that 75 percent of the books Americans buy and 90 percent of the movies they see are Mexican, and that the profits flow across the border to Mexico. If an American does scrape it together to make a movie, the Mexicans won't let him show it in the States, because they own the distribution outlets. If anyone tries to change this ratio, not only the Mexicans but many fellow Americans cry "National chauvinism°," or, even more effectively, "National socialism." After all, the American public prefers the Mexican product. It's what they're used to.

8   Retranslate and you have the current American-Canadian picture. It's changed a little recently, not only on the cultural front. For instance, Canada, some think a trifle late, is attempting to regain control of its own petroleum industry. Americans are predictably angry. They think of Canadian oil as *theirs*.

9   "What's mine is yours," they have said for years, meaning exports; "What's yours is mine" means ownership and profits. Canadians are supposed to do retail buying, not controlling, or what's an empire for? One could always refer Americans to history, particularly that of their own revolution. They objected to the colonial situation when they themselves were a colony; but then, revolution is considered one of a very few home-grown American products that definitely are not for export.

10   Objectively, one cannot become too self-righteous about this state of affairs. Canadians owned lots of things, including their souls, before World War II. After that they sold, some say because they

had put too much into financing the war, which created a capital vacuum° (a position they would not have been forced into if the Americans hadn't kept out of the fighting for so long, say the sore losers). But for whatever reason, capital flowed across the border in the '50s, and Canadians, traditionally sock-under-the-mattress hoarders, were reluctant to invest in their own country. Americans did it for them and ended up with a large part of it, which they retain to this day. In every sellout there's a seller as well as a buyer, and the Canadians did a thorough job of trading their birthright for a mess°.

That's on the capitalist end, but when you turn to the trade 11 union side of things you find much the same story, except that the sellout happened in the '30s under the banner of the United Front. Now Canadian workers are finding that in any empire the colonial branch plants are the first to close, and what could be a truly progressive labor movement has been weakened by compromised bargains made in international union headquarters south of the border.

Canadians are sometimes snippy to Americans at cocktail par- 12 ties. They don't like to feel owned and they don't like having been sold. But what really bothers them—and it's at this point that the United States and Rome part company—is the wide-eyed innocence with which their snippiness is greeted.

Innocence becomes ignorance when seen in the light of interna- 13 tional affairs, and though ignorance is one of the spoils of conquest— the Gauls always knew more about the Romans than the Romans knew about them—the world can no longer afford America's ignorance. Its ignorance of Canada, though it makes Canadians bristle, is a minor and relatively harmless example. More dangerous is the fact that individual Americans seem not to know that the United States is an imperial power and is behaving like one. They don't want to admit that empires dominate, invade and subjugate—and live on the proceeds—or, if they do admit it, they believe in their divine right to do so. The export of divine right is much more harmful than the export of Coca-Cola, though they may turn out to be much the same thing in the end.

Other empires have behaved similarly (the British somewhat 14 better, Genghis Khan decidedly worse); but they have not expected to be *liked* for it. It's the final Americanism, this passion for being liked. Alas, many Americans are indeed likable; they are often more generous, more welcoming, more enthusiastic, less picky and sardonic° than Canadians, and it's not enough to say it's only because they can afford it. Some of that revolutionary spirit still remains: the optimism, the 18th-century belief in the fixability of almost anything, the conviction of the possibility of change. However, at cocktail parties and elsewhere one must be able to tell the difference between an individual and a foreign policy. Canadians can no longer afford to think of Americans as only a spectator sport. If Reagan blows up the world, we will unfortunately be doing more than watching it on television. "No annihilation with[out] representation" sounds good as a slogan, but if we run [it] up the flagpole, who's going to salute?

15   We *are* all in this together. For Canadians, the question is how to survive it. For Americans there is no question, because there does not have to be. Canada is just that vague, cold place where their uncle used to go fishing, before the lakes went dead from acid rain.

16   How do you like Americans? Individually, it's easier. Your average American is no more responsible for the state of affairs than your average man is for war and rape. Any Canadian who is so narrow-minded as to dislike Americans merely on principle is missing out on one of the good things in life. The same might be said, to women, of men. As a group, as a foreign policy, it's harder. But if you like men, you can like Americans. Cautiously. Selectively. Beginning with the feet. One at a time.

MARGARET ATWOOD

Margaret Atwood, the well-known poet and novelist, was born in Ottawa in 1939. She expressed the view in *Survival* that Canadians are content to "get along," unlike the Americans who must "get ahead." She has written numerous collections of poetry and such novels as *The Edible Woman*, *Surfacing*, and *The Handmaid's Tale*.

Words and Meanings

Paragraph

1	jackboots:	large boots coming up above the knees, notorious for having been worn by Nazis
	inegalitarian:	not believing in equality
	alluded:	referred to, hinted at
2	categorically:	without question
3	the Constitution and the Bill of Rights:	documents setting forth the fundamental principles of law and government in the United States
4	quibbles:	minor concerns
	imperialist:	a country that exploits others
5	naïve:	silly, inexperienced
	Gaul:	ancient country in what is now France, conquered by the Romans in 58 B.C.

chauvinism:	extreme patriotism	7
capital vacuum:	shortage of investment money	10
trading their birthright for a mess:	Esau, in the Old Testament, sold his inheritance "for a mess of pottage" (soup)	
sardonic:	sneering, cynical	14

Structure and Strategy

1. With what introductory strategy does Atwood begin her essay?
2. Find three or four particularly effective examples of IRONY in Atwood's essay.
3. Atwood's thesis statement is found in paragraph 5. On what ANALOGY is it based? Do you think the analogy is a valid one?
4. What is the function of paragraph 7? How is it similar to paragraph 2?
5. Identify some of the ways paragraph 16 contributes to the UNITY of this essay.

Content and Purpose

1. The title of this essay, written for Americans and published in an American magazine, is an ALLUSION to Freud's famous question, "Women: what do they want?" Why do you think Atwood chose this title?
2. What causes of anti-Americanism does Atwood identify? (There are at least ten.)
3. According to Atwood, Americans are different from other conquering peoples, ancient and modern. How? Do you think she regards this difference as a strength or a weakness?
4. If you were an American, and therefore part of the audience this essay was written for, how would you react to Atwood's charges? As a Canadian, how valid do you think they are?

Suggestions for Writing

1. Write an essay showing the effects of American influence and domination in a part of the world with which you are familiar.
2. Is there anti-American feeling in the town or city you come from? Write an essay that explains the causes of this anti-Americanism.
3. Mavor Moore once joked that "Canada's national animal isn't the beaver; it's really the carp." What makes Canadians, in Atwood's words, so "picky and sardonic"? Write a short paper outlining the causes of Canadians' well-known tendency to complain about everything.

Let Us Compare Mythologies

WILLIAM THORSELL

1   arly in March [1990], Paul Martin Jr. . . . said this about Canada: "We have declared war on ourselves. We are engaged in a civil war of monumental proportions that simply staggers the mind. East versus West, western alienation against the centre, English versus French—whatever can divide us, we build a monument to it."

2   Civil war overstates it, but Canada is experiencing doubts about its future that are unparalleled in history. Unparalleled because, unlike the period of the Quebec referendum [in 1980], the doubts are spread across a broad swath of Canadians, in all sectors of society and all regions of the country. They are unparalleled because, in some particulars, it is difficult to imagine a way to escape them.

3   How can we explain such angst° at a time when Canada's economy is still strong on its feet after seven years of healthy growth and the national government is secure with a second working majority? Does it all come down to our conflict over constitutional negotiations with Quebec—known as the Meech Lake accord? I think not, for while that conflict is serious, the distress of the Canadian people runs too wide and deep to be explained by one variable alone, no matter how important. In many ways, our constitutional conflict is a symptom, not a cause, of our problems.

4   Instead of focusing on specific issues, I want to explore what you might call the atmospherics of Canada's sour mood today—the context. I will argue that Canada's distress in 1990 cannot be understood without appreciating how much the basic moorings of Canada have been loosened by a series of largely unrelated events. We Canadians have experienced the collapse of several major ideals or mythologies that, until recently, helped to sustain Canada's sense of nationhood. The collapse of these ideals signals the death of Canada as we *knew* it, which is obviously very unsettling to many people. I do not think that Canada as we *know* it is therefore dead or doomed, but the question is certainly in the air.

5   Somewhere in the world today, there may be a country that is

not profoundly changing, or that is not at least confused in a sea of change around it. I might have cited such an example of stolidity° in Mongolia, until February when *The Globe and Mail's* China correspondent visited that vague and forgotten land only to report that it, too, is riding a crest of social change—from green-sequined dancers on local TV to a multiparty system in Ulan Bator.

I am forced, therefore, to cling to Albania, Cuba and the Shining   6
Path guerrillas of Peru as islands of stability in a stream of change— and they are only small islands, surely destined to erode under the insistent pressure that humans feel for individual freedom, the pressure of a global information network and the seductive power of world consumer culture.

Canada, then, is not alone as it grapples with the suddenly   7
shifting foundations of its nationhood and identity. The same forces of globalization that disorient° so many other countries are playing themselves out in Canada to the general consternation° of its people, most of whom would prefer that the future get back where it belongs. But Canada adds its own disturbances.

Let me march quickly through the main traditional myths of   8
Canadian nationhood—myths well rooted in fact once upon a time, but now detached, more obviously every day, from the realities of life as we experience it. These are dead or dying myths, some more important than others, but few of them publicly recognized by our national leaders as having run their course. I will start with a small and simple one.

Myth number one says that Canada is a constitutional monarchy in   9
which the head of state is a king or queen.

Like it or not, this is simply a fiction in the minds of most   10
Canadians who do not conceive° of their country as a monarchy, or Elizabeth II as Canada's head of state, or Prince Charles as its king-in-waiting. The deep monarchist sentiments of some Canadians aside—and I fully respect them—this point hardly needs expansion, it is so obvious a fact in our national life.

I would go as far as to say that, in the unconscious minds of   11
most Canadians, Canada no longer *has* a head of state. There is only a governor-general representing an anachronism°—a shadow symbolizing a memory at the pinnacle of the nation. No leading Canadian politician is willling to say it, but the myth of the monarchy is essentially dead, and our failure to admit it leaves our country headless.

Myth number two says that Canada is a duality—the product of   12
two founding peoples, English and French, who came together in 1867 to form Confederation "from sea unto shining sea."

13   This is the core, binding myth of Canadian nationhood, taught in every school (insofar as schools teach history any more). Precisely because this mythology is so fundamental, very few of Canada's leaders, including its academics, artists and journalists, dare to suggest that this ideal has also seen its best day. (I must observe here that academics and journalists are among the most powerful agents of the status quo in any free society, so their conservative role in this case is entirely predictable.) One need only walk awake through the streets and fields of our country to know that the myth of duality, too, is cracking and breaking under the weight of our daily experience.

14   It is not that duality is untrue, but that it is hopelessly incomplete. Our aboriginal peoples—Inuit, Indian and Métis—challenge the model of two founding peoples that excludes them. They were, after all, here first and there is no logical or moral ground to oppose them on this point. (Members of the government of the Northwest Territories recently dared to ask why English and French were the official languages in the North to the exclusion of native ones.) Less obvious, but just as tenacious°, is the historic and growing presence within Canada of other national backgrounds and races who also see themselves as "founding" peoples.

15   The prairie West was largely settled by the ancestors of its current population a whole generation *after* the original Confederation of 1867. The West was settled, not as a compact° between the two founding peoples, but as a compact among many peoples, notably from continental and central Europe. Western Canadians have never been satisfied to see themselves as late arrivals at someone else's party, and who can blame them? The same can be said of hundreds of thousands of recent immigrants from all over the world who are still coming to Canada's major urban centres. More than 50% of our immigrants now arrive from Asia, Africa and the Caribbean.

16   Canada is not four original provinces frozen in time that can project one moment of their history onto the rest of the land. Canada is 10 provinces, two territories, at least five regions, three city states, many new generations of citizens and continuing immigration from increasingly exotic places in a bewildering flux of time. Canada is alive, and unless we see it as alive, we will not keep it alive.

17   Still, hardly anyone in a position of national influence dares to acknowledge fully that duality is too narrow and dated a concept to contain the reality of Canada as we actually live it. We have invested too much since the 1960s in the historically limited concept of duality to raise common-sense questions about this without scaring ourselves half to death.

18   As in the case of the monarchy, the collapse of this myth happens

in private hearts long before its public funeral. People in the streets are beginning to recognize that the concept of Canada as a duality is essentially academic in most areas of the country—the word "official" in the phrase "official bilingualism" says it all—but we have not yet created another workable concept to take its place. At the heart of our national mythology, then, we are stuck in the purgatory° of pretense that we are something considerably simpler than we actually are. The duality of Canada—which is a truth, but far from the whole truth—is an ideal that is dying on the vine. It leaves our country—which is already headless—drifting without a functioning sense of its own history.

Myth number three says that, unlike the United States, Canada has   19 a mixed economy split between large, state-owned enterprises and private firms. It is habitually said that, without the state-owned firms, there would be no Canada. *L'état, c'est le Crown corporation.*

This myth was quite well founded in history. It grew out of the   20 railroads that were built as a condition of union in 1867 to bind together a far-flung country. It does not matter that the railroads were mostly private undertakings in their beginnings that had to be bailed out of bankruptcy through enormous public subsidies, or nationalized to be saved. The railroads emerged as important symbols of successful national action to build one Canada that could stand independent of the United States in North America.

This symbolism became so powerful that it was imposed on   21 airlines when the time came for a national air system in the 1930s. Despite the intense desire by private entrepreneurs to establish national airlines themselves, Canada's government insisted on a publicly owned air monopoly in the 1930s as another tie to bind the nation.

Electric utilities, telephone systems, hotels, aircraft manufactur-   22 ing firms, oil companies and, of course, a national broadcasting corporation, were added to the stable of public companies meant to serve as bulwarks° of Canadian nationhood in North America. Crown corporations were the flesh on the bones of the state, and in their time, some of these undertakings served their purpose quite well. Now this national security blanket has also been pulled off the bed. For better or worse, the days of economic nationalism appear to be gone.

Privatization of public companies is just one part of a rushing   23 stream of global change that is *de*-nationalizing economics. You can take the cue from the very word "multinational," which describes the main economic engines of the modern world—stateless corporations whose homes are where they find their fat. Throw in the computer revolution that integrates world financial markets, freer trade through the GATT, common markets, multinational passports in Europe, international TV and the vast mobility of modern man and woman in the age of the 747, and the denationalization of economics knocks a giant prop out from beneath all countries that have counted on economic nationalism to define themselves.

24   Think of Mexico, Argentina, Brazil, central Europe, China and the Soviet Union, and the Canadian experience is just a side show in a much bigger play. But, of course, it is *our* side show, so it matters.

25   Our 1988 election debate over free trade with the United States forced us to face up to the myths of economic nationalism much more squarely than those of the monarchy or two founding peoples. We are now trying to articulate new economic ideals calling for excellence, innovation and global competitiveness for Canadian individuals and firms. But the death of the mixed economy in fact, and the acceptance of economic continentalism through free trade by treaty, are still causing a crisis of identity among many Canadians and nostalgia for a Canada we thought we knew just 10 years ago. Headless, and without a functioning sense of history, many Canadians are also feeling a distinct lack of meat on their economic bones.

26   Now I must turn to our fluttering hearts. Other traditional mythologies are also fading at visible cost to our sense of Canadian identity and pride. They include the myth of the helpful fixer in international affairs, where Canadians saw themselves as good-guy mediators serving the interests of peace and justice among bigger powers. We often think of Lester Pearson in the 1950s, but this is the 1990s. Too many new players have arrived on the world scene for Canada to play convincingly its role as Mother Teresa any more.

27   There is also the myth of Canada, the kinder, gentler nation— to borrow a phrase—than the United States, embodying peace, order and good government, humanized by universal medicare, unemployment insurance, old age security, children's allowances and regional development programs. Canadians' hearts are still in the right places here, but their national treasury is empty.

28   As debts and deficits continue to grow, even universal social programs erode before the need for solvency° and the public's resistance to higher taxes. One of the strongest arguments made for universal social programs is the sense of common interest and citizenship they give to everyone in the country. Now this is under pressure, and many Canadians worry that we may be losing our heart in the financial crush.

29   A troubled heart, no head, a poorly functioning history, meat melting from the bones—you can begin to understand the extent of Canada's angst.

And if that is not enough, I would say that democracy itself   30
must be added to the list of ideals in doubt in certain parts of Canada.
In the western and Atlantic provinces particularly, many people feel
that democracy does not function at all well at the national level.
Unlike most federations, we have representation by population in
the House of Commons in Ottawa, unbalanced by a legitimate Sen-
ate speaking up for regional interests. It is shocking but true to say
that the ideal of democracy—which lies at the heart of our body
politic—is now questioned by many thoughtful Canadians. That's
how deep the malaise° has gone. All this adds up to a volatile,
destabilizing mood in Canada. . . .

What are our political leaders doing in this increasingly chippy   31
game? For the most part, they are sticking to a rigid strategy of
defence. The more Canadians are buffeted by change, the more
fervently their leaders exhort them to cling to old verities°. Day after
day in Parliament, we hear calls from the various political parties to
resurrect the mythologies of economic nationalism, Crown corporations, the duality of Canada and official bilingualism as the saviors
of Canadian nationhood. An occasional voice even suggests we rally
around the Queen, but a rally requires more than a dozen people.
None of this addresses what really needs to be done. Indeed, it
exacerbates the sense of unreality that already has the nation so
much on edge.

A particularly depressing example of this occurred in February   32
[1990] when Prime Minister Brian Mulroney threw everything he
had into one small drawer of the status quo. He said—and I quote—
"Simply put, Canada is the coming together of English- and French-
speaking Canadians, and our future lies in the continuing will to
live together. . . . This country will rise or fall on the bilingual nature
of its character. What is Canada without it? There's no country; it's
like an adjunct° of the United States. If you dispose of bilingualism,
if you dispose of the protection of minority language rights, then
you have dealt a lethal° blow to the fundamental tenet° of our
nationhood."

I believe this is a gross overstatement, indeed, a dangerous gross   33
overstatement. The bilingual nature of Canada is an attractive and
important asset, but I don't think most Canadians believe it's the
sine qua non° of our national identity. I don't think most Canadians
believe, to quote the Prime Minister, that "there's no country" without official bilingualism. There was a country called Canada long
before bilingualism appeared as a policy in 1969, and this country
is rooted in much broader ground than that. I firmly support official
bilingualism at the federal level, but little in our experience over the
last 25 years indicates that it is an essential force for keeping Canada
together, within Quebec or elsewhere. It's a good and natural policy

at the federal level, and a good policy in some provincial arenas, but it simply cannot bear the weight of our nationhood from sea to sea.

34   Mulroney is just as silly in saying that our Constitution is "not worth the paper it is written on" because one clause allows legal exemption from the Charter of Rights and Freedoms under certain conditions. Such hyperbole° does not serve the nation well in a time of confusion when Canadians desperately need a ring of truth.

35   Like Argentina, Canada is a richly endowed country sparsely populated by intelligent and cultured people. But we know from observing Argentina that, even with such advantages, things can go terribly wrong. Some observers feel Canadians have developed a bad habit of hectoring° and bitchiness akin to masochism°. We nurture the chips on our shoulders until they become humps on our backs.

36   Yes, we have bad habits, but I am suggesting that more rational explanations exist for our current malaise. We are clinging too loyally to Canada as we knew it, and too cautiously to Canada as we were told to know it.

37   Canada as it actually is need not be an inferior place. On the contrary: Canada is a fully independent, multicultural society, comprising distinctive regions—dare I say, a community of communities—where two major language groups predominate in certain geographic areas, which should be confident enough of their majority rights to value the various minorities among them. . . .

38   Accepting the distinctive cultural histories of regions outside Quebec would . . . make it easier for the rest of the country to live in a more generous national spirit. And it would make it easier to fight the racism stimulated by immigration and the growing presence of visible minorities across the land. People who are secure in their own sense of history tend to be less suspicious of social change. In any case, the history of much of Canada is one of multiculturalism in the first place. Acceptance of diversity is bred in our bone.

39   At the same time, our leadership groups—including artists, intellectuals and even journalists—must stop being so much part of the problem in refusing to face up to change. Whether it be economic nationalism, the nature of social programs, the state of Canada's democracy or the monarchy, the truth will out. Leaders do not deny truth; they work to give it meaning. It is their responsibility to articulate new national ideals that can ease our passage to the future and broaden the consensus needed to reform our federal institutions.

40   I said at the outset that the death of Canada as we *knew* it need not mean the death of Canada as we *know* it. The fundamental threat to Canada is not intolerance—though awful intolerance there be—but hypocrisy. We have nothing to fear from the truth about our

national situation and character, but our leaders keep telling us tales. If we stop lying about ourselves, I believe we can get away from warring among ourselves, and go back to our more familiar national wrestling matches. Wrestling matches give us much better odds on settling our problems. And we have reasons to be optimistic about Canada if we have the wits to be frank°. Like Sigmund Freud, I believe the truth can set you free.

WILLIAM THORSELL

William Thorsell, the editor-in-chief of the *Globe and Mail*, Canada's national newspaper, writes a weekly column on political issues and is a frequent speaker across the country.

Words and Meanings

Paragraph

angst:	anxiety, deep uneasiness	3
stolidity:	resistance to change	5
disorient:	disturb, unsettle	7
consternation:	profound disturbance, sense of disaster	
conceive:	think	10
anachronism:	something left over from another era, outdated	11
tenacious:	strong, persistent	14
compact:	binding agreement	15
purgatory:	state of temporary pain or distress	18
bulwarks:	defences	22
solvency:	condition of having enough money to pay debts	28
malaise:	feeling of depression, hopelessness	30
verities:	truths	31
adjunct:	subordinate part; an add-on	32
lethal:	deadly	
tenet:	principle or doctrine	
sine qua non:	indispensable part	33
hyperbole:	exaggeration	34

35   hectoring: worrying, harassing
     masochism: form of psychological disorder in which the vic-
                              tim derives pleasure from pain and humiliation

40   frank: honest, open, outspoken

Subject and Structure

1. Find Thorsell's statement of subject (paragraph 4) and the six
   myths he identifies as causes of the doubts and distress that he
   sees plaguing Canada today. Then write a thesis statement
   summarizing in a single sentence the causes of our nation's
   "sour mood."
2. What is the function of the last sentences in paragraphs 11 and
   25 and of the first sentences of paragraphs 26 and 29? How
   does Thorsell reinforce his ANALOGY in paragraph 30?
3. Identify the topic sentences and the kinds of support used in
   paragraphs 14 and 22.
4. After discussing the "dead or dying myths" that afflict Canada
   at the beginning of the '90s, Thorsell shifts focus in paragraph 31
   and examines the role our leaders are playing. What examples of
   poor leadership does Thorsell cite to support his point?
5. Study the introductory and concluding paragraphs to this essay.
   How do they contribute to the UNITY of the piece?

Content and Purpose

1. What is a "head of state"? Who is the head of state in Canada?
   Is this concept meaningful to most Canadians? Why or why not?
2. Thorsell sees Canada as only one example of nations undergo-
   ing profound change as we near the end of this century. What
   causes does he identify as contributing to the rising tide of global
   change?
3. Consider each of the six myths that Thorsell claims are "dead
   or dying" in Canada. Do you agree with him? Or do you believe
   some or all of these myths are still valid, still important to Canada's nationhood?
4. In paragraphs 12 to 18, Thorsell points to the inadequacy of the
   notion of Canada as "the product of two founding peoples."
   Whom does this myth exclude? How could Canada revise this
   myth to better reflect the reality of our nation?
5. What would Thorsell think of state-owned enterprises such as
   Air Canada, the CBC, or Petro-Canada? Do they contribute effectively to Canadian unity? Why or why not?
6. Can you think of some examples of what Thorsell means by our
   "familiar national wrestling matches" (paragraph 40)? Do you
   think his metaphor (see FIGURES OF SPEECH) is an effective one?

7. In the last sentence in this essay, Thorsell recalls the famous biblical quotation, "You shall know the truth, and the truth shall make you free." (John 8:32). What is Thorsell's purpose in connecting the quotation to Freud? Does knowing the truth help someone to act more intelligently? More rationally? More tolerantly? How can knowing the "truth" about our country set Canadians free?

Suggestions for Writing

1. Choose one of the myths that Thorsell claims are outmoded or hypocritical, and write an essay explaining why the myth is still important to Canadian unity.
2. Has free trade with the United States benefited or harmed Canada as a nation? Write a causal analysis explaining your views.
3. What would be the effects of abolishing the monarchy in Canada? Write an essay explaining what our country would lose or gain as a result.

Under the Hood

DON SHARP

The owner of this 1966 Plymouth Valiant 1
has made the rounds of car dealers. They will gladly sell him a new car—the latest model of government regulation and industrial enterprise—for $8,000, but they don't want his clattering, emphysemic old vehicle in trade. It isn't worth enough to justify the paperwork, a classified ad, and space on the used-car lot. "Sell it for junk," they tell him. "Scrap iron is high now, and they'll give you $25 for it."

The owner is hurt. He likes this car. It has served him well for 2
90,000-odd miles. It has a functional shape and he can get in and out of it easily. He can roll down his window in a light rain and not get his shoulder wet. The rear windows roll down, and he doesn't need an air conditioner. He can see out of it fore, aft, and abeam. He can hazard° it on urban parking lots without fear of drastic, insurance-deductible casualty loss. His teenage children reject it as passé, so it is always available to him. It has no buzzers, and the

only flashing lights are those he controls himself when signaling a turn. The owner, clearly one of a vanishing tribe, brings the car to a kindred spirit and asks me to rebuild it.

3   We do not discuss the cost. I do not advertise my services and my sign is discreet. My shop is known by word of mouth, and those who spread the word emphasize my house rule: "A blank check and a free hand." That is, I do to your car what I think it needs and you pay for it; you trust me not to take advantage, I guarantee you good brakes, sound steering, and prompt starting, and you pay without quarrel. This kind of arrangement saves a lot of time spent in making estimates and a lot of time haggling over the bill. It also imposes a tremendous burden of responsibility on me, and on those who spread the word, and it puts a burden of trust on those who deliver their cars into my custody.

4   A relationship of that sort is about as profound as any that two people can enjoy, even if it lasts no longer than the time required to reline a set of brakes. I think of hometown farmers who made sharecropping deals for the season on a handshake; then I go into a large garage and see the whitecoated service writer noting the customer's every specification, calling attention to the fine print at the bottom of the work order, and requiring a contractual signature before even a brake-light bulb is replaced. I perceive in their transaction that ignorance of cause and effect breeds suspicion, and I wonder who is the smaller, the customer or the service writer, and how they came to be so small of spirit.

5   Under the hood of this ailing Valiant, I note a glistening line of seeping oil where the oil pan meets the engine block. For thousands of miles, a piece of cork—a strip of bark from a Spanish tree—has stood firm between the pan and the block against churning oil heated to nearly 200 degrees, oil that sought vainly to escape its duty and was forced back to work by a stalwart gasket. But now, after years of perseverance, the gasket has lost its resilience and the craven oil escapes. Ecclesiastes allows a time for all things, and the time for this gasket has passed.

6   Higher up, between the block casting that forms the foundation of the engine and the cylinder-head casting that admits fresh air and exhausts oxidized air and fuel, is the head gasket, a piece of sheet metal as thin as a matchbook cover that has confined the multiple fires built within the engine to their proper domains. Now, a whitish-gray deposit betrays an eroded area from which blue flame spits every time the cylinder fires. The gasket is "blown."

7   Let us stop and think of large numbers. In the four-cycle engines that power all modern cars, a spark jumps a spark-plug gap and sets off a fire in a cylinder every time the crankshaft goes around twice.

The crankshaft turns the transmission shaft, which turns the drive-shaft, which turns the differential gears, which turn the rear axles, which turn the wheels. In 100,000 miles—a common life for modern engines—the engine will make some 260 million turns, and in half of those turns, 130 million of them, a gasoline-fueled fire with a maximum temperature of 2,000 degrees (quickly falling to about 1,200 degrees) is built in each cylinder. The heat generated by the fire raises the pressure in the cylinder to about 700 pounds per square inch, if only for a brief instant before the piston moves and the pressure falls. A head gasket has to contend with heat and pressure like this all the time the engine is running, and, barring mishap°, it will put up with it indefinitely.

This Plymouth has suffered mishap. I know it as soon as I raise   8
the hood and see the telltale line of rust running across the underside of the hood: the mark of overheating. A water pump bearing or seal gave way, water leaked out, and was flung off the fan blades with enough force to embed particles of rust in the undercoating. Without cooling water, the engine grew too hot, and that's why the head gasket blew. In an engine, no cause exists without an effect. Unlike a court of law, wherein criminals are frequently absolved of wrong-doing, no engine component is without duty and responsibility, and failure cannot be mitigated° by dubious explanations such as parental neglect or a crummy neighborhood.

Just as Sherlock Holmes would not be satisifed with one clue if   9
he could find others, I study the oil filter. The block and oil pan are caked with seepings and drippings, but below the filter the caking is visibly less thick and somewhat soft. So: once upon a time, a careless service-station attendant must have ruined the gasket while installing a new oil filter. Oil en route to the bearings escaped and washed away the grime that had accumulated. Odds are that the oil level fell too low and the crankshaft bearings were starved for oil.

Bearings are flat strips of metal, formed into half-circles about   10
as thick as a matchbook match and about an inch wide. The bearing surface itself—the surface that *bears* the crankshaft and that *bears* the load imposed by the fire-induced pressure above the piston— is half as thick. Bearing metal is a drab, gray alloy, the principal component of which is *babbitt*, a low-friction metal porous enough to absorb oil but so soft that it must be allowed to withstand high pressures. When the fire goes off above the piston and the pressure is transmitted to the crankshaft via the connecting rod, the babbitt-alloyed bearing pushes downward with a force of about 3,500 pounds per square inch. And it must not give way, must not be peened° into foil and driven from its place in fragments.

Regard the fleshy end joint of your thumb and invite a 100-   11 pound woman (or a pre-teen child, if no such woman be near to hand) to stand on it. Multiply the sensation by thirty-five and you get an idea of what the bearing is up against. Of course, the bearing enjoys a favorable handicap in the comparison because it works in a metal-to-metal environment heated to 180 degrees or so. The bearing is equal to its task so long as it is protected from direct metal-to-metal contact by a layer of lubricating oil, oil that must be forced into the space between the bearing and the crankshaft against that 3,500 pounds of force. True, the oil gets a lot of help from hydro-dynamic action as the spinning crankshaft drags oil along with it, but lubrication depends primarily on a pump that forces oil through the engine at around 40 pounds of pressure.

12   If the oil level falls too low, the oil pump sucks in air. The oil gets as frothy as whipped cream and doesn't flow. In time, oil pressure will fall so low that the "idiot" light on the dashboard will flash, but long before then the bearing may have run "dry" and suffered considerable amounts of its metal to be peened away by those 3,500-pound hammer blows. "Considerable" may mean only .005 inches, or about the thickness of one sheet of 75-percent-cotton, 25-pound-per-ream dissertation bond°—not much metal, but enough to allow oil to escape from the bearing even after the defective filter gasket is replaced and the oil supply replenished. From the time of oil starvation onward, the beaten bearing is a little disaster waiting to spoil a vacation or a commute to an important meeting.

13   Curious, that an unseen .005 inches of drab, gray metal should enjoy more consequence for human life than almost any equal thickness of a randomly chosen doctoral dissertation. Life is full of ironies.

14   The car I confront does not have an "idiot" light. It has an old-fashioned oil-pressure gauge. As the driver made his rounds from condominium to committee room, he could—if he cared or was ever so alert—monitor the health of his engine bearings by noting the oil pressure. Virtually all cars had these gauges in the old days, but they began to disappear in the mid-'50s, and nowadays hardly any cars have them. In eliminating oil-pressure gauges, the car makers pleaded that, in their dismal experience, people didn't pay much attention to gauges. Accordingly, Detroit switched to the warning light, which was cheaper to manufacture anyway (and having saved a few bucks on the mechanicals, the manufacturer could afford to etch a design in the opera windows; this is called "progress"). Curious, in the midst of all this, that Chrysler Corporation, the maker of Plymouths and the victim of so much bad management over the past fifteen years, should have been the one car manufacturer to constantly assert, via a standard-equipment oil-pressure gauge, a

faith in the awareness, judgment, and responsibility of drivers. That Chrysler did so may have something to do with its current problems.

The other car makers were probably right. Time was when   15
most men knew how to replace their own distributor points, repair a flat tire, and install a battery. Women weren't assumed to know as much, but they were expected to know how to put a gear lever in neutral, set a choke and throttle, and crank a car by hand if the battery was dead. Now, odds are that 75 percent of men and a higher percentage of women don't even know how to work the jacks that come with their cars. To be sure, a bumper jack is an abominable contraption—the triumph of production economies over good sense—but it will do what it is supposed to do, and the fact that most drivers cannot make one work says much about the way motorists have changed over the past forty years.

About all that people will watch on the downslide of this century   16
is the fuel gauge, for they don't like to be balked in their purpose. A lack of fuel will stop a car dead in its tracks and categorically prevent the driver from arriving at the meeting to consider tenure for a male associate professor with a black grandfather and a Chinese mother. Lack of fuel will stall a car in mid-intersection and leave dignity and image prey to the honks and curses of riffraff driving taxicabs and beer trucks, so people watch the fuel gauge as closely as they watch a pubescent daughter or a bearish stock.

But for the most part, once the key goes into the ignition,   17
people assign responsibility for the car's smooth running to someone else—to anybody but themselves. If the engine doesn't start, that's not because the driver has abused it, but because the manufacturer was remiss° or the mechanic incompetent. (Both suspicions are reasonable, but they do not justify the driver's spineless passivity.) The driver considers himself merely a client of the vehicle. He proudly disclaims°, at club and luncheon, any understanding of the dysfunctions of the machine. He must so disclaim, for to admit knowledge or to seek it actively would require an admission of responsibility and fault. To be wrong about inflation or the political aspirations of Albanians doesn't cost anybody anything, but to claim to know why the car won't start and then to be proved wrong is both embarrassing and costly.

Few people would remove $500 from someone's pocket without   18
a qualm° and put it in their own. Yet, the job-lot run of mechanics do it all the time. Mechanics and drivers are alike: they gave up worrying long ago about the intricacies and demands of cause and effect. The mechanics do not attend closely to the behavior of the vehicle. Rather, they consult a book with flowcharts that says, "Try this, and if it doesn't work, try that." Or they hook the engine up

to another machine and read gauges or cathode-ray-tube squiggles, but without realizing that gauges and squiggles are not reality but only tools used to aid perception of reality.

19   Mechanics, like academics and bureaucrats, have retreated too far from the realities of their tasks. An engine runs badly. They consult the book. The book says to replace part A. They replace A. The engine still runs badly, but the mechanic can deny the fact as handily as a socialist can deny that minimum-wage laws eventually lead to unemployment. Just as the driver doesn't care to know why his oil pressure drops from 40 to 30 to 20 pounds and then to zero, so the mechanic cares little for the casuistic° distinctions that suggest that part A is in good order but that some subtle conjunction of wholesome part B with defective part C may be causing the trouble.

20   And why should the mechanic care? He gets paid in any event. From the mechanic's point of view, he should get paid, for he sees a federal judge hire academic consultants to advise about busing, and after the whites have fled before the imperious column of yellow buses and left the schools blacker than ever, the judge hires the consultants again to find out why the whites moved out. The consultant gets paid in public money, whatever effects his actions have, even when he causes things he said would never happen.

21   Consider the garden-variety Herr Doktor° who has spent a pleasant series of warm fall weekends driving to a retreat in the Catskills; his car has started with alacrity and run well despite a stuck choke. Then, when the first blue norther of the season sends temperatures toward zero, the faithful machine must be haggled into action and proceeds haltingly down the road, gasping and backfiring. "Needs a new carburetor," the mechanic says, and, to be sure, once a new carburetor is installed, the car runs well again. Our Herr Doktor is happy. His car did not run well; it got a new carburetor and ran well again; ergo, the carburetor was at fault. Q.E.D.°

22   Curious that in personal matters the classic *post hoc* fallacy° should be so readily accepted when it would be mocked in academic debate. Our Herr Doktor should know, or at least suspect, that the carburetor that functioned so well for the past several months could hardly have changed its nature overnight, and we might expect of him a more diligent inquiry into its problems. But "I'm no mechanic," he chuckles to his colleagues, and they nod agreeably. Such skinned-knuckle expertise would be unfitting in a man whose self-esteem is equivalent to his uselessness with a wrench. Lilies of the postindustrial field must concern themselves with weighty matters beyond the ken of greasy laborers who drink beer at the end of a workday.

23   Another example will illustrate the point. A battery cable has an end that is designed to connect to a terminal on the battery. Both

cable-end and battery-terminal surfaces look smooth, but aren't. Those smooth surfaces are pitted and peaked, and only the peaks touch each other. The pits collect water from the air, and the chemistry of electricity-carrying metals causes lead oxides to form in the pits. The oxides progressively insulate the cable end and battery terminal from each other until the day that turning the key produces only a single, resounding *clunk* and no more. The road service mechanic installs a new $75 battery and collects $25 for his trouble. Removing the cables from the old battery cleans their ends somewhat, so things work for a few days, and then the car again fails to start. The mechanic installs a $110 alternator, applies a $5 charge to the battery, and collects another $25; several days later he gives the battery another $5 charge, installs a $75 starter, and collects $25 more. In these instances, to charge the battery—to send current backwards from cable end to battery terminal—disturbs the oxides and temporarily improves their conductivity. Wriggling the charger clamps on the cable ends probably helps too. On the driver's last $25 visit, the mechanic sells another $5 battery charge and a pair of $25 battery cables. Total bill: $400, and all the car needed was to have its cable ends and battery terminals cleaned. The mechanic wasn't necessarily a thief. Perhaps, like academic education consultants, he just wasn't very smart—and his ilk° abound; they are as plentiful as the drivers who will pay generously for the privilege of an aristocratic disdain of elementary cause and effect in a vehicular electrical system.

After a tolerably long practice as a mechanic, I firmly believe that at least two-thirds of the batteries, starters, alternators, ignition coils, carburetors, and water pumps that are sold are not needed. Batteries, alternators, and starters are sold because battery-cable ends are dirty. A maladjusted or stuck automatic choke is cured by a new carburetor. Water pumps and alternators are sold to correct problems from loose fan belts. In the course of the replacement, the fan belt gets properly tightened, so the original problem disappears in the misguided cure, with mechanic and owner never the wiser.   24

I understand the venality° (and laziness and ignorance) of mechanics, and I understand the shop owner's need to pay a salary to someone to keep up with the IRS and OSHA forms. The shop marks up parts by 50 to 100 percent. When the car with the faulty choke comes in the door, the mechanic must make a choice: he can spend fifteen minutes fixing it and charge a half-hour's labor, or he can spend a half-hour replacing the carburetor (and charge for one hour) with one he buys for $80 and sells for $135. If the shop is a profit-making enterprise, the mechanic can hardly be blamed for selling the unneeded new carburetor, especially if the customer will stand still to be fleeced. Whether the mechanic   25 acts from ignorance or larceny° (the odds are about equal), the result is still a waste, one that arises from the driver's refusal to study the cause and effect of events that occur under the hood of his car.

26   The willingness of a people to accept responsibility for the machines they depend on is a fair barometer of their sense of individual worth and of the moral strength of a culture. According to popular reports, the Russian working folk are a sorrowfully vodka-besotted lot; likewise, reports are that Russian drivers abuse their vehicles atrociously. In our unhappy country, as gauges for battery-changing (ammeters), cooling-water temperature, and oil pressure disappeared from dashboards, they were replaced by a big-brotherly series of cacophonous° buzzers and flashing lights, buzzers and lights mandated° by regulatory edict° for the sole purpose of reminding the driver that the government considers him a hopeless fool. Concurrent with these developments has come social agitation and law known as "consumer protection," which is, in fact, an extension of the philosophy that people are morons for whom the government must provide outpatient care. People pay handsome taxes to be taught that they are not responsible and do not need to be.

27   What is astounding and dismaying is how quickly people came to believe in their own incompetence. In 1951, Eric Hoffer noted in *The True Believer* that a leader so disposed could make free people into slaves easier than he could turn slaves into free people (cf. Moses). Hoffer must be pained by the accuracy of his perception.

28   I do not claim that Everyman can be his own expert mechanic, for I know that precious few can. I do claim that disdain° for the beautiful series of cause-and-effect relationships that move machines, and particularly the automobile, measures not only a man's wit but also a society's morals.

DON SHARP

Don Sharp, a journalist, was born in New Mexico in 1938. He is a graduate of the University of Alaska, in Fairbanks. He taught English in several small colleges in the United States before becoming a free-lance writer and magazine editor. He has published articles in *Harper's* and *Commentary*, and is currently editor of *The Western Boatman*, published in California.

Words and Meanings

hazard:	chance, risk	2
barring mishap:	unless something goes wrong, or there is an accident	7
mitigated:	lessened, diminished	8
peened:	hammered thin	10
dissertation bond:	typing paper	12
remiss: disclaims:	careless, negligent denies any knowledge of	17
qualm:	uneasiness, twinge of conscience	18
casuistic:	fine; quibbling	19
Herr Doktor: Q.E.D.:	highly educated man; university professor *quod erat demonstrandum*, Latin for "proved"	21
post hoc fallacy:	error of assuming that because one event followed another, it was caused by the first event	22
ilk:	like; people similar to him	23
venality: larceny:	lack of principle; greed theft	25
cacophonous: mandated: edict:	harsh-sounding required law	26
disdain:	scorn, contempt	28

Structure and Strategy

1. What introductory strategy does the author use?
2. Study the DICTION of paragraph 5. How does it help to reveal Sharp's attitudes toward machines in general and the automobile in particular?
3. Explain the implied contrast in paragraph 2 that reveals Sharp's opinion of car manufacturers' most recent car designs.
4. Identify the definition Sharp provides in paragraph 10 that is further explained by a comparison in paragraph 11.
5. Identify two of the examples Sharp uses to show that ignorance of mechanical cause-effect relationships is expensive.
6. This essay may be divided into five parts: paragraphs 1 to 4, 5 to 13, 14 to 17, 18 to 25, and 26 to 28. Identify the main idea each part develops.

Content and Purpose

1. What is the basis of an "agreement" and what is the basis of a "contract"? Why does Sharp stress the difference between these two relationships in paragraphs 3 and 4?
2. Summarize the author's reasons for believing that both drivers and mechanics are guilty of ignoring the laws of cause and effect.
3. Who are the "lilies of the postindustrial field" (paragraph 22) and what is Sharp's attitude toward them?
4. What is the author's purpose in comparing mechanics to academics, bureaucrats, and education consultants? What, in Sharp's opinion, do these groups have in common?
5. Why does Sharp dislike "consumer protection" laws? (See paragraph 26.)
6. What is the implied thesis of this essay? (See paragraphs 26 to 28.) Summarize the thesis in your own words.
7. Sharp ends his essay with a credo, a statement of personal philosophy or belief. Summarize his credo. Do you agree or disagree with it?

Suggestions for Writing

1. Write a paper explaining the cause-effect relationship between any two things: two organisms, two parts of a machine, two chemicals, two emotions, two social conditions, or two environmental conditions.
2. We frequently hear that the quality of our school system is deteriorating. Do you think the average high school graduate today is less well-educated than one of twenty years ago? If so, what are some of the causes of this decline in quality? If you don't agree, what are some of the causes of the perceived decline?

Additional Suggestions for Writing: Causal Analysis

Choose one of the topics below and write a paper that explores its causes *or* effects. Write a clear thesis statement and plan the development of each main point before you begin to write the paper.

1. sibling rivalry
2. seat-belt legislation
3. the popularity of a current television series
4. the increasing number of working mothers
5. fascination with the lifestyles of the rich and famous
6. the tendency of people to distrust or dislike people different from themselves
7. the pressure on women to be thin
8. the appeal of television evangelists or preachers
9. peer pressure among adolescents
10. the increasing popularity of foreign-made cars
11. the increasing popularity of French-immersion schooling in Canada
12. the trend to postpone childbearing until a couple reaches their thirties
13. a specific phobia that affects someone you know
14. the attraction of religious cults
15. marriage breakdown
16. alcoholism
17. the popularity of Gordon Korman, or Judy Blume, or any other widely read writer of fiction for adolescents
18. the demand among employers for ever-increasing levels of literacy
19. guilt
20. "Happy families are all alike; every unhappy family is unhappy in its own way." (Tolstoy)

Definition:
Explaining "What"

What? The Definition

Communication between writer and reader cannot take place unless there is a shared understanding of the meaning of the writer's words. Knowing when and how to define terms clearly is one of the most useful skills a writer can learn. Through definition, a writer creates meaning.

In the biblical creation myth, which has endured for millennia (a millennium is a period of a thousand years), the Creator presents the animals to Adam in order that he name them:

And out of the ground the Lord God formed every beast of the field, and every fowl of the air; and brought them to Adam to see what he would call them: and whatsoever Adam called every creature, that was the name thereof.

(Genesis 2:19)

Adam isn't asked to count or catalogue or describe or judge the beasts of creation. They are arrayed before him so that he might *name* them, *define* them, an act which is itself a kind of creation. This capacity to define things through words and to communicate thought by means of those words makes us unique as humans.

There are two basic ways to define terms: the short way and the long way. The short way is sometimes called **formal definition**. The writer very quickly, in a sentence or so, explains a word that may be unknown to the reader. An example of formal definition is the explanation of the word "millennium" in the paragraph above. You should include a definition whenever you introduce an unfamiliar word, or whenever you assign a particular meaning to a general term. If you do not define ambiguous words or phrases, you leave the reader wondering which of several possible meanings you intended. You should also provide definitions when using technical terms, since these are likely to be unfamiliar to at least some readers. For instance, a reader who is not familiar with the term "formal definition" might assume it means "elaborate" or "fancy," when in fact it means a one-sentence definition written in a particular form.

The second way to define a term is through **extended definition**, a form of expository writing in which the word, idea, thing, or phenomenon being defined is the subject of the entire essay or paper. Extended definition is required when the nature of the thing to be defined is complex, and explaining *what it is* in detail is the writer's goal.

Why? The Purpose

In your studies, you have probably already discovered that fully exploring a complex subject requires a detailed explanation of it. Definition papers answer the question, "What does S mean?" For example, the word "myth" used above to describe the creation story does not, in any way, mean "untrue," though that is often the way the word is used. A myth is better defined as a traditional or legendary story that attempts to explain a basic truth. Entire books have been written to define what myth is and how it works in our culture. Obviously, myth is a topic that lends itself to extended definition.

Extended definition is especially useful for three purposes: explaining the abstract, the technical, or the changed meanings of a word or concept. If you were asked in a history class, for example, to define an abstract idea such as "freedom" or "misogyny" or "justice," an extended definition would enable you to establish the meaning of the concept and also to explore your personal commitments and aspirations.

Whatever their professional background, all writers occasionally use technical terms that must be defined for readers who may be unfamiliar with them. For example, a Canadian businessperson with a large potential market in the United States may have to define "free trade" to prospective investors. A social worker would be wise to detail what she means by "substance abuse" in a brochure aimed at teenage drug users. An engineer could not explain concepts such as "gas chromatography" or "atomic absorption" to a non-technical audience without first adequately defining them.

Extended definition can also be used to clarify the way in which a particular term has changed in meaning over the years. For instance, everyone is aware of the way in which the word "gay," which originally meant only "joyful" or "bright," has expanded to include "homosexual," even in its denotative, or dictionary, meaning. Tracking the evolution of a word's meaning can be both an effective and an interesting way to define the term for your readers.

Clearly, extended definition is ideal for explaining because it establishes the boundaries of meaning intended by the writer. In fact, the very word "define" comes from the Latin word *definire*, which means "to put a fence around." But definition is not restricted to its expository function. Defining something in a particular way sometimes involves persuading other people to accept and act on the definition. Our businessperson will probably want to take a stand on free trade after defining it; the social worker's definition of substance abuse might well form the basis of the arguments against drug use. Extended definition is thus a versatile rhetorical strategy that can accommodate the urge we all have to convince and influence the people with whom we're communicating.

How? The Method

Extended definition does not have a single, clear-cut rhetorical pattern unique to itself. Its development relies instead on one or more of the other patterns explained in this text. In other words, depending on the topic and the audience, an extended definition may use any of a variety of forms, or even a combination of forms. For instance, if you wanted to define the term "myth," one way would be by providing *examples* of different myths. Another way would involve *comparing* the terms "myth" and "legend." Or you might choose to explain some of the *effects* of a particular myth on a specific culture. An extended definition of gas chromatography, on the other hand, might focus on the *process* involved in using a chromatograph. An extended definition of substance abuse could *classify* the various addictive drugs. Sometimes a combination of patterns is the best approach. You need to put yourself in your reader's place to determine what questions he or she would be most likely to ask about your topic. Then you'll be able to choose the most appropriate pattern or patterns with which to organize your paper.

It is often helpful to begin your extended definition with a *formal definition*. To write a formal definition, first put the term you are defining into the general class of things to which it belongs; then identify the qualities that set it apart or distinguish it from the others in that class. Here are some examples of formal definitions:

TERM		CLASS	DISTINGUISHING FEATURES
A turtle	is	a shelled reptile	that lives in water.
A tortoise	is	a shelled reptile	that lives on land.
Misogyny	is	a feeling of hatred	against women.
Misanthropy	is	a feeling of hatred	against people in general.
The Gross Domestic Product	is	an economic indicator	derived by establishing the total value of a country's goods and services.
A résumé	is	a written summary	of a job applicant's education, work experience, and personal background.

Constructing a formal definition is a logical way to begin any task of definition. It prevents vague formulations such as "a turtle lives in water" (so does a tuna), or "misanthropy is when you don't like people." (By the way, avoid using "is when" or "is where" in a formal definition—it's bound to be loose and imprecise.) Notice that a formal definition is sometimes a ready-made thesis statement, as in the last two examples given above. An extended definition of the Gross Domestic Product would divide the GDP into its component parts— goods and services—and show how their value is determined. Similarly, an extended definition of a résumé would explain its three essential components: the applicant's education, work experience, and personal background.

There are two pitfalls to avoid when you are writing definitions. First, do not begin with a word-for-word definition copied straight out of the dictionary, even though you may be tempted to do so when you're staring at a piece of blank paper. Resist the temptation. As an introductory strategy, a dictionary definition is both boring and irrelevant. It's *your* meaning the reader needs to understand, not all the potential meanings of the word given in the dictionary. "*Webster's Third International Dictionary* defines love as 'a predilection or liking for anything' " is hardly a useful, let alone an attention-getting, introduction. Second, don't chase your own tail: avoid using in your definition a form of the term you're defining. A definition such as "adolescence is the state of being an adolescent" not only fails to clarify the meaning for your readers, but also wastes their time.

A good definition establishes clearly, logically, and precisely the boundaries of meaning. It communicates the meaning in an organizational pattern appropriate to the term and to the reader. To define is, in many ways, to create, and to do this well is to show respect for the ideas or things you're explaining as well as courtesy to your audience.

Here is an example of an essay that defines a term by exploring its etymological roots.

A Definition of Education

Introduction

Words don't spring into being out of nowhere: they grow out of other words. It is often useful and interesting to explore the etymology, or origins, of the words we use. The word "education," for example, has a meaningful history. It is derived from two different but related Latin words: *educare* and *educere*.

Thesis statement →

First point (developed by definition and quotation)

The Latin verb *educare* is most often translated as "to rear" or "to nourish." Originally, the word was applied to both children and animals, because "rearing" means providing food and basic necessities. The *Oxford English Dictionary* tells us that one of the earliest recorded uses of the word was in the context of animal husbandry. In 1607 a man named Topsell wrote that "horses are not to be despised, if they [are] well bred and educated." The word is not used this way today—we teach a dog new tricks; we don't "educate" him. The word retains something of its earlier meaning, however, in that parents and teachers nourish the young with knowledge, which is digested by relatively passive recipients.

Second point (also developed by definition and quotation)

The Latin verb *educere*, on the other hand, has a different, more active meaning. It means "to lead out" or "to draw forth." The English word "educe," a direct descendant of *educere*, means to infer something, or to come up with ideas oneself. In other words, if I use my own faculties, combined with the knowledge I've gained, I can actively educe or develop new ideas on my own. The

English poet Samuel Taylor Coleridge asserted, "In the education of children, love is first to be instilled, and out of love obedience is to be educed." His use of the word "educed" implies that children can naturally develop obedience out of their own best instincts rather than remain passive receptacles into whom "obedience" is poured (or thrashed). Similarly, a teacher can lead her students or draw them out, but the students must respond actively to develop the behaviour or knowledge themselves. Basically, the *educare* root points to a passive experience in which the learner waits to be filled with facts, while the *educere* root points to a dynamic experience in which the learner interacts creatively with the teacher and the subject matter.

Conclusion
(makes use of a short anecdote to make the general point specific)

This distinction was brought home to me recently as I listened to a hotline radio program in which a grade-ten dropout bemoaned his lack of a job: "Unless my education improves," he began, "I won't have a chance." Interestingly, his phrase lacked a "doer." He seemed to understand education only in the sense that derives from *educare*: the experience of being spoon-fed. To this young man, education was something separate from himself, outside his control—something which, like his chances, could only be altered by outside forces. This attitude is clearly self-defeating. It fails to recognize the meaning of education that derives from *educere*: the experience of actively responding to and developing what a teacher has initiated. The relationship between the learner and what is being learned must be an active one. The learner, in other words, must assume responsibility in the process.

Thus, the roots of the word "education" have something to teach us. We can educe useful knowledge from them even today—hundreds of years after the word itself first appeared in our language.

Don't You Think It's Time to Start Thinking?

NORTHROP FRYE

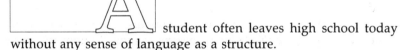

1   student often leaves high school today without any sense of language as a structure.

2   He may also have the idea that reading and writing are elementary skills that he mastered in childhood, never having grasped the fact that there are differences in levels of reading and writing as there are in mathematics between short division and integral calculus.

3   Yet, in spite of his limited verbal skills, he firmly believes that he can think, that he has ideas, and that if he is just given the opportunity to express them he will be all right. Of course, when you look at what he's written you find it doesn't make any sense. When you tell him this he is devastated.

4   Part of his confusion here stems from the fact that we use the word "think" in so many bad, punning ways. Remember James Thurber's Walter Mitty who was always dreaming great dreams of glory. When his wife asked him what he was doing he would say, "Has it ever occurred to you that I might be thinking?"

5   But, of course, he wasn't thinking at all. Because we use it for everything our minds do, worrying, remembering, day-dreaming, we imagine that thinking is something that can be achieved without any training. But again it's a matter of practice. How well we can think depends on how much of it we have already done. Most students need to be taught, very carefully and patiently, that there is no such thing as an inarticulate° idea waiting to have the right words wrapped around it.

6   They have to learn that ideas do not exist until they have been

incorporated into words. Until that point you don't know whether you are pregnant or just have gas on the stomach.

The operation of thinking is the practice of articulating ideas 7 until they are in the right words. And we can't think at random either. We can only add one more idea to the body of something we have already thought about. Most of us spend very little time doing this, and that is why there are so few people whom we regard as having any power to articulate at all. When such a person appears in public life, like Mr. Trudeau, we tend to regard him as possessing a gigantic intellect.

A society like ours doesn't have very much interest in literacy. 8 It is compulsory to read and write because society must have docile and obedient citizens. We are taught to read so that we can obey the traffic signs and to cipher so that we can make out our income tax, but development of verbal competency is very much left to the individual.

And when we look at our day-to-day existence we can see that 9 there are strong currents at work against the development of powers of articulateness. Young adolescents today often betray a curious sense of shame about speaking articulately, of framing a sentence with a period at the end of it.

Part of the reason for this is the powerful anti-intellectual drive 10 which is constantly present in our society. Articulate speech marks you out as an individual, and in some settings this can be rather dangerous because people are often suspicious and frightened of articulateness. So if you say as little as possible and use only stereotyped, ready-made phrases you can hide yourself in the mass.

Then there are various epidemics sweeping over society which 11 use unintelligibility° as a weapon to preserve the present power structure. By making things as unintelligible as possible, to as many people as possible, you can hold the present power structure together. Understanding and articulateness lead to its destruction. This is the kind of thing that George Orwell was talking about, not just in *Nineteen Eighty-Four*, but in all his work on language. The kernel of everything reactionary° and tyrannical° in society is the impoverishment of the means of verbal communication.

The vast majority of things that we hear today are prejudices 12 and clichés, simply verbal formulas that have no thought behind them but are put up as a pretence of thinking. It is not until we realize these things conceal meaning, rather than reveal it, that we can begin to develop our own powers of articulateness.

The teaching of humanities° is, therefore, a militant° job. Teach- 13 ers are faced not simply with a mass of misconceptions° and unexamined assumptions. They must engage in a fight to help the student confront and reject the verbal formulas and stock responses°, to convert passive acceptance into active, constructive power. It is a fight against illiteracy and for the maturation of the mental process, for the development of skills which once acquired will never become obsolete.

```
┌─────────────────────────┐
│                         │
│                         │
└─────────────────────────┘
```

NORTHROP FRYE

Northrop Frye (1912–1991), was born in Sherbrooke, Que., and raised in Moncton, N.B. For many years, he taught English at Victoria College, University of Toronto. His theories of the relationship between myth and reality have had a wide literary and social influence. Among his books are *The Educated Imagination*, *Anatomy of Criticism*, and *The Great Code*.

Words and Meanings

Paragraph

5	inarticulate:	unexpressed; not put into words
11	unintelligibility:	lack of understandable meaning
	reactionary:	ultraconservative
	tyrannical:	like a dictator or tyrant
13	humanities:	the traditional liberal arts subjects, such as philosophy, history, and literature
	militant:	fighting; engaged in battle
	misconception:	mistaken belief
	stock responses:	standard, predictable expressions

Structure and Strategy

1. What is the function of paragraphs 1 to 3 and paragraphs 4 to 6?
2. Why is Frye's allusion to Walter Mitty particularly appropriate in this essay? (If you aren't familiar with the story, look up "The Secret Life of Walter Mitty" in an anthology of James Thurber's short stories.)
3. What metaphor (see FIGURES OF SPEECH) does Frye use in paragraph 6 to help reinforce his point? What connection does Frye imply between pregnancy and thinking?
4. Identify Frye's formal definition of "thinking."
5. What are the reasons Frye offers to support his opinion that thinking isn't often found in our society? How does he develop them (paragraphs 8 to 12)?

Content and Purpose

1. What does Frye mean by "language as structure"? (See paragraph 1.)
2. What does Frye mean by "literacy" and "verbal competency"? (See paragraph 8.)
3. According to Frye, is it possible for an inarticulate person to think? Why?
4. Which groups in our society use "unintelligibility as a weapon"? Why do you think Frye doesn't identify them for us? Why might these groups fear articulateness? (See paragraph 11.)
5. Why are clichés and prejudice enemies of thinking?
6. Explain in your own words what Frye means when he claims that teaching the humanities is "a militant job."

Suggestion for Writing

Write a formal definition of one of the following terms, and develop it by whatever expository techniques you choose into an extended definition: thoughtfulness, imagination, literacy, creativity.

Wrong Ism

J.B. PRIESTLEY

There are three isms that we ought to consider very carefully—regionalism, nationalism, internationalism. Of these three the one there is most fuss about, the one that starts men shouting and marching and shooting, the one that seems to have all the depth and thrust and fire, is of course nationalism. Nine people out of ten, I fancy, would say that of this trio it is the one that really counts, the big boss. Regionalism and internationalism, they would add, are comparatively small, shadowy, rather cranky. And I believe all this to be quite wrong. Like many another big boss, nationalism is largely bogus°. It is like a bunch of flowers made of plastics.

The real flowers belong to regionalism. The mass of people everywhere may never have used the term. They are probably regionalists without knowing it. Because they have been brought

"Wrong Ism" from *Essays of Five Decades* by J.B. Priestley. Copyright 1968 (in association with Little, Brown & Co. and Atlantic Monthly Press). Reprinted by permission of the Peters, Fraser and Dunlop Group, Ltd.

up in a certain part of the world, they have formed perhaps quite unconsciously a deep attachment to its landscape and speech, its traditional customs, its food and drink, its songs and jokes. (There are of course always the rebels, often intellectuals and writers, but they are not the mass of people). They are rooted in their region. Indeed, without this attachment a man can have no roots.

3   So much of people's lives, from earliest childhood onwards, is deeply intertwined with the common life of the region, they cannot help feeling strongly about it. A threat to it is a knife pointing at the heart. How can life ever be the same if bullying strangers come to change everything? The form and colour, the very taste and smell of dear familiar things will be different, alien, life-destroying. It would be better to die fighting. And it is precisely this, the nourishing life of the region, for which common men have so often fought and died.

4   This attachment to the region exists on a level far deeper than that of any political hocus-pocus. When a man says "my country" with real feeling, he is thinking about his region, all that has made up his life, and not about that political entity, the nation. There can be some confusion here simply because some countries are so small—and ours is one of them—and so old, again like ours, that much of what is national is also regional. Down the centuries, the nation, itself, so comparatively small, has been able to attach to itself the feeling really created by the region. (Even so there is something left over, as most people in Yorkshire or Devon, for example, would tell you.) This probably explains the fervent patriotism developed early in small countries. The English were announcing that they were English in the Middle Ages, before nationalism had arrived elsewhere.

5   If we deduct from nationalism all that it has borrowed or stolen from regionalism, what remains is mostly rubbish. The nation, as distinct from the region, is largely the creation of power-men and political manipulators. Almost all nationalist movements are led by ambitious frustrated men determined to hold office. I am not blaming them. I would do the same if I were in their place and wanted power so badly. But nearly always they make use of the rich warm regional feeling, the emotional dynamo of the movement, while being almost untouched by it themselves. This is because they are not as a rule deeply loyal to any region themselves. Ambition and a love of power can eat like acid into the tissues of regional loyalty. It is hard, if not impossible, to retain a natural piety and yet be for ever playing both ends against the middle.

6   Being itself a power structure, devised by men of power, the nation tends to think and act in terms of power. What would benefit the real life of the region, where men, women and children actually

live, is soon sacrificed for the power and prestige of the nation. (And the personal vanity of presidents and ministers themselves, which historians too often disregard.) Among the new nations of our time innumerable peasants and labourers must have found themselves being cut down from five square meals a week to three in order to provide unnecessary airlines, military forces that can only be used against them and nobody else, great conference halls and official yachts and the rest. The last traces of imperialism and colonialism may have to be removed from Asia and Africa, where men can no longer endure being condemned to a permanent inferiority by the colour of their skins; but even so, the modern world, the real world of our time, does not want and would be far better without more and more nations, busy creating for themselves the very parapher- nalia that western Europe is now trying to abolish. You are com- pelled to answer more questions when trying to spend half a day in Cambodia than you are now travelling from the Hook of Holland to Syracuse.

This brings me to internationalism. I dislike this term, which I used only to complete the isms. It suggests financiers and dubious° promoters living nowhere but in luxury hotels; a shallow world of entrepreneurs° and impresarios°. (Was it Sacha Guitry who said that impresarios were men who spoke many languages but all with a foreign accent?) The internationalism I have in mind here is best described as world civilisation. It is life considered on a global scale. Most of our communications and transport already exist on this high wide level. So do many other things from medicine to meteorol- ogy. Our astronomers and physicists (except where they have allowed themselves to be hush-hushed) work here. The UN special agencies, about which we hear far too little, have contributed more and more to this world civilisation. All the arts, when they are arts and not chunks of nationalist propaganda, naturally take their place in it. And it grows, widens, deepens, in spite of the fact that for every dollar, ruble, pound or franc spent in explaining and praising it, a thousand are spent by the nations explaining and praising themselves.

This world civilisation and regionalism can get along together, especially if we keep ourselves sharply aware of their quite different but equally important values and rewards. A man can make his contribution to world civilisation and yet remain strongly regional in feeling: I know several men of this sort. There is of course the danger—it is with us now—of the global style flattening out the regional, taking local form, colour, flavour, away for ever, disinherit- ing future generations, threatening them with sensuous poverty and a huge boredom. But to understand and appreciate regionalism is to be on guard against this danger. And we must therefore make a clear distinction between regionalism and nationalism.

9   It is nationalism that tries to check the growth of world civilisation. And nationalism, when taken on a global scale, is more aggressive and demanding now than it has ever been before. This in the giant powers is largely disguised by the endless fuss in public about rival ideologies, now a largely unreal quarrel. What is intensely real is the glaring nationalism. Even the desire to police the world is nationalistic in origin. (Only the world can police the world.) Moreover, the nation-states of today are for the most part far narrower in their outlook, far more inclined to allow prejudice against the foreigner to impoverish their own style of living, than the old imperial states were. It should be part of world civilisation that men with particular skills, perhaps the product of the very regionalism they are rebelling against, should be able to move easily from country to country, to exercise those skills, in anything from teaching the violin to running a new type of factory to managing an old hotel. But nationalism, especially of the newer sort, would rather see everything done badly than allow a few non-nationals to get to work. And people face a barrage of passports, visas, immigration controls, labour permits; and in this respect are worse off than they were in 1900. But even so, in spite of all that nationalism can do—so long as it keeps its nuclear bombs to itself—the internationalism I have in mind, slowly creating a world civilisation, cannot be checked.

10   Nevertheless, we are still backing the wrong ism. Almost all our money goes on the middle one, nationalism, the rotten meat between the two healthy slices of bread. We need regionalism to give us roots and that very depth of feeling which nationalism unjustly and greedily claims for itself. We need internationalism to save the world and to broaden and heighten our civilisation. While regional man enriches the lives that international man is already working to keep secure and healthy, national man, drunk with power, demands our loyalty, money and applause, and poisons the very air with his dangerous nonsense.

```
┌─────────────────────────┐
│                         │
│                         │
└─────────────────────────┘
```

J.B. PRIESTLEY

J.B. Priestley (1894–1984), the English novelist and dramatist, wrote a number of essays on social and political themes. His best-known novel is *The Good Companions*, while a number of his plays, such as *Time and the Conways*, deal with the nature of time.

Words and Meanings

Paragraph

bogus:	sham, phony	1
dubious:	unreliable, of suspicious character	7
entrepreneur:	self-employed promoter, money-maker	
impresario:	producer, usually of some form of public entertainment	

Structure and Strategy

1. Where and what is Priestley's thesis statement?
2. What SIMILE does Priestley introduce to emphasize the difference between regionalism and nationalism?
3. What expository techniques does Priestley use to develop his definition of regionalism (paragraphs 2 to 4)? How does he develop his definition of nationalism (paragraphs 5 and 6)?
4. What SIMILE in paragraph 5 forcefully communicates Priestley's dislike of the nationalistic spirit?
5. Priestley sums up his attitude to the three "isms" in a METAPHOR in paragraph 10. What is it? How does it contribute to the effectiveness of his conclusion?

Content and Purpose

1. Why has Priestley titled this essay "Wrong Ism"?
2. In a single sentence for each, define "regionalism," "nationalism," and "internationalism."
3. Summarize Priestley's objections to nationalism.
4. Priestley claims that "the nation-states of today are for the most part far narrower in their outlook, far more inclined to allow prejudice against the foreigner to impoverish their own state of living, than the old imperial states were" (paragraph 9). What does he mean by this charge? Can you think of examples to support or to disprove this claim?
5. Canada is often described as "a nation of regions." Do you think this is an accurate description? In other words, has Canada managed to avoid the "rubbish" of nationalism (see paragraphs 5 and 6)?

Suggestions for Writing

1. Write a paper in which you define three fads, personality types, or leisure activities. As Priestley has done in his essay, use comparison and contrast to help make clear to your readers which of the three you favour most and which you like least.
2. Write an essay that defines the region of Canada in which you

live (or have lived). Use examples, comparison and contrast, or any other expository technique to define the region and its unique characteristics.

Beauty

SUSAN SONTAG

1   or the Greeks, beauty was a virtue: a kind of excellence. Persons then were assumed to be what we now have to call—lamely, enviously—*whole* persons. If it did occur to the Greeks to distinguish between a person's "inside" and "outside," they still expected that inner beauty would be matched by beauty of the other kind. The well-born young Athenians who gathered around Socrates° found it quite paradoxical° that their hero was so intelligent, so brave, so honorable, so seductive—and so ugly. One of Socrates' main pedagogical° acts was to be ugly—and teach those innocent, no doubt splendid-looking disciples of his how full of paradoxes life really was.

2   They may have resisted Socrates' lesson. We do not. Several thousand years later, we are more wary° of the enchantments of beauty. We not only split off—with the greatest facility°—the "inside" (character, intellect) from the "outside" (looks); but we are actually surprised when someone who is beautiful is also intelligent, talented, good.

3   It was principally the influence of Christianity that deprived beauty of the central place it had in classical ideals of human excellence. By limiting excellence (*virtus* in Latin) to *moral* virtue only, Christianity set beauty adrift—as an alienated, arbitrary, superficial enchantment. And beauty has continued to lose prestige°. For close to two centuries it has become a convention to attribute beauty to only one of the two sexes: the sex which, however Fair, is always Second. Associating beauty with women has put beauty even further on the defensive, morally.

4   A beautiful woman, we say in English. But a handsome man. "Handsome" is the masculine equivalent of—and refusal of—a compliment which has accumulated certain demeaning overtones, by being reserved for women only. That one can call a man "beautiful"

in French and in Italian suggests that Catholic countries—unlike those countries shaped by the Protestant version of Christianity— still retain some vestiges° of the pagan admiration for beauty. But the difference, if one exists, is of degree only. In every modern country that is Christian or post-Christian, women *are* the beautiful sex—to the detriment° of the notion of beauty as well as of women.

To be called beautiful is thought to name something essential   5 to women's character and concerns. (In contrast to men—whose essence is to be strong, or effective, or competent.) It does not take someone in the throes of advanced feminist awareness to perceive that the way women are taught to be involved with beauty encourages narcissism°, reinforced dependence and immaturity. Everybody (women and men) knows that. For it is "everybody," a whole society, that has identified being feminine with caring about how one *looks*. (In contrast to being masculine—which is identified with caring about what one *is* and *does* and only secondarily, if at all, about how one looks.) Given these stereotypes, it is no wonder that beauty enjoys, at best, a rather mixed reputation.

It is not, of course, the desire to be beautiful that is wrong but   6 the obligation° to be—or to try. What is accepted by most women as a flattering idealization of their sex is a way of making women feel inferior to what they actually are—or normally grow to be. For the ideal of beauty is administered as a form of self-oppression. Women are taught to see their bodies in *parts*, and to evaluate each part separately. Breasts, feet, hips, waistline, neck, eyes, nose, complexion, hair, and so on—each in turn is submitted to an anxious, fretful, often despairing scrutiny°. Even if some pass muster°, some will always be found wanting. Nothing less than perfection will do.

In men, good looks is a whole, something taken in at a glance.   7 It does not need to be confirmed by giving measurements of different regions of the body, nobody encourages a man to dissect his appearance, feature by feature. As for perfection, that is considered trivial— almost unmanly. Indeed, in the ideally good-looking man a small imperfection or blemish is considered positively desirable. According to one movie critic (a woman) who is a declared Robert Redford fan, it is having that cluster of skin-colored moles on one cheek that saves Redford from being merely a "pretty face." Think of the depreciation of women—as well as of beauty—that is implied in that judgment.

"The privileges of beauty are immense," said Cocteau. To be   8 sure, beauty is a form of power. And deservedly so. What is lamentable is that it is the only form of power that most women are encouraged to seek. This power is always conceived in relation to men; it is not the power to do but the power to attract. It is a power that negates° itself. For this power is not one that can be chosen freely—at least, not by women—or renounced° without social censure°.

9   To preen°, for a woman, can never be just a pleasure. It is also a duty. It is her work. If a woman does real work—and even if she has clambered up to a leading position in politics, law, medicine, business, or whatever—she is always under pressure to confess that she still works at being attractive. But in so far as she is keeping up as one of the Fair Sex, she brings under suspicion her very capacity to be objective, professional, authoritative, thoughtful. Damned if they do—women are. And damned if they don't.

10   One could hardly ask for more important evidence of the dangers of considering persons as split between what is "inside" and what is "outside" than that interminable° half-comic half-tragic tale, the oppression of women. How easy it is to start off by defining women as caretakers of their surfaces, and then to disparage° them (or find them adorable) for being "superficial." It is a crude trap, and it has worked for too long. But to get out of the trap requires that women get some critical distance from that excellence and privilege which is beauty, enough distance to see how much beauty itself has been abridged° in order to prop up the mythology of the "feminine." There should be a way of saving beauty *from* women— and *for* them.

```

```

SUSAN SONTAG

Susan Sontag (b. 1933) is an American novelist and essayist best known for her collection *Against Interpretation, and Other Essays*.

Words and Meanings

Paragraph

1	Socrates:	Greek philosopher and teacher (469–399 B.C.) who believed the highest meaning of life is attained through self-knowledge
	paradoxical:	A paradox is a statement or circumstance that seems contradictory, even absurd, at first.
	pedagogical:	teaching
2	wary:	cautious, on guard against
	facility:	ease
3	prestige:	status, influence
4	vestiges:	traces, remains
	detriment:	loss, harm, disadvantage

narcissism:	obsessive self-love	5
obligation:	responsibility	6
scrutiny:	close examination	
pass muster:	be accepted as adequate	
negates:	denies, cancels itself	8
renounced:	rejected, given up	
censure:	disapproval	
preen:	groom oneself, make oneself attractive	9
interminable:	never-ending	10
disparage:	belittle, speak negatively of	
abridged:	diminished, reduced	

Structure and Strategy

1. Sontag defines beauty partly through a series of contrasts. Identify two sets of contrasts that are explained in the first seven paragraphs of the essay.
2. What is the THESIS of "Beauty"? Restate it in your own words.
3. Study the examples Sontag uses in paragraphs 7 and 9. Do they provide effective support for her points? Why?
4. Explain the paradoxes with which Sontag introduces and concludes her essay. How do they contribute to the UNITY of the piece?

Content and Purpose

1. How did the ancient Greeks define beauty? How do we define it today?
2. How, according to Sontag, did Christianity change the classical view of beauty?
3. What difference does Sontag identify in the ways in which men and women define themselves? How has this difference affected our culture's perception of physical attractiveness?
4. How does the "obligation" to be beautiful affect the way women see their bodies?
5. What relationship does Sontag identify between a woman's beauty and power? Do you agree with her?
6. According to this essay, physical beauty puts women in a double bind: they are "damned if they do" and "damned if they don't." What does Sontag mean by this? Do you agree?

Suggestions for Writing

1. Define your own idea of beauty. Is it an internal or external quality?

2. Do you agree or disagree with Sontag that our culture's emphasis on the physical beauty of women is a "crude trap"? Explore
   the relationship between physical attractiveness and power.
3. Read Meredith Chilton's essay, "A Fugitive Pleasure" and write a
   short paper explaining how the process she describes supports
   Sontag's thesis.
4. Read Maggie Helwig's "Hunger" in Further Readings and compare her thesis with Sontag's.

True North

MARGARET ATWOOD

1   Where is the north, exactly? It's not only a
place but a direction, and as such its location is relative: to the
Mexicans, the United States is the north, to Americans Toronto is,
even though it's on roughly the same latitude as Boston.

2   Wherever it is for us, there's a lot of it. You stand in Windsor
and imagine a line going north, all the way to the pole. The same
line going south would end up in South America. That's the sort of
map we grew up with, at the front of the classroom in Mercator
projection°, which made it look even bigger than it was, all that pink
stretching on forever, with a few cities sprinkled along the bottom
edge. It's not only geographical space, it's space related to body
image. When we face south, as we often do, our conscious mind
may be directed down there, towards crowds, bright lights, some
Hollywood version of fame and fortune, but the north is at the back
of our minds, always. There's something, not someone, looking over
our shoulders; there's a chill at the nape of the neck.

3   The north focuses our anxieties. Turning to face north, face the
north, we enter our own unconscious. Always, in retrospect°, the
journey north has the quality of dream.

4   The Acid Rain Dinner, in Toronto's Sheraton Centre, in 1985. The
first of these fund-raising events was fairly small. But the movement
has grown, and this dinner is huge. The leaders of all three provincial
parties are here. So is the minister of the environment from the
federal government. So are several labour leaders, and several high-
ranking capitalists, and representatives of numerous northerly

chambers of commerce, summer residents' associations, tourist-camp runners, outfitters. Wishy-washy urban professionals who say "frankly" a lot bend elbows with huntin', shootin', fishin', and cussin' burnt-necks who wouldn't be caught dead saying "frankly." This is not a good place to be overheard saying that actually acid rain isn't such a bad thing because it gets rid of all that brown scum and leeches in the lake, or who cares because you can water-ski anyway. Teddy Kennedy, looking like a bulky sweater, is the guest speaker. Everyone wears a little gold pin in the shape of a rain drop. It looks like a tear.

Why has acid rain become the collective Canadian nightmare? Why is it—as a good cause—bigger than baby-seal bashing? The reasons aren't just economic, although there are lots of those, as the fishing-camp people and foresters will tell you. It's more than that, and cognate° with the outrage aroused by the uninvited voyage of the American icebreaker *Polar Sea* through the Northwest Passage, where almost none of us ever goes. It's territorial, partly; partly a felt violation of some area in us that we hardly ever think about unless it's invaded or tampered with. It's the neighbours throwing guck into our yard. It's our childhood dying.

In Europe, every scrap of land has been claimed, owned, re-owned, fought over, captured, bled on. The roads are the only no-man's-land. In northern Canada, the roads are civilization, owned by the collective human *we*. Off the road is *other*. Try walking in it, and you'll soon find out why all the early traffic here was by water. "Impenetrable wilderness" is not just verbal.

And suppose you get off the road. Suppose you get lost. Getting lost, elsewhere and closer to town, is not knowing exactly where you are. You can always ask, even in a foreign country. In the north, getting lost is not knowing how to get out.

One way of looking at a landscape is to consider the typical ways of dying in it. Given the worst, what's the worst it could do? Will it be delirium from drinking salty water on the high seas, shrivelling in the desert, snakebite in the jungle, tidal waves on a Pacific isle, volcanic fumes? In the north, there are several hazards. Although you're probably a lot safer there than you are on the highway at rush hour, given the odds, you still have to be a little wary°.

Like most lessons of this sort, those about the north are taught by precept° and example, but also, more enjoyably, by cautionary nasty tale. There is death by blackfly, the one about the fellow who didn't have his shirt cuffs tight enough in the spring and undressed at night only to find he was running with blood, the ones about the lost travellers who bloated up from too many bites and who, when found, were twice the size, unrecognizable, and dead. There is death from starvation, death by animal, death by forest fire; there is death from something called "exposure," which used to confuse me when I heard about men who exposed themselves: why would they intentionally do anything that fatal? There's death by thunderstorm, not to be sneered at: on the open lake, in one of the excessive northern midsummer thunderstorms, a canoe or a bush plane is a vulnerable target. The north is full of Struwwelpeter°-like stories about people who didn't do as they were told and got struck by lightning. Above all, there are death by freezing and death by drowning. Your body's heat-loss rate in the water is twenty times that in air, and northern lakes are cold. Even in a life jacket, even holding on to the tipped canoe, you're at risk. Every summer the numbers pile up.

10   Every culture has its exemplary° dead people, its hagiography° of landscape martyrs, those unfortunates who, by their bad ends, seem to sum up in one grisly episode what may be lurking behind the next rock for all of us, all of us who enter the territory they once claimed as theirs. I'd say that two of the top northern landscape martyrs are Tom Thomson, the painter who was found mysteriously drowned near his overturned canoe with no provable cause in sight, and the Mad Trapper of Rat River, also mysterious, who became so thoroughly bushed° that he killed a Mountie and shot two others during an amazing wintertime chase before being finally mowed down. In our retelling of these stories, mystery is a key element. So, strangely enough, is a presumed oneness with the landscape in question. The Mad Trapper knew his landscape so well he survived in it for weeks, living off the land and his own bootlaces, eluding capture. One of the hidden motifs° in these stories is a warning: maybe it's not so good to get *too* close to Nature.

11   I remember a documentary on Tom Thomson that ended, rather ominously, with the statement that the north had taken him to herself. This was, of course, pathetic fallacy° gone to seed, but it was also a comment on our distrust of the natural world, a distrust that remains despite our protests, our studies in the ethics of ecology°, our elevation of "the environment" to a numinous° noun, our save-the-tree campaigns. The question is, would the trees save us, given the chance? Would the water, would the birds, would the rocks? In the north, we have our doubts.

12   A different part of the north. We're sitting around the table, by lamplight—it is still the old days here, no electricity—talking about bad hunters. Bad hunters, bad fishers, everyone has a story. You come upon a campsite, way in the back of beyond, no roads into the lake, they must have come in by float plane, and there it is, garbage all over the place, beer cans, blobs of human poop flagged by melting toilet paper, and twenty-two fine pickerel left rotting on

a rock. Business executives who get themselves flown in during hunting season with their high-powered rifles, shoot a buck, cut off the head, fill their quota°, see another one with a bigger spread of antlers, drop the first head, cut off the second. The woods are littered with discarded heads, and who cares about the bodies?

New way to shoot polar bear: you have the natives on the ground finding them for you, then they radio the location in to the base camp, the base camp phones New York, fellow gets on the plane, gets himself flown in, they've got the rifle and the clothing all ready for him, fly him to the bear, he pulls the trigger from the plane, doesn't even get out of the g.d. *plane*, they fly him back, cut off the head, skin it, send the lot down to New York.   13

These are the horror stories of the north, one brand. They've replaced the ones in which you got pounced upon by a wolverine or had your arm chewed off by a she-bear with cubs or got chased into the lake by a moose in rut°, or even the ones in which your dog got porcupine quills or rolled in poison ivy and gave it to you. In the new stories, the enemies and the victims of old have done a switch. Nature is no longer implacable°, dangerous, ready to jump you; it is on the run, pursued by a number of unfair bullies with the latest technology.   14

One of the key nouns in these stories is "float plane." These outrages, this banditry°, would not be possible without them, for the bad hunters are notoriously weak-muscled and are deemed° incapable of portaging° a canoe, much less paddling one. Among their other badnesses, they are sissies. Another key motif is money. What money buys these days, among other things, is the privilege of no-risk slaughter.   15

As for us, the ones telling the stories, tsk-tsking by lamplight, we are the good hunters, or so we think. We've given up saying we only kill to eat; Kraft dinner and freeze-dried food have put paid° to that one. Really there's no excuse for us. However, we do have some virtues left. We can still cast a fly. We don't cut off heads and hang them stuffed on the wall. We would never buy an ocelot coat. We paddle our own canoes.   16

We're sitting on the dock at night, shivering despite our sweaters, in mid-August, watching the sky. There are a few shooting stars, as there always are at this time in August, as the earth passes through the Perseids°. We pride ourselves on knowing a few things like that, about the sky; we find the Dipper, the North Star, Cassiopeia's Chair, and talk about consulting a star chart, which we know we won't actually do. But this is the only place you can really *see* the stars, we tell each other. Cities are hopeless.   17

Suddenly, an odd light appears, going very fast. It spirals around   18 like a newly dead firecracker, and then bursts, leaving a cloud of luminous° dust, caught perhaps in the light from the sun, still up there somewhere. What could this be? Several days later, we hear that it was part of an extinct Soviet satellite, or that's what they say. That's what they would say, wouldn't they? It strikes us that we don't really know very much about the night sky at all any more. There's all kinds of junk up there: spy planes, old satellites, tin cans, man-made matter gone out of control. It also strikes us that we are totally dependent for knowledge of these things on a few people who don't tell us very much.

19   Once, we thought that if the balloon ever went up we'd head for the bush and hide out up there, living—we naively supposed— off the land. Now we know that if the two superpowers begin hurling things at each other through the sky, they're likely to do it across the Arctic, with big bangs and fallout all over the north. The wind blows everywhere. Survival gear and knowing which moss you can eat is not going to be a large help. The north is no longer a refuge.

20   Driving back towards Toronto from the Near North, a small reprise° runs through my head:

> Land of the septic tank,
> Home of the speedboat,
> Where still the four-wheel-drive
> Wanders at will,
> Blue lake and tacky shore,
> I will return once more:
> Vroom-diddy-vroom-vroom
> Vroom-diddy-vroom-vroom
> Vroo-OO-oo-oom.

Somehow, just as the drive north inspires saga° and tragedy, the drive south inspires parody°. And here it comes: the gift shops shaped like teepees, the maple-syrup emporiums° that get themselves up like olde-tyme sugaring-off huts; and, farther south, the restaurants that pretend to offer wholesome farm fare, the stores that pretend to be general stores, selling quilts, soap shaped like hearts, high-priced fancy conserves° done up in frilly cloth caps, the way Grandma (whoever she might be) was fondly supposed to have made them.

21   And then come the housing developments, acres of prime farm-land turning overnight into Quality All-Brick Family Homes; and then come the Industrial Parks; and there, in full anti-bloom, is the city itself, looming like a mirage or a chemical warfare zone on the

horizon. A browny-grey scuzz hovers above it, and we think, as we always do when facing re-entry, we're going into *that*? We're going to breathe *that*?

But we go forward, as we always do, into what is now to us   22
the unknown. And once inside, we breathe the air, not much bad happens to us, we hardly notice. It's as if we've never been anywhere else. But that's what we think, too, when we're in the north.

+------------------------------------+
| |
| |
+------------------------------------+

MARGARET ATWOOD

Margaret Atwood, the well-known poet and novelist, was born in Ottawa in 1939. She expressed the view in *Survival* that Canadians are content to "get along," unlike the Americans who must "get ahead." She has written numerous collections of poetry and such novels as *The Edible Woman*, *Surfacing*, and *The Handmaid's Tale*.

Words and Meanings

Paragraph

Mercator projection:	a flat map of the world on which the representation of distances and land masses is increasingly distorted between the equator and the poles (e.g., Greenland looks to be roughly the same size as South America)	2
retrospect:	looking back	3
cognate:	akin to, related to	5
wary:	cautious	8
precept:	unwritten law or principle	9
Struwwelpeter:	disobedient little boy in German folk tale	
exemplary:	ideal, serving as an example to be imitated	10
hagiography:	literature of saints' lives and legends	
bushed:	form of insanity brought on by prolonged isolation in the wilderness	
motifs:	recurring themes	
pathetic fallacy:	figure of speech in which the landscape is described as having human feelings	11
ecology:	study of relationship between living things and their environment	
numinous:	sacred	
quota:	number of game animals a hunter is allowed by law to kill	12

14	rut:	sexual excitement of male animals during mating season
	implacable:	unforgiving, relentless
15	banditry:	actions of bandits or outlaws
	deemed:	thought
	portaging:	carrying a canoe overland
16	put paid to:	finished, ended
17	Perseids:	constellation of stars (as are the Dipper and Cassiopeia's Chair)
18	luminous:	filled with light
20	reprise:	a repetition of a song or other musical passage
21	saga:	heroic tale
	parody:	mimicking or imitating something to poke fun at it
	emporiums:	stores
	conserves:	jams or jellies

Structure and Strategy

1. This essay is divided into six main sections: paragraphs 1 to 3, 4 to 7, 8 to 11, 12 to 16, 17 to 19, and 20 to 22. Identify the main point of each section. How does each section contribute to Atwood's definition of "north"?
2. What method of development does Atwood use in paragraphs 8 to 11? paragraph 12? paragraph 13? paragraphs 20 to 21?
3. What contrast does Atwood develop in paragraphs 6 to 7? paragraphs 15 to 16? How do these contrasts contribute to our understanding of "north"?
4. Find three or four particularly effective examples of IRONY in this essay.

Content and Purpose

1. The first three paragraphs of Atwood's essay explore the indefinable, shifting quality of the concept of "north." What does she mean when she states, "The north focuses our anxieties. . . . Turning to face north, face the north, we enter our own unconscious."
2. According to this essay, "the north" is not only a direction and a place, but also much more. What, according to Atwood, does "the north" signify for us?
3. How do paragraphs 3 and 4 contribute to Atwood's purpose? What is there about acid rain that provokes concern among people from all walks of life?

4. What, according to Atwood, is the significance of the float plane? How has technology changed our experience of the north?
5. What is the purpose of the ANECDOTE in paragraphs 17 to 18? What comparisons can be made between the landscape of the north and the reaches of outer space?
6. What contrasts between "north" and "south" does Atwood point to in this essay? Do you agree with her?

Suggestions for Writing

1. Write an extended definition of your concept of "neighbourhood," "homeland," "province," "village," or other place of origin.
2. Most of Canada's population is strung out along a narrow strip of land just north of the U.S. border. Write your own analysis of the ways in which the popular notion of "the great, white north" affects Canadians' sense of themselves as a nation.
3. After the failure of the Meech Lake Accord in 1990 and the recommendations of Quebec's Belanger-Campeau Commission in 1991, it has been stated that Quebeckers know who and what they are, but the rest of Canada does not. Write an essay in which you define what "being Canadian" means to you.

"I'm Not Racist But . . ."

NEIL BISSOONDATH

Someone recently said that racism is as 1 Canadian as maple syrup. I have no argument with that. History provides us with ample proof. But, for proper perspective, let us remember that it is also as American as apple pie, as French as croissants, as Jamaican as ackee, as Indian as aloo, as Chinese as chow mein, as. . . . Well, there's an entire menu to be written. This is not by way of excusing it. Murder and rape, too, are international, multicultural, as innate° to the darker side of the human experience.

But we must be careful that the inevitable rage evoked does not blind us to the larger context.

2   The word "racism" is a discomforting one: It is so vulnerable to manipulation. We can, if we so wish, apply it to any incident involving people of different colour. And therein lies the danger. During the heat of altercation°, we seize, as terms of abuse, on whatever is most obvious about the other person. It is, often, a question of unfortunate convenience. A woman, because of her sex, easily becomes a female dog or an intimate part of her anatomy. A large person might be dubbed "a stupid ox," a small person "a little" whatever. And so a black might become "a nigger," a white "a honky," an Asian "a paki," a Chinese "a chink," an Italian "a wop," a French-Canadian "a frog."

3   There is nothing pleasant about these terms; they assault every decent sensibility°. Even so, I once met someone who, in a stunning surge of naiveté°, used them as simple descriptives and not as terms of racial abuse. She was horrified to learn the truth. While this may have been an extreme case, the point is that the use of such patently° abusive words may not always indicate racial or cultural distaste. They may indicate ignorance or stupidity or insensitivity, but pure racial hatred—such as the Nazis held for Jews, or the Ku Klux Klan for blacks—is a thankfully rare commodity.

4   Ignorance, not the willful kind but that which comes from lack of experience, is often indicated by that wonderful phrase, "I'm not racist but. . . . " I think of the mover, a friendly man, who said, "I'm not racist, but the Chinese are the worst drivers on the road." He was convinced this was so because the shape of their eyes, as far as he could surmise°, denied them peripheral° vision.

5   Or the oil company executive, an equally warm and friendly man, who, looking for an apartment in Toronto, rejected buildings with East Indian tenants not because of their race—he was telling me this, after all—but because he was given to understand that cockroaches were symbols of good luck in their culture and that, when they moved into a new home, friends came by with gift-wrapped roaches.

6   Neither of these men thought of himself as racist, and I believe they were not, deep down. (The oil company executive made it clear he would not hesitate to have me as a neighbour; my East Indian descent was of no consequence to him, my horror of cockroaches was.) Yet their comments, so innocently delivered, would open them to the accusation, justifiably so if this were all one knew about them. But it is a charge which would undoubtedly be wounding to them. It is difficult to recognize one's own misconceptions°.

7   True racism is based, more often than not, on willful° ignorance, and an acceptance of—and comfort with—stereotype°. We like to

think, in this country, that our multicultural mosaic will help nudge us into a greater openness. But multiculturalism as we know it indulges in stereotype, depends on it for a dash of colour and the flash of dance. It fails to address the most basic questions people have about each other: Do those men doing the Dragon Dance really all belong to secret criminal societies? Do those women dressed in saris really coddle cockroaches for luck? Do those people in dreadlocks all smoke marijuana and live on welfare? Such questions do not seem to be the concern of the government's multicultural programs, superficial and exhibitionistic as they have become.

So the struggle against stereotype, the basis of all racism,   8
becomes a purely personal one. We must beware of the impressions we create. A friend of mine once commented that, from talking to West Indians, she has the impression that their one great cultural contribution to the world is in the oft-repeated boast that "We (unlike everyone else) know how to party."

There are dangers, too, in community response. We must be   9
wary of the self-appointed activists who seem to pop up in the media at every given opportunity spouting the rhetoric of retribution°, mining distress for personal, political and professional gain. We must be skeptical about those who depend on conflict for their sense of self, the non-whites who need to feel themselves victims of racism, the whites who need to feel themselves purveyors° of it. And we must be sure that, in addressing the problem, we do not end up creating it. Does the *Miss Black Canada Beauty Contest* still exist? I hope not. Not only do I find beauty contests offensive, but a racially segregated one even more so. What would the public reaction be, I wonder, if every year CTV broadcast the *Miss White Canada Beauty Pageant*? We give community-service awards only to blacks: Would we be comfortable with such awards only for whites? In Quebec, there are The Association of Black Nurses, The Association of Black Artists, The Congress of Black Jurists. Play tit for tat: The Association of White Nurses, White Artists, White Jurists: visions of apartheid. Let us be frank, racism for one is racism for others.

Finally, and perhaps most important, let us beware of abusing   10
the word itself.

NEIL BISSOONDATH

Neil Bissondath (b. 1955) is a Trinidad-born Canadian writer whose works include *A Casual Brutality* (1988) and *Digging Up the Mountains: Selected Stories* (1985).

Words and Meanings

1	innate:	natural, inborn
2	altercation:	quarrel, dispute
3	sensibility:	feeling
	naiveté:	simple ignorance; lack of sophistication
	patently:	obviously, clearly
4	surmise:	figure out, guess
	peripheral:	side
6	misconceptions:	mistaken beliefs
7	willful:	deliberate, stubborn
	stereotype:	see List of Useful Terms
9	rhetoric of retribution:	language of revenge, of retaliation
	purveyors:	providers

Structure and Strategy

1. With what ANALOGY does Bissoondath introduce this essay? Why is it effective?
2. This essay is divided into three parts. Identify the main point of paragraphs 2 to 6, 7 to 8, and 9 to 10.
3. Identify the sentence that most clearly defines what Bissoondath thinks racism is.
4. Do you think the CONCLUSION of this essay is effective? Explain.

Content and Purpose

1. In paragraph 3, Bissoondath draws a distinction between "igno- rance or stupidity or insensitivity" and "pure racial hatred." Into which category does he place the kind of racial epithets cited in paragraph 2?
2. What is the difference between the kind of ignorance repre- sented by the examples in paragraphs 4 and 5 and "true racism" as Bissoondath sees it?
3. What does Bissoondath think of Canada's multicultural policies and programs? Do you agree with him?
4. In paragraph 8, Bissoondath maintains that we "must beware of the impressions we create" in the struggle against racism. Do you agree that ethnic groups are to some extent responsible for their own stereotyping? Is it reasonable to make an ethnic group responsible for counteracting the stereotypical image other groups have of them?
5. What does Bissoondath think of beauty contests, clubs, or orga-

nizations that limit participation to a particular ethnic group? Do
you think he would be in favour of or opposed to affirmative
action programs?

Suggestions for Writing

1. Have you ever experienced the kind of racist stereotyping that
   Bissoondath describes in this essay? Write a paper explaining
   the incident, or series of incidents, and its effects on you.
2. Write an essay in which you agree or disagree with Bissoondath's opinion that awards, associations, and competitions that
   are restricted to people of colour are racist.
3. Read Walter Stewart's "Good Old Us" and write a paper contrasting his view of Canadian racism with Bissoondath's.

Altruism

LEWIS THOMAS

Altruism has always been one of biology's   1
deep mysteries. Why should any animal, off on its own, specified
and labeled by all sorts of signals as its individual self, choose to
give up its life in aid of someone else? Nature, long viewed as a
wild, chaotic battlefield swarmed across by more than ten million
different species, comprising unnumbered billions of competing
selves locked in endless combat, offers only one sure measure of
success: survival. Survival, in the cool economics of biology, means
simply the persistence of one's own genes in the generations to
follow.

At first glance, it seems an unnatural act, a violation of nature,   2
to give away one's life, or even one's possessions, to another. And
yet, in the face of improbability, examples of altruism abound. When
a worker bee, patrolling the frontiers of the hive, senses the nearness
of a human intruder, the bee's attack is pure, unqualified suicide;
the sting is barbed, and in the act of pulling away the insect is fatally
injured. Other varieties of social insects, most spectacularly the ants
and higher termites, contain castes of soldiers for whom self-sacrifice
is an everyday chore.

It is easy to dismiss the problem by saying that "altruism" is the   3 wrong technical term for behavior of this kind. The word is a human word, pieced together to describe an unusual aspect of human behavior, and we should not be using it for the behavior of mindless automata°. A honeybee has no connection to creatures like us, no brain for figuring out the future, no way of predicting the inevitable outcome of that sting.

4   But the meditation of the 50,000 or so connected minds of a whole hive is not so easy to dismiss. A multitude of bees can tell the time of day, calculate the geometry of the sun's position, argue about the best location for the next swarm. Bees do a lot of close observing of other bees; maybe they know what follows stinging and do it anyway.

5   Altruism is not restricted to the social insects, in any case. Birds risk their lives, sometimes lose them, in efforts to distract the attention of predators from the nest. Among baboons, zebras, moose, wildebeests, and wild dogs there are always stubbornly fated guardians, prepared to be done in first in order to buy time for the herd to escape.

6   It is genetically determined behavior, no doubt about it. Animals have genes for altruism, and those genes have been selected in the evolution of many creatures because of the advantage they confer for the continuing survival of the species. It is, looked at in this way, not the emotion-laden problem that we feel when we try to put ourselves in the animal's place; it is just another plain fact of life, perhaps not as hard a fact as some others, something rather nice, in fact, to think about.

7   J.B.S. Haldane, the eminent British geneticist, summarized the chilly arithmetic of the problem by announcing, "I would give up my life for two brothers or eight cousins." This calculates the requirement for ultimate self-interest: the preservation and survival of an individual's complement of genes. Trivers, Hamilton, and others have constructed mathematical models to account nicely for the altruistic behavior of social insects, quantifying the self-serving profit for the genes of the defending bee in the act of tearing its abdomen apart. The hive is filled with siblings, ready to carry the *persona* of the dying bee through all the hive's succeeding generations. Altruism is based on kinship; by preserving kin, one preserves one's self. In a sense.

8   Haldane's prediction has the sound of a beginning sequence: two brothers, eight (presumably) first cousins, and then another series of much larger numbers of more distant relatives. Where does the influence tail off? At what point does the sharing of the putative° altruist's genes become so diluted as to be meaningless? Would the line on a graph charting altruism plummet to zero soon after those eight cousins, or is it a long, gradual slope? When the combat marine

throws himself belly-down on the live grenade in order to preserve the rest of his platoon, is this the same sort of altruism, or is this an act without any technically biological meaning? Surely the marine's genes, most of them, will be blown away forever; the statistical likelihood of having two brothers or eight cousins in that platoon is extremely small. And yet there he is, belly-down as if by instinct, and the same kind of event has been recorded often enough in wartime to make it seem a natural human act, normal enough, even though rare, to warrant the stocking of medals by the armed services.

At what point do our genetic ties to each other become so remote 9
that we feel no instinctual urge to help? I can imagine an argument about this, with two sides, but it would be a highly speculative discussion, not by any means pointless but still impossible to settle one way or the other. One side might assert, with total justification, that altruistic behavior among human beings has nothing at all to do with genetics, that there is no such thing as a gene for self-sacrifice, not even a gene for helpfulness, or concern, or even affection. These are attributes that must be learned from society, acquired by cultures, taught by example. The other side could maintain, with equal justification, since the facts are not known, precisely the opposite position: we get along together in human society because we are genetically designed to be social animals, and we are obliged, by instructions from our genes, to be useful to each other. This side would argue further that when we behave badly, killing or maiming or snatching, we are acting on misleading information learned from the wrong kinds of society we put together; if our cultures were not deformed, we would be better company, paying attention to what our genes are telling us.

For the purposes of the moment I shall take the side of the 10
sociobiologists because I wish to carry their side of the argument a certain distance afield, beyond the human realm. I have no difficulty in imagining a close enough resemblance among the genomes° of all human beings, of all races and geographic origins, to warrant a biological mandate° for all of us to do whatever we can to keep the rest of us, the species, alive. I maintain, despite the moment's evidence against the claim, that we are born and grow up with a fondness for each other, and we have genes for that. We can be talked out of it, for the genetic message is like a distant music and some of us are hard-of-hearing. Societies are noisy affairs, drowning out the sound of ourselves and our connection. Hard-of-hearing, we go to war. Stone-deaf, we make thermonuclear missiles. Nonetheless, the music is there, waiting for more listeners.

But the matter does not end with our species. If we are to take 11
seriously the notion that the sharing of similar genes imposes a responsibility on the sharers to sustain each other, and if I am right

in guessing that even very distant cousins carry at least traces of this responsibility and will act on it whenever they can, then the whole world becomes something to be concerned about on solidly scientific, reductionist, genetic grounds. For we have cousins more than we can count, and they are all over the place, run by genes so similar to ours that the differences are minor technicalities. All of us, men, women, children, fish, sea grass, sandworms, dolphins, hamsters, and soil bacteria, everything alive on the planet, roll ourselves along through all our generations by replicating DNA° and RNA°, and although the alignments of nucleotides within these molecules are different in different species, the molecules themselves are fundamentally the same substance. We make our proteins in the same old way, and many of the enzymes most needed for cellular life are everywhere identical.

12   This is, in fact, the way it should be. If cousins are defined by common descent, the human family is only one small and very recent addition to a much larger family in a tree extending back at least 3.5 billion years. Our common ancestor was a single cell from which all subsequent cells derived, most likely a cell resembling one of today's bacteria in today's soil. For almost three-fourths of the earth's life, cells of that first kind were the whole biosphere°. It was less than a billion years ago that cells like ours appeared in the first marine invertebrates, and these were somehow pieced together by the joining up and fusion of the earlier primitive cells, retaining the same blood lines. Some of the joiners, bacteria that had learned how to use oxygen, are with us still, part of our flesh, lodged inside the cells of all animals, all plants, moving us from place to place and doing our breathing for us. Now there's a set of cousins!

13   Even if I try to discount the other genetic similarities linking human beings to all other creatures by common descent, the existence of these beings in my cells is enough, in itself, to relate me to the chestnut tree in my backyard and to the squirrel in that tree.

14   There ought to be a mathematics for connections like this before claiming any kinship function, but the numbers are too big. At the same time, even if we wanted to, we cannot think the sense of obligation away. It is there, maybe in our genes for the recognition of cousins, or, if not, it ought to be there in our intellects for having learned about the matter. Altruism, in its biological sense, is required of us. We have an enormous family to look after, or perhaps that assumes too much, making us sound like official gardeners and zookeepers for the planet, responsibilities for which we are probably not yet grown-up enough. We may need new technical terms for concern, respect, affection, substitutes for altruism. But at least we should acknowledge the family ties and, with them, the obligations. If we do it wrong, scattering pollutants, clouding the atmosphere

with too much carbon dioxide, extinguishing the thin carapace° of ozone, burning up the forests, dropping the bombs, rampaging at large through nature as though we owned the place, there will be a lot of paying back to do and, at the end, nothing to pay back with.

```
┌──────────────────────┐
│                      │
│                      │
└──────────────────────┘
```

LEWIS THOMAS

Chancellor of New York's Sloan-Kettering Center, the largest cancer research hospital in the world, Dr. Lewis Thomas combines the careers of research scientist, physician, teacher, and writer. The recipient of many scientific and academic awards, Lewis Thomas strives in his essays to humanize science and to remind us that medicine is an art. A recurring theme in books such as *The Lives of a Cell* (1974), *The Medusa and the Snail* (1979) and *The Youngest Science* (1983) is the interrelatedness of all life forms.

Words and Meanings

Paragraph

automata:	unthinking, machinelike organisms	3
putative:	supposed	8
genomes:	chromosomal structures	10
mandate:	contract, requirement	
DNA	deoxyribonucleic acid; the molecule that carries genetic information	11
RNA	ribonucleic acid; the substance that transmits genetic information from the nucleus to the surrounding cellular material	
biosphere:	earth's zone of life—from crust to atmosphere— encompassing all living organisms	12
carapace:	outer shell, such as on a crab or tortoise	14

Structure and Strategy

1. What two ABSTRACT terms does Thomas define in his introductory paragraph? How does he do so?
2. The body of this essay can be divided into sections, as follows: paragraphs 2 to 5, 6 to 8, 9 to 10, 11 to 13. Identify the main idea Thomas develops in each of these four sections, and list some of the expository techniques he uses in his development.
3. From paragraphs 1 to 8, Thomas writes in the third person. Why does he shift to the first person in paragraph 9 and continue in first person until the end? To understand the different effects of

the two POINTS OF VIEW, try rewriting some of the sentences in paragraph 14 in the third person.

4. In paragraph 10, Thomas introduces and develops a SIMILE to explain his faith in the "genetic message." Identify the simile and explain how it helps prepare the reader for the conclusion.
5. What concluding strategy does Thomas use in paragraph 14? How does his conclusion contribute to the UNITY of the essay?

Content and Purpose

1. What is Thomas's thesis? Can you summarize it in a single sentence?
2. In paragraph 1, Thomas introduces the fundamental IRONY on which this essay is based. Explain in your own words the ironic connection between altruism and survival.
3. Identify six or seven specific examples of animals that, according to Thomas, display altruistic behaviour. What ILLUSTRATION does Thomas use to show the altruistic behaviour of human beings?
4. Explain in your own words Thomas's claim that altruism is not an "emotion-laden problem" but that it is based on self-interest (see paragraph 7).
5. In paragraph 9, Thomas identifies two opposing explanations for altruistic behaviour: the cultural and the sociobiological. Summarize these in your own words. Which side does Thomas take and why? (See paragraphs 10 to 13.)

Suggestions for Writing

1. Write an extended definition of the term "parenthood." Explain the reasons why people choose to have children, an act that involves a considerable amount of self-sacrifice.
2. Define another abstract term such as "wisdom," "integrity," "freedom," "evil," "success." Attempt to define it as clearly and concretely as Thomas does "altruism."

Additional Suggestions for Writing: Definition

Write an extended definition of one of the topics below.

addiction

team spirit

superstition

maturity

elitism

conspicuous
    consumption

wisdom

terrorism

creativity

censorship

physical fitness

generosity

a typical Canadian

a Yuppie

chauvinism

sin

recession

a conservative

a liberal

the ideal job (boss, employee, parent,
    roommate, friend, spouse, child)

_____

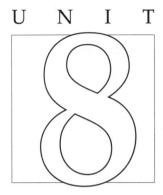

U N I T

Argument and Persuasion: Appealing to Reason and Emotion

What? The Definition

We all know what is meant by the word **persuasion**. It's bringing someone over to our side, sometimes with a nod, a wink, usually with a word or two. The meaning of the word **argument** is reasonably clear as well. An argument is a disagreement, an altercation, a verbal brawl of sorts; an argument may occur when someone resists our attempts at persuasion. As Unit Seven on definition pointed out, however, occasionally words have specific meanings different from their generally accepted meanings.

Persuasion is more than encouraging someone to come on side; argument means more than disagreement. In the context of writing, argument and persuasion refer to a kind of writing that has a particular purpose—one that differs in degree, if not in kind, from the purpose of expository prose.

The introductions to the first seven units of this text have explained structural patterns commonly found in *exposition*—writing intended primarily to explain. It is true that many explanations contain some element of argument or persuasion: consider Mitford's indictment of embalming in Unit Three, for instance. Nevertheless, the primary purpose of expository writing is to *inform* the reader.

Argument and persuasion have a different primary purpose; they attempt to lead the reader to share the writer's belief and, perhaps, even to act on this belief. Naturally, readers are not likely to be persuaded of anything unless the concept is first clearly explained to them. In this chapter, we will consider argument and persuasion as writing strategies designed to *convince* the reader of an opinion, judgment, or course of action.

There are two ways to convince people: through their minds or through their hearts. *Argument* is the term often applied to the logical approach, convincing a person by way of the mind. *Persuasion* is the term often applied to the emotional approach, convincing a person by way of the heart. Often we can use both routes. We decide which approach to use, logical or emotional—or a combination of the two—depending on the issue we are discussing. For instance, if we want to persuade someone to give money for famine relief, we might appeal to the reader's emotions with descriptions of blighted landscapes, emaciated adults, and starving children. We want our readers to feel the victims' plight and support the cause. However, if we want to argue that a highway needs widening, there is likely to be little emotional punch. In a case like this, we would appeal to the reader's mind by providing logical, well-developed reasons. The issue itself determines which approach is the best one to take.

An important part of convincing the reader is getting the facts straight. An argument is only as strong as the logic behind it. Even when appealing primarily to the reader's feelings, the writer must do so reasonably or risk producing a paper that is sentimental, bullying, or manipulative, and therefore not persuasive. Most of us have been pestered by "persuaders" who attempt to convince us that water fluoridation is a Communist plot, or that all Irish are drunkards, or that people who smoke marijuana inevitably get addicted to heroin. The reasoning that leads to such conclusions is faulty. To be convincing, the reasoning must be sound; if it is not, readers are likely to be confused or insulted rather than convinced.

There are two fundamental ways of reasoning: **induction** and **deduction**. Exploring these logical processes will help you to clarify your own ideas before you try to convince someone else.

Inductive reasoning is the logical process of examining a number of individual cases and coming to a general conclusion. For example, if you order pizza from Guido's Pizzeria once and it's cold when delivered, a one-time-only delay may have occurred. But if you get cold pizzas three times in a row from Guido's, and talk to four friends who have likewise got cold pizza from Guido's, it is fair to make a generalization: Guido's pizzas are usually cold by the time they get to you. You'd better phone another pizzeria. This simple example illustrates the straightforward, let's-look-at-the-facts approach of inductive reasoning. On a more lofty level, we find that induction is also the reasoning of the science laboratory and the law court. For example, if a microbiologist finds bacillus X in the bloodstreams of a significant number of flu victims, she may eventually generalize that bacillus X is the cause of that particular strain of flu.

To use inductive reasoning effectively, you must make sure that your evidence is solid, that it isn't just hearsay or unsupported opinion. You must also ensure that you have sampled enough evidence. You may know three teenage mothers who do not take good care of their babies, but three instances are not enough evidence to dismiss all teenagers as poor mothers.

Deductive reasoning is the flip side of inductive reasoning. Instead of considering specific cases to come up with a general statement, deduction applies a general statement to a specific instance and reasons through to a conclusion. Deduction is the formal logic of the syllogism, a traditional three-part formula:

MAJOR PREMISE: All humans are mortal.
MINOR PREMISE: Socrates[1] is human.
CONCLUSION: Socrates is mortal.

Deductive logic is only as solid as its premises. Deducing specifics from faulty generalizations is dangerous reasoning, as the next example shows:

MAJOR PREMISE: All Iraqis are terrorists.
MINOR PREMISE: Yusuf is Iraqi.
CONCLUSION: Yusuf is a terrorist.

Given the flawed nature of the major premise, the conclusion is erroneous. It is also the product of a bigoted mind.

In short, any writing intended to convince must be grounded in sound logic. Both inductive and deductive reasoning are only as sound as the observations or the premises on which they are based. If your readers are able to detect logical gaps, faulty premises, or unsupportable generalizations in your reasoning, they will not be convinced of anything you say.

---

[1]Socrates (469–399 B.C.) was a Greek thinker and teacher who, along with his disciples Plato and Aristotle, is considered the founder of Western philosophy.

Why? The Purpose

Papers designed to convince the reader answer the question, "What are the reasons for—or against—S?" To answer this question, you must first critically assess the belief, proposal, or course of action on which your paper is based. Keep in mind that "critical" means to make a judgment—for or against—not just to "find fault." Once you have tested the logic of your viewpoint, you can use argument and persuasion to accomplish one of two purposes—and sometimes both.

You may simply want your readers to share your opinion, to agree with the argument you present. You may want to bring them over to your side. For instance, you could try to convince readers that Canada's involvement in space exploration is valuable both economically and technologically.

On the other hand, you may intend not only to convince your readers to agree with you but also to convince them to *do* something, to act in some way, based on your opinion. For example, you might argue that regular exercise promotes health and lengthens life expectancy; hence, the reader should get involved in a regular exercise program. Usually, you need to accomplish the first aim, getting the reader's agreement (especially if the topic is a controversial one), before you attempt the second, moving the reader to act. For instance, a writer might argue for mandatory jail sentences for drunk drivers. The writer might then go on to urge readers to write letters, circulate petitions, and pressure legislators to enact such a law. Proposals such as this one require that you first convince your readers of the validity of your opinion and then motivate them to support your cause.

Learning about the logical processes that underlie argumentation and persuasion has another purpose, one that extends beyond the act of writing. The "hidden agenda" in mastering this rhetorical mode is that learning to reason well enables us to detect other people's attempts to pull persuasive wool over our eyes. If we know the rules of sound logical argument, we can see through the tricks of those who would like to manipulate or lie to us. We frequently meet relatively innocuous examples, such as the promises of television commercials: Drink Blue—you'll be part of the crowd; brush with Glitzodent—you'll get your man; buy a diamond—your marriage will last forever. At other times, we encounter profoundly disturbing distortions and lies: Blacks are inferior—they should not be allowed to vote; the Holocaust never happened—the millions who were "murdered" never existed. It is imperative that we recognize the twisted logic of those who would persuade us to evil. It was, after all, Adolf Hitler who forewarned in *Mein Kampf*: "The broad mass of a

nation . . . will more easily fall victim to a big lie than to a small one."
A person aware of the principles of sound reasoning is not easily
victimized by lies, big or small.

How? The Technique

Persuasive papers can be developed in a variety of ways. It is possible, as you will see in the readings for this unit, to use a number of
different structural patterns to convince your readers. For instance,
a *cause-effect* structure might be an ideal way to urge action to end
the sulphur emissions that cause acid rain. *Comparison* might offer
an opportunity to assess the efficiency of Canada's regulated airline
industry as opposed to the deregulated industry in the United States
and to argue in favour of one approach. Most of the expository
patterns can be adapted to persuasive purposes.

Two patterns are specific to argument and persuasion. One is
the classic *their side–my side* strategy, which is particularly useful
when you are arguing a controversial position that will provoke serious dispute. This pattern involves presenting the "con" (or
"against") points of your opponents first, then refuting them with the
"pro" (or "for") side of your argument. For example, if a writer
were to argue that women in the Canadian Armed Forces should
participate in combat, she might choose to present the opposing
view and then counter each point with well-reasoned arguments of
her own. Such a strategy impresses readers with its fairness and
tends to neutralize opposition.

The second structural pattern specific to argument and persuasion makes use of the familiar thesis statement. The first step in this
procedure is discovering, examining, and stating an *opinion* about
an issue. Of course, the logic of your opinion must be scrutinized
carefully before the opinion can serve as the subject of a persuasive
paper. Here are three examples of clearly stated opinions that could
be expanded into thesis statements:

1. General education is an essential part of the college curriculum.
    (See " 'Why Are We Reading This Stuff, Anyway?' ")
2. Cheating is pervasive in college sports. (See Harry Bruce's
    essay, "And May the Best Cheater Win.")
3. The North American idea of manhood is pitiful. (See Paul
    Theroux, "Being a Man.")

The crucial test for a satisfactory statement of opinion is that
someone could argue the contrary point of view: "General education
is not an essential part of the college curriculum"; "Cheating is not
often found in college sports"; "The North American idea of manhood is noble."

Once the opinion is clearly stated, the second step is to assemble *reasons* to support it. Here again, logic is essential. Apply the rules of evidence, as they are called in courtrooms. Your reasons should be *accurate*, *relevant*, and *complete*. Facts, especially statistics, must be precise. For example, a recent letter to the *Globe and Mail* lamented that only 32 percent of the books purchased by the Toronto Public Library were written by women, while 48 percent of the fiction purchased by the Antigonish Public Library was written by women. Given that no totals were provided, that the categories of books are different, and that Toronto and Antigonish are hardly comparable in size and diversity of population, the statistic was misleading and made the writer's entire argument suspect. As Britain's eminently quotable Prime Minister, Benjamin Disraeli, once said, "There are three kinds of lies: lies, damned lies, and statistics." The writer of a persuasive paper, like the witness in a courtroom, should tell the truth, the whole truth, and nothing but the truth.

Once you have ensured that your reasons are accurate, relevant (clearly related to the stated opinion), and complete (omitting no vital premise), the next step is to arrange these reasons in order. The usual arrangement is climactic order, which means building from least important to most important. In climactic order, you save your most compelling reasons for the end of the paper when the reader may already be inclined to accept your point of view. For example, you might argue that censorship of books is dangerous because it restricts an individual's right to read, it impedes artists' ability to create, and it jeopardizes an entire society's freedom of expression. Arranged in this order, the argument proceeds from the individual level to the threat to the artistic community and on to the larger implications of censorship for society as a whole. The reasons are separate, yet linked, and build upon each other convincingly.

The last step is to link the opinion to the reasons in a grammatically parallel thesis statement (**O** stands for your statement of opinion; **1**, **2**, and **3** represent your reasons):

> O because of 1, 2, and 3.

Example: Censorship of books is dangerous because it restricts the individual's right to read, impedes artists' ability to create, and jeopardizes society's freedom of expression.

Example: General education is an essential part of the college curriculum because it enhances one's ability to build a career and to live a full life.

Clearly, bringing someone over to our side through well-chosen words is a challenge. Argument and persuasion are probably the most formidable writing tasks that we undertake, yet they may also be the most important. When we are engaged in argument and persuasion, we distinguish ourselves from those who can only nod, grunt, wag a tail, or brandish a club over another's head. It is possible to convince others to agree with us and even prevail upon them to act, armed with nothing more than our logic, our feelings, our words and, ultimately, our integrity. Effective persuasion is an art that truly deserves to be called civilized.

The essay that follows expands one of the thesis statements given above into a convincing argument:

"Why Are We Reading This Stuff, Anyway?"

Introduction (uses an anecdote to ask an important question)

As an English teacher in a community college, I encounter large numbers of bright, highly motivated students who are committed to particular career paths. English is not their favourite subject. One of these students—a would-be microbiologist—challenged me as we worked our way through a Faulkner piece one gray, wintry Monday morning. "Why," he demanded, "are we reading this stuff, anyway?" Not being especially quick on my verbal feet so early in the morning, I burbled something about the value of literature and of empathy, the ability to see the world through someone else's eyes. I could tell by his glower that he was unconvinced.

Now I'd like to step back and answer the larger question inherent in my student's query. Why do colleges require anything other than skills training? Why bother with the seemingly unrelated, "irrelevant" part of the curriculum called "general education"? To my microbiology student and the many others who ask this question, I would

Thesis statement

like to respond: general education is an essential part of the curriculum because it enhances one's ability to build a career and to live a full life.

First point
(the reason is
developed through
well-chosen
examples)

Skills training alone is enough to get you a job. College or university training will provide you with the entry-level professional skills that most employers require. The important word here, however, is "entry-level." Your degree or diploma does not entitle you to an executive suite; it enables you to find a footing on the very first rung of the ladder. To proceed up that ladder, to build a career, you must continue to learn and to develop numerous other skills. You must be able to read quickly and thoroughly, to analyze all kinds of information logically, to solve problems effectively, and to communicate both in speech and in writing in an articulate and reasonably sophisticated way. In addition, you will be expected to function in a world where people are comfortable with ideas. The latest television miniseries, fashion fad, or hockey brawl will not always be appropriate conversational fare. You may be expected to know who Sigmund Freud, John Maynard Keynes, or Charlotte Brontë was. To be unaware of great cultural epochs or accomplishments, to fail to read significant new publications, to be ignorant of the difference between the Great War and the Black Death will mark you as uneducated and possibly unsuited to high career achievement. The skills and knowledge described here are developed in the "general education" portion of your education, in courses such as history, English, psychology, philosophy, and the natural sciences.

Second point
(again, note use
of examples to
develop the
reason)

Secondly, one pursues an education to improve the overall quality of life. Working is only one part of living. Most of us hope that it is the means to an end: a comfortable life shared with other people in a way that will bring happiness to ourselves and those

Conclusion
(ties the essay
together by
citing a quotation
from the writer
mentioned in
the introductory
paragraph)

around us. We may marry and have children; we will surely make friends; and we will want to contribute to the communities in which we live. The education we acquire will contribute to our family's well-being in a spiritual and cultural sense as well as an economic one. Our education will enable us to make thoughtful choices; it will arm us against manipulation by sham ideas and charlatans. It will even help us to acquire some measure of wisdom and courage and serenity as we face whatever joys and perils life holds for us.

Grand promises? Perhaps. However, people with a solid, well-rounded education tend to thrive in the same way that civilizations that place a premium on education continue to flourish. With these thoughts in mind, I return to my young microbiology student and remind him of some lines by William Faulkner, the author whose text we were studying that dreary Monday:

I believe that man will not merely endure: he will prevail. He is immortal, not because he alone among creatures has an inexhaustible voice, but because he has a soul, a spirit capable of compassion and sacrifice and endurance. The poet's, the writer's, duty is to write about these things. It is his privilege to help man endure by lifting his heart, by reminding him of the courage and honor and hope and pride and compassion and pity and sacrifice which have been the glory of his past. The poet's voice need not merely be the record of man, it can be one of the props, the pillars to help him endure and prevail.[2]

[2]William Faulkner, Nobel Prize acceptance speech, 1949.

And May the Best Cheater Win

HARRY BRUCE

Every youth knows he can get into deep   1
trouble by stealing cameras, peddling dope, mugging winos, forging
cheques or copying someone else's answers during an exam. Those
are examples of not playing by the rules. Cheating. But every youth
also knows that in organized sports across North America, cheating is not only perfectly okay, it's *recommended*. "The structure of
sport . . . actually promotes deviance," says U.S. sport sociologist
D.S. Eitzen.

The downy-cheeked hockey player who refuses to play dirty   2
may find himself fired off the team. The boy soccer player who
refuses to rough up a superior striker to "throw him off his game"
may find himself writhing under a coach's tongue-lashing. The
basketball player who refuses to foul a goal-bound enemy star in
the last seconds of a close game may find himself riding the bench
next week. Thus, we have that cynical paradox, "the good foul," a
phrase that makes about as much sense as "a beneficial outbreak of
bubonic plague."

If organized sports offer benefits to youngsters, they also offer   3
a massive program of moral corruption. The recruiting of college
athletes in the United States, and the use of academic fraud to
maintain their "eligibility," stunk so powerfully in 1980 that *Newsweek* decided "cheating has become the name of the game," and
spoke of the fear on U.S. campuses of "an epidemic of corruption."
But the epidemic had already arrived, and what really worried
Newsweek was national acceptance of corruption as normal: "Many
kids are admitting that they have tried to take the bribes and induce-
ments on the sleazy terms with which they are offered. Their complaints are not so much that illegalities exist, but that they aren't
getting their share of the goodies." Fans, alumni, coaches, college
administrators, players and their parents all believed nothing could
ever be more important than winning (or more disgraceful than
losing), and that cheating in victory's cause was therefore com-
mendable°.

"And May the Best Cheater Win" by Harry Bruce from *Quest Magazine*. Copyright
November 1984. Reprinted with the permission of Bella Pomer Agency, Inc.

4   "Candidates for big-time sport's Hall of Shame have seemed
suddenly to break out all over like an ugly rash," William Oscar
Johnson wrote last year in *Sports Illustrated*. He constructed a dismal
catalogue of assaults on cops, drunken brawls, adventures in the
cocaine trade, credit-card frauds and other sordid activities by rich
professional athletes who, in more naive times, might have earned
the adulation° of small boys. Jim Finks, then Chicago Bears general
manager, speculated that the trouble with the younger lawbreakers
was that they had "been looked after all the way from junior high
school. Some of them have had doctored grades. This plus the
affluence [astronomical salaries] means there has never been any
pressing need for them to work things out for themselves. They
have no idea how to face reality."

5   No one in all their lives had taught them about fair play. "In the
early days of playground and high-school leagues, one of the key
issues was moral regulation," says Alan Ingham, a teacher at the
University of Washington. "You got sports, and you got Judeo-
Christian principles thrown in, too." Now, however, "the majority
of things taught in sports are performance things." John Pooley of
the School of Recreation, Physical and Health Education at Dalhousie University, Nova Scotia, asked Calvin Hill, a former Dallas Cowboy, what percentage of all the football rookies he'd ever met had
said that, as college players, they'd encountered no cheating. Hill's
reply was short: "None."

6   So here we have the most powerful nation in the world, and it
blithely corrupts children so they'll mature as athletic machines
without an ounce of the moral sense that might prevent their sniffing
cocaine or complicate their lust for victory. Pray for nuclear disarmament, fans.

7   Still, Canadians are little better. We all know who invented the
game that inspired Paul Newman to star in *Slap Shot*, a black and
bloody comedy about butchery on ice. We can't argue that it's only
American coaches who teach peewees to draw tripping penalties
rather than let an enemy player continue a breakaway on your goal.
Moreover, I happen to live in Halifax, where only last winter St.
Mary's University was disgraced for allowing a ringer from Florida
to play varsity basketball. The coach of a rival but inferior team
ferreted out the truth about the player's ineligibility. In doing so, he
imported one of the fine old traditions of amateur sports in the
States: if you can't beat them, hire a private dick. Oh well, that's
what universities are supposed to be all about: the pursuit of truth.

8   Pursuing another truth, Pooley of Dalhousie surveyed recent
graduates of three down-east universities. The grads were both men
and women, and they had all played intercollegiate field hockey,
ice hockey, soccer or basketball. "With one exception [a woman field

hockey player], all felt there was immense pressure to win," Pooley said. Typical responses: "Winning is everything in university sport. . . . The measure of success was not how well you played but the win-loss record. . . . There is incredible pressure to perform because there are always two or three guys on the bench ready to take your place."

Half said their coaches had urged "winning at any cost." One   9
grad revealed, "Some coaches send their players 'out to get' a good player on the other team." Another described "goon coaches who stressed intimidation and rough play." Coaches had not only con-doned° tactical fouls, but had actually taught the arts of fouling during routine practice. A player who had competed against British and Bermudian teams said they played "intensely but fairly" while the Maritimers "sometimes used dirty tactics" or "blatantly tried to stop a player."

Pooley wondered if the grads, after years in intercollegiate sport,   10
felt it had promoted fair play. Only the field-hockey players said yes. Answers from the others were shockers: "Everyone cheats and the best cheater wins. . . . Fair play and sportsmanship are *not* pro-moted. This is a joke. . . . You did whatever you could to win. . . . You are taught to gain an advantage, whatever it takes." Such cynicism, from people so young they've barely doffed their mortar-boards°, confirms the sad opinion of one Kalevi Heinila, who told a world scientific congress in 1980 that fair play was "ripe to be dumped in the waste basket of sport history."

The irony in all this—and it's both ludicrous and nauseating—is   11
that universities defend their expensive programs for intercollegiate sports with lip service to the notion that keen teamwork in clean competition nurtures good citizens. Fair play in sports, don't you know, spawns fair players for the worlds of politics, the professions and business.

That's a crock. What intercollegiate sport really teaches is how   12
to get away with murder, how to be crooked within the law. Just listen to one of the fresh-faced grads in Pooley's survey as he sets out to make his way in the world, his eyes shining with idealism: "University sport teaches you to play as close to the limits as possible; and this is the attitude that will get you ahead in the business world." Another acknowledged that his "concept of fair play decreased"; but, on the other hand, he had learned to "stretch the rules to my advantage." A young woman confided, "University sport has made me tough, less sensitive to other people's feelings." Still others stressed that college sport had prepared them for "the real world," for "real life," in which winning was all.

Cheating in amateur sport, Pooley says, "gives it a hollow feel-   13
ing. Many coaches do not have integrity. I'm still sickened by that.

It upsets me, at all levels." A tall, talkative, forceful man with a bony face and a thick brush of steely hair, Pooley has coached soccer in six countries, once played for professional teams in Britain, and now, at 53, cavorts on a team for men over 35. "I'm still playing league soccer," he wrote in a paper for the 1984 Olympic Scientific Congress in Eugene, Oregon, "because: a) I helped to organize and plan my own youth soccer experiences; b) coming second or being beaten was okay; c) I was always much more interested in playing well than playing to win; d) I never minded playing less well than I'd earlier played; and e) I always felt successful at the level played."

14   Those are highly un-American reasons for playing any sport, but Pooley is originally from northern England, the nation that invented "fair play" and knew that certain things just weren't cricket°. That was in a time long before Americans institutionalized cheating even in soap box derbies, before athletes gobbled steroids, before universities invented courses in weight lifting and racquetball so quarterbacks could qualify as "students." Moreover, Pooley believes that the few adults who stick with team sports until middle age do so because, as youngsters, "They preferred the feel of the ball, the pass well made, the sweetness of the stroke or the power in the shot, rather than whether they won or lost the game." Such people don't need to cheat.

15   Some scholars believe that the sleaziness of organized sports simply reflects the sleaziness of our entire culture. Pooley points out, for instance, that one sociologist offers two reasons why cheating in sports shouldn't be "disproportionately reprimanded." The first is that it's "endemic° in society," and the second is that even more cheating probably occurs in other fields. Pooley disagrees. He says this argument is like saying you should not disproportionately reprimand the clergy for being dishonest. Poor Pooley. He has such quaint ideas about sports. He actually believes they should not be immoral, and should be fun.

```
┌─────────────────────────┐
│                         │
│                         │
└─────────────────────────┘
```

HARRY BRUCE

Toronto-born Harry Bruce began his career as a journalist with the *Ottawa Citizen* in 1955. He has written articles and columns for leading magazines and newspapers across the country. *Each Moment As It Flies* is a collection of articles and essays in which Bruce explores a number of subjects such as the lives of famous Canadians, recollections of his childhood experiences, environmental issues, and family life. Bruce now makes his home in Halifax.

Words and Meanings

Paragraph

commendable:	praiseworthy, something to be congratulated for	3
adulation:	excessive praise; hero-worship	4
condoned:	excused, overlooked	9
doffed their mortarboards:	taken off the caps worn during graduation ceremonies	10
weren't cricket:	British expression for "socially unacceptable"	14
endemic:	widespread, pervasive	15

Structure and Strategy

1. What two methods of paragraph development has Bruce used in paragraph 1? What is the effect of the one-word sentence fragment in this paragraph?
2. In paragraph 3, Bruce claims that cheating in sports has become "an epidemic of corruption." Find three or four instances of this METAPHOR elsewhere in the essay and explain how it contributes to the UNITY of the whole piece.
3. What FIGURES OF SPEECH make the first sentence of paragraph 4 particularly effective?
4. What is the TOPIC SENTENCE of paragraph 12, and how does Bruce develop it?
5. Study the direct quotations Bruce uses as evidence in his essay. Why are they effective in supporting his argument?
6. Paragraph 6 consists of two seemingly unrelated sentences. Explain the connection between them that Bruce implies.

Content and Purpose

1. Summarize the opinion and supporting reasons that form the thesis of this essay.
2. What is Bruce's attitude toward cheating in college sports? Why does he take the matter so seriously?
3. What is wrong with the argument that "cheating in sports shouldn't be disproportionately reprimanded" because cheating is "endemic in society"? (See paragraph 15.)
4. What connection does Bruce establish between corruption in organized sports and the decline in moral standards of society as a whole?
5. Explain why Bruce sees organized sports at their best as a form of training for responsible citizenship.

Suggestions for Writing

1. Write a paper persuading your readers that Canadians are (or are not) the world's best hockey players, professional peace-keepers, or most devoted sports fans.
2. Write a paper arguing that some form of cheating is necessary (or unnecessary) in a particular situation, such as in a sport, a business, an exam, a personal relationship, preparing one's income tax, or filling out a job application.

A Planet for the Taking

DAVID SUZUKI

1   Canadians live under the remarkable illusion that we are technologically advanced people. Everything around us denies that assumption. We are, in many ways, a Third World country, selling our natural resources in exchange for the high technology of the industrialized world. Try going through your home and looking at the country of origin of your clothes, electrical appliances, books, car. The rare technological product that does have Canada stamped on it is usually from a branch plant of a multinational company centred in another country. But we differ from traditional Third World countries. We have a majority population of Caucasians and a very high level of literacy and affluence. And we have been able to maintain our seemingly advanced social state by virtue of an incredible bounty of natural resources.

2   Within the Canadian mystique there is also a sense of the vastness of this land. The prairies, the Arctic, the oceans, the mountains are ever present in our art and literature. This nation is built on our sense of the seeming endlessness of the expanse of wilderness and the output of nature and we have behaved as if this endlessness were real. Today we speak of renewable resources but our "harvest" procedures are more like a mining operation. We extract raw resources in the crudest of ways, gouging the land to get at its inner core, spewing our raw wastes into the air, water and soil in massive amounts while taking fish, birds, animals and trees in vast quantities without regard to the future. So we operate under a strange duality

"A Planet for the Taking" by David Suzuki. Originally published in *Canadian Forum*, February 1985. Reprinted with the permission of the author.

of mind: we have both a sense of the importance of the wilderness and space in our culture and an attitude that it is limitless and therefore we needn't worry.

Native cultures of the past may have been no more conserva-   3
tion-minded than we are but they lacked the technology to make the kind of impact that we do today. Canadians and Americans share one of the great natural wonders, the Great Lakes, which contain 20 percent of the world's fresh water, yet today even this massive body of water is terribly polluted and the populations of fish completely mixed-up by human activity. We speak of "managing" our resources but do it in a way that resembles the sledgehammer-on-the-head cure for a headache. On the west coast of Canada, Natives lived for millenia° on the incredible abundance of five species of salmon. Today, the massive runs are gone and many biologists fear that the fish may be in mortal jeopardy because of both our fishing and management policies. Having improved fishing techniques this century to the point of endangering runs yet still knowing very little of the biology of the fish, we have assumed that we could build up the yield by simply dumping more back. But it wasn't known that sockeye salmon fry°, for example, spend a year in a freshwater lake before going to sea. Millions of sockeye fry were dumped directly into the Fraser River where they died soon after. In Oregon, over-fishing and hydroelectric dams had decimated coho° populations in the Columbia River. In one year, over 8 million fry were released of which only seven were ever caught. No one knows what's happening to the rest.

We act as if a fish were a fish, a duck a duck or a tree a tree. If   4
we "harvest" one, we renew it by simply adding one or two back. But what we have learned is that all animals and plants are not equivalent. Each organism reflects the evolutionary° history of its progenitors°; in the case of salmon, each race and subrace of fish has been exquisitely honed by nature to return to a very specific part of the Pacific watershed. Similarly, in the enormous area of prairie pothole country in the centre of the continent, migratory birds do not just space themselves out according to the potholes that are empty. Scientists have discovered that the birds have been selected to return to a very restricted part of that area. And of course, our entire forestry policy is predicated° on the ridiculous idea that a virgin stand° of fir or cedar which has taken millenia to form and clings to a thin layer of topsoil can be replaced after clear-cut logging simply by sticking seedlings into the ground. How can anyone with even the most rudimentary° understanding of biology and evolution ignore the realities of the complex interaction between organisms and the environment and attempt to manipulate wild populations as if they were tomato plants or chickens?

5   I believe that in large part our problems rest on our faith in the power of science and technology. At the beginning of this century, science, when applied by industry and medicine, promised a life immeasurably better and there is no doubt that society, indeed the planet, has been transformed by the impact of new ideas and inventions of science. Within my lifetime, I've seen the beginning of television, oral contraception, organ transplants, space travel, computers, jets, nuclear weapons, satellite communication, and polio vaccine. Each has changed society forever and made the world of my youth recede into the pages of history. But we have not achieved a technological utopia°. The problems facing us today are immense and many are a direct consequence of science and technology. What has gone wrong?

6   I believe that the core of our 20th century dilemma lies in a fundamental limitation of science that most scientists, especially those in the life sciences, fail to recognize. Most of my colleagues take it for granted that our studies will ultimately be applicable to the "big picture," that our research will have beneficial payoffs to society eventually. That is because the thrust of modern science has been predicated on the Newtonian idea that the universe is like an enormous machine whose entire system will be reconstructed on the basis of our understanding of the parts. This is the fundamental reductionist faith in science: the whole is equal to the sum of its parts. It does make a lot of sense—what distinguishes science from other activities that purport° to provide a comprehensive "world view" is its requirement that we focus on a part of nature isolated to as great an extent as possible from the rest of the system of which it is a part. This has provided enormous insights into that fragment of nature, often accompanied by power to manipulate it. But when we attempt to tinker with what lies in the field of our view, the effects ripple far beyond the barrel of the microscope. And so we are constantly surprised at the unexpected consequences of our interference. Scientists only know nature in "bits and pieces" and assume that higher levels of organization are simply the expression of the component parts. This is what impels neurobiologists to study the chemical and electrical behaviour of single neurons in the faith that it will ultimately lead to an understanding of what creativity and imagination are, a faith that I don't for a moment think will ever be fulfilled (although a lot of useful information will accrue°).

7   Physicists, who originally set this view in motion, have this century, with the arrival of relativity and quantum theory, put to rest the notion that we will ever be able to reconstruct the entire universe from fundamental principles. Chemists know that a complete physical description of atoms of oxygen and hydrogen is of little value in predicting the behaviour of a water molecule. But

biologists scream that any sense that there are properties of organization that don't exist at lower levels is "vitalism," a belief that there is some mystical life force in living organisms. And so biochemists and molecular biologists are intent on understanding the workings of organisms by learning all they can about sub-cellular° organization.

Ironically, ecology°, long scorned by molecular biologists as an   8
inexact science, is now corroborating physics. In studying ecosystems, we are learning that a simple breakdown into components and their behaviour does not provide insight into how an entire collection of organisms in a natural setting will work. While many ecologists do continue to "model" ecosystems in computers in the hope that they will eventually derive a predictive tool, their science warns of the hazards of treating it too simply in management programs.

At present, our very terminology suggests that we think we can   9
manage wild plants and animals as though they were domesticated° organisms. We speak of "herds" of seals, of "culling," "harvesting," "stocks." The ultimate expression of our narrow view (and self-interested rationalizations) is seen in how we overlook the enormous environmental impact of our pollution, habitat destruction and extraction and blame seals and whales for the decline in fish populations or wolves for the decrease in moose—and then propose bounties° as a solution!

But Canadians do value the spiritual importance of nature and   10
want to see it survive for future generations. We also believe in the power of science to sustain a high quality of life. And while the current understanding of science's power is, I believe, misplaced, in fact the leading edges of physics and ecology may provide the insights that can get us off the current track. We need a very profound perceptual shift and soon.

DAVID SUZUKI

David Suzuki (b. 1936) is a well-known Canadian scientist, educator, journalist, and broadcaster. He earned his Ph.D. in genetics and became a professor at the University of British Columbia, a post he held until 1975. Suzuki currently hosts the CBC's acclaimed series, "The Nature of Things," and writes for a wide range of publications.

Words and Meanings

Paragraph

millenia: thousands of years   3

| fry: | salmon in their second year of life |
| coho: | species of salmon |

4 | evolutionary: | continuous genetic adaptation of living things to their environment |
progenitors:	ancestors; previous generations
predicated:	based
virgin stand:	group of trees that have never been logged
rudimentary:	basic

5 | utopia: | perfect world |

6 | purport: | intend or seem to |
| accrue: | result |

7 | sub-cellular: | particle or particles smaller than a single cell |

8 | ecology: | study of the interrelationships between organisms and their environment |

9 | domesticated: | tame; raised in controlled environment for human use |
| bounties: | sums of money paid to individuals who have killed "nuisance" animals, e.g., wolves |

Structure and Strategy

1. Identify five examples Suzuki uses to support his contention that Canada is recklessly abusing its abundant natural resources. Find three or four examples of DICTION that reinforce this contention.
2. What is the topic of paragraph 4? How is the topic supported or developed?

Content and Purpose

1. What are the "illusions" deceiving Canadians that Suzuki identifies in paragraphs 1, 2, and 3?
2. What two reasons does Suzuki identify for Canadians' belief that the "harvesting" of our natural resources is not a cause for serious concern? How does Suzuki attempt to convince us that our notion of "limitless" natural resources is dangerously naïve?
3. Suzuki's essay is both an argument and a warning. Is his primary purpose to convince his readers of the validity of his opinion or to move them to act in some way?
4. Why does Suzuki believe that biologists are lagging behind chemists and physicists in their understanding of the world in which we live?

Suggestions for Writing

1. Suzuki is a scientist, yet he believes that "in large part, our problems rest on our faith in the power of science and technology." Write a persuasive essay in which you agree or disagree with Suzuki. Use at least three well-developed examples to support your argument.

2. Read Margaret Atwood's "True North" and write an essay in which you compare her view of the vast Canadian wilderness with that of Suzuki in "A Planet for the Taking."

The Harvest, the Kill

JANE RULE

I live among vegetarians of various persua- 1
sions and moral meat eaters; therefore when I have guests for dinner, I pay rather more attention to the nature of food than I would, left to my own imagination.

The vegetarians who don't eat meat because they believe it to 2
be polluted with cancer-causing hormones or because they identify their sensitive digestive tracts with herbivore° ancestors are just cautious folk similar to those who cross the street only at the corner with perhaps a hint of the superstition found in those who don't walk under ladders. They are simply taking special care of their lives without further moral deliberation°.

Those who don't eat meat because they don't approve of killing 3
aren't as easy for me to understand. Yesterday, as I pried live scallops from their beautiful, fragile shells and saw them still pulsing in the bowl, ready to cook for friends for whom food from the sea is acceptable, it felt to me no less absolute an act of killing than chopping off the head of a chicken. But I also know in the vegetable garden that I rip carrots untimely° from their row. The fact that they don't twitch or run around without their heads doesn't make them less alive. Like me, they have grown from seed and have their own natural life span which I have interrupted. It is hard for me to be hierarchical° about the aliveness of living things.

There are two vegetarian arguments that bear some guilty 4
weight for me. The first is the number of acres it takes to feed beef

cattle as compared to the number of acres it takes to feed vegetarians. If there ever were a large plan to change our basic agriculture in order to feed everyone more equably°, I would support it and give up eating beef, but until then my not eating beef is of no more help than my eating my childhood dinner was to the starving Armenians. The second is mistreatment of animals raised for slaughter. To eat what has not been a free-ranging animal is to condone° the abuse of animals. Again, given the opportunity to support laws for more humane treatment of the creatures we eventually eat, I would do so, but I probably wouldn't go so far as to approve of chickens so happy in life that they were tough for my table.

5   The moral meat eaters are those who believe that we shouldn't eat what we haven't killed ourselves, either gone to the trouble of stalking it down or raising it, so that we have proper respect for the creatures sacrificed for our benefit.

6   I am more at home with that view because my childhood summers were rural. By the time I was seven or eight, I had done my share of fishing and hunting, and I'd been taught also to clean my catch or kill. I never shot anything larger than a pigeon or rabbit. That I was allowed to use a gun at all was the result of a remarkably indulgent° father. He never took me deer hunting, not because I was a girl but because he couldn't bear to shoot them himself. But we ate venison° brought to us by other men in the family.

7   I don't remember much being made of the sacredness of the life we took, but there was a real emphasis on fair play, much of it codified° in law, like shooting game birds only on the wing, like not hunting deer with flashlights at night, like not shooting does°. But my kinfolk frowned on bait fishing as well. They were sportsmen who retained the wilderness ethic of not killing more than they could use. Strictly speaking, we did not need the food. (We could get meat in a town ten miles down the road.) But we did eat it.

8   Over the years, I became citified. I still could and did put live lobsters and crab in boiling water, but meat came from the meat market. Now that I live in the country again, I am much more aware of the slaughter that goes on around me, for I not only eat venison from the local hunt but have known the lamb and kid on the hoof (even in my rhododendrons°, which is good for neither them nor the rhododendrons) which I eat. The killers of the animals are my moral, meat-eating neighbors. I have never killed a large animal, and I hope I never have to, though I'm not particularly tender-hearted about creatures not human. I find it hard to confront the struggle, smell, and mess of slaughter. I simply haven't the stomach for it. But, if I had to do it or go without meat, I would learn how.

9   It's puzzling to me that cannibalism is a fascinating abomination to vegetarian and meat eater alike, a habit claimed by only the most vicious and primitive tribes. We are scandalized by stories of the

Donner Party or rumors of cannibalism at the site of a small plane crash in the wilderness, a boat lost at sea. Yet why would it be so horrifying for survivors to feed on the flesh of those who have died? Have worms and buzzards more right to the carcass?

We apparently do not think of ourselves as part of the food chain, except by cruel and exceptional accident. Our flesh, like the cow in India, is sacred and taboo°, thought of as violated° even when it is consigned° to a mass grave. We bury it to hide a truth that still must be obvious to us, that as we eat so are we eaten. Why the lowly maggot is given the privilege (or sometimes the fish or the vulture) denied other living creatures is a complex puzzle of hygiene, myth and morality in each culture.

Our denial that we are part of nature, our sense of superiority to it, is our basic trouble. Though we are not, as the producers of margarine would make us believe, what we eat, we are related to what we harvest and kill. If being a vegetarian or a moral meat eater is a habit to remind us of that responsibility, neither is to be disrespected. When habit becomes a taboo, it blinds us to the real meaning. We are also related to each other, but our general refusal to eat our own flesh has not stopped us from slaughtering each other in large and totally wasted numbers.

I am flesh, a flesh eater, whether the food is carrot or cow. Harvesting and killing are the same activity, the interrupting of one life cycle for the sake of another. We don't stop at eating either. We kill to keep warm. We kill for shelter.

Back there in my rural childhood, I had not only a fishing rod and rifle, I had a hatchet, too. I cleared brush, cut down small trees, chopped wood. I was present at the felling of a two-thousand-year-old redwood tree, whose impact shook the earth I stood on. It was a death more simply shocking to me than any other I've ever witnessed. The house I lived in then was made of redwood. The house I live in now is cedar.

My ashes may nourish the roots of a living tree, pitifully small compensation for the nearly immeasurable acres I have laid waste for my needs and pleasures, even for my work. For such omnivorous° creatures as we are, a few frugal° habits are not enough. We have to feed and midwife° more than we slaughter, replant more than we harvest, if not with our hands, then with our own talents to see that it is done in our name, that we own to it.

The scallop shells will be finely cleaned by raccoons, then made by a neighbor into wind chimes, which may trouble my sleep and probably should until it is time for my own bones to sing.

10

11

12

13

14

15

JANE RULE

Jane Rule, the novelist and essayist, was born in 1931 in Plainfield, N.J., and educated at Mills College, California, and University College, London. She moved to Vancouver in 1956 and in 1976 settled on Galiano Island, B.C. Among her novels are *Desert of the Heart*, *The Young in One Another's Arms*, and *Contract with the World*.

Words and Meanings

Paragraph

2	herbivore:	creature that eats only plants
	deliberation:	thought, consideration
3	untimely:	before they are fully grown
	hierarchical:	organized in order of rank or importance
4	equably:	evenly, fairly
	condone:	forgive, excuse
6	indulgent:	the opposite of strict
	venison:	deer meat
7	codified:	written down as rules or laws
	does:	female deer
8	rhododendrons:	large, flowering bushes common in B.C. gardens
10	taboo:	forbidden
	violated:	abused, dishonoured
	consigned:	delivered, handed over to
14	omnivorous:	creatures that eat both animals and plants
	frugal:	saving, conserving
	midwife:	assist in the reproduction of animals

Subject and Structure

1. In paragraph 1, Rule divides her neighbours into two categories: vegetarians and moral meat eaters. What is the function of paragraphs 2 to 4? 5 to 7? What relation do they have to the opening paragraph?

2. In which paragraph does Rule explicitly state the opinion that forms the basis for her argument? Why do you think she introduces this statement so late in the essay?

3. Explain what makes the concluding sentence of this essay effective and memorable. What powerful images come together to reinforce Rule's point about the interdependency of all forms of life?

Content and Purpose

1. What two classes of vegetarians does Rule identify?
2. What are the "two vegetarian arguments" presented in paragraph 3? Do they appeal to the intellect or to the emotions? Do you find either of these arguments persuasive? Why is Rule not a vegetarian herself?
3. What is a "moral meat eater"? Does Rule herself fit into this category?
4. What childhood experiences contributed to Rule's adult views about the morality of "harvesting and killing"?
5. According to Rule, why is there such a strong taboo on cannibalism? (See paragraphs 9 to 11.)
6. According to Rule, what do humans deny about themselves that leads to an absence of responsibility for the natural world? How does she relate this denial to burial rituals?
7. Paragraphs 12 to 14 illustrate how we exploit nature, consuming far more than we return. What, according to Rule, do we need to acknowledge before we can correct this imbalance?

Suggestions for Writing

1. Write an essay persuading the reader to adopt a vegetarian lifestyle. Appeal to your readers' intellect and emotions in your attempt to convince them to give up meat.
2. Do you agree or disagree with the contention that wearing fur or leather clothing is a violation of animal rights? Write an essay in which you convince your reader of the reasonableness of your opinion.
3. Compare Rule's thesis in "The Harvest, the Kill" with Suzuki's in "A Planet for the Taking," or with Atwood's in "True North." What premises do the writers share about the relationship between human life and the life of other species on our planet?

Being a Man

PAUL THEROUX

1   here is a pathetic sentence in the chapter "Fetishism" in Dr. Norman Cameron's book *Personality Development and Psychopathology*. It goes, "Fetishists are nearly always men; and their commonest fetish° is a woman's shoe." I cannot read that sentence without thinking that it is just one more awful thing about being a man—and perhaps it is an important thing to know about us.

2   I have always disliked being a man. The whole idea of manhood in America is pitiful, in my opinion. This version of masculinity is a little like having to wear an ill-fitting coat for one's entire life (by contrast, I imagine femininity to be an oppressive sense of naked-ness). Even the expression "Be a man!" strikes me as insulting and abusive. It means: Be stupid, be unfeeling, obedient, soldierly and stop thinking. Man means "manly"—how can one think about men without considering the terrible ambition of manliness? And yet it is part of every man's life. It is a hideous and crippling lie; it not only insists on difference and connives° at superiority, it is also by its very nature destructive—emotionally damaging and socially harmful.

3   The youth who is subverted, as most are, into believing in the masculine ideal is effectively separated from women and he spends the rest of his life finding women a riddle and a nuisance. Of course, there is a female version of this male affliction. It begins with mothers encouraging little girls to say (to other adults) "Do you like my new dress?" In a sense, little girls are traditionally urged to please adults with a kind of coquettishness°, while boys are enjoined to behave like monkeys towards each other. The nine-year-old coquette proceeds to become womanish in a subtle power game in which she learns to be sexually indispensable, socially decorative and always alert to a man's sense of inadequacy.

4   Femininity—being lady-like—implies needing a man as witness and seducer; but masculinity celebrates the exclusive company of men. That is why it is so grotesque; and that is also why there is no

manliness without inadequacy—because it denies men the natural friendship of women.

It is very hard to imagine any concept of manliness that does   5
not belittle women, and it begins very early. At an age when I wanted to meet girls—let's say the treacherous years of thirteen to sixteen—I was told to take up a sport, get more fresh air, join the Boy Scouts, and I was urged not to read so much. It was the 1950s and if you asked too many questions about sex you were sent to camp—boy's camp, of course: the nightmare. Nothing is more unnatural or prison-like than a boy's camp, but if it were not for them we would have no Elks' Lodges°, no pool rooms, no boxing matches, no Marines.

And perhaps no sports as we know them. Everyone is aware of   6
how few in number are the athletes who behave like gentlemen. Just as high school basketball teaches you how to be a poor loser, the manly attitude towards sports seems to be little more than a recipe for creating bad marriages, social misfits, moral degenerates, sadists, latent rapists and just plain louts. I regard high school sports as a drug far worse than marijuana, and it is the reason that the average tennis champion, say, is a pathetic oaf.

Any objective study would find the quest for manliness essen-   7
tially right-wing, puritanical, cowardly, neurotic and fueled largely by a fear of women. It is also certainly philistine°. There is no book-hater like a Little League coach. But indeed all the creative arts are obnoxious to the manly ideal, because at their best the arts are pursued by uncompetitive and essentially solitary people. It makes it very hard for a creative youngster, for any boy who expresses the desire to be alone seems to be saying that there is something wrong with him.

It ought to be clear by now that I have something of an objection   8
to the way we turn boys into men. It does not surprise me that when the President of the United States has his customary weekend off he dresses like a cowboy—it is both a measure of his insecurity and his willingness to please. In many ways, American culture does little more for a man than prepare him for modeling clothes in the L.L. Bean° catalogue. I take this as a personal insult because for many years I found it impossible to admit to myself that I wanted to be a writer. It was my guilty secret, because being a writer was incompatible with being a man.

There are people who might deny this, but that is because the   9
American writer, typically, has been so at pains to prove his manliness that we have come to see literariness and manliness as mingled qualities. But first there was a fear that writing was not a manly profession—indeed, not a profession at all. (The paradox in American letters is that it has always been easier for a woman to write and

for a man to be published.) Growing up, I had thought of sports as
wasteful and humiliating, and the idea of manliness was a bore. My
wanting to become a writer was not a flight from that oppressive
role-playing, but I quickly saw that it was at odds with it. Everything
in stereotyped manliness goes against the life of the mind. The
Hemingway personality is too tedious to go into here, and in any
case his exertions are well-known, but certainly it was not until this
aberrant° behavior was examined by feminists in the 1960s that any
male writer dared question the pugnacity° in Hemingway's fiction.
All the bullfighting and arm wrestling and elephant shooting diminished Hemingway as a writer, but it is consistent with a prevailing
attitude in American writing: one cannot be a male writer without
first proving that one is a man.

10   It is normal in America for a man to be dismissive or even
somewhat apologetic about being a writer. Various factors make it
easier. There is a heartiness about journalism that makes it acceptable—journalism is the manliest form of American writing and,
therefore, the profession the most independent-minded women
seek (yes, it is an illusion, but that is my point). Fiction-writing is
equated with a kind of dispirited failure and is only manly when it
produces wealth—money is masculinity. So is drinking. Being a
drunkard is another assertion, if misplaced, of manliness. The American male writer is traditionally proud of his heavy drinking. But we
are also a very literal-minded people. A man proves his manhood
in America in old-fashioned ways. He kills lions, like Hemingway;
or he hunts ducks, like Nathanael West; or he makes pronouncements like, "A man should carry enough knife to defend himself
with," as James Jones once said to a *Life* interviewer. Or he says he
can drink you under the table. But even tiny drunken William
Faulkner loved to mount a horse and go fox hunting, and Jack
Kerouac roistered up and down Manhattan in a lumberjack shirt
(and spent every night of *The Subterraneans* with his mother in
Queens). And we are familiar with the lengths to which Norman
Mailer is prepared, in his endearing way, to prove that he is just as
much a monster as the next man.

11   When the novelist John Irving was revealed as a wrestler, people
took him to be a very serious writer; and even a bubble reputation
like Eric (*Love Story*) Segal's was enhanced by the news that he ran
the marathon in a respectable time. How surprised we would be if
Joyce Carol Oates were revealed as a sumo wrestler or Joan Didion
active in pumping iron. "Lives in New York City with her three
children" is the typical woman writer's biographical note, for just
as the male writer must prove he has achieved a sort of muscular
manhood, the woman writer—or rather her publicists—must prove
her motherhood.

There would be no point in saying any of this if it were not   12
generally accepted that to be a man is somehow—even now in
feminist-influenced America—a privilege. It is on the contrary an
unmerciful and punishing burden. Being a man is bad enough;
being manly is appalling (in this sense, women's lib has done much
more for men than for women). It is the sinister silliness of men's
fashions, and a clubby attitude in the arts. It is the subversion of
good students. It is the so-called "Dress Code" of the Ritz-Carlton
Hotel in Boston, and it is the institutionalized cheating in college
sports. It is the most primitive insecurity.

And this is also why men often object to feminism but are afraid   13
to explain why: of course women have a justified grievance, but
most men believe—and with reason—that their lives are just as bad.

[ ]

PAUL THEROUX

Paul Theroux is an American-born novelist, travel writer, critic, and poet.
After graduating from university, Theroux spent ten years travelling abroad,
teaching in Malawi, Uganda, Italy, and Singapore before settling in England.
Much of his writing centres on characters whose experiences of a foreign
culture have left them disillusioned and critical of the values of their own
society. Among his best-known works are *The Mosquito Coast* (1981), *Picture Palace* (1977), *The Great Railway Bazaar* (1975), and *Kingdom by the Sea* (1983).

Words and Meanings

Paragraph

fetish:	object to which one is irrationally devoted or attached; here, in the sense of sexual arousal	1
connives:	schemes or co-operates secretly	2
coquettishness:	flirtatiousness	3
Elks' Lodges:	kind of club; fraternal society for men	5
philistine:	anti-intellectual	7
L. L. Bean catalogue:	American mail-order catalogue for fashionable sportswear, hunting and camping equipment	8
aberrant:	erratic or abnormal	9
pugnacity:	quarrelsome tendency; desire to fight	

Structure and Strategy

1.   How successful is the first paragraph in catching the reader's interest?

2. What is the TONE of paragraphs 5 to 8?
3. What is the topic sentence of paragraph 9 and how is it developed in the next two paragraphs?
4. Do paragraphs 12 and 13 form a successful conclusion to this essay? Why or why not?

Content and Purpose

1. What idea or concept does Theroux present in this essay? Is his argument successful or unsuccessful in your opinion?
2. What does Theroux mean when he says he has always "disliked being a man"? What is the distinction between "being a man" and "being manly"?
3. In what ways are both the masculine ideal and the feminine ideal damaging to one's identity and personality? (See paragraphs 3 and 4.)
4. What are the reasons Theroux objects to the way North American society rears male children, the way we "turn boys into men"?
5. Would you describe Theroux as a feminist? Why or why not?

Suggestions for Writing

1. Think of a particular man or some men whom you admire and write an essay defining what it means to be a man.
2. Theroux discusses the difficulty of being a man. Are there difficulties associated with being a woman? Write an essay in which you persuade your readers of the difficulties (or privileges) of being a woman.

A Farewell to Work

BARBARA EHRENREICH

1   he media just buried the last yuppie, a pathetic creature who had not heard the news that the great pendulum of public consciousness has just swung from Greed to Compassion and from Tex-Mex to meatballs. Folks lined up outside the mausoleum° bearing many items he had hoped to take with him, including a quart bottle of raspberry vinegar and the Cliffs notes for *The Wealth of Nations*°. I also brought something to throw onto the

funeral pyre—the very essence of yupdom, its creed and its meaning. Not the passion for money, not even the lust for tiny vegetables, but the work ethic.

Yes, I realize how important the work ethic is. I understand that   2
it occupies the position in the American constellation of values once held by motherhood and Girl Scout cookies. But yuppies took it too far; they *abused* it.

One of the reasons they only lived for three years (1984–1987)   3
was that they *never* rested, never took the time to chew between bites or gaze soulfully past their computer screens. What's worse, the mere rumor that someone—anyone—was not holding up his or her end of the work ethic was enough to send them into tantrums. They blamed lazy workers for The Decline of Productivity. They blamed lazy welfare mothers for The Budget Deficit. Their idea of utopia° (as once laid out in that journal of higher yup thought, *The New Republic*) was the "Work Ethic State": no free lunches, no handouts, and too bad for all the miscreants° and losers who refuse to fight their way up to the poverty level by working 80 hours a week at Wendy's.

Personally, I have nothing against work, particularly when per-   4
formed, quietly and unobtrusively°, by someone else. I just don't happen to think it's an appropriate subject for an "ethic." As a general rule, when something gets elevated to apple-pie status in the hierarchy of American values, you have to suspect that its actual monetary value is skidding toward zero. Take motherhood: nobody ever thought of putting it on a moral pedestal until some brash feminists pointed out, about a century ago, that the pay is lousy and the career ladder nonexistent. Same thing with work: would we all be so reverent about the "work ethic" if it weren't for the fact that the average working stiff's hourly pay is shrinking, year by year, toward the price of a local phone call?

In fact, let us set the record straight: the work ethic is not a   5
"traditional value." It is a johnny-come-lately value, along with thin thighs and nonsmoking hotel rooms. In ancient times, work was considered a disgrace inflicted upon those who had failed to amass a nest egg through imperial conquest or other forms of organized looting. Only serfs, slaves, and women worked. The yuppies of ancient Athens—which we all know was a perfect cornucopia° of "traditional values"—passed their time rubbing their bodies with olive oil and discussing the Good, the True, and the Beautiful.

The work ethic came along a couple of millennia° later, in the   6
form of Puritanism—the idea that the amount of self-denial you endured in this life was a good measure of the amount of fun awaiting you in the next. But the work ethic only got off the ground

with the Industrial Revolution and the arrival of the factory system. This was—let us be honest about it—simply a scheme for extending the benefits of the slave system into the age of emancipation°.

7   Under the new system (aka° capitalism, in this part of the world), huge numbers of people had to be convinced to work extra hard, at pitifully low wages, so that the employing class would not have to work at all. Overnight, with the help of a great number of preachers and other well-rested propagandists, work was upgraded from an indignity to an "ethic."

8   But there was a catch: the aptly named *working* class came to resent the *resting* class. There followed riots, revolutions, graffiti. Quickly the word went out from the robber barons to the swelling leisure class of lawyers, financial consultants, plant managers, and other forerunners of the yuppie: Look busy! Don't go home until the proles° have punched out! Make 'em think *we're* doing the work and that they're lucky to be able to hang around and help out!

9   The lawyers, managers, etc., were only too happy to comply, for as the perennially clever John Kenneth Galbraith° once pointed out, they themselves constituted a "new leisure class." Of course, they "work," but only under the most pleasant, air-conditioned, centrally heated, and fully carpeted conditions, and then only in a sitting position. It was in their own interest to convince the working class that what looks like lounging requires intense but invisible effort.

10   The yuppies, when they came along, had to look more right-eously busy than anyone, for the simple reason that they did nothing at all. Workwise, that is. They did not sow, neither did they reap, but rather sat around pushing money through their modems° in games known as "corporate takeover" and "international currency speculation." Hence their rage at anyone who actually works—the "unproductive" American worker, or the woman attempting to raise a family on welfare benefits set below the average yuppie's monthly spa fee.

11   So let us replace their cruel and empty slogan—"Go for it!"— with the cry that lies deep in every true worker's heart: "Gimme a break!" What this nation needs is not the work ethic, but a *job* ethic: if it needs doing—highways repaired, babies changed, fields plowed—let's get it done. Otherwise, take five. Listen to some new wave music, have a serious conversation with a three-year-old, write a poem, look at the sky. Let the yuppies Rest In Peace. The rest of us deserve a break.

```

```

BARBARA EHRENREICH

The editor of *Seven Days* magazine, Barbara Ehrenreich is a well-known writer of essays on social history and contemporary culture, with particular emphasis on women's issues. Her books include *The Hearts of Men: American Dreams and the Flight from Commitment* (1983).

Words and Meanings

Paragraph

mausoleum:	a tomb or burial structure	1
The Wealth of Nations:	Adam Smith's theory of capitalism, written in the eighteenth century	
utopia:	an ideal state; a social and political paradise	3
miscreants:	villains, crooks	
unobtrusively:	unnoticeably	4
cornucopia:	abundance, overflowing supply	5
millennia:	thousands of years	6
emancipation:	freedom	
aka	also known as	7
proles:	slang for "proletarians," the working classes	8
Galbraith:	Canadian-born U.S. economist and diplomat (b. 1908)	9
modems:	computer link-ups	10

Structure and Strategy

1. What TONE is established early in the essay with phrases such as "the essence of yupdom," and "the lust for tiny vegetables" (paragraph 1)?
2. What is the THESIS of this essay? Restate it in a single-sentence thesis statement.
3. In paragraphs 5 to 7, Ehrenreich condenses into three paragraphs a huge span of human history. What eras does she highlight? Why? Is hers a traditional view of history?
4. What concluding strategy does Ehrenreich use in paragraph 11? How does this paragraph contribute to the UNITY of the essay as a whole?
5. Is Ehrenreich appealing primarily to our reason or to our emotions in this essay? Do you think her appeal is effective? Why (or why not)?

Content and Purpose

1. What does Ehrenreich want to bury (or, more specifically, cremate) along with the yuppies? Why?
2. To what does Ehrenreich attribute the short life span of the yuppie lifestyle?
3. What differences does the essay identify between the working conditions of industrialized workers and those of the "new leisure class" (paragraphs 8 and 9)? Who, according to Ehrenreich, really works?
4. Is Ehrenreich's goal to convince her readers of the validity of her point of view, or does she want to motivate her readers to take action? If so, what sort of action? How do you think her readers are likely to respond to her argument?

Suggestions for Writing

1. Read Amy Willard Cross's essay, "Life in the Stopwatch Lane," and compare her view of the yuppie lifestyle with that of Ehrenreich in "A Farewell to Work."
2. Consider your own goals and those of your friends. What kinds of jobs and lives do people today want for themselves and their families? Write an essay in which you identify these goals and argue that they are (or are not) realistic.
3. "A Farewell to Work" is a controversial essay designed to provoke thought, not to be traditionally "objective" or "fair." It criticizes many different professional groups: lawyers, managers, and businesspeople, to name a few. Write a short essay in which you challenge one or more of Ehrenreich's contentions: for example, the assumption that well-paid professionals who work in pleasant surroundings are not productive.

The Huxleyan Warning

NEIL POSTMAN

1   here are two ways by which the spirit of a culture may be shriveled. In the first—the Orwellian°—culture

"The Huxleyan Warning" from *Amusing Ourselves to Death: Public Discourse in the Age of Show Business* by Neil Postman. Copyright 1985 by Neil Postman. Used by permission of Viking Penguin, a division of Penguin Books USA, Inc.

becomes a prison. In the second—the Huxleyan°—culture becomes a burlesque°.

No one needs to be reminded that our world is now marred by many prison-cultures whose structure Orwell described accurately in his parables. If one were to read both *1984* and *Animal Farm*, and then for good measure, Arthur Koestler's *Darkness at Noon*, one would have a fairly precise blueprint of the machinery of thought-control as it currently operates in scores of countries and on millions of people. Of course, Orwell was not the first to teach us about the spiritual devastations of tyranny. What is irreplaceable about his work is his insistence that it makes little difference if our wardens are inspired by right- or left-wing ideologies. The gates of the prison are equally impenetrable, surveillance equally rigorous, icon-worship equally pervasive.

What Huxley teaches is that in the age of advanced technology, spiritual devastation is more likely to come from an enemy with a smiling face than from one whose countenance exudes suspicion and hate. In the Huxleyan prophecy, Big Brother° does not watch us, by his choice. We watch him, by ours. There is no need for wardens or gates or Ministries of Truth. When a population becomes distracted by trivia, when cultural life is redefined as a perpetual round of entertainments, when serious public conversation becomes a form of baby-talk, when, in short, a people become an audience and their public business a vaudeville act, then a nation finds itself at risk; culture-death is a clear possibility.

In America, Orwell's prophecies are of small relevance, but Huxley's are well under way toward being realized. For America is engaged in the world's most ambitious experiment to accommodate itself to the technological distractions made possible by the electric plug. This is an experiment that began slowly and modestly in the mid-nineteenth century and has now, in the latter half of the twentieth, reached a perverse maturity in America's consuming love-affair with television. As nowhere else in the world, Americans have moved far and fast in bringing to a close the age of the slow-moving printed word, and have granted to television sovereignty over all of their institutions. By ushering in the Age of Television, America has given the world the clearest available glimpse of the Huxleyan future.

Those who speak about this matter must often raise their voices to a near-hysterical pitch, inviting the charge that they are every-thing from wimps to public nuisances to Jeremiahs°. But they do so because what they want others to see appears benign°, when it is not invisible altogether. An Orwellian world is much easier to recognize, and to oppose, than a Huxleyan. Everything in our back-ground has prepared us to know and resist a prison when the gates begin to close around us. We are not likely, for example, to be indifferent to the voices of the Sakharovs° and the Timmermans° and the Walesas°. We take arms against such a sea of troubles, buttressed by the spirit of Milton°, Bacon°, Voltaire°, Goethe° and Jefferson°. But what if there are no cries of anguish to be heard? Who is prepared to take arms against a sea of amusements? To whom do we complain, and when, and in what tone of voice, when serious discourse dissolves into giggles? What is the antidote° to a culture's being drained by laughter?

6   I fear that our philosophers have given us no guidance in this matter. Their warnings have customarily been directed against those consciously formulated ideologies that appeal to the worst tendencies in human nature. But what is happening in America is not the design of an articulated ideology. No *Mein Kampf°* or *Communist Manifesto°* announced its coming. It comes as the unintended consequence of a dramatic change in our modes of public conversation. But it is an ideology nonetheless, for it imposes a way of life, a set of relations among people and ideas, about which there has been no consensus, no discussion and no opposition. Only compliance. Public consciousness has not yet assimilated° the point that technology is ideology. This, in spite of the fact that before our very eyes technology has altered every aspect of life in America during the past eighty years. For example, it would have been excusable in 1905 for us to be unprepared for the cultural changes the automobile would bring. Who could have suspected then that the automobile would tell us how we were to conduct our social and sexual lives? Would reorient our ideas about what to do with our forests and cities? Would create new ways of expressing our personal identity and social standing?

7   But it is much later in the game now, and ignorance of the score is inexcusable. To be unaware that a technology comes equipped with a program for social change, to maintain that technology is neutral, to make the assumption that technology is always a friend to culture is, at this late hour, stupidity plain and simple. Moreover, we have seen enough by now to know that technological changes in our modes of communication are even more ideology-laden than changes in our modes of transportation. Introduce the alphabet to a culture and you change its cognitive habits°, its social relations, its notions of community, history and religion. Introduce the printing press with movable type, and you do the same. Introduce speed-of-light transmission of images and you make a cultural revolution. Without a vote. Without polemics°. Without guerrilla resistance. Here is ideology, pure if not serene. Here is ideology without words, and all the more powerful for their absence. All that is required to make it stick is a population that devoutly believes in the inevitabil-

ity of progress. And in this sense, all Americans are Marxists, for we believe nothing if not that history is moving us toward some preordained paradise and that technology is the force behind that movement.

Thus, there are near insurmountable difficulties for anyone who   8
has written such a book as this, and who wishes to end it with some remedies for the affliction. In the first place, not everyone believes a cure is needed, and in the second, there probably isn't any. But as a true-blue American who has imbibed the unshakable belief that where there is a problem there must be a solution, I shall conclude with the following suggestions.

We must, as a start, not delude° ourselves with preposterous   9
notions such as the straight Luddite° position as outlined, for ex- ample, in Jerry Mander's *Four Arguments for the Elimination of Televi- sion*. Americans will not shut down any part of their technological apparatus, and to suggest that they do so is to make no suggestion at all. It is almost equally unrealistic to expect that nontrivial modifi- cations in the availability of media will ever be made. Many civilized nations limit by law the amount of hours television may operate and thereby mitigate° the role television plays in public life. But I believe that this is not a possibility in America. Once having opened the Happy Medium to full public view, we are not likely to counte- nance even its partial closing. Still, some Americans have been think- ing along these lines. As I write, a story appears in *The New York Times* (September 27, 1984) about the plans of the Farmington, Con- necticut, Library Council to sponsor a "TV Turnoff." It appears that such an effort was made the previous year, the idea being to get people to stop watching television for one month. The *Times* reports that the turnoff the previous January was widely noted by the media. Ms. Ellen Babcock, whose family participated, is quoted as saying, "It will be interesting to see if the impact is the same this year as last year, when we had terrific media coverage." In other words, Ms. Babcock hopes that by watching television, people will learn that they ought to stop watching television. It is hard to imagine that Ms. Babcock does not see the irony in this position. It is an irony that I have confronted many times in being told that I must appear on television to promote a book that warns people against television. Such are the contradictions of a television-based culture.

In any case, of how much help is a one-month turnoff? It is a   10
mere pittance°; that is to say, a penance°. How comforting it must be when the folks in Farmington are done with their punishment and can return to their true occupation. Nonetheless, one applauds their effort, as one must applaud the efforts of those who see some relief in limiting certain kinds of content on television—for example,

excessive violence, commercials on children's shows, etc. I am particularly fond of John Lindsay's suggestion that political commercials be banned from television as we now ban cigarette and liquor commercials. I would gladly testify before the Federal Communications Commission as to the manifold merits of this excellent idea. To those who would oppose my testimony by claiming that such a ban is a clear violation of the First Amendment, I would offer a compromise: Require all political commercials to be preceded by a short statement to the effect that common sense has determined that watching political commercials is hazardous to the intellectual health of the community.

11   I am not very optimistic about anyone's taking this suggestion seriously. Neither do I put much stock in proposals to improve the quality of television programs. Television, as I have implied earlier, serves us most usefully when presenting junk-entertainment; it serves us most ill when it co-opts° serious modes of discourse°— news, politics, science, education, commerce, religion—and turns them into entertainment packages. We would all be better off if television got worse, not better. "The A-Team" and "Cheers" are no threat to our public health. "60 Minutes," "Eye-Witness News" and "Sesame Street" are.

12   The problem, in any case, does not reside in *what* people watch. The problem is in *that* we watch. The solution must be found in *how* we watch. For I believe it may fairly be said that we have yet to learn what television is. And the reason is that there has been no worthwhile discussion, let alone widespread public understanding, of what information is and how it gives direction to a culture. There is a certain poignancy° in this, since there are no people who more frequently and enthusiastically use such phrases as "the information age," "the information explosion," and "the information society." We have apparently advanced to the point where we have grasped the idea that a change in the forms, volume, speed and context of information *means* something, but we have not got any further.

13   What is information? Or more precisely, what *are* information? What are its various forms? What conceptions of intelligence, wisdom and learning does each form insist upon? What conceptions does each form neglect or mock? What are the main psychic effects of each form? What is the relation between information and reason? What is the kind of information that best facilitates thinking? Is there a moral bias to each information form? What does it mean to say that there is too much information? How would one know? What redefinitions of important cultural meanings do new sources, speeds, contexts and forms of information require? Does television, for example, give a new meaning to "piety," to "patriotism," to "privacy"? Does television give a new meaning to "judgment" or

to "understanding"? How do different forms of information persuade? Is a newspaper's "public" different from television's "public"? How do different information forms dictate the type of content that is expressed?

These questions, and dozens more like them, are the means   14
through which it might be possible for Americans to begin talking back to their television sets. For no medium is excessively dangerous if its users understand what its dangers are. It is not important that those who ask the questions arrive at my answers or Marshall McLuhan's° (quite different answers, by the way). This is an instance in which the asking of the questions is sufficient. To ask is to break the spell. To which I might add that questions about the psychic, political and social effects of information are as applicable to the computer as to television. Although I believe the computer to be a vastly overrated technology, I mention it here because, clearly, Americans have accorded it their customary mindless inattention; which means they will use it as they are told, without a whimper. Thus, a central thesis of computer technology—that the principal difficulty we have in solving problems stems from insufficient data— will go unexamined. Until, years from now, when it will be noticed that the massive collection and speed-of-light retrieval of data have been of great value to large-scale organizations but have solved very little of importance to most people and have created at least as many problems for them as they may have solved.

In any case, the point I am trying to make is that only through   15
a deep and unfailing awareness of the structure and effects of information, through a demystification of media, is there any hope of our gaining some measure of control over television, or the computer, or any other medium. How is such media consciousness to be achieved? There are only two answers that come to mind, one of which is nonsense and can be dismissed almost at once; the other is desperate but it is all we have.

The nonsensical answer is to create television programs whose   16
intent would be, not to get people to stop watching television but to demonstrate how television ought to be viewed, to show how television recreates and degrades our conception of news, political debate, religious thought, etc. I imagine such demonstrations would of necessity take the form of parodies, along the lines of "Saturday Night Live" and "Monty Python," the idea being to induce a nationwide horse laugh over television's control of public discourse. But, naturally, television would have the last laugh. In order to command an audience large enough to make a difference, one would have to make the programs vastly amusing, in the television style. Thus, the act of criticism itself would, in the end, be co-opted by television.

The parodists would become celebrities, would star in movies, and would end up making television commercials.

17   The desperate answer is to rely on the only mass medium of communication that, in theory, is capable of addressing the problem: our schools. This is the conventional American solution to all dangerous social problems, and is, of course, based on a naive and mystical faith in the efficacy° of education. The process rarely works. In the matter at hand, there is even less reason than usual to expect it to. Our schools have not yet even got around to examining the role of the printed word in shaping our culture. Indeed, you will not find two high school seniors in a hundred who could tell you—within a five-hundred-year margin of error—when the alphabet was invented. I suspect most do not even know that the alphabet *was* invented. I have found that when the question is put to them, they appear puzzled, as if one had asked, When were trees invented, or clouds? It is the very principle of myth, as Roland Barthes pointed out, that it transforms history into nature, and to ask of our schools that they engage in the task of de-mythologizing media is to ask something the schools have never done.

18   And yet there is reason to suppose that the situation is not hopeless. Educators are not unaware of the effects of television on their students. Stimulated by the arrival of the computer, they discuss it a great deal—which is to say, they have become somewhat "media conscious." It is true enough that much of their consciousness centers on the question, How can we use television (or the computer, or word processor) to control education? They have not yet got to the question, How can we use education to control television (or the computer, or word processor)? But our reach for solutions ought to exceed our present grasp, or what's our dreaming for? Besides, it is an acknowledged task of the schools to assist the young in learning how to interpret the symbols of their culture. That this task should now require that they learn how to distance themselves from their forms of information is not so bizarre an enterprise that we cannot hope for its inclusion in the curriculum; even hope that it will be placed at the center of education.

19   What I suggest here as a solution is what Aldous Huxley suggested, as well. And I can do no better than he. He believed with H.G. Wells that we are in a race between education and disaster, and he wrote continuously about the necessity of our understanding the politics and epistemology° of media. For in the end, he was trying to tell us that what afflicted the people in *Brave New World* was not that they were laughing instead of thinking, but that they did not know what they were laughing about and why they had stopped thinking.

NEIL POSTMAN

Neil Postman, the American advocate of radical educational reform, lives in Flushing, New York, and is a professor of communication arts and sciences at New York University. Among his many books are *Teaching as a Subversive Activity*, *The Disappearance of Childhood*, and *Amusing Ourselves to Death*. In the chapters that precede the excerpt above, Postman argues that our society expects and requires its politics, religion, education, news and commerce to be delivered in the form of entertainment—a demand that ultimately trivializes them.

Words and Meanings

Paragraph

Orwellian:	reference to George Orwell's *1984*, a novel about dictatorship through thought-control	1
Huxleyan:	reference to Aldous Huxley's *Brave New World*, a contrasting view of future society	
burlesque:	farce	
Big Brother	dictator in *1984* whose image controls the masses	3
Jeremiahs:	prophets of doom	5
benign:	harmless, or even good	
the Sakharovs, Timmermans and Walesas:	Russian, Argentinian, and Polish dissidents	
Milton:	seventeenth-century English poet who celebrated liberty	
Bacon:	Francis Bacon, seventeenth-century English essayist	
Voltaire:	eighteenth-century French writer	
Goethe:	nineteenth-century German philosopher and poet	
Jefferson:	Thomas Jefferson, one of the "fathers of America" who helped draft the Declaration of Independence	
antidote:	remedy, cure	
Mein Kampf:	Adolf Hitler's autobiography	6
Communist Manifesto:	Karl Marx's 1848 indictment of capitalism	
assimilated:	digested, absorbed; fully understood	
cognitive habits:	ways of knowing	7
polemics:	controversial discussions; debates	
delude:	deceive	9
Luddite:	follower of eighteenth-century workman, Ned Ludd, who thought he could halt technological progress by destroying the machines threatening the workers' livelihood	

	mitigate:	moderate, diminish
10	pittance:	small amount, trifle
	penance:	self-imposed punishment
11	co-opts:	adopts, absorbs
	discourse:	verbal communication
12	poignancy:	painful sharpness
14	Marshall McLuhan:	philosopher of the media, coiner of the phrase "the medium is the message"
17	efficacy:	power, effectiveness
19	epistemology:	the study of the origin, nature, and limits of knowledge

Structure and Strategy

1. In paragraph 1, Postman introduces a contrast that forms the basis of the first section of this essay. How does he develop that contrast in paragraphs 2 to 5?
2. Identify the main point Postman develops in each of the following sections: paragraphs 6 to 8, 9 to 11, 12 to 14, and 15. How does paragraph 15 serve as a TRANSITION?
3. Explore the ALLUSION in paragraph 5. (Hint: see *Hamlet*, III, i, 59.)
4. Identify three or four particularly effective examples of IRONY in this essay.
5. Postman attempts to appeal to his readers' emotions as well as to their reason in this essay. Identify two or three examples of his use of DICTION to affect our emotions.
6. What concluding strategy does Postman use? Is it effective?

Content and Purpose

1. Does Postman intend simply to convince his readers that his point of view is a valid one, or does he want his readers to act in some way as a result of his message? What are his purposes in writing this essay?
2. Why does Postman regard Huxley's prophecies as more dangerous to our culture than Orwell's (paragraph 3)?
3. In paragraph 4, Postman claims that Americans live in an Age of Television more than any other people in the world. To what extent do you think Canadians share the Americans' "consuming love-affair with television" and, therefore, share the risk of "culture-death"?
4. Explain what Postman means when he asserts that technology

is not neutral. What examples does he use to support this contention? (See paragraphs 6 and 7.)

5. Why does Postman reject "Luddite" solutions in America and regard the campaign against television as ironic?

6. Why does Postman believe that "we would all be better off if television got worse, not better"?

7. What is Postman's solution? Why does he see the problem as "a race between education and disaster," as H.G. Wells described it?

Suggestions for Writing

1. Postman writes about the pervasive influence of television in America, but he does not mention the pervasive influence of America on the rest of the world, an influence that is largely attributable to American media. Many countries, Canada included, regard the influence of American television as cultural imperialism. However, some people in Canada want access to American television at all costs and are not in the least worried about Canada's identity as a nation. Write an essay in which you attempt to convince your readers that American television programs should (or should not) be severely restricted in Canada.

2. Write an essay in which you argue that television is a positive influence in our society.

Additional Suggestions for Writing:
Argument and Persuasion

Choose one of the topics below and write an essay based on it. Think through your position carefully, formulate your opinion, and identify logical reasons for holding that opinion. Construct a clear thesis statement before you begin to write the paper.

1. Equal pay for work of equal value is (or is not) an impractical goal in Canada.
2. Canada Post should (or should not) provide home mail delivery to everyone.
3. The overall quality of Canadian life is improving (or declining).
4. Violence against an established government is (or is not) justified in certain circumstances.
5. Private religious schools should (or should not) receive government subsidies.
6. The federal government should (or should not) make significant changes to the unemployment insurance plan.
7. It is too easy (or too difficult) to get a divorce in Canada.
8. A teacher should (or should not) aim most of the course work at the weakest students in the class.
9. A couple should (or should not) live together before marriage.
10. Smoking should (or should not) be banned in all public buildings.
11. The government of Canada should (or should not) decriminalize the use of "soft" drugs.
12. Blondes do (or do not) have more fun.
13. Boys and girls should (or should not) play on the same sports teams.
14. Critically ill patients should (or should not) be permitted to end their lives if and when they choose.
15. The government of Canada is (or is not) helpless to deal effectively with acid rain (or any other environmental hazard).
16. Physical education should (or should not) be compulsory for all able-bodied students throughout the high school years.
17. Fully subsidized day-care is (or is not) in the best interests of the whole community.
18. A gay parent should (or should not) be eligible to gain custody of his or her children after a divorce.
19. Dishonesty is sometimes (is never) the best policy.
20. "It is a truth universally acknowledged that a single man in possession of a good fortune must be in want of a wife." (Jane Austen)

Further Reading

The Game

KEN DRYDEN

he Forum is disturbingly empty: just a few players sit quietly cocooned away in a dressing room; twenty-five or thirty staff work in distant upstairs offices; throughout the rest of its vast insides a few dozen men are busy washing, painting, fixing, tidying things up. There is one other person. Entering the corridor to the dressing room, I hear muffled, reverberating sounds from the ice, and before I can see who it is, I know it's Lafleur. Like a kid on a backyard rink, he skates by himself many minutes before anyone joins him, shooting pucks easily off the boards, watching them rebound, moving skates and gloved hands wherever his inventive instincts direct them to go. Here, far from the expedience of a game, away from defenders and linemates who shackle him to their banal predictability, alone with his virtuoso skills, it is his time to create.

The Italians have a phrase, *inventa la partita*. Translated, it means to "invent the game." A phrase often used by soccer coaches and journalists, it is now, more often than not, used as a lament. For in watching modern players with polished but plastic skills, they wonder at the passing of soccer *genius*—Pele, di Stefano, Puskas—players whose minds and bodies in not so rare moments created something unfound in coaching manuals, a new and continuously changing game for others to aspire to.

It is a loss they explain many ways. In the name of team play, there is no time or place for individual virtuosity, they say; it is a game now taken over by coaches, by technocrats and autocrats who empty players' minds to control their bodies, reprogramming them with X's and O's, driving them to greater *efficiency* and *work rate*, to move *systems* faster, to move games faster, until achieving mindless pace. Others fix blame more on the other side: on smothering defenses played with the same technical sophistication, efficiency, and work rate, but in the nature of defense, easier to play. Still others argue it is the professional sports culture itself which says that games are not won on good plays, but by others' mistakes, where the safe and sure survive, and the creative and not-so-sure may not.

But a few link it to a different kind of cultural change, the loss of what they call "street soccer": the mindless hours spent with a ball next to your feet, walking with it as if with a family pet, to school, to a store, or anywhere, playing with it, learning new things about it and about yourself, in time, as with any good companion, developing an *understanding*. In a much less busy time undivided by TV, rock music, or the clutter of modern lessons, it was a child's diversion from having nothing else to do. And, appearances to the contrary, it was creative diversion. But now, with more to do, and with a sophisticated, competitive society pressing on the younger and younger the need for training and skills, its time has run out. Soccer has moved away from the streets and playgrounds to soccer fields, from impromptu games to uniforms and referees, from any time to specific, scheduled time; it has become an *activity* like anything else, organized and maximized, done right or not at all. It has become something to be taught and learned, then tested in games; the answer at the back of the book, the one and only answer. So other time, time not spent with teams in practices or games, deemed wasteful and inefficient, has become time not spent at soccer.

Recently, in Hungary, a survey was conducted asking soccer players from 1910 to the present how much each practiced a day. The answer, on a gradually shrinking scale, was three hours early in the century to eight minutes a day today. Though long memories can forget, and inflate what they don't forget, if the absolute figures are doubtful, the point is none the less valid. Today, except in the barrios of Latin America, in parts of Africa and Asia, "street soccer" is dead, and many would argue that with it has gone much of soccer's creative opportunity.

When Guy Lafleur was five years old, his father built a small rink in the backyard of their home in Thurso, Quebec. After school and on weekends, the rink was crowded with Lafleur and his friends, but on weekdays, rushing through lunch before returning to school, it was his alone for half an hour or more. A few years later, anxious for more ice time, on Saturday and Sunday mornings he would sneak in the back door of the local arena, finding his way unseen through the engine room, under the seats, and onto the ice. There, from 7:30 until just before the manager awakened about 11, he played alone; then quickly left. Though he was soon discovered, as the manager was also coach of his team Lafleur was allowed to continue, by himself, and then a few years later with some of his friends.

There is nothing unique to this story; only its details differ from many others like it. But because it's about Lafleur it is notable. At the time, there were thousands like him across Canada on other noon-hour rinks, in other local arenas, doing the same. It was when he got older and nothing changed that his story became special. For as others in the whirl of more games, more practices, more off-ice diversions, more travel and everything else gave up solitary time as boring and unnecessary, Lafleur did not. When he moved to Quebec City at fourteen to play for the Remparts, the ice at the big Colisée was unavailable at other times, so he began arriving early for the team's 6 P.M. practices, going on the ice at 5, more than thirty minutes before any of his teammates joined him. Now, many years later, the story unchanged, it seems more and more remarkable to us. In clichéd observation some would say it is a case of the great and dedicated superstar who is first on the ice, last off. But he is not. When practice ends, Lafleur leaves, and ten or twelve others remain behind, skating and shooting with Ruel. But every day we're in Montreal, at 11 A.M., an hour before Bowman steps from the dressing room as signal for practice to begin, Lafleur goes onto the ice with a bucket of pucks to be alone.

Not long ago, thinking of the generations of Canadians who learned hockey on rivers and ponds, I collected my skates and with two friends drove up the Gatineau River north of Ottawa. We didn't know it at the time, but the ice conditions we found were rare, duplicated only a few times the previous decade. The combination of a sudden thaw and freezing rain in the days before had melted winter-high snow, and with temperatures dropping rapidly overnight, the river was left with miles of smooth glare ice. Growing up in the suburbs of a large city, I had played on a river only once before, and then as a goalie. On this day, I came to the Gatineau to find what a river of ice and a solitary feeling might mean to a game.

We spread ourselves rinks apart, breaking into river-wide openings for passes that sometimes connected, and other times sent us hundreds of feet after what we had missed. Against the wind or with it, the sun glaring in our eyes or at our backs, we skated for more than three hours, periodically tired, continuously renewed. The next day I went back again, this time alone. Before I got bored with myself an hour or two later, with no one watching and nothing to distract me, loose and daring, joyously free, I tried things I had never tried before, my hands and feet discovering new patterns and directions, and came away feeling as if something was finally clear.

The Canadian game of hockey was weaned on long northern winters uncluttered by things to do. It grew up on ponds and rivers, in big open spaces, unorganized, often solitary, only occasionally moved into arenas for practices or games. In recent generations, that has changed. Canadians have moved from farms and towns to cities and suburbs; they've discovered skis, snowmobiles, and southern vacations; they've civilized winter and moved it indoors. A game we once played on rivers and ponds, later on streets and driveways and in backyards, we now play in arenas, in full team uniform, with coaches and referees, or to an ever-increasing extent we don't play at all. For, once a game is organized, unorganized games seem a wasteful use of time; and once a game moves indoors, it won't move outdoors again. Hockey has become suburbanized, and as part of our suburban middle-class culture, it has changed.

Put in uniform at six or seven, by the time a boy reaches the NHL, he is a veteran of close to 1,000 games—30-minute games, later 32-, then 45-, finally 60-minute games, played more than twice a week, more than seventy times a year between late September and late March. It is more games from a younger age, over a longer season than ever before. But it is less hockey than ever before. For, every time a twelve-year-old boy plays a 30-minute game, sharing the ice with teammates, he plays only about ten minutes. And ten minutes a game, anticipated and prepared for all day, travelled to and from, dressed and undressed for, means ten minutes of hockey a day, more than two days a week, more than seventy days a hockey season. And every day that a twelve-year-old plays only ten minutes, he doesn't play two hours on a backyard rink, or longer on school or playground rinks during weekends and holidays.

It all has to do with the way we look at free time. Constantly preoccupied with time and keeping ourselves busy (we have come to answer the ritual question "How are you?" with what we apparently equate with good health, "Busy"), we treat non-school, non-sleeping or non-eating time, unbudgeted free time, with suspicion and no little fear. For, while it may offer opportunity to learn and do new things, we worry that the time we once spent reading, kicking a ball, or mindlessly coddling a puck might be used destructively, in front of TV, or "getting into trouble" in endless ways. So we organize free time, scheduling it into lessons—ballet, piano, French—into organizations, teams, and clubs, fragmenting it into impossible-to-be-boring segments, creating in ourselves a mental metabolism geared to moving on, making free time distinctly unfree.

It is in free time that the special player develops, not in the competitive expedience of games, in hour-long practices once a week, in mechanical devotion to packaged, processed, coaching-manual, hockey-school skills. For while skills are necessary, setting out as they do the limits of anything, more is needed to transform those skills into something special. Mostly it is time—unencumbered, unhurried, time of a different quality, more time, time to find wrong answers to find a few that are right; time to find your own right answers; time for skills to be practiced to set higher limits, to settle and assimilate and become fully and completely yours, to organize and combine with other skills comfortably and easily in some uniquely personal way, then to be set loose, trusted, to find new instinctive directions to take, to create.

But without such time a player is like a student cramming for exams. His skills are like answers memorized by his body, specific, limited to what is expected, random and separate, with no overviews to organize and bring them together. And for those times when more is demanded, when new unexpected circumstances come up, when answers are asked for things you've never learned, when you must intuit and piece together what you already know to find new answers, memorizing isn't enough. It's the difference between knowledge and understanding, between a super-achiever and a wise old man. And it's the difference between a modern suburban player and a player like Lafleur.

For a special player has spent time with his game. On backyard rinks, in local arenas, in time alone and with others, time without short-cuts, he has seen many things, he has done many things, he has *experienced* the game. He understands it. There is *scope* and *culture* in his game. He is not a born player. What he has is not a gift, random and otherworldly, and unearned. There is surely something in his genetic make-up that allows him to be great, but just as surely there are others like him who fall short. He is, instead, *a natural*.

"Muscle memory" is a phrase physiologists sometimes use. It means that for many movements we make, our muscles move with no message from the brain telling them to move, that stored in the muscles is a learned capacity to move a certain way, and, given stimulus from the spinal cord, they move that way. We see a note on a sheet of music, our fingers move; no thought, no direction, and because one step of the transaction is eliminated—the information-message loop through the brain—we move faster as well.

When first learning a game, a player thinks through every step of what he's doing, needing to direct his body the way he wants it to go. With practice, with repetition, movements get memorized, speeding up, growing surer, gradually becoming part of the muscle's memory. The great player, having seen and done more things, more different and personal things, has in his muscles the memory of more notes, more combinations and patterns of notes, played in more different ways. Faced with a situation, his body responds. Faced with something more, something new, it finds an answer he didn't know was there. He *invents the game.*

Listen to a great player describe what he does. Ask Lafleur or Orr, ask Reggie Jackson, O. J. Simpson, or Julius Erving what makes them special, and you will get back something frustratingly unrewarding. They are inarticulate jocks, we decide, but in fact they can know no better than we do. For ask yourself how you walk, how your fingers move on a piano keyboard, how you do any number of things you have made routine, and you will know why. Stepping outside yourself you can think about it and decide what *must* happen, but you possess no inside story, no great insight unavailable to those who watch. Such movement comes literally from your body, bypassing your brain, leaving few subjective hints behind. Your legs, your fingers move, that's all you know. So if you want to know what makes Orr or Lafleur special, watch their bodies, fluent and articulate; let them explain. They know.

When I watch a modern suburban player, I feel the same as I do when I hear Donnie Osmond or René Simard sing a love song. I hear a skillful voice, I see closed eyes and pleading outstretched fingers, but I hear and see only fourteen-year-old boys who can't tell me anything.

· Hockey has left the river and will never return. But like the "street," like an "ivory tower," the river is less a physical place than an *attitude,* a metaphor for unstructured, unorganized time alone. And if the game no longer needs the place, it needs the attitude. It is the rare player like Lafleur who reminds us.

KEN DRYDEN

Ken Dryden, the hockey player, was born in Hamilton, Ont., in 1947. He kept goal for the Montreal Canadiens and played for Team Canada in 1972 against the USSR. He is a lawyer and the author of *The Game*, a best-selling study of hockey.

Return of the Battle of the Monster Trucks

TOM HAWTHORN

Up there atop Bigfoot sits Ken Koelling, strapped into seven tons of mean machine, his Missouri butt just inches from a 429-cubic-inch boss Ford hemi V-6 power plant. The Crunch Bunch in the stands are on their feet in delirium over The Clash of Titans, which begins as soon as this Monster Truck does some righteous damage to those eight dead sedans parked door-to-door on the floor of the hockey arena. Rest assured, Ken knows his bruising beast sometimes flips and sometimes careens crazily into the seats, but all he can think about as he looks out on those cars is, "I sure wish that were a mud pit."

A mud pit is a challenge to a man of Koelling's skills. They make this giant bog of mud and muck for the Monster Truck drivers to plow through. Only slick handling saves a driver and his rig from sinking into the goo, but this here dinky rink at Copps Coliseum in Hamilton is simply too small for a quagmire. All Ken has to do tonight is stomp on dead cars in Bigfoot, a task he finds about as sporting as squirrel hunting with a cannon. "From what I understand," he had said in his slow Midwest drawl, "we're going to go out there and crush cars just to crush 'em."

A Mercury Monarch is the first to go. Koelling slips Bigfoot into gear, rocketing his mutant truck towards the cars. Four huge tires start their climb onto the Monarch's roof with a jolt. A roar louder than Bigfoot's engine goes up from the stands, and cameras flash. The Monarch caves in easily, followed in quick succession by a Cordoba, a Galaxy, a Capri, an Aspen, some big boat of a Chrysler and pair of LTDs, each crunch raising another cheer from the Crunch

Bunch. Bigfoot turns around and drives over them again to complete the freestyle portion of the program. That done, Koelling backs his truck against the end boards, pops the clutch, puts the pedal to the metal, and as his tires hit the first car he soars into the air, landing in a cloud of paint chips on the roof of an LTD 28 feet from where he became airborne.

It is ten o'clock Friday evening in Steeltown, the first of two nights of The Return of the Battle of the Monster Trucks. Top ticket costs $18.50 and it's a poor night for Hamilton's babysitters. Eight thousand fans, maybe half of them kids, are revved up for some gear-grinding, axle-busting, flame-throwing fun. The kids are here for the Monster Trucks, lured by their fascination for things that are big, loud and powerful. The adults, who better appreciate the rear-wheel dragsters and modified four-wheel-drive Hot Rods that haul 50,000-pound sleds to open the show, are here for the same reason. "The power of the machines . . . I think that gets everybody," says a carpenter, his Ford cap pushed back on his head. "I have a four-wheel-drive of my own . . . and I'd just love to get behind the wheel of one of *those*, to feel that power under me."

You can see it now, the man's sensible Ford Ranger chassis plopped precariously atop a giant rubbery block of Super Terra-Grips as tall as a man. The hulking mass of metal would be the greatest status item in the neighborhood, besting even the humongous satellite dish in the front yard down the street. The other guys with trucks would park near by to gawk. "Hell, I wouldn't mind driving that thing in a traffic jam," one'd say. But you'd need more than just big tires. Big engine (preferably on the outside where the flywheel and the header could shine in the sun), nice hand-rubbed lacquer paint job, a pair of thin racing stripes painted along the panels and maybe even a sword-wielding babe with billowing science-fiction breasts—but no, the wife wouldn't go for that. And after you'd finished hopping up the truck, a slow cruise would be in order, elbow out the window, the steering wheel controlled by the open palm of your right hand. And in that rumbling truck, with a two-four of Molson on the floor and burger in hand, a little bit of hot-rod heaven will have been discovered.

The temptation would be to unleash the 400 horsepower straining under the hood, but it's embarrassing to lay smoke when you're 38, an age better given to burning leaves than burning rubber. So the carpenter just uses his truck to haul the occasional load of wood, and tonight it's brought him and his 11-year-old son to the arena where he can dream of being in Ken Koelling's place, with all that liberating internal-combustion power underneath.

It is garish spectacle, and the snooty can seek all form of explanation for its meaning. Some would see this as clear evidence of Western bourgeois decadence, the purposefully wasteful destruction of goods with wanton disregard for all those who lack cars. Others would see it as a product of worker alienation, all the riveters from the Ford assembly line in nearby Oakville here to wreak vengeance on the oppressive monster that forced them to create the cars now getting crunched. Still others would see the horror of gladiator culture, a celebration of Road Warrior Rambos tooling about in two-ton phalli.

It is, however, none of these. Where road racing is still a serious sport—with its specter of imminent spectacular death—Monster Trucks are the punchline of car culture. They are the Liberace, the Elvis, the Shrine of Ste. Anne de Beaupre of four-wheel drive.

Bigfoot is the Hulk Hogan of Monster Truckdom, but new heroes are making the scene. The Virginia Beach Beast and Bear Foot Trax are two trucks with tank treads instead of tires. Where Bigfoot stomps cars dead, these monsters shred them open like tin cans. When tank trucks jump, they land with a spray of sparks. Everyone says the tank trucks are the next big thing in the world's fastest growing motor sport.

Monster Trucks have all the making of becoming one of the great good ol' boy sports, like Indy racing or stock cars. Racing the Indianapolis 500, a 500-mile road race run round and round an oval track, is a matter of sticking the biggest engine imaginable on the sleekest body engineers can design, strapping some nut to the works and telling him to keep turning left. Monster Trucks work on a similar principle, except speed is replaced by brute force. But it's all too lowbrow for the sports pages, because the big tire and car companies haven't yet thrown their full financial weight behind Monster Trucks, and until they do the sport is not going to have the status that would permit the sports pages to ignore its humble beginnings. The sons of Alabama were racing their monster stock cars across dirt tracks all over the South for years before Goodyear and Quaker State and Valvoline and STP twigged on that millions of car-driving Southerners identified with the Junior Johnsons and Lee Pettys risking their necks at 160 mph. The cars nowadays are mobile billboards, and TV provides up to eight different angles— camera in the pits, camera on the blimp, camera behind the driver, even a Bumpercam—for the big crashes. Monster Trucks are far from the big time, although The Sports Network airs regular weekend truck- and tractor-pull shows for Canadian audiences.

"The kids can watch more of it on TV than they've ever been able to," says Jim Harris, a promoter. "And they have access to fan clubs of the trucks. Boys and trucks. Boys and trucks, that's what it is."

Harris, 31, books the trucks, puts in the dirt track and inspects the vehicles to make sure no one is accidentally barbecued. For four years, he has been running SRO Pace Promotions, which created the U.S. Hot Rod Association, out of Hot Springs, Ark. He designs formats for the shows and brooks no talk of his competitions being choreographed like wrestling.

"We could put a bit more character into this sport if we wanted to stage it all, know who was going to do what, know who was going to win the event before it even started. That way you could always put on a better show. With this, I don't even know who's going to do what when they get out there."

Like the time in Maryland when the Monster Truck crushed a bunch of cars, and everyone was hooting and hollering even as the damn thing headed into the seats. "It was someone who just couldn't stop," Harris shrugs. His job during showtime is to make sure no such mishaps occur, so as the trucks and the tanks turn the beater cars into so much scrap metal, he scurries along awful close to the jumping machines. "If a throttle sticks on one of those trucks, he's gonna go up into the stands. He'll climb to the middle level. So they have kill switches on them that are accessible to the driver inside the truck and to someone outside the truck. Like myself. That's why I stand close to the trucks when they're going over the cars. There's a kill switch on the back bumper with a two-inch diameter ring on it that I can pull to stop the truck. I'm there to protect the people in the seats to make sure somethin' doesn't happen. A driver can get knocked out even with a helmet on."

Thrills, chills, spills, and the whole freaking concept was an accident. Fellow out of St. Louis by the name Bob Chandler . . . ah, announcer Brent Kepner knows the story. "Ladies and gentlemen," he says, standing on the floor of the arena with a microphone on a long cord, "back in 1973, he decided to create a four-wheel-drive pickup truck that would draw attention to his off-road shop. Not even Bob Chandler had any idea of what he was creating. What he created was an entire sport. Were it not for that man, and the trucks he has produced since then, we would not be here tonight watching these machines. Those trucks have gone on to appear in virtually every country in front of the Iron Curtain." Where, undoubtedly, slave-labor Monster Trucks are inferior to free-enterprise Monster Trucks. No matter. Bob Chandler is the Abner Doubleday of Monster Trucks, the visionary whose gimmick has become a favored pastime for millions, who has added another chapter to the history of car culture. Bob Chandler now has six Bigfoots, so on any given night six American cities are being converted to his cause. Ken Koelling, the man who misses his mud pit, usually drives the original Bigfoot, but tonight he's handling Bigfoot III. Each machine costs $125,000 (U.S.), but what with poster and T-shirt sales, and sponsors in Ford and McDonald's restaurants, and the $50,000 he'll earn when Bigfoot III finishes its current 12-city tour, not to mention how all the attention hasn't hurt business at Chandler Auto Sales back home, Bob Chandler is not wanting for money.

It only takes the Monster Trucks about 20 minutes to finish squishing, so The Return of the Battle of the Monster Trucks is padded by more than two hours of sled pulls. The program is the same as the tour travels its circuit from Anaheim, Calif., to Alexandria, Va. The announcer is perhaps the most important participant, as his steady patter keeps things moving. Brent Kepner has been doing this for ten years. He's both barker and pitchman, though sometimes his rhetoric hits the wrong note.

"I ask you to stand," he says, "as we salute the greatest country on the face of the earth—our national anthem." The anthem is "The Star-Spangled Banner." In the garage beneath the stands, mechanics and drivers doff their caps to place them over their hearts.

"How many Chevrolet fans do we have here? How many Ford fans? Come on, Fords, I wanna hear you yell." The world thus divided, the competition begins. A black truck called the Tasmanian Devil bucks across the dirt. It is the first of a dozen modified 4WDs that will be attached to a sled with an adjustable weight. They start at 50,000 pounds and will end at 80,000. The sled is called the Humiliator. The object is to drag it all the way across the floor—Full Pull!—without causing the engine to seize. Where farmers once competed by hauling heavy logs with a team of horses, their modern counterpart does the same with horsepower.

The cognoscenti wear industrial earmuffs from home. Others stuff their ears with yellow plugs. Those without protection soon suffer from a skull-splitting ache, as this motorized extravaganza takes its toll. Kids cry. And on the floor of the arena, the Tasmanian Devil is kicking up a bejeezus spray of sand as the Humiliator lives up to its name. Tires spinning and steam spraying, the truck is stranded 15 meters from its goal. "One thing's for sure," shouts Kepner, "the Devil's driver wasn't afraid to keep his right foot planted!" The parade continues. There's Charlie's L'il Angel out of Michigan lugging 604 cubic inches; Positively Wicked from Rhode Island with a 454 stock block inside the body of a '49 Chevy pickup; and Wild Child from Connecticut, a '53 Chevy found rusting in a field, which body-shop-owner Rob Peradi has home-built with steely-grey dual fuel injectors jabbing out from under its crimson hood. "It probably broke his heart to cut open that hood," Kepner sympathizes, the crowd roaring as twin blue flames burst from the injectors. One driver comes within a hair of an engine meltdown in a futile effort to snag a share of the purse. "It doesn't take a nuclear physicist to figure out why that pull didn't work. The young man was *brutalizing* his equipment!" A '68 military jeep with camouflage coloring called Gone A.W.O.L. finally pulls the 80,000-pound sled more than 155 feet to win the pull-off.

In between sales pitches for the hot rod association's "official wall-quality calendar" and its most recent video (*Blood, Sweat and Gears*), a trio of funny cars struts its stuff. One has four rear wheels and two front ones. It rears on its back tires as it tries to pull the sled. "What a beautiful and outrageous wheelie by War Lord!" Kepner says. Another has a hydraulic flip-top mechanism that raises the entire chassis of the truck to expose its engine parts in all their shiny splendor.

The funny cars are a throwback to the glory days of hot rodding and customizing. Detroit was cookie-cutting millions of lookalike cars after the war. They had engines big enough to power a tank— no problem there—but the '55 Mercury you bought was exactly the same as the one your old man brought home. The young went for baroque, adding dynamic curvilinear ornamentation to their Motown wheels. Jack the back, Mac. Chrome! Decorate the Mae Wests up front with a line of hand-painted flame in yellow and red, and maybe a manic cartoon character. But that's all show, no go. So boost the HP to blow your old man's doors in. Then that awful day came when factory options killed the hot rod. Detroit would do all the custom work and all the engine revamping for a few C-notes, and suddenly any squirrel boy with a see-through mustache was tearing down the highway. Hell, they *bought* their decals. Even the local Canadian Tire was selling those angry Woody Woodpeckers chomping on a cigar.

But in small towns like Latrobe, Pa., and Rockville, R.I., and Amelia, Ohio, and Hope, B.C., and Cayuga, Ont., the car and truck lovers can be found covered in the black grease of their hobby. They work on their wheels and dream of tearing down the never-ending blacktop that rushes past their garage. Once they make it on the truck show circuit, travelling the black ribbon becomes as much a part of their day as another's bus ride.

"It's a busy life," says Ken Koelling. "You drive all night, come here and you put it together and you wait. After the show, you tear down and head back home."

After Bigfoot wins the Battle of the Monster Trucks, mechanics and drivers gather in the concrete garage to swig brew and suck back methanol exhaust. It's well below freezing, but this is one of the rare nights when the roustabouts don't have to take the trucks apart for the long haul to the next stop. There is a lot of chatting and story-telling going on.

"I remember when Freddie rolled Bear Foot," Bigfoot's mechanic is telling a driver from Rhode Island. "Oh, hell, he turned that sumbitch over. I ran over and pulled him out. He was upside down when he landed, so it took a little while to get him out 'cause the shoulder harness had him. He was shakin' so hard you coulda used him for a vibrator."

Rhode Island doesn't cotton to talk about getting hurt: "Don't say that in no concrete building when there ain't no pieces of wood to knock on." He doesn't laugh.

Gene Fanning stands off to one side, his pockets filled with beer cans. He wears a full-length camouflage suit to match that of his truck, Gone A.W.O.L. It took almost three years to build the truck, a project he started after getting laid off from a steel factory in Derby, Pa. "I haven't been looking for another job with any heart," Fanning admits. "I'm just trying to make a go of this pulling. I'm tryin' real hard for sponsors, but it's tough. I've made a pretty good enough name for myself, but I just cain't get no money out of anybody." His latest brainstorm is to contact the brewers of Rolling Rock beer in nearby Latrobe, which was bought recently by a Canadian brewer. "I'm a local boy," he says. "I can do a lot of good for them."

Fanning, 26, has been working trucks since he graduated from high school. Gone A.W.O.L. cost him $30,000 to build, which some spend on an engine alone. He's tempted to invest in another pulling truck, or perhaps a funny car. "You got exhibition, you got guaranteed income. Funny cars, you know that money's coming in."

It's a precarious and not very lucrative life, but it suits Fanning fine. He likes trucks, and he likes it when others like his trucks. "I have another truck that I run on the streets of Derby. It's camouflage, a beater truck, just a snow-plowing, four-wheel-drive, hunting truck. It turns heads, and I figured if that ugly thing could turn heads, then I just had to get a nice one."

TOM HAWTHORN

Tom Hawthorn was born in 1960 in Winnipeg, Manitoba. He is a free-lance writer whose pieces frequently appear in *The Globe and Mail*.

The Greater Evil

MARGARET LAURENCE

I have a troubled feeling that I may be capable of doublethink, the ability to hold two opposing beliefs simultaneously. In the matter of censorship, doublethink seems, alas, appropriate. As a writer, my response to censorship of any kind is that I am totally opposed to it. But when I consider some of the vile material that is being peddled freely, I want to see some kind of control. I don't think I am being hypocritical. I have a sense of honest bewilderment. I have struggled with this inner problem for years, and now, with the spate of really bad video films and porn magazines flooding the market, my sense of ambiguity grows. I am certain of one thing, though. I cannot be alone in my uncertainty.

I have good reason to mistrust and fear censorship. I have been burned by the would-be book censors. Not burned in effigy, nor suffered my books being burned, not yet anyhow. But burned nonetheless, scorched mentally and emotionally. This has happened in more than one part of Canada, but the worst experience for me was in my own county of Peterborough a few years ago, when a group of people, sincere within their limited scope, no doubt, sought to have my novel, *The Diviners*, banned from the Grade 13 course and the school libraries. The book was attacked as obscene, pornographic, immoral and blasphemous. It is, I need hardly say, none of these things. Open meetings of the school board were held. Letters, pro and con, appeared in the local newspaper. Some awful things were said about the book and about me personally, mostly by people who had not read the book or met me. In retrospect, some of the comments seem pretty funny, but at the time I was hurt and furious. One person confidently stated that "Margaret Laurence's aim in life is to destroy the home and the family." In an interview, another person claimed that the novel contained a detailed account, calculated to titillate, of the sex life of the housefly. I couldn't recollect any such scene. Then I remembered that when Morag, as a child, is embarrassed by the sad, self-deprecating talk of her stepmother, the gentle, obese Prin, the girl seeks anything at all to focus on, so she need not listen. "She looked at two flies fucking, buzzing as they did it." Beginning and end of sensational scene. The reporter asked if the fundamentalist minister himself had found the scene sexually stimulating. "Oh no," was the reply. "I am a happily married man." At one open meeting, a man rose to condemn the novel and said that he spoke for a delegation of seven: himself, his wife, their four children—and God. In another county, a bachelor pharmacist accused me of adding to the rate of venereal disease in Canada by writing my books. He claimed that young people should not be given any information about sex until they are physically mature— "at about the age of 21." I hoped his knowledge of pharmacy was greater than his knowledge of biology.

Many readers, teachers and students did speak out for the novel, which was ultimately restored to the Grade 13 course. But the entire episode was enough to make me come down heavily against censorship, and especially against self-appointed groups of vigilantes. At the time I made a statement, which said, in part: "Surely it cannot do other than help in the growing toward a responsible maturity, for our young people to read novels in which many aspects of human life are dealt with, by writers whose basic faith is in the unique and irreplaceable value of the human individual."

I hold to that position. Artists of all kinds have been persecuted, imprisoned, tortured and killed, in many countries and at many times throughout history, for portraying life as they honestly saw it. Artistic suppression and political suppression go hand in hand, and always have. I would not advocate the banning of even such an evil and obscene book as Hitler's *Mein Kampf*. I think we must learn to recognize our enemies, to counter inhuman ranting with human and humane beliefs and practices. With censorship, the really bad stuff would tend to go underground and flourish covertly, while works of genuine artistic merit might get the axe (and yes, I know that "genuine artistic merit" is very difficult to define). I worry that censorship of any kind might lead to the suppression of anyone who speaks out against anything in our society, the suppression of artists, and the eventual clamping down on ideas, human perceptions, questionings. I think of our distinguished constitutional lawyer and poet F.R. Scott. In an essay written in 1933, he said: " 'The time, it is to be hoped, has gone by,' wrote John Stuart Mill, 'when any defence would be necessary of the principle of freedom of speech.' His hope was vain. The time for defending freedom never goes by. Freedom is a habit that must be kept alive by use."

And yet—my ambiguity remains. The pornography industry is now enormous, and includes so-called "kiddie porn." Most of us do not look at this stuff, nor do we have any notion how widespread it is, nor how degrading and brutal toward women and children, for it is they who are the chief victims in such magazines and films. Let me make one thing clear. I do not object to books or films or anything else that deals with sex, if those scenes are between two adults who are entering into this relationship of their own free will. (You may well say—what about *Lolita*? I hated the book, as a matter of fact, and no, I wouldn't advocate banning Nabokov. Ambiguity.) I do not object to the portrayal of social injustice, of terrible things done to one human by another or by governments or groups of whatever kind, as long as this is shown for what it is. But when we see films and photographs, *making use of real live women and children*, that portray horrifying violence, whether associated with sex or simply violence on its own, as being acceptable, on-turning, a thrill a minute, then I object.

The distinction must be made between erotic and pornographic. Eroticism is the portrayal of sexual expression between two people who desire each other and who have entered this relationship with mutual agreement. Pornography, on the other hand, is the portrayal of coercion and violence, usually with sexual connotations, and, like rape in real life, it has less to do with sex than with subjugation and cruelty. Pornography is not in any sense life-affirming. It is a denial of life. It is a repudiation of any feelings of love and tenderness and mutual passion. It is about hurting people, mainly women, and having that brutality seen as socially acceptable, even desirable.

As a woman, a mother, a writer, I cannot express adequately my feelings of fear, anger and outrage at this material. I have to say that I consider visual material to be more dangerous than any printed verbal material. Possibly I will be accused of being elitist and of favoring my own medium, the printed word, and possibly such a charge could be true. I just don't know. The reason I feel this way, however, is that these films and photographs make use of living women and children—not only a degradation of them, but also a strong suggestion to the viewer that violence against women and children, real persons, is acceptable. One of the most sinister aspects of these films and photographs is that they frequently communicate the idea that not only is violence against women OK—women actually *enjoy* being the subject of insanely brutal treatment, actually enjoy being chained, beaten, mutilated and even killed. This aspect of pornography, of course, reinforces and purports to excuse the behavior of some men who do indeed hate women. I could weep in grief and rage when I think of this attitude. As for the use of children in pornography, this is unspeakable and should be forbidden by law. The effect of this material is a matter of some dispute, and nothing can be proved either way, but many people believe that such scenes have been frighteningly re-enacted in real life in one way or another.

But is censorship, in any of the media involved, the answer? I think of John Milton's *Areopagitica; A Speech for the Liberty of Unli-*

censed Printing to the Parliament of England, in 1644, in which these words appear: "He that can apprehend and consider vice with all her baits and seeming pleasures, and yet abstain, and yet distinguish, and yet prefer that which is truly better, he is the true wayfaring Christian. I cannot praise a fugitive and cloistered virtue, unexercised and unbreathed, that never sallies out and sees her adversary, but slinks out of the race, where that immortal garland is to be run for, not without dust and heat." Obviously, Milton was not thinking of the sort of video films that anyone can now show at home, where any passing boy child can perhaps get the message that cruelty is OK and fun, and any passing girl child may wonder if that is what will be expected of her, to be a victim. All the same, we forget Milton's words at our peril.

The situation is not without its ironies. It has created some very strange comrades-in-arms. We find a number of feminists taking a strong stand *for* censorship, and being praised and applauded by people whose own stance is light-years away from feminism, the same people who would like my books, Alice Munro's books, W.O. Mitchell's books, banned from our high schools. We see civil libertarians who are *against* censorship and for free expression arguing that "anything goes," a view that must rejoice the hearts of purveyors of this inhumane material, but certainly distresses mine.

I consider myself to be both a feminist and a strong supporter of civil liberties and free speech, but there is no way I want to be on the same team as the would-be book-banning groups who claim that no contemporary novels should be taught or read in our schools. There is no way, either, that I want to be on the same team as the pornographers.

What position can a person like myself honestly take? The whole subject is enormously complex, but I must finally come down against a censorship board, whether for the visual media or for the printed word. I think that such boards tend to operate by vague and ill-defined standards. What can "acceptable community standards" possibly mean? It depends on which community you're talking about, and within any one community, even the smallest village, there are always going to be wide differences. Censorship boards tend to be insufficiently accountable. I believe that in cases of obscenity, test cases have to be brought before the courts and tried openly in accordance with our federal obscenity laws. The long-term solution, of course, is to educate our children of both sexes to realize that violence against women and children, against anyone, is not acceptable, and to equalize the status of women in our society.

What about Section 159 of the Criminal Code, "Offences Tending to Corrupt Morals"? My impression of federal law in this area is that its intentions are certainly right, its aims are toward justice, and it is indeed in some ways woefully outdated and in need of clarification. Clarification and amendment have not been and will not be easy. The clause that is most widely known to the general public is Section 159(8): "For the purpose of this Act, any publication a dominant characteristic of which is the undue exploitation of sex, or of sex and any one or more of the following subjects, namely, crime, horror, cruelty and violence, shall be deemed to be obscene." I think the first use of the words "of sex" could be deleted. How much sex between consenting adults is too much? Are three scenes OK but ten excessive? Frankly, among the many things I worry about in my life, as a citizen and as a writer, this is not one of them. But how are we to enshrine in our laws the idea that the degradation and coercion of women and children, of anyone, is dreadful, without putting into jeopardy the portrayal of social injustice seen as injustice? How are we to formulate a law that says the use of real women and children in situations of demeanment and violence, shown as desirable fun stuff, is not acceptable, while at the same time not making it possible for people who don't like artists questioning the status quo to bring charges against those who must continue to speak out against the violation of the human person and spirit?

In one case cited in the Criminal Code, the judge declares: "The onus of proof upon the Crown may be discharged by simply producing the publication without expert opinion evidence. Furthermore, where, although the book has certain literary merit particularly for the more sophisticated reader, it was available for the general public to whom the book was neither symbolism nor a psychological study, the accused cannot rely on the defence of public good." "Public good" is later defined as "necessary or advantageous to religion or morality, to the administration of justice, the pursuit of science, literature or art, or other objects of general interest." If this precedent means what it appears to say, it alarms me. It appears to put works of "literary merit" into some jeopardy, especially as expert opinion evidence need not be heard. If a book of mine were on trial, I would certainly want expert opinion evidence. I do not always agree with the views of the literary critics, or of teachers, but at least, and reassuringly, many of them know how to read with informed skill.

Realizing the difficulty of accurate definitions, I think that violence itself, shown as desirable, must be dealt with in some way in this law. It is *not* all right for men to beat and torture women. *It is wrong*. I also think that the exploitation of real live children for "kiddie porn" should be dealt with as a separate issue in law and should not be allowed, ever.

The more I think about it, the more the whole question becomes disturbingly complicated. Yet I believe it is a question that citizens,

Parliament and the legal profession must continue to grapple with. It is not enough for citizens to dismiss our obscenity laws as inadequate and outdated, and then turn the whole matter over to censorship boards. Our laws are not engraved on stone. They have been formulated carefully, although sometimes not well, but with a regard to a general justice. The law is not perfect, but it *is* public. It can be changed, but not upon the whim of a few. An informed and alert public is a necessary component of democracy. When laws need revision, we must seek to have them revised, not toward any narrowing down but toward a greater justice for all people, children, women and men, so that our lives may be lived without our being victimized, terrorized or exploited. Freedom is more fragile than any of us in Canada would like to believe. I think again of F.R. Scott's words: "Freedom is a habit that must be kept alive by use." Freedom, however, means responsibility and concern toward others. It does not mean that unscrupulous persons are permitted to exploit, demean and coerce others. It is said, correctly, that there is a demand for pornography. But should this demand be used to justify its unchallenged existence and distribution? Some men are said to "need" pornography. To me this is like saying some men "need" to beat up their wives or commit murder. Must women and children be victims in order to assuage the fears and insecurities of those men who want to feel they are totally powerful in a quite unreal way? I don't think so. If some men "need" pornography, then I as a woman will never be a party to it, not even by the tacit agreement of silence. We and they had better try together to control and redirect those needs. I think that citizens can and should protest in any nonviolent way possible against the brutalities and callousness of pornography, including one area I haven't even been able to deal with here, the demeanment of women in many advertisements.

In the long run, it is all-important to raise our children to know the reality of others; to let them know that sex can and should be an expression of love and tenderness and mutual caring, not hatred and domination of the victor/victim kind; to communicate to our daughters and our sons that to be truly human is to try to be loving and responsible, strong not because of power but because of self-respect and respect for others.

In *Areopagitica*, Milton said: "That which purifies us is trial, and trial is by what is contrary." In the final analysis, we and our society will not stand or fall by what we are "permitted" to see or hear or read, but by what we ourselves choose. We must, however, have some societal agreement as to what is acceptable in the widest frame of reference possible, but still within the basic concept that *damaging people is wrong*. Murder is not acceptable, and neither is the abasement, demeanment and exploitation of human persons, whatever their race, religion, age or gender. Not all of this can be enshrined in law. Laws can never make people more understanding and compassionate toward one another. That is what individual people try to do, in our imperfect and familial ways. What the law *can* do is attempt to curb, by open process in public courts, the worst excesses of humankind's always-in-some-way-present inhumanity to humankind.

This is as close as I can get to formulating my own beliefs. It is an incomplete and in many ways a contradictory formulation, and I am well aware of that. Perhaps this isn't such a bad thing. I don't think we can or should ever get to a point where we feel we know, probably in a simplistic way, what all the answers are or that we ourselves hold them and no one else does. The struggle will probably always go on, as it always has in one way or another. The new technology has brought its own intricacies. I doubt that the human heart and conscience will ever be relieved of their burdens, and I certainly hope they are not. This particular struggle, *for* human freedom and *against* the awfulness that seeks to masquerade as freedom but is really slavery, will not ever be easy or simple, but it is a struggle that those of us who are concerned must never cease to enter into, even though it will continue to be, in Milton's words, "not without dust and heat."

MARGARET LAURENCE

Margaret Laurence (1926–1987) was born in the prairie town of Neepawa, Man., which appears in her fiction as Manawaka. Her best-known novels include *The Stone Angel, A Jest of God,* and *The Fire-Dwellers.* Her articles and essays are collected in *Heart of a Stranger.*

What If Shakespeare Had Had a Sister?

VIRGINIA WOOLF

It is a perennial puzzle why no woman wrote a word of that extraordinary literature [of the time of Elizabeth I] when every man, it seemed, was capable of song or sonnet. What were the conditions in which women lived, I asked myself; for fiction, imaginative work, that is, is not dropped like a pebble upon the ground, as science may be; fiction is like a spider's web, attached ever so lightly perhaps, but still attached to life at all four corners. Often the attachment is scarcely perceptible: Shakespeare's plays, for instance, seem to hang there complete by themselves. But when the web is pulled askew, hooked up at the edge, torn in the middle, one remembers that these webs are not spun in midair by incorporeal creatures, but are the work of suffering human beings, and are attached to grossly material things, like health and money and the houses we live in.

I went, therefore, to the shelf where the histories stand and took down one of the latest, Professor Trevelyan's *History of England*. Once more I looked up Women, found "position of," and turned to the pages indicated. "Wife-beating," I read, "was a recognised right of man, and was practised without shame by high as well as low. . . . Similarly," the historian goes on, "the daughter who refused to marry the gentleman of her parents' choice was liable to be locked up, beaten and flung about the room, without any shock being inflicted on public opinion. Marriage was not an affair of personal affection, but of family avarice, particularly in the 'chivalrous' upper classes. . . . Betrothal often took place while one or both of the parties was in the cradle, and marriage when they were scarcely out of the nurses' charge." That was about 1470, soon after Chaucer's time. The next reference to the position of women is some two hundred years later, in the time of the Stuarts. "It was still the exception for women of the upper and middle class to choose their own husbands, and when the husband had been assigned, he was lord and master, so far at least as law and custom could make him. Yet even so," Professor Trevelyan concludes, "neither Shakespeare's women nor those of authentic seventeenth-century memoirs, like the Verneys and the Hutchinsons, seem wanting in personality and character." Certainly, if we consider it, Cleopatra must have had a way with her; Lady Macbeth, one would suppose, had a will of her own; Rosalind, one might conclude, was an attractive girl. Professor Trevelyan is speaking no more than the truth when he remarks that Shakespeare's women do not seem wanting in personality and character. Not being a historian, one might go even further and say that women have burnt like beacons in all the works of all the poets from the beginning of time—Clytemnestra, Antigone, Cleopatra, Lady Macbeth, Phedre, Cressida, Rosalind, Desdemona, the Duchess of Malfi, among the dramatists; then among the prose writers: Millamant, Clarissa, Becky Sharp, Anna Karenina, Emma Bovary, Madame de Guermantes—the names flock to mind, nor do they recall women "lacking in personality and character." Indeed, if woman had no existence save in the fiction written by men, one would imagine her a person of the utmost importance; very various; heroic and mean; splendid and sordid; infinitely beautiful and hideous in the extreme; as great as a man, some think even greater. But this is woman in fiction. In fact, as Professor Trevelyan points out, she was locked up, beaten and flung about the room.

A very queer, composite being thus emerges. Imaginatively she is of the highest importance; practically she is completely insignificant. She pervades poetry from cover to cover; she is all but absent from history. She dominates the lives of kings and conquerors in fiction; in fact, she was the slave of any boy whose parents forced a ring upon her finger. Some of the most inspired words, some of the most profound thoughts in literature fall from her lips; in real life she could hardly read, could scarcely spell, and was the property of her husband.

It was certainly an odd monster that one made up by reading the historians first and the poets afterwards—a worm winged like an eagle; the spirit of life and beauty in a kitchen chopping up suet. But these monsters, however amusing to the imagination, have no existence in fact. What one must do to bring her to life was to think poetically and prosaically at one and the same moment, thus keeping in touch with fact—that she is Mrs. Martin, aged thirty-six, dressed in blue, wearing a black hat and brown shoes; but not losing sight of fiction either—that she is a vessel in which all sorts of spirits and forces are coursing and flashing perpetually. The moment, however, that one tries this method with the Elizabethan woman, one branch of illumination fails; one is held up by the scarcity of facts. One knows nothing detailed, nothing perfectly true and substantial about her. History scarcely mentions her. . . .

Here am I asking why women did not write poetry in the Elizabethan age, and I am not sure how they were educated; whether they were taught to write; whether they had sitting-rooms to themselves; how many women had children before they were twenty-one; what, in short, they did from eight in the morning till eight at night. They had no money evidently; according to Professor Trevelyan they were married whether they liked it or not before they were out of the nursery, at fifteen or sixteen very likely. It would have been extremely odd, even upon this showing, had one of them suddenly written the plays of Shakespeare, I concluded, and I thought of that old gentleman, who is dead now, but was a bishop, I think, who declared that it was impossible for any woman, past, present, or to come, to have the genius of Shakespeare. He wrote to the papers about it. He also told a lady who applied to him for information that cats do not as a matter of fact go to heaven, though they have, he added, souls of a sort. How much thinking those old gentlemen used to save one! How the borders of ignorance shrank back at their approach! Cats do not go to heaven. Women cannot write the plays of Shakespeare.

Be that as it may, I could not help thinking, as I looked at the works of Shakespeare on the shelf, that the bishop was right at least in this; it would have been impossible, completely and entirely, for any woman to have written the plays of Shakespeare in the age of Shakespeare. Let me imagine, since facts are so hard to come by, what would have happened had Shakespeare had a wonderfully gifted sister, called Judith, let us say. Shakespeare himself went, very probably—his mother was an heiress—to the grammar school, where he may have learnt Latin—Ovid, Virgil and Horace—and the elements of grammar and logic. He was, it is well known, a wild boy who poached rabbits, perhaps shot a deer, and had, rather sooner than he should have done, to marry a woman in the neighborhood, who bore him a child rather quicker than was right. That escapade sent him to seek his fortune in London. He had, it seemed, a taste for the theatre; he began by holding horses at the stage door. Very soon he got work in the theatre, became a successful actor, and lived at the hub of the universe, meeting everybody, knowing everybody, practising his art on the boards, exercising his wits in the streets, and even getting access to the palace of the queen. Meanwhile his extraordinarily gifted sister, let us suppose, remained at home. She was as adventurous, as imaginative, as agog to see the world as he was. But she was not sent to school. She had no chance of learning grammar and logic, let alone of reading Horace and Virgil. She picked up a book now and then, one of her brother's perhaps, and read a few pages. But then her parents came in and told her to mend the stockings or mind the stew and not moon about with books and papers. They would have spoken sharply but kindly, for they were substantial people who knew the conditions of life for a woman and loved their daughter—indeed, more likely than not she was the apple of her father's eye. Perhaps she scribbled some pages up in an apple loft on the sly, but was careful to hide them or set fire to them. Soon, however, before she was out of her teens, she was to be betrothed to the son of a neighboring wool-stapler. She cried out that marriage was hateful to her, and for that she was severely beaten by her father. Then he ceased to scold her. He begged her instead not to hurt him, not to shame him in this matter of her marriage. He would give her a chain of beads or a fine petticoat, he said; and there were tears in his eyes. How could she disobey him? How could she break his heart? The force of her own gift alone drove her to it. She made up a small parcel of her belongings, let herself down by a rope one summer's night and took the road to London. She was not seventeen. The birds that sang in the hedge were not more musical than she was. She had the quickest fancy, a gift like her brother's for the tune of words. Like him, she had a taste for the theatre. She stood at the stage door; she wanted to act, she said. Men laughed in her face. The manager—a fat, loose-lipped man—guffawed. He bellowed something about poodles dancing and women acting—no woman, he said, could possibly be an actress. He hinted—you can imagine what. She could get no training in her craft. Could she even seek her dinner in a tavern or roam the streets at midnight? Yet her genius was for fiction and lusted to feed abundantly upon the lives of men and women and the study of their ways. At last—for she was very young, oddly like Shakespeare the poet in her face, with the same grey eyes and rounded brows— at last Nick Greene the actor-manager took pity on her; she found herself with child by that gentleman and so—who shall measure the heat and violence of the poet's heart when caught and tangled in a woman's body?—killed herself one winter's night and lies buried at some crossroads where the omnibuses now stop outside the Elephant and Castle.

That, more or less, is how the story would run, I think, if a woman in Shakespeare's day had had Shakespeare's genius. But for my part, I agree with the deceased bishop, if such he was—it is unthinkable that any woman in Shakespeare's day should have had Shakespeare's genius. For genius like Shakespeare's is not born among laboring, uneducated, servile people. It was not born in England among the Saxons and the Britons. It is not born today among the working classes. How, then, could it have been born among women whose work began, according to Professor Trevelyan, almost before they were out of the nursery, who were forced to it by their parents and held to it by all the power of law and custom? Yet genius of a sort must have existed among women as it must have existed among the working classes. Now and again an Emily Brontë or a Robert Burns blazes out and proves its presence. But certainly it never got itself on to paper. When, however, one reads of a witch being ducked, of a woman possessed by devils, or a wise woman selling herbs, or even of a very remarkable man who had a mother, then I think we are on the track of a lost novelist, a suppressed poet, of some mute and inglorious Jane Austen, some Emily Brontë who dashed her brains out on the moor or mopped and mowed about the highways crazed with the torture that her gift had put her to. Indeed, I would venture to guess that Anon, who wrote so many poems without signing them, was often a woman. It was a woman Edward Fitzgerald, I think, suggested who made the ballads and the folk-songs, crooning them to her children, beguiling her spinning with them, or the length of the winter's night.

This may be true or it may be false—who can say?—but what is true in it, so it seemed to me, reviewing the story of Shakespeare's sister as I had made it, is that any woman born with a great gift in the sixteenth century would certainly have gone crazed, shot herself, or ended her days in some lonely cottage outside the village, half witch, half wizard, feared and mocked at. For it needs little skill in psychology to be sure that a highly gifted girl who had tried to use her gift for poetry would have been so thwarted and hindered by other people, so tortured and pulled asunder by her own contrary instincts, that she must have lost her health and sanity to a certainty. No girl could have walked to London and stood at a stage door and forced her way into the presence of actor-managers without doing herself a violence and suffering an anguish which may have been irrational—for chastity may be a fetish invented by certain societies for unknown reasons—but were none the less inevitable. Chastity had then, it has even now, a religious importance in a woman's life, and has so wrapped itself round with nerves and instincts that to cut it free and bring it to the light of day demands courage of the rarest. To have lived a free life in London in the sixteenth century would have meant for a woman who was poet and playwright a nervous stress and dilemma which might well have killed her. Had she survived, whatever she had written would have been twisted and deformed, issuing from a strained and morbid imagination. And undoubtedly, I thought, looking at the shelf where there are no plays by women, her work would have gone unsigned. That refuge she would have sought certainly. It was the relic of the sense of chastity that dictated anonymity to women even so late as the nineteenth century. Currer Bell, George Eliot, George Sand, all the victims of inner strife as their writings prove, sought ineffectively to veil themselves by using the name of a man. Thus they did homage to the convention, which if not implanted by the other sex was liberally encouraged by them (the chief glory of a woman is not to be talked of, said Pericles, himself a much-talked-of man), that publicity in women is detestable. Anonymity runs in their blood. . . .

I told you in the course of this paper that Shakespeare had a sister; but do not look for her in Sir Sidney Lee's life of the poet. She died young—alas, she never wrote a word. She lies buried where the omnibuses now stop, opposite the Elephant and Castle. Now my belief is that this poet who never wrote a word and was buried at the crossroads still lives. She lives in you and in me, and in many other women who are not here tonight, for they are washing up the dishes and putting the children to bed. But she lives; for great poets do not die; they are continuing presences; they need only the opportunity to walk among us in the flesh. This opportunity, as I think, it is now coming within your power to give her. For my belief is that if we live another century or so—I am talking of the common life which is the real life and not of the little separate lives which we live as individuals—and have five hundred a year each of us and rooms of our own; if we have the habit of freedom and the courage to write exactly what we think; if we escape a little from the common sitting-room and see human beings not always in their relation to each other but in relation to reality; and the sky, too, and the trees or whatever it may be in themselves; if we look past Milton's bogey, for no human being should shut out the view; if we face the fact, for it is a fact, that there is no arm to cling to, but that we go alone and that our relation is to the world of reality and not only to the world of men and women, then the opportunity will come and the dead poet who was Shakespeare's sister will put on the body which she has so often laid down. Drawing her life from the lives of the unknown who were her forerunners, as her brother did before her, she will be born. As for her coming without that preparation, without that effort on our part, without that determination that when she is born again she shall find it possible to live and write her poetry, that we cannot expect, for that would be impossible. But I maintain that she would come if we worked for her, and that so to work, even in poverty and obscurity, is worth while.

VIRGINIA WOOLF

Virginia Woolf (1882–1941) was born into an intellectually distinguished family and became the focal point of an influential group of thinkers, writers, and artists, known as the Bloomsbury Circle, in London in the early 1900s. A critic and essayist of great power, she is considered the most important English woman writer of the century. Her novels include *Jacob's Room* (1922), *Mrs. Dalloway* (1925), *To the Lighthouse* (1927), and *Orlando* (1928).

The Necessary Enemy

KATHERINE ANNE PORTER

She is a frank, charming, fresh-hearted young woman who married for love. She and her husband are one of those . . . good-looking young pairs who ornament this modern scene rather more in profusion perhaps than ever before in our history. They are handsome, with a talent for finding their way in their world, they work at things that interest them, their tastes agree and their hopes. They intend in all good faith to spend their lives together, to have children and do well by them and each other—to be happy, in fact, which for them is the whole point of their marriage. And all in stride, keeping their wits about them. Nothing romantic, mind you; their feet are on the ground.

Unless they were this sort of person, there would be not much point to what I wish to say; for they would seem to be an example of the high-spirited, right-minded young whom the critics are always invoking to come forth and do their duty and practice all those sterling old-fashioned virtues which in every generation seem to be falling into disrepair. As for virtues, these young people are more or less on their own, like most of their kind; they get very little moral or other aid from their society; but after three years of marriage this very contemporary young woman finds herself facing the oldest and ugliest dilemma of marriage.

She is dismayed, horrified, full of guilt and forebodings because she is finding out little by little that she is capable of hating her husband, whom she loves faithfully. She can hate him at times as fiercely and mysteriously, indeed in terribly much the same way, as often she hated her parents, her brothers and sisters, whom she loves, when she was a child. Even then it had seemed to her a kind of black treacherousness in her, her private wickedness that, just the same, gave her her only private life. That was one thing her parents never knew about her, never seemed to suspect. For it was never given a name. They did and said hateful things to her and to each other as if by right, as if in them it was a kind of virtue. But when they said to her, "Control your feelings," it was never when she was amiable and obedient, only in the black times of her hate.

So it was her secret, a shameful one. When they punished her, sometimes for the strangest reasons, it was, they said, only because they loved her—it was for her good. She did not believe this, but she thought herself guilty of something worse than ever they had punished her for. None of this really frightened her: the real fright came when she discovered that at times her father and mother hated each other; this was like standing on the doorsill of a familiar room and seeing in a lightning flash that the floor was gone, you were on the edge of a bottomless pit. Sometimes she felt that both of them hated her, but that passed, it was simply not a thing to be thought of, much less believed. She thought she had outgrown all this, but here it was again, an element in her own nature she could not control, or feared she could not. She would have to hide from her husband, if she could, the same spot in her feelings she had hidden from her parents, and for the same no doubt disreputable, selfish reason: she wants to keep his love.

Above all, she wants him to be absolutely confident that she loves him, for that is the real truth, no matter how unreasonable it sounds, and no matter how her own feelings betray them both at times. She depends recklessly on his love; yet while she is hating him, he might very well be hating her as much or even more, and it would serve her right. But she does not want to be served right, she wants to be loved and forgiven—that is, to be sure he would forgive her anything, if he had any notion of what she had done. But best of all she would like not to have anything in her love that should ask forgiveness. She doesn't mean about their quarrels— they are not so bad. Her feelings are out of proportion, perhaps. She knows it is perfectly natural for people to disagree, have fits of temper, fight it out; they learn quite a lot about each other that way, and not all of it disappointing either. When it passes, her hatred seems quite unreal. It always did.

Love. We are early taught to say it. I love you. We are trained to the thought of it as if there were nothing else, or nothing else worth having without it, or nothing worth having which could not bring with it. Love is taught, always by precept, sometimes by example. Then hate, which no one meant to teach us, comes of itself. It is true that if we say I love you, it may be received with doubt, for there are times when it is hard to believe. Say I hate you, and the one spoken to believes it instantly, once for all.

Say I love you a thousand times to that person afterward and mean it every time, and still it does not change the fact that once we said I hate you, and meant that too. It leaves a mark on that surface love had worn so smooth with its eternal caresses. Love must be learned, and learned again and again; there is no end to it.

Hate needs no instruction, but waits only to be provoked . . . hate, the unspoken word, the unacknowledged presence in the house, that faint smell of brimstone among the roses, that invisible tongue-tripper, that unkempt finger in every pie, that sudden oh-so-curiously *chilling* look—could it be boredom?—on your dear one's features, making them quite ugly. Be careful: love, perfect love, is in danger.

If it is not perfect, it is not love, and if it is not love, it is bound to be hate sooner or later. This is perhaps a not too exaggerated statement of the extreme position of Romantic Love, more especially in America, where we are all brought up on it, whether we know it or not. Romantic Love is changeless, faithful, passionate, and its sole end is to render the two lovers happy. It has no obstacles save those provided by the hazards of fate (that is to say, society), and such sufferings as the lovers may cause each other are only another word for delight: exciting jealousies, thrilling uncertainties, the ritual dance of courtship within the charmed closed circle of their secret alliance; all *real* troubles come from without, they face them unitedly in perfect confidence. Marriage is not the end but only the beginning of true happiness, cloudless, changeless to the end. That the candidates for this blissful condition have never seen an example of it, nor ever knew anyone who had, makes no difference. That is the ideal and they will achieve it.

How did Romantic Love manage to get into marriage at last, where it was most certainly never intended to be? At its highest it was tragic: the love of Héloïse and Abélard. At its most graceful, it was the homage of the trouvère for his lady. In its most popular form, the adulterous strayings of solidly married couples who meant to stray for their own good reasons, but at the same time do nothing to upset the property settlements or the line of legitimacy; at its most trivial, the pretty trifling of shepherd and shepherdess.

This was generally condemned by church and state and a word of fear to honest wives whose mortal enemy it was. Love within the sober, sacred realities of marriage was a matter of personal luck, but in any case, private feelings were strictly a private affair having, at least in theory, no bearing whatever on the fixed practice of the rules of an institution never intended as a recreation ground for either sex. If the couple discharged their religious and social obligations, furnished forth a copious progeny, kept their troubles to themselves, maintained public civility and died under the same roof, even if not always on speaking terms, it was rightly regarded as a successful marriage. Apparently this testing ground was too severe for all but the stoutest spirits; it too was based on an ideal, as impossible in its way as the ideal Romantic Love. One good thing to be said for it is that society took responsibility for the conditions of marriage, and the sufferers within its bounds could always blame the system, not themselves. But Romantic Love crept into the marriage bed, very stealthily, by centuries, bringing its absurd notions about love as eternal springtime and marriage as a personal adventure meant to provide personal happiness. To a Western romantic such as I, though my views have been much modified by painful experience, it still seems to me a charming work of the human imagination, and it is a pity its central notion has been taken too literally and has hardened into a convention as cramping and enslaving as the older one. The refusal to acknowledge the evils in ourselves which therefore are implicit in any human situation is as extreme and unworkable a proposition as the doctrine of total depravity; but somewhere between them, or maybe beyond them, there does exist a possibility for reconciliation between our desires for impossible satisfactions and the simple unalterable fact that we also desire to be unhappy and that we create our own sufferings; and out of these sufferings we salvage our fragments of happiness.

Our young woman who has been taught that an important part of her human nature is not real because it makes trouble and interferes with her peace of mind and shakes her self-love, has been very badly taught; but she has arrived at a most important stage of her re-education. She is afraid her marriage is going to fail because she has not love enough to face its difficulties; and this because at times she feels a painful hostility toward her husband, and cannot admit its reality because such an admission would damage in her own eyes her view of what love should be, an absurd view, based on her vanity of power. Her hatred is real as her love is real, but her hatred has the advantage at present because it works on a blind instinctual level, it is lawless; and her love is subjected to a code of ideal conditions, impossible by their very nature of fulfillment, which prevents its free growth and deprives it of its right to recognize its human limitations and come to grips with them. Hatred is natural in a sense that love, as she conceives it, a young person brought up in the tradition of Romantic Love, is not natural at all. Yet it did not come by hazard, it is the very imperfect expression of the need of the human imagination to create beauty and harmony out of chaos, no matter how mistaken its notion of these things may be, nor how clumsy its methods. It has conjured love out of the air, and seeks to preserve it by incantations; when she spoke a vow to love and honor her husband until death, she did a very reckless thing, for it is not possible by an act of the will to fulfill such an engagement. But it was the necessary act of faith performed in defense of a mode of feeling, the statement of honorable intention to practice as well as she is able the noble, acquired faculty of love,

that very mysterious overtone to sex which is the best thing in it.
Her hatred is part of it, the necessary enemy and ally.

KATHERINE ANNE PORTER

Katherine Anne Porter (1890–1980) was a Texas-born newspaper writer,
actress, teacher, and novelist. She is best remembered for the novels *Pale
Horse, Pale Rider* and *Ship of Fools* as well as many short stories and
essays.

Hunger

MAGGIE HELWIG

Consider that it is now normal for North
American women to have eating disorders. Consider that anorexia—
deliberate starvation—and bulimia—self-induced vomiting—and
obsessive patterns for weight-controlling exercise are now the ordinary thing for young women, and are spreading at a frightening
rate to older women, to men, to ethnic groups and social classes that
were once "immune." Consider that some surveys suggest that
80 per cent of the women on an average university campus have
borderline-to-severe eating disorders; that it is almost impossible to
get treatment unless the problem is life-threatening; that, in fact, if
it is not life-threatening it is not considered a problem at all. I once
sat in a seminar on nutritional aspects of anorexia, and ended up
listening to people tell me how to keep my weight down. All this is
happening in one of the richest countries in the world, a society
devoted to consumption. Amazing as it may seem, we have normal-
ized anorexia and bulimia, even turned them into an industry.

   We've also trivialized them: made them into nothing more than
an exaggerated conformity with basically acceptable standards of
behavior. Everyone wants to be thin and pretty, after all. Some
people take it a little too far; you have to get them back on the right
track, but it's all a question of knowing just how far is proper.

   The consumer society has gone so far we can even buy into
hunger.

But that is not what it's about. You do not stuff yourself with food and force yourself to vomit just because of fashion magazines. You do not reduce yourself to the condition of a skeleton in order to be attractive. This is not just a problem of proportion. This is the nightmare of consumerism acted out in women's bodies.

This is what we are saying as we starve: it is not all right. It is not all right. It is not all right.

There've always been strange or disordered patterns of eating, associated mainly with religious extremism or psychological problems (which some, not myself, would say were the same thing). But the complex of ideas, fears, angers and actions that make up contemporary anorexia and bulimia seems to be of fairly recent origin. Anorexia did not exist as a recognized pattern until the 1960s, and bulimia not until later than that—and at first they were deeply shocking. The idea that privileged young women (the first group to be affected) were voluntarily starving themselves, sometimes to death, or regularly sticking their fingers down their throats to make themselves throw up, shook the culture badly. It was a fad, in a sense, the illness of the month, but it was also a scandal, and a source of something like horror.

Before this, though, before anorexia had a widely recognized name, one of the first women to succumb to it had made her own scandalous stand, and left a body of writing that still has a lot to say about the real meaning of voluntary hunger.

Simone Weil was a brilliant, disturbed, wildly wrong-headed and astonishingly perceptive young French woman who died from the complications of self-starvation in America during World War II, at the age of 34. She never, of course, wrote directly about her refusal to eat—typically for any anorexic, she insisted she ate perfectly adequate amounts. But throughout her philosophical and theological writing (almost all of it fragments and essays collected after her death), she examines and uses the symbolism of hunger, eating and food.

Food occupied, in fact, a rather important and valued position in her philosophy—she once referred to food as "the irrefutable proof of the reality of the universe," and at another time said that the foods served at Easter and Christmas, the turkey and *marron glacés*, were "the true meaning of the feast"; although she could also take the more conventional puritan position that desire for food is a "base motive." She spoke often of eating God (acceptable enough in a Christian context) and of being eaten by God (considerably less so). The great tragedy of our lives, she said, is that we cannot really eat God; and also "it may be that vice, depravity and crime are almost always . . . attempts to eat beauty."

But it is her use of the symbolism of hunger that explains her death. "We have to go down into ourselves to the abode of the desire which is not imaginary. Hunger: we imagine kinds of food, but the hunger itself is real: we have to fasten onto the hunger."

Hunger, then, was a search for reality, for the irreducible need that lies beyond all imaginary satisfactions. Weil was deeply perturbed by the "materialism" of her culture; though she probably could not have begun to imagine the number of imaginary and illusory "satisfactions" now available. Simply, she wanted truth. She wanted to reduce herself to the point where she would *know* what needs, and what foods, were real and true.

Similarly, though deeply drawn to the Catholic faith, she refused to be baptized and to take Communion (to, in fact, eat God). "I cannot help wondering whether in these days when so large a proportion of humanity is sunk in materialism, God does not want there to be some men and women who have given themselves to him and to Christ and who yet remain outside the Church." For the sake of honesty, of truth, she maintained her hunger.

Weil, a mystic and a political activist simultaneously until the end of her short life—she was one of the first French intellectuals to join the Communist party and one of the first to leave, fought in the Spanish civil war and worked in auto factories—could not bear to have life be less than a total spiritual and political statement. And her statement of protest, of dissatisfaction, her statement of hunger, finally destroyed her.

The term anorexia nervosa was coined in the 19th century, but it was not until sometime in the 1960s that significant—and constantly increasing—numbers of well-off young women began dying of starvation, and not until the early 1970s that it became public knowledge.

It is the nature of our times that the explanations proffered were psychological and individualistic; yet, even so, it was understood as being, on some level, an act of protest. And of course symbolically, it could hardly be other—it was, simply, a hunger strike. The most common interpretation, at that point, was that it was a sort of adolescent rebellion against parental control, an attempt, particularly, to escape from an overcontrolling mother. It was a fairly acceptable paradigm for the period, although many mothers were justifiably disturbed; sometimes deeply and unnecessarily hurt. The theory still has some currency, and is not entirely devoid of truth.

But can it be an accident that this happened almost precisely to coincide with the growth of the consumer society, a world based on a level of material consumption that, by the end of the 1960s, had become very nearly uncontrollable? Or with the strange, underground guilt that has made "conspicuous consumption" a matter of consuming vast amounts and *hiding it*, of million-dollar minimalism?

With the development of what is possibly the most emotionally depleted society in history, where the only "satisfactions" seem to be the imaginary ones, the material buy-offs?

To be skeletally, horribly thin makes one strong statement. It says, I am hungry. What I have been given is not sufficient, not real, not true, not acceptable. I am starving. To reject food, whether by refusing it or by vomiting it back, says simply, I will not consume. I will not participate. This is not real.

Hunger is the central nightmare image of our society. Of all the icons of horror the last few generations have offered us, we have chosen, above all, pictures of hunger—the emaciated prisoners of Auschwitz and Belsen, Ethiopian children with bloated bellies and stick-figure limbs. We carry in our heads these nightmares of the extreme edge of hunger.

And while we may not admit to guilt about our level of consumption in general, we admit freely to guilt about eating, easily equate food with "sin." We cannot accept hunger of our own, cannot afford to consider it.

It is, traditionally, women who carry our nightmares. It was women who became possessed by the Devil, women who suffered from "hysterical disorders," women who, in all popular culture, are the targets of the "monster." One of the roles women are cast in is that of those who act out the subconscious fears of their society. And it is women above all, in this time, who carry our hunger.

It is the starving women who embody the extremity of hunger that terrifies and fascinates us, and who insist that they are not hungry. It is the women sticking their fingers down their throats who act out the equation of food and sin, who deny hunger and yet embody endless, unfulfilled appetite. It is these women who live through every implication of our consumption and our hunger, our guilt and ambiguity and our awful need for something real to fill us.

We have too much; and it is poison.

It was first—in fact exclusively—feminist writers who began to explore the symbolic language of anorexia and bulimia; Sheila MacLeod (*The Art of Starvation*), Susie Orbach (*Hunger Strike*), and others. However, as their work began to appear, a new presentation of eating disorders was entering the general consciousness, one that would no longer permit them to be understood as protest at *any* level.

For, as eating disorders became increasingly widespread, they also became increasingly trivialized, incorporated into a framework already "understood" all too well. Feminist writers had, early on, noted that anorexia had to be linked with the increasing thinness of models and other glamor icons, as part of a larger cultural trend. This is true enough as a starting point, for the symbolic struggle being waged in women's bodies happens on many levels, and is not limited to pathology cases. Unfortunately, this single starting point was seized on by "women's magazines" and popularizing accounts in general. Anorexia was now understandable, almost safe really, it was just fashion gone out of control. Why, these women were *accepting* the culture, they just needed a sense of proportion. What a relief.

Now it could be condoned. Now it could, in fact, become the basis for an industry; could be incorporated neatly into consumer society. According to Jane Fonda the solution to bulimia is to remain equally unhealthily thin by buying the 20-minute workout and becoming an obsessive fitness follower (at least for those who can afford it). The diet clinic industry, the Nutrisystem package, the aerobics boom. An advertising industry that plays equally off desire and guilt, for they now reinforce each other. Thousands upon thousands of starving, tormented women, not "sick" enough to be taken seriously, not really troubled at all.

One does not reduce oneself to the condition of a skeleton in order to be fashionable. One does not binge and vomit daily as an acceptable means of weight control. One does not even approach or imagine or dream of these things if one is not in some sort of trouble. If it were as simple as fashion, surely we would not be so ashamed to speak of these things, we would not feel that either way, whether we eat or do not eat, we are doing something wrong.

I was anorexic for eight years. I nearly died. It was certainly no help to me to be told I was taking fashion too far—I knew perfectly well that had nothing to do with it. It did not help much to be told I was trying to escape from my mother, since I lived away from home and was in only occasional contact with my family; it did not help much to be approached on an individualistic, psychological level. In fact, the first person I was able to go to for help was a charismatic Catholic, who at least understood that I was speaking in symbols of spiritual hunger.

I knew that I had something to say, that things were not all right, that I had to make that concretely, physically obvious. I did not hate or look down on my body—I spoke through it and with it.

Women are taught to take guilt, concern, problems, onto themselves personally; and especially onto their bodies. But we are trying to talk about something that is only partly personal. Until we find new ways of saying it and find the courage to talk to the world about the world, we will speak destruction to ourselves.

We must come to know what we are saying—and say it.

MAGGIE HELWIG

Maggie Helwig (b. 1961) is a Canadian poet and editor whose published works include *Talking Prophet Blues*.

The Space Crone

URSULA K. LE GUIN

he menopause is probably the least glamorous topic imaginable; and this is interesting, because it is one of the very few topics to which cling some shreds and remnants of taboo. A serious mention of menopause is usually met with uneasy silence; a sneering reference to it is usually met with relieved sniggers. Both the silence and the sniggering are pretty sure indications of taboo.

Most people would consider the old phrase "change of life" a euphemism for the medical term "menopause," but I, who am now going through the change, begin to wonder if it isn't the other way round. "Change of life" is too blunt a phrase, too factual. "Menopause," with its chime-suggestion of a mere pause after which things go on as before, is reassuringly trivial.

But the change is not trivial, and I wonder how many women are brave enough to carry it out wholeheartedly. They give up their reproductive capacity with more or less of a struggle, and when it's gone they think that's all there is to it. Well, at least I don't get the Curse any more, they say, and the only reason I felt so depressed sometimes was hormones. Now I'm myself again. But this is to evade the real challenge, and to lose, not only the capacity to ovulate, but the opportunity to become a Crone.

In the old days women who survived long enough to attain the menopause more often accepted the challenge. They had, after all, had practice. They had already changed their life radically once before, when they ceased to be virgins and became mature women/wives/matrons/mothers/mistresses/whores/etc. This change involved not only the physiological alterations of puberty—the shift from barren childhood to fruitful maturity—but a socially recognized alteration of being: a change of condition from the sacred to the profane.

With the secularization of virginity now complete, so that the once awesome term "virgin" is now a sneer or at best a slightly dated word for a person who hasn't copulated yet, the opportunity of gaining or regaining the dangerous/sacred condition of being at the Second Change has ceased to be apparent.

Virginity is now a mere preamble or waiting room to be got out of as soon as possible; it is without significance. Old age is similarly a waiting room, where you go after life's over and wait for cancer or a stroke. The years before and after the menstrual years are vestigial: the only meaningful condition left to women is that of fruitfulness. Curiously, this restriction of significance coincided with the development of chemicals and instruments that make fertility itself a meaningless or at least secondary characteristic of female maturity. The significance of maturity now is not the capacity to conceive but the mere ability to have sex. As this ability is shared by pubescents and by postclimacterics, the blurring of distinctions and elimination of opportunities is almost complete. There are no rites of passage because there is no significant change. The Triple Goddess has only one face: Marilyn Monroe's, maybe. The entire life of a woman from ten or twelve through seventy or eighty has become secular, uniform, changeless. As there is no longer any virtue in virginity, so there is no longer any meaning in menopause. It requires fanatical determination now to become a Crone.

Women have thus, by imitating the life condition of men, surrendered a very strong position of their own. Men are afraid of virgins, but they have a cure for their own fear and the virgin's virginity: fucking. Men are afraid of crones, so afraid of them that their cure for virginity fails them; they know it won't work. Faced with the fulfilled Crone, all but the bravest men wilt and retreat, crestfallen and cockadroop.

Menopause Manor is not merely a defensive stronghold, however. It is a house or household, fully furnished with the necessities of life. In abandoning it, women have narrowed their domain and impoverished their souls. There are things the Old Woman can do, say, and think that the Woman cannot do, say, or think. The Woman has to give up more than her menstrual periods before she can do, say, or think them. She has got to change her life.

The nature of that change is now clearer than it used to be. Old age is not virginity but a third and new condition; the virgin must be celibate, but the crone need not. There was a confusion there, which the separation of female sexuality from reproductive capacity, via modern contraceptives, has cleared up. Loss of fertility does not mean loss of desire and fulfillment. But it does entail a change, a change involving matters even more important—if I may venture a heresy—than sex.

The woman who is willing to make that change must become pregnant with herself, at last. She must bear herself, her third self, her old age, with travail and alone. Not many will help her with that birth. Certainly no male obstetrician will time her contractions, inject her with sedatives, stand ready with forceps, and neatly stitch up the torn membranes. It's hard even to find an old-fashioned midwife, these days. That pregnancy is long, that labor is hard. Only one is harder, and that's the final one, the one that men also must suffer and perform.

It may well be easier to die if you have already given birth to others or yourself, at least once before. This would be an argument for going through all the discomfort and embarrassment of becoming a Crone. Anyhow it seems a pity to have a built-in rite of passage and to dodge it, evade it, and pretend nothing has changed. That is to dodge and evade one's womanhood, to pretend one's like a man. Men, once initiated, never get the second chance. They never change again. That's their loss, not ours. Why borrow poverty?

Certainly the effort to remain unchanged, young, when the body gives so impressive a signal of change as the menopause, is gallant; but it is a stupid, self-sacrificial gallantry, better befitting a boy of twenty than a woman of forty-five or fifty. Let the athletes die young and laurel-crowned. Let the soldiers earn the Purple Hearts. Let women die old, white-crowned, with human hearts.

If a space ship came by from the friendly natives of the fourth planet of Altair, and the police captain of the space ship said, "We have room for one passenger; will you spare us a single human being, so that we may converse at leisure during the long trip back to Altair and learn from an exemplary person the nature of the race?"—I suppose what most people would want to do is provide them with a fine, bright, brave young man, highly educated and in peak physical condition. A Russian cosmonaut would be ideal (American astronauts are mostly too old). There would surely be hundreds, thousands of volunteers, just such young men, all worthy. But I would not pick any of them. Nor would I pick any of the young women who would volunteer, some out of magnanimity and intellectual courage, others out of a profound conviction that Altair couldn't possibly be any worse for a woman than Earth is.

What I would do is go down to the local Woolworth's, or the

local village marketplace, and pick an old woman, over sixty, from behind the costume jewelry counter or the betel-nut booth. Her hair would not be red or blonde or lustrous dark, her skin would not be dewy fresh, she would not have the secret of eternal youth. She might, however, show you a small snapshot of her grandson, who is working in Nairobi. She is a bit vague about where Nairobi is, but extremely proud of the grandson. She has worked hard at small, unimportant jobs all her life, jobs like cooking, cleaning, bringing up kids, selling little objects of adornment or pleasure to other people. She was a virgin once, a long time ago, and then a sexually potent fertile female, and then went through menopause. She has given birth several times and faced death several times—the same times. She is facing the final birth/death a little more nearly and clearly every day now. Sometimes her feet hurt something terrible. She never was educated to anything like her capacity, and that is a shameful waste and a crime against humanity, but so common a crime should not and cannot be hidden from Altair. And anyhow she's not dumb. She has a stock of sense, wit, patience, and experiential shrewdness, which the Altaireans might, or might not, perceive as wisdom. If they are wiser than we, then of course we don't know how they'd perceive it. But if they are wiser than we, they may know how to perceive that inmost mind and heart which we, working on mere guess and hope, proclaim to be humane. In any case, since they are curious and kindly, let's give them the best we have to give.

The trouble is, she will be very reluctant to volunteer. "What would an old woman like me do on Altair?" she'll say. "You ought to send one of those scientist men, they can talk to those funny-looking green people. Maybe Dr. Kissinger should go. What about sending the Shaman?" It will be very hard to explain to her that we want her to go because only a person who has experienced, accepted, and acted the entire human condition—the essential quality of which is Change—can fairly represent humanity. "Me?" she'll say, just a trifle slyly. "But I never did anything."

But it won't wash. She knows, though she won't admit it, that Dr. Kissinger has not gone and will never go where she has gone, that the scientists and the shamans have not done what she has done. Into the space ship, Granny.

URSULA K. LE GUIN

Ursula K. Le Guin (b. 1929) is a distinguished writer who was born in California and graduated from Radcliffe and Columbia University. She has written many award-winning short stories, poems, and novels including *The*

Left Hand of Darkness, The Dispossessed, and *The Earthsea Trilogy,* a fantasy trio of novels intended for young people.

Father, Where Are You?

RUDY WIEBE

When I was a child, my parents were classic, western Canadians: immigrant homesteaders. With their children they were trying to build a livable farm out of a poplar-covered quarter section of land. The fact that they, as 1930 refugees from the Soviet Union, had to choose the stony bush near Turtle Lake, Saskatchewan, during a worldwide depression, made their work all the harder. I was the family baby and so had the privilege of watching the others without doing much myself, but as I grew older, one thing puzzled me. My father was rarely at home. And if he was, it was not for long.

A few early memories of him remain. Of him setting up a tent for us one summer evening because our log house—he and my two brothers built it, I was born in it—had to be fumigated with formaldehyde to kill the lice that kept moving in from the bush; father made an enormous fire from our lousy straw mattress that blazed up against the towering thunderheads and the dark house, its windows and log cracks and doors stuffed tight with grass. Of him walking so easily into the yard and beating a strange range bull, who had terrorized us all afternoon roaring about the yard, over the head with a poplar stick until the beast fled like a whipped cur. Of his beautiful tenor rising above all the men's voices behind me in our small church.

Lovely memories indeed; nevertheless, for most of my childhood he seemed to be missing. And it was in that very church where the most powerful image of my childhood was impressed upon me in every hymn, sermon, prayer, and Bible reading: God is our Father. Tenderly He cares for us, nurtures, teaches, comforts, but also punishes hard if necessary. When I began school, every day all 27 children together addressed Him, aloud, that father, and the prayer for me went far beyond word recitation into something powerfully searching: "Our Father, which art in heaven, Hallowed. . . ." In my child's mind the possible picture of "father" shifted, fluid as fish in the spring creeks. The questions "Where is he?" and "Where is He?" slid in and out of each other, wavered into one.

By the third grade, I had read a shortened version of *The Odyssey*. It begins with the boy Telemachus asking passing strangers whether in their travels they have seen his father, who left home 10 years ago. With such an absence, he says, "It is a wise child indeed that knows its own father."

Those famous words memorialize the profound mystery that has forever surrounded the facts of fatherhood. The facts of motherhood are plain: this is the child that she carried within herself, to which she gave birth at such a time and in such a place, and which she now feeds. The facts of fatherhood, however, seem not to exist. The instant of begetting is unknown to anyone; the begotten child grows hidden in the mother's body, and the man (the father?) can at best be an attentive watcher at its birth.

In my case, as a child I had no sense of a mother or a father's activities before my birth because I was taught unambiguously that children were "a gift from God." I never made any connection between the farm births of animals and the appearance of new babies in our small community where everyone came to church on Sunday. Animals gave birth, sometimes in a bloody, horrible mess as I once saw my brother pull a calf from a cow, but children were a divine gift; rocking me against her warm, huggable body, my mother told me that again and again. I was told nothing about human sexual behavior, certainly never stumbled on any, and, as the youngest in the family, I never saw my mother grow pregnant. For all I could imagine, babies arrived all pink-faced from God up in Heaven, beautifully wrapped in their Sunday cap and blankets exactly the way they were carried in their mothers' arms into the church babyroom.

HAVE WE NOT ALL ONE FATHER? HATH NOT ONE GOD CREATED US?
MALACHI 2:10

A mother (my mother) was a mother because she was always there, caring for her child (me) and never once leaving home (as I did not). A mother was someone who, as I discovered with amazement from a nursing woman who lived nearby, could unbutton the top of her dress and silence her screaming baby by holding it against her bare skin, which bulged there like some marvellous, glowing fruit. And answer your staring question with complete calm:

"He was hungry, and so he's eating."

"What's he eating?"

"Milk."

And when you ask, ever more astonished, "Where's it from?" can answer, "Me, it comes from me." And show you a milky nipple to prove it.

Which of course makes perfect sense, since your mother is always feeding you too, though in different ways. And when you ask her about this strange arrangement Mrs. ——— has for feeding her baby, she explains that's the way all infants are fed, but that you're too big, you already have teeth to chew potatoes and meat and can sit in a chair at the table and drink the milk warm from cows.

O, as a child I understood what a mother was very well; she displayed most of the characteristics ascribed to God. So what was a father?

The Second World War was being fought then, and it provided for many missing fathers. Mine was not one of them. The world war he had fought was the first of this century, not as a military combatant but as a conscientious objector. The Czar allowed Russian Mennonites an extended term of alternative service (usually hospital or forestry work) in lieu of compulsory military training, but in 1914 my father was barely home from three years of that when the Great War broke out and he was conscripted again. He spent another three years in the forests of Siberia until the Russian government fell; in the resulting chaos of civil war, he disguised himself in a soldier's uniform and rode freight trains back to his home village. By 1940, after 10 years in Canada, he was too old for so understandable a form of "missing" as military service, even if he had accepted it. Which I know now he never would have.

I know now, and knew even then, the ostensible reason for his being away so much. He was "working out," as we called it. In the spring, he would clamber over the wooden planks of one of those tall, square-cabbed trucks, vintage 1928, to breathe dust 300 gravel miles to Swift Current, Saskatchewan, or 400 to Nemiskam, Alberta, where the big farmers hired laborers for their huge War Effort crops. By the middle of summer, he would be working his way north with the harvest, pitching bundles onto the hayracks (field pitcher: the toughest job on the crew) for hauling to the giant threshing machines, and as he approached home he would sometimes return for a Sunday and leave immediately after with his own rack and team (he could earn up to $3.50 a day that way). Eventually the enormous steam tractor, blasting woodsmoke, would drag the threshing machine into our yard and manoeuvre it against our granary. If he had threshed long enough, he would have earned the price of threshing our own small crop. It seemed our bush clearing was always the last on that long harvesting trail north, a circumstance about which my mother complained bitterly as rain and then snow increased.

But with that late return, my father would remain home only until the winter settled in; by early November he would harness our two best horses to the heaviest working sleigh, heap it with hay and oat bundles, and drive north to the sawmills near Paradise Hill, or even as far as Cold Lake, Alberta. He would skid logs out of the bush with the team, and always be home for Christmas, but after New Year's he would be gone again to the mills if there was any work; during the war there always was.

> I THINK A CHILD SHOULD BE ALLOWED TO TAKE HIS FATHER'S OR HIS MOTHER'S NAME AT WILL ON COMING OF AGE. PATERNITY IS A LEGAL FICTION.
> JAMES JOYCE. LETTER. 18 SEPTEMBER, 1905

My mother and brother (beginning in his teens) farmed our homestead, and I have since learned that my father worked away from home so much not only to earn money to keep that bush farm barely alive. Nor was he lazy, far from it; he was physically very strong and he worked longer, harder, than anyone I have ever known. But long ago my mother told me he hired out because he was a man who did not make good decisions. This was not only so in Canada, she said; it had been that way in Russia too. It seemed he could not anticipate, seemed unable to foresee consequences. He worked tirelessly at the most thankless jobs, but though he knew a great deal about farming, he could not make the myriad, small decisions necessary to build up a marginal farm in Canada. He worked best when told what to do. He was not, it seems, a leader.

Many, perhaps most, men aren't. And why the elementary physical ability of being able to impregnate a woman, why a momentary sexual spasm of uncertain time and always unknown effectiveness, should, somehow, direct the qualities of human leadership toward the male remains an unfathomed mystery to me. In our family our mother was the leader; we all knew that. The Judeo-Christian teaching of God as Father, man as head, made little sense in my family. God always away? God told what to do and doing it? We were biblically wrong, all upside down or inside out, reversed, faintly freaks.

For me this was a private matter, and I would no more have admitted it than go about naked in public. But I longed to be "normal," as I believed other families to be, and what concerns me now is the contradictory understanding of "father" I grew up with. It was not my father who guided me into the great mysteries of life. Death? The whole community gathered together for the arrival of death. Since before I can remember, I saw the profiled bodies of people I had known alive lying uncovered on the steps of the church, a surround of relatives weeping about the coffin while someone took pictures that I would see above the family table when we went there to visit. Sex? I was to eventually have my nose (as it were) rubbed into the mechanics of human sex through the conjunction of a giant stallion, the mare I usually rode to school, and a snickering neighbor boy somewhat older than myself. The mechanical facts as presented to my eight-year-old eyes seemed to me so savagely brutal that for as long as I could I refused to believe them; the humane facts, of course, required more time than that.

My father did not punish me; he was absent too much, and my mother did not trust him not to overdo it when he was present. Nor did he advise me about my life's work. True, his example taught me the value of hard physical work, especially after we left the homestead in Saskatchewan to my brother and moved to a small town in Alberta where he worked for the rest of his life as a farm laborer. But he could tell me nothing about growing up in Canada; he was over 40 when he arrived here and never understood more than the most minimal of spoken English.

> YOU MUST DEAL WITH THE MEMORY OF A FATHER. OFTEN THE
> MEMORY IS MORE POTENT THAN THE LIVING PRESENCE, IS AN
> INNER VOICE COMMANDING. . . . AT WHAT POINT DO YOU
> BECOME YOURSELF? NEVER, WHOLLY, YOU ARE ALWAYS PARTLY
> HIM.
>
> DONALD BARTHELME, THE DEAD FATHER

Such a gulf between father and child is, I believe, no longer unique to immigrants; most families experience it today. The technological revolution has made much of men's traditional work obsolete; more importantly, the social revolution of personal and racial rights, women's rights, and individual moral value has, I believe, made implausible our traditional Judeo-Christian patterns of authority.

Whether we know it or not, for most western men the problem is this: because we can no longer say in the traditional Judeo-Christian way, "This is what God says. Now do it," therefore men also can no longer say, "This is what I (the father, the man) say. Now do it." How can a father establish his role today?

As far as I can see, there is nothing inherent in the male that would give him primacy over the human race. In fact, his momentary and invisible role before birth, his secondary role after (he can at best feed the mother who must feed the child), makes him naturally subordinate to the female. Brute strength alone cannot, I believe, confirm his dominance with humanity, any more than can the early

Jewish idea of fatherhood, based on Yahweh, a sort of perfect Middle Eastern desert patriarch. It seems to me that no thoughtful man facing the 1990s can believe in such an image of himself as "father". Such a certain male confidence is today a fatal delusion. The ideas of "a self-evident, worldwide male superiority", of "my belief (or race, or nation) is stronger than yours and I'll kill you to prove it": such traditional male western thinking can no longer hold our fragile, entangled global humanity together. Probably not even until the twenty-first century.

> MY FATHER IS GATHERED TO HIS FATHERS,
> GOD REST HIS WRAITH!
> AND HIS SON
> IS A PAUPER IN SPIRIT, A BEGGAR IN PIETY,
> CUT OFF WITHOUT A PENNY'S WORTH OF FAITH.
>
> A.M. KLEIN,
> "CHILDE HAROLD'S PILGRIMAGE"

Which returns me to my original question: "Father, where are you?" The cemetery where his body was buried 14 years ago tells me nothing, but perhaps my memories of him, filtered now through my own sometimes sad 30-year experience as a father, can discover a little.

Unlike the God I heard thunder (with the voices of men only) in church, my father never gave me specific instructions. On the other hand, despite the disasters of his life, he lived his 86 years with a humble grace I think about more and more. For him there was work: whatever you must do (he rarely had any choice), no matter how miserable, you did it as well as you possibly could. There was also life: you killed animals for the necessity of food, but otherwise life was sacred. I never saw him touch a gun; he did not want one in the house, because "A gun can do only one thing."

Finally, for him there was faith: faith in the God revealed in the German Bible, which he studied with absolute devotion, and faith in his family. He was anchored by and, especially in later life, anchored in turn my mother; together they lived through 61 years. And he believed in his children.

For example, he was amazed that I, the child of peasants, should be successful at university. He could not read my writing (it was all English to him), but when my first novel, *Peace Shall Destroy Many*, highly critical of the patriarchal Mennonite community, caused a Canada-wide controversy in the church, he defied the preachers and supported me. He laughed with delight that a child of his could create such an uproar among all those "big men," as he called them, and he never doubted that I had written a "good book."

It seems to be that physical birth itself establishes a woman's primary claim as "mother." What kind of a mother she becomes, of course, is defined by her continuing life with or without the child she has borne, but the almost total irrelevance of the man in that very birthing gives him no such irrefutable beginning. He can only begin and must continue to prove himself "fatherly" by the way he lives. When I now look at pictures of my ageing father, I see a resolute, determined, occasionally intense, and almost defiant face, characteristics that, as a child, I do not remember seeing.

It cannot be the defiance of autocratic, patriarchal command, because none of his children experienced his life that way. It can, I think, only be the resolute defiance of a humble life lived, despite great difficulties, with some firm, certain convictions he never tried to force on anyone, not even his own children. It seems to me now that he was a very good father to have had in the twentieth century. Perhaps even for the twenty-first.

RUDY WIEBE

Rudy Wiebe (b. 1934) comes from a Saskatchewan Mennonite family. He is a professor of English at the University of Alberta in Edmonton. Among his many published works are the novels *The Mad Trapper* (1980) and *My Lovely Enemy* (1983).

Politics and the English Language

GEORGE ORWELL

ost people who bother with the matter at all would admit that the English language is in a bad way, but it is generally assumed that we cannot by conscious action do anything about it. Our civilization is decadent and our language—so the argument runs—must inevitably share in the general collapse. It follows that any struggle against the abuse of language is a senti-

"Politics and the English Language" from *Shooting an Elephant and Other Essays* by George Orwell. Copyright 1950, 1978. Reprinted with the permission of A.M. Heath & Company Limited on behalf of the estate of the late Sonia Brownell Orwell and Secker and Warburg Limited.

mental archaism, like preferring candles to electric light or hansom cabs to aeroplanes. Underneath this lies the half-conscious belief that language is a natural growth and not an instrument which we shape for our own purpose.

Now, it is clear that the decline of a language must ultimately have political and economic causes: it is not due simply to the bad influence of this or that individual writer. But an effect can become a cause, reinforcing the original cause and producing the same effect in an intensified form, and so on indefinitely. A man may take to drink because he feels himself to be a failure, and then fail all the more completely because he drinks. It is rather the same thing that is happening to the English language. It becomes ugly and inaccurate because our thoughts are foolish, but the slovenliness of our language makes it easier for us to have foolish thoughts. The point is that the process is reversible. Modern English, especially written English, is full of bad habits which spread by imitation and which can be avoided if one is willing to take the necessary trouble. If one gets rid of these habits one can think more clearly, and to think clearly is a necessary first step towards political regeneration: so that the fight against bad English is not frivolous and is not the exclusive concern of professional writers. I will come back to this presently, and I hope that by that time the meaning of what I have said here will have become clearer. Meanwhile, here are five specimens of the English language as it is now habitually written.

These five passages have not been picked out because they are especially bad—I could have quoted far worse if I had chosen—but because they illustrate various of the mental vices from which we now suffer. They are a little below the average, but are fairly representative samples. I number them so that I can refer back to them when necessary:

(1) I am not, indeed, sure whether it is not true to say that the Milton who once seemed not unlike a seventeenth-century Shelley had not become, out of an experience ever more bitter in each year, more alien [sic] to the founder of that Jesuit sect which nothing could induce him to tolerate.

Professor Harold Laski (Essay in *Freedom of Expression*)

(2) Above all, we cannot play ducks and drakes with a native battery of idioms which prescribes such egregious collocations of vocables as the Basic *put up with* for *tolerate* or *put at a loss* for *bewilder*.

Professor Lancelot Hogben (*Interglossa*)

(3) On the one side we have the free personality: by definition it is not neurotic, for it has neither conflict nor dream. Its desires, such as they are, are transparent, for they are just what institutional approval keeps in the forefront of consciousness; another institutional pattern would alter their

number and intensity; there is little in them that is natural, irreducible, or culturally dangerous. But *on the other side*, the social bond itself is nothing but the mutual reflection of these self-secure integrities. Recall the definition of love. Is not this the very picture of a small academic? Where is there a place in this hall of mirrors for either personality or fraternity?

Essay on psychology in *Politics* (New York)

(4) All the "best people" from the gentlemen's clubs, and all the frantic fascist captains, united in common hatred of Socialism and bestial horror of the rising tide of the mass revolutionary movement, have turned to acts of provocation, to foul incendiarism, to medieval legends of poisoned wells, to legalize their own destruction of proletarian organizations, and rouse the agitated petty-bourgeoisie to chauvinistic fervor on behalf of the fight against the revolutionary way out of the crisis.

Communist pamphlet

(5) If a new spirit *is* to be infused into this old country, there is one thorny and contentious reform which must be tackled, and that is the humanization and galvanization of the B.B.C. Timidity here will bespeak cancer and atrophy of the soul. The heart of Britain may be sound and of strong beat, for instance, but the British lion's roar at present is like that of Bottom in Shakespeare's *Midsummer Night's Dream*—as gentle as any sucking dove. A virile new Britain cannot continue indefinitely to be traduced in the eyes or rather ears, of the world by the effete languors of Langham Place, brazenly masquerading as "standard English." When the Voice of Britain is heard at nine o'clock, better far and infinitely less ludicrous to hear aitches honestly dropped than the present priggish, inflated, inhibited, school-ma'amish arch braying of blameless bashful mewing maidens!

Letter in *Tribune*

Each of these passages has faults of its own, but, quite apart from avoidable ugliness, two qualities are common to all of them. The first is staleness of imagery; the other is lack of precision. The writer either has a meaning and cannot express it, or he inadvertently says something else, or he is almost indifferent as to whether his words mean anything or not. The mixture of vagueness and sheer incompetence is the most marked characteristic of modern English prose, and especially of any kind of political writing. As soon as certain topics are raised, the concrete melts into the abstract and no one seems to think of turns of speech that are not hackneyed: prose consists less and less of *words* chosen for the sake of their meaning, and more and more of *phrases* tacked together like the sections of a prefabricated henhouse. I list below, with notes and examples, various of the tricks by means of which the work of prose-construction is habitually dodged:

Dying Metaphors

A newly invented metaphor assists thought by evoking a visual image, while on the other hand a metaphor which is technically "dead" (e.g., *iron resolution*) has in effect reverted to being an ordinary word and can generally be used without loss of vividness. But in between these two classes there is a huge dump of worn-out metaphors which have lost all evocative power and are merely used because they save people the trouble of inventing phrases for themselves. Examples are: *ring the changes on, take up the cudgels for, toe the line, ride roughshod over, stand shoulder to shoulder with, play into the hands of, no axe to grind, grist to the mill, fishing in troubled waters, rift within the lute, on the order of the day, Achilles' heel, swan song, hotbed.* Many of these are used without knowledge of their meaning (what is a "rift," for instance?), and incompatible metaphors are frequently mixed, a sure sign that the writer is not interested in what he is saying. Some metaphors now current have been twisted out of their original meaning without those who use them even being aware of the fact. For example, *toe the line* is sometimes written *tow the line.* Another example is *the hammer and the anvil,* now always used with the implication that the anvil gets the worst of it. In real life it is always the anvil that breaks the hammer, never the other way about: a writer who stopped to think what he was saying would be aware of this, and would avoid perverting the original phrase.

Operators or Verbal False Limbs

These save the trouble of picking out appropriate verbs and nouns, and at the same time pad each sentence with extra syllables which give it an appearance of symmetry. Characteristic phrases are: *render inoperative, militate against, make contact with, be subjected to, give rise to, give grounds for, have the effect of, play a leading part (role) in, make itself felt, take effect, exhibit a tendency to, serve the purpose of,* etc., etc. The keynote is the elimination of simple verbs. Instead of being a single word, such as *break, stop, spoil, mend, kill,* a verb becomes a *phrase,* made up of a noun or adjective tacked on to some general-purpose verb such as *prove, serve, form, play, render.* In addition, the passive voice is wherever possible used in preference to the active, and noun constructions are used instead of gerunds (*by examination of* instead of *by examining*). The range of verbs is further cut down by means of the *-ize* and *de-* formation, and the banal statements are given an appearance of profundity by means of the *not un-* formation. Simple conjunctions and prepositions are replaced by such phrases as *with respect to, having regard to, the fact that, by dint of, in view of, in the interests of, on the hypothesis that;* and the ends of sentences are saved from anticlimax by such resounding common-places as *greatly to be desired, cannot be left out of account, a development to be expected in the near future, deserving of serious consideration, brought to a satisfactory conclusion,* and so on and so forth.

Pretentious Diction

Words like *phenomenon, element, individual* (as noun), *objective, categorical, effective, virtual, basic, primary, promote, constitute, exhibit, exploit, utilize, eliminate, liquidate,* are used to dress up simple statements and give an air of scientific impartiality to biased judgments. Adjectives like *epoch-making, epic, historic, unforgettable, triumphant, age-old, inevitable, inexorable, veritable,* are used to dignify the sordid processes of international politics, while writing that aims at glorifying war usually takes on an archaic color, its characteristic words being: *realm, throne, chariot, mailed fist, trident, sword, shield, buckler, banner, jackboot, clarion.* Foreign words and expressions such as *cul de sac, ancien régime, deus ex machina, mutatis mutandis, status quo, gleichschaltung, weltanschauung,* are used to give an air of culture and elegance. Except for the useful abbreviations *i.e., e.g.,* and *etc.,* there is no real need for any of the hundreds of foreign phrases now current in English. Bad writers, and especially scientific, political and sociological writers, are nearly always haunted by the notion that Latin or Greek words are grander than Saxon ones, and unnecessary words like *expedite, ameliorate, predict, extraneous, deracinated, clandestine, subaqueous* and hundreds of others constantly gain ground from their Anglo-Saxon opposite numbers.[1] The jargon peculiar to Marxist writing (*hyena, hangman, cannibal, petty bourgeois, these gentry, lackey, flunkey, mad dog, White Guard,* etc.) consists largely of words and phrases translated from Russian, German, or French; but the normal way of coining a new word is to use a Latin or Greek root with the appropriate affix and, where necessary, the *-ize* formation. It is often easier to make up words of this kind (*deregionalize, impermissible, extramarital, nonfragmentatory* and so forth) than to think up the English words that will cover one's meaning. The result, in general, is an increase in slovenliness and vagueness.

---

[1]An interesting illustration of this is the way in which the English flower names which were in use till very recently are being ousted by Greek ones, *snapdragon* becoming *antirrhinum, forget-me-not* becoming *myosotis,* etc. It is hard to see any practical reason for this change of fashion: it is probably due to an instinctive turning-away from the more homely word and a vague feeling that the Greek word is scientific.

Meaningless Words

In certain kinds of writing, particularly in art criticism and literary criticism, it is normal to come across long passages which are almost completely lacking in meaning.[2] Words like *romantic, plastic, values, human, dead, sentimental, natural, vitality*, as used in art criticism, are strictly meaningless in the sense that they not only do not point to any discoverable object, but are hardly ever expected to do so by the reader. When one critic writes, "The outstanding feature of Mr. X's work is its living quality," while another writes, "The immediately striking thing about Mr. X's work is its peculiar deadness," the reader accepts this as a simple difference of opinion. If words like *black* and *white* were involved, instead of the jargon words *dead* and *living*, he would see at once that language was being used in an improper way. Many political words are similarly abused. The word *Fascism* has now no meaning except in so far as it signifies "something not desirable." The words *democracy, socialism, freedom, patriotic, realistic, justice*, have each of them several different meanings which cannot be reconciled with one another. In the case of a word like *democracy*, not only is there no agreed definition, but the attempt to make one is resisted from all sides. It is almost universally felt that when we call a country democratic we are praising it: consequently the defenders of every kind of régime claim that it is a democracy, and fear that they might have to stop using the word if it were tied down to any one meaning. Words of this kind are often used in a consciously dishonest way. That is, the person who uses them has his own private definition, but allows his hearer to think he means something quite different. Statements like *Marshal Pétain was a true patriot, The Soviet Press is the freest in the world, The Catholic Church is opposed to persecution*, are almost always made with intent to deceive. Other words used in variable meanings, in most cases more or less dishonestly, are: *class, totalitarian, science, progressive, reactionary, bourgeois, equality*.

Now that I have made this catalogue of swindles and perversions, let me give another example of the kind of writing that they lead to. This time it must of its nature be an imaginary one. I am going to translate a passage of good English into modern English of the worst sort. Here is a well-known verse from *Ecclesiastes*:

---

[2]Example: "Comfort's catholicity of perception and image, strangely Whitmanesque in range, almost the exact opposite in aesthetic compulsion, continues to evoke that trembling atmospheric accumulative hinting at a cruel, an inexorably serene timelessness. . . . Wrey Gardiner scores by aiming at simple bull's-eyes with precision. Only they are not so simple, and through this contented sadness runs more than the surface bitter-sweet of resignation." (*Poetry Quarterly*)

I returned and saw under the sun, that the race is not to the swift, nor the battle to the strong, neither yet bread to the wise, nor yet riches to men of understanding, nor yet favour to men of skill; but time and chance happeneth to them all.

Here it is in modern English:

Objective consideration of contemporary phenomena compels the conclusion that success or failure in competitive activities exhibits no tendency to be commensurate with innate capacity, but that a considerable element of the unpredictable must invariably be taken into account.

This is a parody, but not a very gross one. Exhibit (3), above, for instance, contains several patches of the same kind of English. It will be seen that I have not made a full translation. The beginning and ending of the sentence follow the original meaning fairly closely, but in the middle the concrete illustrations—race, battle, bread—dissolve into the vague phrase "success or failure in competitive activities." This had to be so, because no modern writer of the kind I am discussing—no one capable of using phrases like "objective consideration of contemporary phenomena"—would ever tabulate his thoughts in that precise and detailed way. The whole tendency of modern prose is away from concreteness. Now analyze these two sentences a little more closely. The first contains forty-nine words but only sixty syllables, and all its words are those of everyday life. The second contains thirty-eight words of ninety syllables: eighteen of its words are from Latin roots, and one from Greek. The first sentence contains six vivid images, and only one phrase ("time and chance") that could be called vague. The second contains not a single fresh, arresting phrase, and in spite of its ninety syllables it gives only a shortened version of the meaning contained in the first. Yet without a doubt it is the second kind of sentence that is gaining ground in modern English. I do not want to exaggerate. This kind of writing is not yet universal, and outcrops of simplicity will occur here and there in the worst-written page. Still, if you or I were told to write a few lines on the uncertainty of human fortunes, we should probably come much nearer to my imaginary sentence than to the one from *Ecclesiastes*.

As I have tried to show, modern writing at its worst does not consist in picking out words for the sake of their meaning and inventing images in order to make the meaning clearer. It consists in gumming together long strips of words which have already been set in order by someone else, and making the results presentable by sheer humbug. The attraction of this way of writing is that it is easy. It is easier—even quicker once you have the habit—to say *In my opinion it is a not unjustifiable assumption that* than to say *I think.* If you use ready-made phrases, you not only don't have to hunt about for words; you also don't have to bother with the rhythms of your sentences, since these phrases are generally so arranged as to be more or less euphonious. When you are composing in a hurry— when you are dictating to a stenographer, for instance, or making a public speech—it is natural to fall into a pretentious, Latinized style. Tags like *a consideration which we should do well to bear in mind* or *a conclusion to which all of us would readily assent* will save many a sentence from coming down with a bump. By using stale metaphors, similes and idioms, you save much mental effort, at the cost of leaving your meaning vague, not only for your reader but for your-self. This is the significance of mixed metaphors. The sole aim of a metaphor is to call up a visual image. When these images clash—as in *The Fascist Octopus has sung its swan song, the jackboot is thrown into the melting pot*—it can be taken as certain that the writer is not seeing a mental image of the objects he is naming; in other words he is not really thinking. Look again at the examples I gave at the beginning of this essay. Professor Laski (1) uses five negatives in fifty-three words. One of these is superfluous, making nonsense of the whole passage, and in addition there is the slip *alien* for *akin*, making further nonsense, and several avoidable pieces of clumsiness which increase the general vagueness. Professor Hogben (2) plays ducks and drakes with a battery which is able to write prescriptions, and, while disap-proving of the everyday phrase *put up with*, is unwilling to look *egregious* up in the dictionary and see what it means. (3), if one takes an uncharitable attitude towards it, is simply meaningless: probably one could work out its intended meaning by reading the whole of the article in which it occurs. In (4), the writer knows more or less what he wants to say, but an accumulation of stale phrases chokes him like tea leaves blocking a sink. In (5), words and meaning have almost parted company. People who write in this manner usually have a general emotional meaning—they dislike one thing and want to express solidarity with another—but they are not interested in the detail of what they are saying. A scrupulous writer, in every sentence that he writes, will ask himself at least four questions, thus: What am I trying to say? What words will express it? What image or idiom will make it clearer? Is this image fresh enough to have an effect? And he will probably ask himself two more: Could I put it more shortly? Have I said anything that is avoidably ugly? But you are not obliged to go to all this trouble. You can shirk it by simply throwing your mind open and letting the ready-made phrases come crowding in. They will construct your sentences for you—even think your thoughts for you, to a certain extent—and at need they will perform the important service of partially concealing your meaning even from yourself. It is at this point that the special connection between politics and the debasement of language becomes clear.

In our times it is broadly true that political writing is bad writing. Where it is not true, it will generally be found that the writer is some kind of rebel, expressing his private opinions and not a "party line." Orthodoxy, of whatever color, seems to demand a lifeless, imitative style. The political dialects to be found in pamphlets, leading articles, manifestos, White Papers and the speeches of under-secretaries do, of course, vary from party to party, but they are all alike in that one almost never finds in them a fresh, vivid, home-made turn of speech. When one watches some tired hack on the platform mechanically repeating the familiar phrases—*bestial atrocities, iron heel, bloodstained tyranny, free peoples of the world, stand shoulder to shoulder*—one often has a curious feeling that one is not watching a live human being but some kind of dummy, a feeling which suddenly becomes stronger at moments when the light catches the speaker's spectacles and turns them into blank discs which seem to have no eyes behind them. And this is not altogether fanciful. A speaker who uses that kind of phraseology has gone some distance towards turning himself into a machine. The appropriate noises are coming out of his larynx, but his brain is not involved as it would be if he were choosing his words from himself. If the speech he is making is one that he is accustomed to make over and over again, he may be almost unconscious of what he is saying, as one is when one utters the responses in church. And this reduced state of consciousness, if not indispensable, is at any rate favorable to political conformity.

In our time, political speech and writing are largely the defense of the indefensible. Things like the continuance of British rule in India, the Russian purges and deportations, the dropping of the atom bombs on Japan, can indeed be defended, but only by arguments which are too brutal for most people to face, and which do not square with the professed aims of political parties. Thus political language has to consist largely of euphemism, question-begging and sheer cloudy vagueness. Defenseless villages are bombarded from the air, the inhabitants driven out into the countryside, the cattle machine-gunned, the huts set on fire with incendiary bullets: this is called *pacification*. Millions of peasants are robbed of their farms and sent trudging along the roads with no more than they can carry: this is called *transfer of population* or *rectification of frontiers*. People are imprisoned for years without trial, or shot in the back of the neck or sent to die of scurvy in Arctic lumber camps: this is called *elimination of unreliable elements*. Such phraseology is needed if one wants to name things without calling up mental pictures of them. Consider for instance some comfortable English professor defending

Russian totalitarianism. He cannot say outright, "I believe in killing off your opponents when you can get good results by doing so." Probably, therefore, he will say something like this:

"While freely conceding that the Soviet régime exhibits certain features which the humanitarian may be inclined to deplore, we must, I think, agree that a certain curtailment of the right to political opposition is an unavoidable concomitant of transitional periods, and that the rigors which the Russian people have been called upon to undergo have been amply justified in the sphere of concrete achievement."

The inflated style is itself a kind of euphemism. A mass of Latin words falls upon the facts like soft snow, blurring the outlines and covering up all the details. The great enemy of clear language is insincerity. When there is a gap between one's real and one's declared aims, one turns as it were instinctively to long words and exhausted idioms, like a cuttlefish squirting out ink. In our age there is no such thing as "keeping out of politics." All issues are political issues, and politics itself is a mass of lies, evasions, folly, hatred and schizophrenia. When the general atmosphere is bad, language must suffer. I should expect to find—this is a guess which I have not sufficient knowledge to verify—that the German, Russian and Italian languages have all deteriorated in the last ten or fifteen years, as a result of dictatorship.

But if thought corrupts language, language can also corrupt thought. A bad usage can spread by tradition and imitation, even among people who should and do know better. The debased language that I have been discussing is in some ways very convenient. Phrases like *a not unjustifiable assumption, leaves much to be desired, would serve no good purpose, a consideration which we should do well to bear in mind*, are a continuous temptation, a packet of aspirins always at one's elbow. Look back through this essay, and for certain you will find that I have again and again committed the very faults I am protesting against. By this morning's post I have received a pamphlet dealing with conditions in Germany. The author tells me that he "felt impelled" to write it. I open it at random, and here is almost the first sentence that I see: "(The Allies) have an opportunity not only of achieving a radical transformation of Germany's social and political structure in such a way as to avoid a nationalistic reaction in Germany itself, but at the same time of laying the foundations of a co-operative and unified Europe." You see, he "feels impelled" to write—feels, presumably, that he has something new to say—and yet his words, like cavalry horses answering the bugle, group themselves automatically into the familiar dreary pattern. This invasion of one's mind by ready-made phrases (*lay the foundations, achieve a radical transformation*) can only be prevented if one is constantly on guard against them, and every such phrase anaesthetizes a portion of one's brain.

I said earlier that the decadence of our language is probably curable. Those who deny this would argue, if they produced an argument at all, that language merely reflects existing social conditions, and that we cannot influence its development by any direct tinkering with words and constructions. So far as the general tone or spirit of a language goes, this may be true, but it is not true in detail. Silly words and expressions have often disappeared, not through any evolutionary process but owing to the conscious action of a minority. Two recent examples were *explore every avenue* and *leave no stone unturned*, which were killed by the jeers of a few journalists. There is a long list of flyblown metaphors which could similarly be got rid of if enough people would interest themselves in the job; and it should also be possible to laugh the *not un-* formation out of existence,[3] to reduce the amount of Latin and Greek in the average sentence, to drive out foreign phrases and strayed scientific words, and, in general, to make pretentiousness unfashionable. But all these are minor points. The defense of the English language implies more than this, and perhaps it is best to start by saying what it does *not* imply.

To begin with it has nothing to do with archaism, with the salvaging of obsolete words and turns of speech, or with the setting up of a "standard English" which must never be departed from. On the contrary, it is especially concerned with the scrapping of every word or idiom which has outworn its usefulness. It has nothing to do with correct grammar and syntax, which are of no importance so long as one makes one's meaning clear, or with the avoidance of Americanisms, or with having what is called a "good prose style." On the other hand, it is not concerned with fake simplicity and the attempt to make written English colloquial. Nor does it even imply in every case preferring the Saxon word to the Latin one, though it does imply using the fewest and shortest words that will cover one's meaning. What is above all needed is to let the meaning choose the word, and not the other way about. In prose, the worst thing one can do with words is to surrender to them. When you think of a concrete object, you think wordlessly, and then, if you want to describe the thing you have been visualizing you probably hunt about till you find the exact words that seem to fit. When you think of something abstract, you are more inclined to use words from the start, and unless you make a conscious effort to prevent it, the existing dialect will come rushing in and do the job for you, at the

---

[3] One can cure oneself of the *not un-* formation by memorizing this sentence: *A not unblack dog was chasing a not unsmall rabbit across a not ungreen field.*

expense of blurring or even changing your meaning. Probably it is better to put off using words as long as possible and get one's meaning as clear as one can through pictures or sensations. Afterwards one can choose—not simply *accept*—the phrases that will best cover the meaning, and then switch round and decide what impression one's words are likely to make on another person. This last effort of the mind cuts out all stale or mixed images, all prefabricated phrases, needless repetitions, and humbug and vagueness generally. But one can often be in doubt about the effect of a word or a phrase, and one needs rules that one can rely on when instinct fails. I think the following rules will cover most cases:

(i) Never use a metaphor, simile or other figure of speech which you are used to seeing in print.
(ii) Never use a long word where a short one will do.
(iii) If it is possible to cut a word out, always cut it out.
(iv) Never use the passive where you can use the active.
(v) Never use a foreign phrase, a scientific word or jargon word if you can think of an everyday English equivalent.
(vi) Break any of these rules sooner than say anything outright barbarous.

These rules sound elementary, and so they are, but they demand a deep change in attitude in anyone who has grown used to writing in the style now fashionable. One could keep all of them and still write bad English, but one could not write the kind of stuff that I quoted in those five specimens at the beginning of this article.

I have not here been considering the literary use of language, but merely language as an instrument for expressing and not for concealing or preventing thought. Stuart Chase and others have come near to claiming that all abstract words are meaningless, and have used this as a pretext for advocating a kind of political quietism. Since you don't know what Fascism is, how can you struggle against Fascism? One need not swallow such absurdities as this, but one ought to recognize that the present political chaos is connected with the decay of language, and that one can probably bring about some improvement by starting at the verbal end. If you simplify your English, you are freed from the worst follies of orthodoxy. You cannot speak any of the necessary dialects, and when you make a stupid remark, its stupidity will be obvious, even to yourself. Political language—and with variations this is true of all political parties, from Conservatives to Anarchists—is designed to make lies sound truthful and murder respectable, and to give an appearance of solidity to pure wind. One cannot change this all in a moment, but one can at least change one's own habits, and from time to time one can even, if one jeers loudly enough, send some worn-out and useless phrase—some *jackboot, Achilles' heel, hotbed, melting pot, acid test, veritable inferno* or other lump of verbal refuse—into the dustbin where it belongs.

GEORGE ORWELL

George Orwell (1903–1950), the essayist and novelist, was born in India and died in London. He was a critic of colonialism and an advocate of clear thinking and writing. His two famous works of fiction are *Animal Farm* and *Nineteen Eighty-Four*. Also highly readable are such autobiographical books as *Down and Out in Paris and London* and *The Road to Wigan Pier*.

A Modest Proposal . . .

JONATHAN SWIFT

It is a melancholy object to those who walk through this great town[1] or travel in the country, when they see the streets, the roads, and cabin doors, crowded with beggars of the female sex, followed by three, four, or six children, all in rags and importuning every passenger for an alms. These mothers, instead of being able to work for their honest livelihood, are forced to employ all their time in strolling to beg sustenance for their helpless infants, who, as they grow up, either turn thieves for want of work, or leave their dear native country to fight for the Pretender in Spain, or sell themselves to the Barbadoes.

I think it is agreed by all parties that this prodigious number of children in the arms, or on the backs, or at the heels of their mothers, and frequently of their fathers, is in the present deplorable state of the kingdom a very great additional grievance; and therefore whoever could find out a fair, cheap, and easy method of making these children sound, useful members of the commonwealth would deserve so well of the public as to have his statue set up for a preserver of the nation.

But my intention is very far from being confined to provide only for the children of professed beggars; it is of a much greater extent, and shall take in the whole number of infants at a certain age who

[1]Dublin, 1729.

are born of parents in effect as little able to support them as those who demand our charity in the streets.

As to my own part, having turned my thoughts for many years upon this important subject, and maturely weighed the several schemes of other projectors, I have always found them grossly mistaken in their computation. It is true, a child just dropped from its dam may be supported by her milk for a solar year, with little other nourishment; at most not above the value of two shillings, which the mother may certainly get, or the value in scraps, by her lawful occupation of begging; and it is exactly at one year old that I propose to provide for them in such a manner as instead of being a charge upon their parents or the parish, or wanting food and raiment for the rest of their lives, they shall on the contrary contribute to the feeding, and partly to the clothing, of many thousands.

There is likewise another great advantage in my scheme, that it will prevent those voluntary abortions, and that horrid practice of women murdering their bastard children, alas, too frequent among us, sacrificing the poor innocent babes, I doubt, more to avoid the expense than the shame, which would move tears and pity in the most savage and inhuman breast.

The number of souls in this kingdom being usually reckoned one million and a half, of these I calculate there may be about two hundred thousand couples whose wives are breeders; from which number I subtract thirty thousand couples who are able to maintain their own children, although I apprehend there cannot be so many under the present distresses of the kingdom; but this being granted, there will remain an hundred and seventy thousand breeders. I again subtract fifty thousand for those women who miscarry, or whose children die by accident or disease within the year. There only remain an hundred and twenty thousand children of poor parents annually born. The question therefore is, how this number shall be reared and provided for, which, as I have already said, under the present situation of affairs, is utterly impossible by all the methods hitherto proposed. For we can neither employ them in handicraft nor agriculture; we neither build houses (I mean in the country) nor cultivate land. They can very seldom pick up a livelihood by stealing till they arrive at six years old, except where they are of towardly parts; although I confess they learn the rudiments much earlier, during which time they can however be looked upon only as probationers, as I have been informed by a principal gentleman in the county of Cavan, who protested to me that he never knew above one or two instances under the age of six, even in a part of the kingdom so renowned for the quickest proficiency in that art.

I am assured by our merchants that a boy or a girl before twelve years old is no salable commodity; and even when they come to this age, they will not yield above three pounds, or three pounds and half a crown at most on the Exchange; which cannot turn to account either to the parents or the kingdom, the charge of nutriment and rags having been at least four times that value.

I shall now therefore humbly propose my own thoughts, which I hope will not be liable to the least objection.

I have been assured by a very knowing American of my acquaintance in London, that a young healthy child well nursed is at a year old a most delicious, nourishing, and wholesome food, whether stewed, roasted, baked, or boiled; and I make no doubt that it will equally serve in a fricassee or a ragout.

I do therefore humbly offer it to public consideration that of the hundred and twenty thousand children, already computed, twenty thousand may be reserved for breed, whereof only one fourth part to be males, which is more than we allow to sheep, black cattle, or swine; and my reason is that these children are seldom the fruits of marriage, a circumstance not much regarded by our savages, therefore one male will be sufficient to serve four females. That the remaining hundred thousand may at a year old be offered in sale to the persons of quality and fortune through the kingdom, always advising the mother to let them suck plentifully in the last month, so as to render them plump and fat for a good table. A child will make two dishes at an entertainment for friends; and when the family dines alone, the fore or hind quarter will make a reasonable dish, and seasoned with a little pepper or salt will be very good boiled on the fourth day, especially in winter.

I have reckoned upon a medium that a child just born will weigh twelve pounds, and in a solar year if tolerably nursed increaseth to twenty-eight pounds.

I grant this food will be somewhat dear, and therefore very proper for landlords, who, as they have already devoured most of the parents, seem to have the best title to the children.

Infant's flesh will be in season throughout the year, but more plentiful in March, and a little before and after. For we are told by a grave author, an eminent French physician, that fish being a prolific diet, there are more children born in Roman Catholic countries about nine months after Lent, than at any other season; therefore, reckoning a year after Lent, the markets will be more glutted than usual, because the number of popish infants is at least three to one in this kingdom; and therefore it will have one other collateral advantage, by lessening the number of Papists among us.

I have already computed the charge of nursing a beggar's child (in which list I reckon all cottagers, laborers, and four fifths of the farmers) to be about two shillings per annum, rags included; and I believe no gentleman would repine to give ten shillings for the carcass of a good fat child, which, as I have said, will make four dishes of excellent nutritive meat, when he hath only some particular friend or his own family to dine with him. Thus the squire will learn to be a good landlord, and grow popular among the tenants; the mother will have eight shillings net profit, and be fit for work till she produces another child.

Those who are more thrifty (as I must confess the times require) may flay the carcass; the skin of which artificially dressed will make admirable gloves for ladies, and summer boots for fine gentlemen.

As to our city of Dublin, shambles may be appointed for this purpose in the most convenient parts of it, and butchers we may be assured will not be wanting; although I rather recommend buying the children alive, and dressing them hot from the knife as we do roasting pigs.

A very worthy person, a true lover of his country, and whose virtues I highly esteem, was lately pleased in discoursing on this matter to offer a refinement upon my scheme. He said that many gentlemen of his kingdom, having of late destroyed their deer, he conceived that the want of venison might be well supplied by the bodies of young lads and maidens, not exceeding fourteen years of age nor under twelve, so great a number of both sexes in every county being now ready to starve for want of work and service; and these to be disposed of by their parents, if alive, or otherwise by their nearest relations. But with due deference to so excellent a friend and so deserving a patriot, I cannot be altogether in his sentiments; for as to the males, my American acquaintance assured me from frequent experience that their flesh was generally tough and lean, like that of our schoolboys, by continual exercise, and their taste disagreeable; and to fatten them would not answer the charge. Then as to the females, it would, I think with humble submission, be a loss to the public, because they soon would become breeders themselves; and besides, it is not improbable that some scrupulous people might be apt to censure such a practice (although indeed very unjustly) as a little bordering upon cruelty; which, I confess, hath always been with me the strongest objection against any project, how well soever intended.

But in order to justify my friend, he confessed that this expedient was put into his head by the famous Psalmanazar, a native of the island Formosa, who came from thence to London above twenty years ago, and in conversation told my friend that in his country when any young person happened to be put to death, the executioner sold the carcass to the persons of quality as a prime dainty; and that in his time the body of a plump girl of fifteen, who was crucified for an attempt to poison the emperor, was sold to his

Imperial Majesty's prime minister of state, and other great mandarins of the court, in joints from the gibbet, at four hundred crowns. Neither indeed can I deny that if the same use were made of several plump young girls in this town, who without one single groat to their fortunes cannot stir abroad without a chair, and appear at the playhouse and assemblies in foreign fineries which they never will pay for, the kingdom would not be the worse.

Some persons of a desponding spirit are in great concern about that vast number of poor people who are aged, diseased, or maimed, and I have been desired to employ my thoughts what course may be taken to ease the nation of so grievous an encumbrance. But I am not in the least pain upon that matter, because it is very well known that they are every day dying and rotting by cold and famine, and filth and vermin, as fast as can be reasonably expected. And as to the younger laborers, they are now in almost as hopeful a condition. They cannot get work, and consequently pine away for want of nourishment to a degree that if any time they are accidentally hired to common labor, they have not strength to perform it; and thus the country and themselves are happily delivered from the evils to come.

I have too long digressed, and therefore shall return to my subject. I think the advantages by the proposal which I have made are obvious and many, as well as of the highest importance.

For first, as I have already observed, it would greatly lessen the number of Papists, with whom we are yearly overrun, being the principal breeders of the nation as well as our most dangerous enemies; and who stay at home on purpose to deliver the kingdom to the Pretender, hoping to take their advantage by the absence of so many good Protestants, who have chosen rather to leave their country than to stay at home and pay tithes against their conscience to an Episcopal curate.

Secondly, the poorer tenants will have something valuable of their own, which by law may be made liable to distress, and help to pay their landlord's rent, their corn and cattle being already seized and money a thing unknown.

Thirdly, whereas the maintenance of an hundred thousand children, from two years old and upwards, cannot be computed at less than ten shillings a piece per annum, the nation's stock will be thereby increased fifty thousand pounds per annum, besides the profit of a new dish introduced to the tables of all gentlemen of fortune in the kingdom who have any refinement in taste. And the money will circulate among ourselves, the goods being entirely of our own growth and manufacture.

Fourthly, the constant breeders, besides the gain of eight shillings sterling per annum by the sale of their children, will be rid of the charge for maintaining them after the first year.

Fifthly, this food would likewise bring great custom to taverns, where the vintners will certainly be so prudent as to procure the best receipts for dressing it to perfection, and consequently have their houses frequented by all the fine gentlemen, who justly value themselves upon their knowledge in good eating; and a skillful cook, who understands how to oblige his guests, will contrive to make it as expensive as they please.

Sixthly, this would be a great inducement to marriage, which all wise nations have either encouraged by rewards or enforced by laws and penalties. It would increase the care and tenderness of mothers toward their children, when they were sure of a settlement for life to the poor babes, provided in some sort by the public, to their annual profit instead of expense. We should see an honest emulation among the married women, which of them could bring the fattest child to the market. Men would become as fond of their wives during the time of their pregnancy as they are now of their mares in foal, their cows in calf, or sows when they are ready to farrow; nor offer to beat or kick them (as is too frequent a practice) for fear of a miscarriage.

Many other advantages might be enumerated. For instance, the addition of some thousand carcasses in our exportation of barreled beef, the propagation of swine's flesh, and improvements in the art of making good bacon, so much wanted among us by the great destruction of pigs, too frequent at our tables, which are no way comparable in taste or magnificence to a well-grown, fat, yearling child, which roasted whole will make a considerable figure at a lord mayor's feast or any other public entertainment. But this and many others I omit, being studious of brevity.

Supposing that one thousand families in this city would be constant customers for infants' flesh, besides others who might have it at merry meetings, particularly weddings and christenings, I compute that Dublin would take off annually about twenty thousand carcasses, and the rest of the kingdom (where probably they will be sold somewhat cheaper) the remaining eighty thousand.

I can think of no one objection that will possibly be raised against this proposal, unless it should be urged that the number of people will be thereby much lessened in the kingdom. This I freely own, and it was indeed one principal design in offering it to the world. I desire the reader will observe, that I calculate my remedy for this one individual kingdom of Ireland and for no other that ever was, is, or I think ever can be upon earth. Therefore, let no man talk to me of other expedients: of taxing our absentees at five shillings a pound: of using neither clothes nor household furniture except what is of our own growth and manufacture: of utterly rejecting the materials and instruments that promote foreign luxury: of curing the expensiveness of pride, vanity, idleness, and gaming in our women: of introducing a vein of parsimony, prudence, and temperance: of learning to love our country, in the want of which we differ even from Laplanders and the inhabitants of Topinamboo: of quitting our animosities and factions, nor acting any longer like the Jews, who were murdering one another at the very moment their city was taken: of being a little cautious not to sell our country and conscience for nothing: of teaching landlords to have at least one degree of mercy toward their tenants: lastly, of putting a spirit of honesty, industry, and skill into our shopkeepers; who, if a resolution could now be taken to buy only our native goods, would immediately unite to cheat and exact upon us in the price, the measure, and the goodness, nor could ever yet be brought to make one fair proposal of just dealing, though often and earnestly invited to it.[2]

Therefore, I repeat, let no man talk to me of these and the like expedients, till he hath at least some glimpse of hope that there will ever be some hearty and sincere attempt to put them in practice.

But as to myself, having been wearied out for many years with offering vain, idle, visionary thoughts, and at length utterly despairing of success, I fortunately fell upon this proposal, which, as it is wholly new, so it hath something solid and real, of no expense and little trouble, full in our own power, and whereby we can incur no danger in disobliging England. For this kind of commodity will not bear exportation, the flesh being of too tender a consistence to admit a long continuance in salt, although perhaps I could name a country which would be glad to eat up our whole nation without it.

After all, I am not so violently bent upon my own opinion as to reject any offer proposed by wise men, which shall be found equally innocent, cheap, easy, and effectual. But before something of that kind shall be advanced in contradiction to my scheme, and offering a better, I desire the author or authors will be pleased maturely to consider two points. First, as things now stand, how they will be able to find food and raiment for an hundred thousand useless mouths and backs. And secondly, there being a round million of creatures in human figure throughout this kingdom, whose sole subsistence put into a common stock would leave them in debt two millions of pounds sterling, adding those who are beggars by profession to the bulk of farmers, cottagers, and laborers, with their wives and children who are beggars in effect; I desire those politicians who dislike my overture, and may perhaps be so bold to

[2]Swift himself had made these various proposals in previous works.—EDS.

attempt an answer, that they will first ask the parents of these mortals whether they would not at this day think it a great happiness to have been sold for food at a year old in this manner I prescribe, and thereby have avoided such a perpetual scene of misfortunes as they have since gone through by the oppression of landlords, the impossibility of paying rent without money or trade, the want of common sustenance, with neither house nor clothes to cover them from the inclemencies of the weather, and the most inevitable prospect of entailing the like or great miseries upon their breed forever.

I profess, in the sincerity of my heart, that I have not the least personal interest in endeavoring to promote this necessary work, having no other motive than the public good of my country, by advancing our trade, providing for infants, relieving the poor, and giving some pleasure to the rich. I have no children by which I can propose to get a single penny; the youngest being nine years old, and my wife past childbearing.

JONATHAN SWIFT

Jonathan Swift (1667–1745) is considered the greatest satirist of English literature. The Irish-born son of English parents, Swift became Dean of St. Patrick's Cathedral in Dublin in 1713. He became beloved by the Irish as a defender of their rights against the English. Swift is best remembered for his work, *Gulliver's Travels* (1726).

GLOSSARY

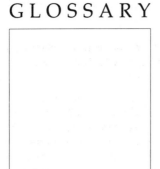

List of
Useful Terms

ABSTRACT and CONCRETE are terms used to describe two kinds of language. *Abstract* words are for ideas, terms, feelings, qualities, measurements— concepts we understand through our minds. For example, *idea, term, feeling, quality,* and *measurement* are all abstract words. *Concrete* words, on the other hand, are for things we perceive through our senses: we can see, hear, touch, taste, or smell what they stand for. *Knee, song, carburetor, apple,* and *smoke* are all concrete words.

ALLUSION is a reference to something—a person, a concept, a quotation, or a character—from literature, history, mythology, politics, or any other field familiar to your readers. For instance, in an essay on different kinds of employees, we might call one individual "the Woody Allen type." Immediately, the reader can picture a slight, indecisive, funny character.

The secret of the effective use of allusions is to allude to events, books, people, or quotations that are known to your readers. Suppose one of the references in an essay on employee types is to a Morel type. Can you picture this type? Are you any better informed? If not, the allusion is a poor one.

Be sure your allusions are clear, single, and unambiguous. A reference to "King" could mean Mackenzie King, King Hussein (or any other male monarch), or Martin Luther King. Or perhaps it refers to the King of Rock. Who knows? Imagine the confusion if the reader has the wrong King in mind.

AMBIGUITY: An ambiguous statement is one that has at least two different and conflicting interpretations. Similarly, an ambiguous action is one that can be understood in various ways. When it's used deliberately and carefully, ambiguity can add richness of meaning to your writing; however, most of the time ambiguity is not planned. It is the result of imprecise use of language. For instance, the statement, "He never has enough money" could mean that he is always broke, or that he is never satisfied no matter how much money he has. As a general rule, it is wise to avoid ambiguity in your writing.

ANALOGY is an extended comparison. Writers explain complicated or unfamiliar concepts by comparing them to simple or familiar ones. For instance, one could draw an analogy between life's experience and a race: the stages in life—infancy, childhood, adolescence, maturity, old age—become the laps of the race, and the problems or crises of life become the hurdles of an obstacle course. If we "fall down," we have let a problem get the better of us; if we "get up again," we are refusing to let a problem beat us. (See Tom Wolfe's "O Rotten Gotham" in Unit Six for an example of an extended analogy.)

ANALYSIS means looking at the parts of something individually and considering how they contribute to the whole. In essay writing, the common kinds of analysis are process analysis and causal analysis. See the introductions to Unit Three and Unit Six for a more detailed explanation.

ANECDOTE is a little story—an account of an incident—often humorous, that is used to catch the reader's interest. Writers frequently use this technique to introduce an essay. See paragraphs 2 to 4 of Pearson's "The Cat in the Bag . . . " in Unit Two for an example of the effective use of anecdote.

ARGUMENT: See RHETORICAL MODES.

AUDIENCE is the writer's intended reader or readers. Knowledge of their level of understanding, their expectations, is critically important to the writer. Tone, level of vocabulary, the amount of detail included, even the organizational structure, will all be influenced by the needs of the audience.

You know instinctively that when you speak or write to children, you use simple, direct language and, usually, short sentences. You adapt your style to suit your listeners. Before you begin to write, think about their knowledge of your subject, their educational background, their probable age level. Never talk down to your readers; but don't talk over their heads either, or they will stop reading in frustration.

For example, suppose you were preparing an article on the appeal of sports cars to the public. For a popular women's magazine, you would probably stress style, economy, comfort, and reliability, and you would support your thesis with examples of well-known women who love the sports cars they drive. You would not include much technical automotive jargon. If you were writing about the same topic for a general-audience consumers' magazine, however, you would include more specifics about price, ease of maintenance and cost, gas consumption, reliability under various weather and road conditions, with detailed figures comparing several popular makes. But if you were writing for a publication such as *Popular Mechanics* or *Road and Track*, you would stress performance, handling under high speed or unusual road conditions, and the ease or difficulty with which owners could maintain their cars themselves.

CHRONOLOGICAL ORDER means time order; items or ideas that are introduced chronologically are discussed in order of *time sequence*. Historical accounts are usually presented chronologically. In a chronological sequencing, connectives such as *first, second, third, next, then, after that*, and *finally*, are helpful to keep your reader on track. See the Introduction to Unit Three for further details.

CLICHÉ is a trite and familiar expression that was once colourful and original; now it's so familiar it's boring. Clichés often appear in similes or comparisons: for example, your writing will be as "dull as dishwater" and your reader will be "bored stiff" if you are "as stubborn as a mule" and keep on using them. See also STEREOTYPES.

CLIMACTIC ORDER means order of importance. In this ordering pattern, writers arrange their main points so that the most important or strongest point comes last. Thus, the paper builds up to a *climax.*

COHERENCE means a clear connection among the ideas or parts of a piece of writing. In a coherent paper, one paragraph leads logically to the next: ideas are clearly sequenced; the subject is consistent throughout; and the writer has supplied carefully chosen and logical TRANSITIONS such as *also, however, nevertheless, on the other hand, first, second, thus*, etc. If a paper is coherent, it is probably unified as well. (See UNITY.)

COLLOQUIALISM: Colloquial language is the language we speak. Expressions such as *well, okay, a lot*, or *kids* are perfectly acceptable in informal speech but are not appropriate in essays, papers, or reports. Contractions (such as *they're, isn't, it's*, or *let's)* and abbreviations *(*such as *TV, ads*, or *photos)* that are often used in speech are appropriate in writing only if the writer is consciously trying to achieve a casual, informal effect.

CONCLUSION: The conclusion of any piece of writing determines what will stay with your reader; therefore, it should be both logical and memorable. A good conclusion contributes to the overall UNITY of the piece. This is no place to throw in a new point you just thought of, or a few minor details. Your conclusion should reinforce your THESIS, but it should not simply restate it, or repeat it word for word, which is even more boring. Here are five effective strategies you can choose from when writing a conclusion:

1. *Refer back to your introduction.* This does *not* mean simply repeating the opening lines of your paper; instead, allude to its content and draw the connections for your reader. See the conclusion of "The Social Value of Education" in Unit Two.

2. *Conclude with a relevant, thought-provoking quotation.* See the conclusion of " 'Why Are We Reading This Stuff, Anyway?' " in Unit Eight.

3. *Ask a rhetorical question*—one that is asked to emphasize a point, not to elicit an answer. See the concluding paragraph of "Bumblers, Martinets, and Pros" in Unit Four.

4. *Issue a challenge.* See the conclusion of "Flunking with Style" in Unit Three.

5. *Highlight the value or significance of your subject.* See the last paragraph of "Why Do They Fail?" in Unit Six.

There are still other techniques you can use to conclude effectively: by providing a suggestion for change, offering a solution, making a prediction, or ending with an ANECDOTE that perfectly illustrates your thesis. Whatever strategy you choose, you should leave your reader with a sense of your paper's unity and completeness.

CONNOTATION and DENOTATION: The *denotation* of a word is its literal or dictionary meaning. *Connotation* refers to the emotional overtones the word has in the reader's mind. Some words have only a few connotations, while others have many. For instance, "house" is a word whose denotative meaning is familiar to all and which has few connotations. "Home," on the other hand, is also denotatively familiar, but has a rich connotative meaning that differs from reader to reader.

To take another example, the word "prison" is denotatively a "place of confinement for lawbreakers who have been convicted of serious crimes." But the connotations of the word are much deeper and broader: when we hear or read the word "prison," we think of colours like grey and black; we hear sounds of clanging doors, jangling keys, or wailing sirens; and we associate with the word emotions like anger, fear, despair, or loneliness. A careful writer will not use this word lightly: to refer to your job as a "prison" is a strong statement. It would not be appropriate to use this phrase simply because you don't like the location or the lunch break.

CONTEXT is the verbal background of a word or phrase—the words that come before and after it and fix its meaning. For example, the word "manual," which in most contexts means an instruction book, means a non-electric typewriter in Peter Gzowski's essay.

When a word or phrase is taken *out of context*, it is often difficult to determine what it originally meant. Therefore, when you are quoting from another writer, be sure to include enough of the context so the meaning is clear to your reader.

DEDUCTION is the logical process of applying a general statement to a specific instance and reasoning through to a conclusion about that instance. See the introduction to Unit Eight.

DESCRIPTION: See RHETORICAL MODES.

DICTION refers to the selection and arrangement of words in a piece of writing. Effective diction depends upon the writer's careful choice of a level of vocabulary suited to both the reader and the subject. A careful writer does not mix formal with colloquial language; standard English with dialect or slang; or informal language with technical jargon or archaisms (outmoded, antique phrases). Good diction is that which is appropriate to the subject, the reader, and the writer's purpose. Writing for a general audience about the closing of the local A&P store, a careful writer would not say, "The retail establishment for the purveyance of merchandise relative to the sustaining of life has cemented its portals," which is pretentious nonsense. "The corner grocery store is closed" conveys the same meaning more appropriately and more concisely.

EMPHASIS: A writer can emphasize or highlight key points in several ways: by repetition; by placement (the essay's first and last sections are the most prominent positions); or by phrasing. Careful phrasing can call attention to a particular point: parallel structure, a very short sentence or paragraph, even a deliberate sentence fragment. These are all emphatic devices. A writer can also add emphasis by developing an idea at greater length, or by calling attention to its significance directly, by inserting expressions such as *most important is* or *significantly*. TONE, particularly IRONY or even sarcasm, can be used to add emphasis. Finally, distinctive diction is an emphatic device. (See Wolfe's piece, "O Rotten Gotham," in Unit Six for a good example of the use of distinctive diction.)

EVIDENCE in a piece of writing functions the same way it does in a court of law: it proves the point. Evidence can consist of statistical data, examples, references to authorities in the field, surveys, illustrations, quotations, or facts. Charts, graphs, and maps are also forms of evidence and are well suited to particular kinds of reports.

A point cannot be effectively explained, let alone proved, without evidence. For instance, it is not enough to say that computers are displacing many office workers. You need to find specific examples of companies, jobs, and statistics to prove the connection. After all, the number of dogs in Ontario has increased almost as much as the number of computers. Does that prove that dogs breed computers? What makes a paper credible and convincing is the evidence presented and the COHERENCE with which you present it.

EXPOSITION: See RHETORICAL MODES.

FIGURES of SPEECH are words or phrases that mean something more than the literal meanings of the individual words or phrases. Writers choose to use figurative language when they want the reader to associate one thing with another. Some of the more common figures of speech include similes, metaphors, personifications, and puns.

A *simile* is a comparison in which the author uses "like" or "as." For example, "She is as slow as an arthritic turtle" is a simile. Effective similes are both appropriate and imaginative: trotting out old clichés such as "cool as a cucumber" or "busy as a bee" will only bore, not enlighten, your reader.

A *metaphor* does not use "like" or "as": it claims one thing *is* another. For example, if you write, "My supervisor wallowed in his chair," you are implicitly comparing your boss to a pig. "My boss is a pig" is a metaphor, but it is unoriginal and inappropriate. Choose your metaphors with care: they should enlighten your readers with fresh and original insight, not confuse or tire them with an inappropriate comparison or a cliché.

Personification is a figure of speech in which the writer gives human qualities to an inanimate object or an abstract idea. For instance, if you write, "The brakes screeched when he hit them," you are comparing the sound of the car's brakes to a human voice. Strive for original and insightful personifications; otherwise, you will be trapped by clichés such as "The solution to the problem was staring me in the face."

A *pun* is the use of language so that one word or phrase brings to the reader's mind two different meanings. Max Eastman, in *Enjoyment of Laughter*, classifies puns into three sorts: atrocious, witty, and poetic. The person who wrote, "How does Dolly Parton stack up against Mae West?"

was guilty of an atrocious pun. Barry Callaghan's title, "Canadian Wry," contains a witty pun. Poetic puns go beyond the merely humorous double meaning and offer the reader a concise, pointed, original comparison of two entities, qualities, or ideas. Dylan Thomas's "Do not go gentle into that good night" is an example of a poetic pun. See Callaghan's "Canadian Wry" in Unit Two for numerous examples of puns.

GENERAL and SPECIFIC: *General* words refer to classes or groups of things. "Animal" is a general word; so is "fruit." *Specific* words limit or narrow down the class of things to something very specific such as "wolf" or "lemon." Good writing is a careful blend of general and specific language. (See also ABSTRACT/CONCRETE.)

GOBBLEDYGOOK is a type of JARGON distinguished by language that is both pretentious and wordy and highly ABSTRACT and vague. George Orwell's famous essay "Politics and the English Language" (Unit Nine) contains several examples of gobbledygook.

ILLUSTRATION: See the Introduction to Unit Two.

INDUCTION is the logical process of looking at a number of specific instances and reasoning through to a general conclusion about them. See the Introduction to Unit Eight.

INTRODUCTION: The introduction to any piece of writing is crucial to its success. A good introduction indicates the THESIS of the piece, establishes the TONE, and secures the reader's attention. The introduction is the "hook" with which you catch your reader's interest and make him want to read what you have to say. Here are five different "attention-getters" you can use:

1. *Begin with a story of an interesting incident.* The story or ANECDOTE should be related to your subject. See the first paragraph of " 'Why Are We Reading This Stuff, Anyway?' " in Unit Eight.

2. *Offer a dramatic statistic or striking fact.* See "Why Do They Fail?" in Unit Six.

3. *Begin with a relevant quotation.* Make it interesting but keep it short. See the first paragraph of "Bumblers, Martinets, and Pros" in Unit Four.

4. *Begin by stating a commonly held opinion that you intend to challenge.* See "Flunking with Style" in Unit Three.

5. *Set up a contrast to "hook" your reader.* The opening paragraph of "College or University?" contrasts the post-secondary educational scene in the United States with that in Canada. See the comparison in Unit Five.

Other strategies you might want to experiment with include posing a question, offering a definition—make sure it's yours, not the dictionary's—or even telling a joke. You know how important first impressions are when you meet someone. Treat your introductory paragraph with the same care you would take when you want to make a good first impression on a person. If you bait the hook attractively, your reader will want to read on—and that, after all, is your goal.

IRONY is a statement or situation that means the opposite of what it appears to mean. To call a hopelessly ugly painting a masterpiece is ironic—it's an example of verbal irony, to be exact. Irony of situation occurs when a twist of fate reverses an expected outcome: for example, a man defers all the pleasure in his life to scrimp and save for his retirement but wins a million-dollar lottery at age 65.

Irony is an effective technique because it forces readers to think about the relationship between seemingly different things or ideas. Jonathan Swift's "A Modest Proposal" is a famous example of extended irony. Although he appears to recommend a barbarous solution to poverty in Ireland (eating the children of the poor), Swift in reality forces his readers to consider the desperate plight of the Irish peasantry.

JARGON is the specialized language used within a particular trade, discipline, or profession. Among members of that trade or profession, jargon is perfectly appropriate; indeed, such highly technical language is an efficient, time-saving means of communication. Outside the context of the trade or profession, however, jargon is inappropriate, because it inhibits rather than promotes the reader's understanding. Another meaning of jargon, the meaning usually intended when the word is used in this text, is GOBBLEDYGOOK.

METAPHOR: See FIGURES OF SPEECH.

NARRATION: See RHETORICAL MODES.

ORDER refers to the arrangement of information or points in a piece of prose. While you are still in the planning stages, choose the order most appropriate to your subject. There are four main ways to arrange your points:

1. *Chronological order* means in order of time, from first to last.

2. *Climactic order* means in order of importance, leading up to the climax. Usually you would present your strongest or most important point last, your second-strongest point first, and the others in between, where they will attract less attention.

3. *Causal* or *logical order* means that the points are connected in such a way that one point must be explained before the next can be understood. Often used in cause/effect patterns, this order is appropriate when there is a direct and logical connection between one point and the next.

4. *Random order* is a shopping-list kind of arrangement: the points can be presented in any order. Random order is appropriate only when the points are all equal in significance and not logically or causally linked.

PARAGRAPH refers to a unit of composition, usually from five to ten sentences long, all dealing with one topic. In an essay, you present several main ideas, all related to your subject. The main ideas are broken down into points or topics, each of which is developed in a paragraph.

Every paragraph should have a *topic sentence*—a sentence that states clearly what the paragraph is about. It is often the first or second sentence of the paragraph. The rest of the paragraph consists of sentences that develop the topic, perhaps with examples, a description, a definition, a quotation, a comparison—or a combination of these strategies. There should be no sentence in the paragraph that is not clearly related to its topic. A paragraph should lead smoothly into the next (see TRANSITION), and it must also possess internal COHERENCE and UNITY. The essays by Bertrand Russell and Martin Luther King, Jr., (Unit Four) deserve careful analysis: their paragraphs are models of form.

PARALLEL STRUCTURE means similarity of grammatical form. In a sentence, for example, all items in a series would be written in the same grammatical form: single words, phrases, or clauses. Julius Caesar's famous pronouncement, "I came; I saw; I conquered" is a classic example of parallelism.

Parallelism creates symmetry that is pleasing to the reader. Lack of parallelism, on the other hand, can be jarring: "His favourite sports are skiing, skating, and he particularly loves sailing." Such potholes in your prose should be fixed up before you hand in a paper. For example, "What Carol says, she means; and she delivers what she promises, too" would be much more effective if rewritten in parallel form: "What Carol says, she means; what she promises, she delivers."

Because the human mind responds favourably to the repetition of rhythm, parallelism is an effective device for adding EMPHASIS. King's "Dimensions of a Complete Life" (Unit Four) contains many examples of emphatic parallel structure.

PARAPHRASE is putting another writer's ideas into your own words. Of course, you acknowledge the original writer as the source of the idea—if you don't, you are guilty of plagiarism.

You will find paraphrasing very useful when you are writing a research paper. Once you have gathered the information you need from your various sources and organized your ideas into an appropriate order, you then write the paper, drawing on your sources for supporting ideas, but expressing them in your own words.

A paraphrase should reflect both the meaning and the general TONE of the original. It may be the same length or shorter than the original, but it is not a PRÉCIS.

PERSONIFICATION: See FIGURES OF SPEECH.

PERSUASION: See RHETORICAL MODES and the Introduction to Unit Eight.

POINT OF VIEW, in exposition, means the grammatical angle of the essay. (In persuasion, point of view can mean either the grammatical angle or an opinion.)

If the writer identifies himself as "I," we have the first-person point of view; in this case, we expect to find the writer's own opinions and first-hand experiences. All the essays in Unit One, Narration and Description, are written in the first person.

If the writer addresses the readers as "you," we have the second-person point of view, as in Berton's "Baked Beans" (Unit Three). Second person lends itself to a fairly informal style.

If the writer—or reader—is not grammatically "present" in the material, we have the third-person point of view. Chilton's "A Fugitive Pleasure: Perfume in the 18th Century" (Unit Three) is an example. The writer uses "one," "he," "they," and the result is a more formal essay than one written in the first or second person.

A careful writer maintains point of view consistently throughout an essay; if a shift occurs, it should be for a good reason, with a particular effect in mind. Careless shifts in point of view throw the reader off track. See paragraph 9 of Lewis Thomas's "Altruism" (in Unit Seven) for an example of a purposeful change in point of view.

PRÉCIS is a condensed summary of an article or essay. It is one-quarter to one-third the length of the original. The examples and illustrations are omitted, and the prose is tightened up as much as possible. All the main ideas are included; most of the development is not.

PROCESS ANALYSIS: See the Introduction to Unit Three.

PUN: See FIGURES OF SPEECH.

PURPOSE means the writer's intent: to inform, to persuade, or to amuse, or a combination of these. See RHETORICAL MODES.

RHETORICAL MODES: The word "rhetoric" simply means the art of using language effectively. There are four classic modes, or kinds, of writing: exposition, narration, description, and argument. The writer's choice of mode is often dependent on his or her PURPOSE.

Exposition is writing intended to inform or explain. If the writer's purpose is to inform, this mode is a likely choice. Expository writing can be personal or impersonal, serious or light-hearted. The various methods of exposition (such as exemplification, definition, comparison, and the rest) are sometimes called rhetorical forms.

Narration tells a story. It is the mode used for fiction. Examples of narrative writing are sometimes found within expository prose: in anecdotes or illustrations, for example. George Jonas's "Why I Love Opera . . . " and Emily Carr's "Sophie" (Unit One) are good examples of the use of narration to help explain a thesis.

Description is used to make a reader see, hear, taste, smell, or feel something. Good descriptive writing re-creates a sensory experience in the reader's imagination. Descriptive writing is also sometimes found in expository prose. In addition to the essays in Unit One, see the essays by Ken Dryden, Tom Hawthorn, and Rudy Wiebe in Unit Nine for examples of effective description.

Argument, sometimes called *persuasion*, is writing that sets out not to explain something, but to convince the reader of the validity of the writer's opinion on an issue. Sometimes its purpose goes even further, and the writer attempts to motivate the reader to act in some way. Like exposition, argument conveys information to the reader, but not solely for the purpose of making a subject clear. Argument seeks to reinforce or to change a reader's opinion about an issue.

SATIRE is a form of humour, sometimes light-hearted, sometimes biting, in which the writer deliberately attacks and ridicules something: a person, a political decision, an event, an institution, a philosophy, or a system. The satirist uses exaggeration, ridicule, and IRONY to achieve his or her effect.

There is often a social purpose in satire: the writer points to the difference between the ideal—a world based on common sense and moral standards—and the real, which may be silly, vicious, alienating, or immoral, depending on the object of the satirist's attack. The essays by Mitford and Syfers (Units Three and Four) in this text are examples of satire.

SIMILE: See FIGURES OF SPEECH.

STEREOTYPE refers to a character, situation, or idea that is trite, unoriginal, and conventional. Stereotypes are based on automatic, widely known, and usually incorrect assumptions: all women are poor drivers; all truck drivers are illiterate; all teenagers are boors; all Scots are tight with money. Stereotypical notions about races and nationalities are particularly dangerous: think of the well-known "Newfie" jokes, for example.

A careful writer avoids stereotypes, unless he or she is using them for satiric purposes. Unthinking acceptance of others' assumptions is a sure sign of a lazy mind.

STYLE refers to the distinctive way a person writes. When two writers approach the same subject, even if they share many of the same ideas, the resulting works will be different. That difference is the result of personal style. DICTION, sentence structure, sentence length, TONE, and level of formality all contribute to an individual's style. Compare Wolfe's "O Rotten Gotham—Sliding Down into the Behaviorial Sink" (Unit Six) and Martin Luther King's "The Dimensions of a Complete Life" (Unit Four) as examples of unique styles.

Good writers adapt their style to their audience; one doesn't write the same way in the business world as one does in the academic world, for example. In this sense, "good style" means one that suits the writer's PURPOSE, subject, and AUDIENCE. An informal and humorous style full of slang expressions would be inappropriate in a paper on teenage suicide. Similarly, a stiff, formal style would hardly be suitable for an article on new toys for the Christmas season.

SUMMARY is a brief statement, in sentence or paragraph form, of the main ideas of an article or essay. See also PRÉCIS and PARAPHRASE.

SYNTAX means the arrangement of words in a sentence. Good syntax means not only grammatical correctness, but also an effective word order and a variety of sentence patterns. Good writers use short sentences and long ones, simple sentences and complex ones, and natural-order sentences and inverted-order ones. The choice depends on the meaning the writer wishes to convey.

THESIS is the main idea or point the writer wants to communicate to the reader in an essay. It is often expressed in a *thesis statement*. (See "How to Write to Be Understood" in the Introduction.) Sometimes the thesis is not stated, but implied. Whether stated or implied, however, the thesis is the central idea that everything in the essay is designed to support and explain.

TONE reflects the writer's attitude to the subject and to the presumed audience. For instance, a writer who is looking back with longing to the past will use a nostalgic tone. An angry writer might use an indignant, outraged tone, or an understated, ironic tone—depending on the subject and purpose of the piece.

Through DICTION, POINT OF VIEW, sentence structure, PARAGRAPH development, and STYLE, a writer modulates the message to suit the knowledge, attitudes, and taste of the people who will read it. Contrast the carping, negative tone of Atwood's "Canadians: What Do They Want?" with the poignant yet somehow positive tone of Finn's "Reflections on My Brother's Murder" in Unit Six. Other examples of superb control of tone are Mitford's scathing "Behind the Formaldehyde Curtain" (Unit Three), Ignatieff's sympathetic "Deficits" (Unit One), and Syfers's ironic "I Want a Wife" (Unit Four).

TOPIC SENTENCE is a sentence that identifies the topic, or main idea, of a paragraph; it is usually found at or near the beginning of the paragraph.

TRANSITIONS are linking words or phrases. They help connect a writer's sentences and paragraphs so that the whole piece flows smoothly and logically. Here are some of the most common transitions used to show relationships between ideas:

1. *to show a time relation*: first, second, third, next, before, during, after, now, then, finally, last
2. *to add an idea or example*: in addition, also, another, furthermore, similarly, for example, for instance
3. *to show contrast*: although, but, however, instead, nevertheless, on the other hand, in contrast, on the contrary
4. *to show a cause-effect relation*: as a result, consequently, because, since, therefore, thus
   See also COHERENCE.

UNITY: A piece of writing has unity if all its parts work together; each part contributes to the ultimate effect. The unified work has one subject and one tone. Unity is an important quality of a good paragraph: each sentence must be related to and develop the central idea expressed or implied in the TOPIC SENTENCE.

AUTHOR INDEX